OBSESSION

The FBI's Legendary Profiler Probes the Psyches of Killers, Rapists, and Stalkers and Their Victims and Tells How to Fight Back

JOHN DOUGLAS
AND MARK OLSHAKER

A LISA DREW BOOK

SCRIBNER

A LISA DREW BOOK/SCRIBNER
1230 Avenue of the Americas
New York, NY 10020

Set in Bembo

DESIGNED BY ERICH HOBBING

Manufactured in the United States of America

1   3   5   7   9   10   8   6   4   2

Library of Congress Cataloging-in-Publication Data
Douglas, John E.
Obsession : the FBI's legendary profiler probes the
psyches of killers, rapists, and stalkers and their victims and
tells how to fight back / John Douglas and Mark Olshaker.
p.   cm.
Includes index.
1. Serial muderers—United States—Psychology.
2. Serial murders—United States—Case studies. 3. Serial murder
investigation—United States. 4. Sex offenders—United States.
5. Victims of crimes—United States. 6. Self-defense—United
States. I. Olshaker, Mark, 1951– . II. Title.
HV7914.D67   1998
364.15'0973—dc21   97-48654
CIP

ISBN 0-684-84560-1

For
JACK DOUGLAS

March 19, 1918–May 14, 1997

Father, friend,
and our greatest supporter

With love, and the hope
you're just as proud
of this one

Authors' Note

Our deepest and most heartfelt appreciation goes out to the team that has made this book possible: our intrepid editor, Lisa Drew; her able assistant, Blythe Grossberg; our own talented assistant and researcher, Ann Hennigan; our agent, manager and confidant, Jay Acton; all of our friends at Scribner and Pocket Books; and, of course, Mark's wife Carolyn, our Mindhunters chief of staff.

We're also profoundly indebted to all of the heroic people who shared their insights, their professional experience and, in some very real instances, their lives. These are, strictly in alphabetical order: David Beatty, Director of Public Policy of the National Victim Center; Jack and Trudy Collins; Carroll Ann Ellis, Director of the Fairfax County, Virginia, Victim-Witness Unit; Linda A. Fairstein, Chief of the Sex Crimes Prosecution Unit of the New York County District Attorney's Office; Hans Hageman, Director of the East Harlem School at Exodus House; Katie and Steven Hanley; Dr. Stanton Samenow; Gene, Jeni and Peggy Schmidt; Kansas State Attorney General Carla Stovall; and Sandy Witt, Victim Coordinator of the Fairfax County Victim-Witness Unit.

As always, the work of colleagues Dr. Ann Burgess and Roy Hazelwood has proved invaluable. We'd also like to thank: Jim Adler; Lynn Allen; Richard Berlin; Det. Dick Cline; Gavin de Becker; Dr. Park Dietz; Darron and Kelli Farha; Heather Haas; Inge Hanson; Det. Dennis Harris; Shannon Marsh; Det. Bob Murphy; Stacey Payne; Eric Rittenhouse; Chief M. Douglas Scott; Bill Whildin; and all of John's colleagues and Mark's friends at the FBI.

Finally, we'd like to take this opportunity to pay special tribute to John's father, Jack Douglas, who passed away on the morning of May

AUTHORS' NOTE

14, 1997, as we were writing this book. We had no greater or more enthusiastic supporter and we will miss him very much, which is why this book is dedicated to him.

—John Douglas and Mark Olshaker

CONTENTS

1. Motivation X — 15

2. The Hunter and the Hunted — 33

3. A Tale of Two Rapists — 51

4. The Dimensions of Rape — 91

5. What Actually Happened in Central Park? — 117

6. The Survivor's Journey — 139

7. Katie's Story — 165

8. For the Victims — 199

9. Stalking — 223

10. If I Can't Have You, Nobody Will — 265

11. Buffalo Bill and Beyond — 291

12. Speak Out for Stephanie — 319

13. Knowledge Is Power — 355

Index — 367

The mind is its own place, and in itself
Can make a heav'n of hell, a hell of heav'n.

—John Milton,
Paradise Lost

"Nothing happened to me, Officer Starling. *I* happened. You can't reduce me to a set of influences. You've given up good and evil for behaviorism, Officer Starling. You've got everybody in moral dignity pants—nothing is ever anybody's fault. Look at me, Officer Starling. Can you stand to say I'm evil? Am I evil, Officer Starling?"

—Thomas Harris,
The Silence of the Lambs

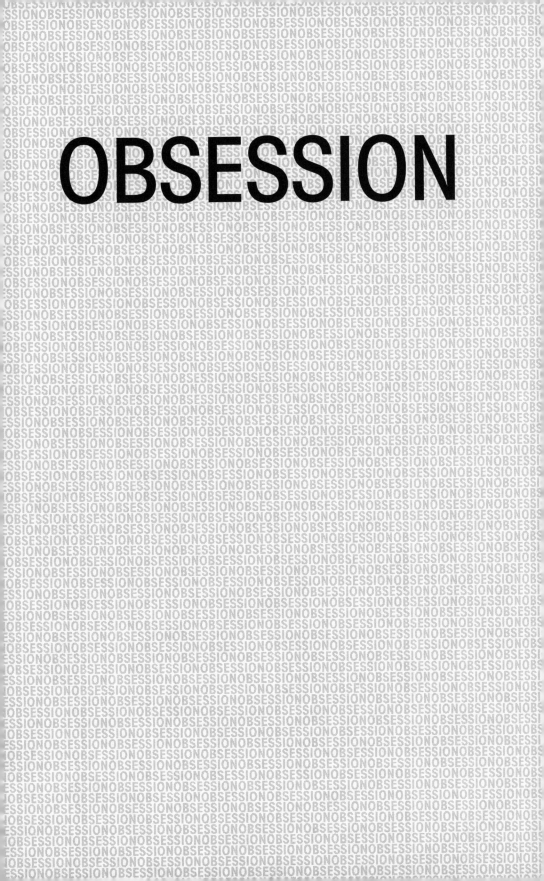

CHAPTER ONE

MOTIVATION X

They were all dead. All four of them. The entire family.

It was 1979. I sat at my desk at Quantico concentrating on the color crime-scene photos. Mr. and Mrs. Kenneth Peterson were in the bedroom of their one-story wood home in this medium-sized Mid-Atlantic city—he on the bed, his wife, Sarah, nude on the floor, her head sprawled to one side. Both had been bound with black electrical tape and white venetian-blind cords, which, from the ligature marks encircling their necks, appeared to be the means of death. Thankfully, their eyes were closed, but there was no peace evident on their bloodied and swollen faces. Eleven-year-old Melissa was in the basement, bound upright by white cords and tied by her neck to a drainpipe. She was gagged with a towel, naked below the waist except for her socks, panties bunched around her ankles. I stared at the close-up of her head, her long, dark hair sprawled in matted tufts across her face. She looked as though she had been a pretty girl, but it's always hard to tell from crime-scene photos. Violence robs a person of so much; violent death robs her of everything. Daniel, nicknamed Danny, was only nine. He was lying on the floor of his own bedroom next to his bed, fully clothed, bound with cord with a plastic bag over his head. Whatever other wounds were evidenced on each body, both kids also died from ligature strangulation. The butchery had occurred between about eight and ten o'clock on a Wednesday morning in February of 1974—more than five years ago. Now there were two, possibly three, more killings, and an unknown subject—UNSUB— still apparently active. That's why the local police had called us in.

The names and some of the details in this case have been changed for reasons that will become apparent. The facts, however, speak for themselves.

I studied the other pictures in the Peterson file and the detectives' reports. Despite the mayhem at the scene, this was not a haphazard or opportunistic crime. There was no sign of forced entry, but one photo showed that the telephone line had been cut before the intruder entered the house, and a search by detectives indicated that the binding cord had been brought to the scene. Whoever had done this had it all planned out.

I was unclear what, if anything, was missing from the house, but the family car had been stolen. Police found it abandoned in a food-store parking lot.

In 1979, our profiling program was just getting established. I'd only been at Quantico for two years, first as a National Academy counselor, then as an instructor, after serving stints as a field agent in Detroit and then Milwaukee. FBI director William Webster had recently given the Behavioral Science Unit official approval to offer psychological profiling consultation as an adjunct to our educational and research responsibilities. A few years later, I would be the first to move over from training to full-time profiling, but at this point, my main job was still teaching, specifically the Applied Criminal Psychology course given to new agents and police fellows from around the United States and the world. Bob Ressler, Roy Hazelwood, and a few of the other instructors were also starting to consult as their teaching schedules allowed.

Even though we were new and still relatively unknown, we'd already developed a procedure: Send us your crime-scene photos and officer-on-the-scene accounts, witness statements, autopsy photos, protocols and medical-examiner reports, maps of crime scenes and/or body dump sites, anything else that might be relevant to the case. Tell us anything you know about the victims, their habits, their lifestyles. But don't give us your suspect list, if you have one, or tell us who you think might have done it; we don't want to be influenced by your opinion.

Kenneth Peterson was forty-one at the time of death. His wife, Sarah, had been thirty-four, the same age I was now as I sat here reading this. Kenneth had retired from the Army, where he'd been stationed in Germany. He came with his family back to the United States, settled in this pleasant Eastern-seaboard city, and worked as a pilot and mechanic at a small airfield just south of the metropolitan area. Roughly a month before, the Petersons had moved into the house in which they died.

I glanced through the cold, clinical facts of the four autopsy reports.

Just as the crime-scene photos suggested, all four of them had died of asphyxia due to compression of the larynx by ligature, causing pulmonary edema and congestion of the viscera. There were other wounds on Sarah, and the Gross Description noted that Melissa was also wearing a white bra, which had been cut in the front. Yet there was no evidence of sexual assault on either female.

Though there were no bullet wounds on any of the bodies, I figured he had to have had a gun. Otherwise, he couldn't have controlled that many people at the same time, particularly when one was a former military man. But clearly, he never intended to use the gun except as a last resort to save his own life. He definitely went in intending to kill—no chance this was a burglary or robbery gone bad—but he wasn't interested in killing quickly and "cleanly" with a bullet.

The police had come up with a number of well-publicized suspects, but none of them was strong. Then in October, a local newspaper editor received a phone call directing him to look in a particular book in the main branch of the public library. Inside was a letter purporting to be from the killer. It claimed that the suspects the police had examined "know nothing at all." To authenticate his claim of responsibility, under the heading "PETERSON CASE," he typed out specific descriptions of each victim, including position, type of binding, clothing, and means of death. He also threw in additional random "Comments" under each victim, such as the fact that Kenneth had thrown up and that Sarah had not made the bed. He even complained that the car he stole was dirty inside and practically out of gas.

I read the grayish photocopy, each sheet protected by a plastic sleeve. *What are you going to tell me about yourself from this?* I wondered.

The text that followed the descriptions was only semicoherent, going on for several paragraphs about how hard it was to control himself and that, since the murders, he didn't have any effective way of dealing with the urge to kill, since he couldn't approach anyone else about his problem.

"When this monster enters my brain I never know. But, it is here to stay. How does one cure himself? If you ask for help after you have killed four people they will laugh or hit the panic button and call the cops."

In a way, it reminded me of the crime-scene plea of William Heirens, the seventeen-year-old college-student serial killer in 1940s Chicago who had used the lipstick of one of his victims to scrawl on

17

her wall, "For heAVens Sake cAtch Me BeFore I Kill More. I cannot control myselF." He had been caught and attributed his kills to a George Murman (probably short for "Murder Man"), who he eventually acknowledged lived inside him. He was tried and sentenced to life in prison, where Bob Ressler and I had recently interviewed him as part of our Criminal Personality Research Project. The difference, though, was that whereas there might have been something heartfelt in Heirens's lipsticked plea, this guy was playing with his audience.

He described his modus operandi (MO): ". . . following them, checking up on them, waiting in the dark, waiting, waiting." Like Heirens, he attempted to split off responsibility, saying, "Maybe you can stop him. I can't. He has already chosen his next victim or victims and I don't know who they are yet," then finished the note with, "Good luck with your hunting," before signing off, "YOURS, TRULY GUILTILY."

He added a PS: "Since sex criminals do not change their M.O. or by nature cannot do so, I will not change mine. The code words for me will be . . . Search and Destroy."

That was the key, I realized. Not only is he taking credit for the murders, he's putting his own stamp on them, giving himself a persona. Whatever else this guy has accomplished in life, and my guess was it wasn't much, this is the thing he was most proud of. This is the thing he spends most of his time thinking and fantasizing about. He sees himself as an artist and this is his "art," his life's work. The second part of the letter is just an explanation, a facile excuse, for why he's going to keep doing it. This is what makes him feel most alive. For this moment, he can get away from his inadequate, ineffectual existence and exercise the ultimate power over other people. No matter what they are or have been, he's more powerful than they are. This is the thing he wants to be known for.

That was it for a while, as far as anyone could tell. No more crimes, no more communications.

But even without the documentary evidence I had in front of me, it was clear this UNSUB wasn't finished. I took a closer look at the first page of the letter. The detail was incredible; I'd never seen anything quite like it. He even noted where Melissa's glasses were left lying. How'd he do this? Was he compulsive enough to go through the entire house taking meticulous notes? He sure as hell wasn't doing it from memory eight months later.

Of course not! He was looking at crime-scene photographs, just as I was. Only he'd made his own. He'd brought a camera to the scene or, more likely, taken one from the Petersons. Unless you know to look for it, that's not the kind of thing that would be missed. And unless he was a photography buff himself with his own darkroom setup, it had to be a Polaroid. He couldn't take a chance on sending film out with those images on it.

And why had he made the photos? Not to be able to recount the scene to the police and media, though he certainly got a charge out of that. He made the pictures, I realized, so he could relive the moment over and over. Some guys take jewelry or underwear. This guy takes crime-scene photos. Of course he was going to keep killing. He was enjoying it too much not to. And he'd start again as soon as his memories didn't do the job for him any longer.

The next murder in the suspected series occurred a little more than three years later, in May of 1977. A white male forced his way into Frances Farrell's house at gunpoint. He locked her three children— two boys and a girl—in a bathroom, then tied up and strangled their mother, twenty-seven-year-old Frances. A ringing telephone apparently scared away the intruder before he could complete his agenda. The children managed to free themselves and call the police. If it was the same guy, he'd neglected to cut the phone line this time, or maybe it wasn't accessible. Police got a few more details to add to the composite descriptions of witnesses who thought they'd seen someone around the Peterson house. One of Frances's sons had been stopped on the street that morning by the man he thought was the killer, asking for directions in the neighborhood.

The crime-scene photos of Frances Farrell were pretty horrific, possibly even more so than those of the Petersons. Like Sarah Peterson, she was nude, bound with black electrical tape and white venetian-blind cord. Her arms were tied behind her back with the tape and cord and a pair of her own stockings. As with Danny Peterson, Frances had been found with a plastic bag tied over her head. When it was removed at the crime scene, her face was almost completely blackish red from cyanosis and hemorrhaging, and bloody vomit was dried around her nose and mouth. Yet the autopsy report noted no defense wounds on the hands nor evidence of sexual assault.

Then on November 6 of the same year, twenty-three-year-old Lori

Gallagher returned home and was surprised by an intruder who had come in through the bedroom window. This time, he had cut the phone line. She was facedown on her bed, clad in a pink, long-sleeved sweater with her panties pulled down, her own panty hose binding her wrists behind her. There were additional pairs of panty hose of various colors that had been fashioned into a gag around her neck and across her mouth, which, along with her nose, had been bleeding. Her entire body had a reddish cast from petechial hemorrhage. Again, no defense wounds and no apparent vaginal or anal assault. And again, the cause of death was ligature strangulation.

Most noteworthy about this particular murder was the way police found out about it. The next morning, the killer called them and directed officers to the scene. The police traced the call to a public phone booth on a busy downtown corner. A couple of witnesses vaguely recalled seeing a tall blond man using the phone at about the right time.

Near the beginning of February 1978, the killer mailed a poem to the local newspaper, but it somehow found its way to the circulation department, where no one noticed it for several days. Evidently ticked off over this slight, not to mention the lack of publicity he so desperately craved, the UNSUB took a different tack, sending a letter to a television station that served a large part of the region. Not only did he reassert credit for the Peterson murders, he also claimed responsibility for Farrell and Gallagher.

The station immediately brought the letter to the police, who took it seriously.

The letter's description of the Farrell and Gallagher murders was just as detailed as the original depictions of the Petersons had been. He said how lucky the Farrell children had been that the phone had rung, saving their lives. He had intended to kill them as he had Danny Peterson. Only this time, his letter gave an even greater insight into his methods and motivations. At the end of the paragraphs on both Farrell and Gallagher, he had written identical commentaries: "Chosen at random with little planning, Motivation X."

And he promised another one, in a scenario similar to the one in which he had killed Melissa Peterson, a scenario he described in hideous and vulgar detail. She would be chosen at random with a little more planning this time. And the driving force, again, would be "Motivation X."

"How many do I have to kill before I get my name in the paper or some national attention?" he practically pleaded. "Do the cops think that all those deaths are not related? Yes, the M.O. is different in each, but look at the pattern that is developing."

As if he hadn't made himself clear enough already, he explained, "You don't understand these things because you're not under the influence of Motivation X. The same thing that made Son of Sam, Jack the Ripper, the Boston Strangler, the Hillside Strangler, Ted [Bundy] of the West Coast and many more infamous characters."

He called his affliction "a terrible nightmare," but admitted he didn't "lose any sleep over it. After a thing like Gallagher I come home and go about life like anyone else. And I will be like that until the urge hits me again."

Even as early in my profiling career as this was, I knew he wasn't going home and going about life like anyone else. But I'd already learned how to read the deeper message, the "subtext," as actors call it, and here he was saying something profoundly accurate, not only about himself but about virtually all serial predators. And that is, on an everyday basis, they do appear to go about their business and ordinary lives just like the rest of us. Even though they're monsters, they don't look or act like monsters, and that is why they become successful. We see them, but we look right through them. What makes them monsters is not how they look; it's that they "don't lose any sleep" over what they do.

He closed by appealing, "How about some name for me?" and suggested, formally this time, "SEARCH AND DESTROYER."

Technically speaking, I suppose, it should have been Searcher and Destroyer, but even with the shoddy syntax, he'd managed to get his point across. He hadn't spent much time on his style, but he'd sure as hell spent a lot of time working on his image. If we were going to catch him, we'd have to play his game.

The police had already made a good first step before they even came to us. Not only had they formed a task force to assimilate all the evidence and leads and hunt for the killer, the same day the letter came in to the television station, the chief held a press conference and publicly announced the communication and the department's belief in its authenticity.

"I want to restate that there is no question in our minds but that the person who wrote the letter killed these people. This person has consistently identified himself with the phrase Search and Destroy and wants to be known as the Search and Destroyer. Because we are sure this man is responsible for six murders, we wish to enlist the assistance of each citizen of this community."

As new as I was at profiling and criminal investigative analysis, I already knew how good the chief's instincts were, a feeling that has only strengthened in me throughout my law enforcement career.

There is a tendency in this kind of work to want to withhold and control information, and sometimes, of course, that is necessary. In each open case, you have to keep certain details secret so you can evaluate and authenticate your various suspects and witnesses. Any sensational crime or crime series, and Search and Destroyer certainly qualified as that, is bound to have a bunch of crazies coming out of the woodwork claiming credit. In other words, you're going to have confessions from people who'd like to have done what the killer did, but couldn't, so this is an attempt to get the recognition and have the fantasy come to life as it had for the real offender. And there's got to be a way to screen them out before they waste too much of your time.

But on the whole, I have found over and over and over again that the public is almost always your best and most effective partner in bringing UNSUBs to justice. Someone out there knows him. Someone out there has seen or heard something. Someone out there has the missing piece to the puzzle. "Douglas's First Rule of Crime-Solving" states that the more you share with the public, the more they're going to be able to help you.

Partially because of this, I wasn't the first to offer a "profile" of Search and Destroyer. The media went crazy with "Motivation X," with psychiatrists and psychologists weighing in on what it meant and how the UNSUB had come to be the way he was. There was actually merit in some of what was stated, but our approach to profiling is, by its very nature, going to be much different from that of most of the mental health community. It's their job to use raw psychological data to tell them how he became the way he is. It's my job to use the material to figure out what he's like right now, how we can recognize him, and what we can do to catch him before he does any more.

For example, one psychologist wrote a column theorizing that the killer had studied extensively in medical or psychological journals trying to better understand himself and the motivations for his deadly acts, and that he had sought counseling as far back as adolescence to deal with his impulsive feelings and violent fantasies.

Maybe, maybe not. What I was seeing, from a practical criminal-profiling perspective, was a guy fascinated with police life, procedure, and culture. He was either in some form of law enforcement or very much wanted to be and fantasized about the power that status would give him. Not only was I convinced he was taking crime-scene photos as the real police would, his written descriptions of the bodies and scenes were methodical, procedural, and full of police-type jargon, such as giving north-south, east-west orientations to how the bodies were placed or found. With the kind of pictures he was taking, I wouldn't be surprised if he was also making sketches, fantasizing and planning the future crimes he promised in his letter.

The offices of the Behavioral Science Unit were in a subbasement at Quantico, sixty feet underground. The suite had originally been designed as a relocation center for the national law enforcement brain trust in case of national emergency. The bunker mentality might be a good one in case of enemy attack, but on a daily basis I found it some-what stifling. So when I had a case that I really wanted to think about and focus on, I used to go over to an adjacent building, up to the top floor of the library, where the Legal Unit did its research, and isolate myself with the case materials. I would sit there by myself and try to visualize the scene as it was happening—what must have taken place between the victim and the subject. I would try to do an extensive analysis of the victim, what we came to call victimology, equally impor-tant as understanding the perpetrator in getting a handle on the crime.

And unlike my tiny basement office, the library had windows and plenty of light. You didn't feel as if you were working in a crypt.

As my first step, I tried to imagine how each particular victim would have reacted when confronted by the subject. I would analyze the wounds, try to interpret them to understand why the victim was treated as she was.

For example, if you found out from your research that this would have been a compliant victim, but you found evidence of torture on the body, that would tell you something about the UNSUB and his signature. It would tell you that he inflicted pain for its own sake, that that's what he needed to make the crime satisfying.

I tried to visualize, to internalize, the terror young Melissa Peterson, this eleven-year-old child, must have gone through as her attacker forced her at gunpoint to undress, as he bound her wrists together, as he tied her around the waist and legs. Had he already killed her parents? My guess was that he had—you have to neutralize the greatest threat first. Did she know they were dead and couldn't come to her aid? She must have heard the commotion, heard them scream or beg for their and their children's lives. Did she know that this would only turn on her tormentor even more? My stomach churned and I became almost physically ill as I imagined him cinching the cord ligature tighter and tighter. He knew that the image of him, her torturer, would be the last thing this young girl ever saw, and he must have reveled in the thought. How could anyone do such a thing to another person, much less someone this young and blameless? Once you've seen pictures like this, how can you not be obsessed about hunting down the one who did it?

Melissa, I cannot now, nor will I ever be able to, put you out of my mind, or stop thinking about your mother and father and brother, and all the others like you, who are dead now because someone else decided you should be. And just because other people have not seen what I have seen does not mean it could not have happened to them just as easily as it happened to you and your wonderful family. You could be any of us, and any of us could be you.

And yet, merely being angry, merely craving the blood of the guilty to avenge the blood of the innocent, accomplishes nothing. What does the evidence tell you? What could I intuit from the crime-scene photos and the other material I had to work with?

Later, we would come to use terms such as *organized* and *disorganized* to characterize offenders. What I could say as I looked at the evidence was that this one certainly seemed to have his act together in terms of implementing what he set out to do. I saw no evidence that he knew the victims personally, which meant he had been surveilling them (another thing he'd consider policelike) and constructing his fantasy of control, degradation, and murder before he went in. Because that was one thing we knew from our prison interviews and research: with sexual predators, the fantasy always precedes the act.

The police report described semen found on Melissa's leg. No surprise; we see a lot of predators masturbate at the scene. But how does it tie in with the rest of the behavioral evidence?

He's very visual, I noted. Not only does he take photos and take pains to describe the scene, he stages his victims the way he wants to.

This was particularly true of Melissa, to whom he seemed to have devoted the most time and attention. What this meant to me was that even though he's sexually obsessed, he feels deeply inadequate and therefore more comfortable with children than with his chronological peers. His inadequacy is evident by the fact that even though he strips the women, he doesn't penetrate them. Instead, he just uses them as props for his masturbatory fantasies. In fact, he probably jerked off on her after she was already dead.

Though he certainly puts his victims through a horrible ordeal, it is not physical torture in the sense that we see it in sexual sadists, who have to inflict intense physical pain to get off. The torture is mostly mental, his way of asserting power and superiority. Though he may fantasize about physical torture, this is no more a part of his signature than actual intercourse with his victims.

His arrested development would probably have shown up first in Peeping Tom or voyeuristic situations, which would tie in with his propensity for surveillance. He spent so much time with the victims that he had to feel confident he was in control of the environment. He had to know that there were only four members of the family and no one else was likely to break in on him.

Just as significant as what he did to Melissa was what he did to her little brother. In one of his letters he stated that he placed the bag over the boy's head to suffocate him, just as he claimed he intended to do to Frances Farrell's sons before he was interrupted by the telephone. But he also used ligature strangulation on young Daniel, just as he did to his parents and sister. So the bag was, in our terminology, overkill, which meant there had to be another reason for it. And the reason, I felt confident, was that, unlike the others, he didn't feel good about this kill. He wanted to cover it up and also prevent Danny's dead eyes from accusing him.

Why? Because this was the one he identified with, just as he identified with Frances Farrell's young boys and shut them up in the bathroom so they wouldn't see what he was going to do to their mother. Whether he would have treated the girl in the same way remains open to speculation.

Sitting alone at the library table, I began constructing my profile, longhand on a yellow legal pad, heading the first page "MULTIPLE HOMICIDES," with the name of the city.

I began with what had already become our usual disclaimer, "It should be noted that the attached analysis is not a substitute for a thorough and well-planned investigation," and went on to point out that the information contained in the profile was based on our knowledge of behavior in similar cases, but that no two criminal acts or criminal personalities are exactly alike.

I then went on to describe the Search and Destroy murders as the result of fantasies acted out by an inadequate type, a nobody, who, for the first time in his life, has placed himself in a position of importance and control, finally receiving the recognition he believes has been his due for many years. He's so inadequate, however, that he can't even come up with original crimes and has to pattern himself after other well-publicized criminals. He's so jealous of other killers' publicity that he seizes on the Son of Sam as a model, even though the Peterson murders took place before Son of Sam was even active. In other words, he looks to killers who began after him in a wretched attempt to define himself.

The UNSUB would be a white male in his twenties or early thirties. He could be married, but if he was, there would be ongoing problems of both a personality and sexual type.

This guy is alienated, lonely, and withdrawn. He's probably never had a normal heterosexual experience with a woman. His victims appear to be people who, unlike him, are outgoing and loved by others, so he renders them worse off than himself—not only vulnerable but completely helpless, begging for their lives.

Based on the profiles we'd composed of similar offenders in our prison interviews, I expected the UNSUB to come from a broken family and to have been raised primarily by an overbearing mother who was inconsistent in her discipline. She may have been highly religious and placed a burden of guilt on her son from an early age. His father probably left home or died when the UNSUB was young, maybe around Danny's age or even younger. I wouldn't have been surprised to learn he was raised by foster parents.

In school, he would have been an average student, but more interested in disrupting the class than in doing his work. His language certainly suggests interest in law enforcement, but it could also mean that he's been in the military. This was underscored by his use of the phrase *search and destroy,* but I didn't make too much of it. In 1974, Vietnam was so much in the public consciousness that virtually everyone was familiar with the term. In his case, it could represent just one more bit of fantasy.

Any arrest record he'd have racked up so far would involve breaking and entering or voyeurism. Unlike a lot of sexual predators, we wouldn't expect to see any outright rapes in his past.

He chooses the neighborhoods for his crimes based on his comfort level, where he has a choice of several different targets and where there is always an easy escape route or place to hide, such as a park. His targets, as he himself suggests, are a combination of some planning and then opportunity—the available victim when he has the urge to kill.

The extended periods between the murders could have had several causes. He might have been in the service or out of the area for some other reason. He could have been institutionalized in a mental facility, or he could have been incarcerated on an unrelated charge, such as B&E.

We know from his own words that he is closely monitoring the media and craves the recognition they offer. What we would also expect for a police buff of this type is that he would somehow attempt to inject himself into the investigation, such as by frequenting police hangouts where he could ingratiate himself with the cops and/or overhear conversations. This will make him feel like "one of them," which is what he wants to be, and at the same time make him feel superior, which he needs to so as to assuage his own inadequacy, since he has been able to outwit law enforcement and create a high level of fear in the community. If he starts feeling sufficiently superior, he could offer more communication, either by phoning the police directly or by sending them or the press actual photos he's taken at a crime scene. Because we could expect him to kill again and keep killing, perfecting his fantasy and gaining confidence each time he gets away with it.

A profile is an important tool, but it is only one of several. If the investigators believe in it, it can help them narrow down a suspect list or recognize a hot prospect when they see him. This is particularly true in situations in which we advise the police that they've probably already interviewed the UNSUB as part of their initial inquiries. But just as important, if not more so, is understanding the meaning of the profile enough to translate it into proactive techniques, and that had to be the next phase of our advice.

What we had to play on, I felt, was his overwhelming self-centeredness and arrogance. Somewhere along the line, he will brag to a friend or acquaintance or possibly even family member and let slip something about what he's done. The police fascination could work to our advantage, too. If he's not actually a member of some law enforcement agency, even if he's just a security guard or part-time rent-a-cop at night, he might try to impersonate a police officer. From his interest in bondage, he probably reads the "true detective" magazines, since bondage and depiction of various forms of domination of women are staples of such publications. As a result, he'll know from the ads how easy it is to send away for an authentic-looking police or detective badge, which he'll carry on his person. In fact, he may even use this MO to gain admittance into his victims' homes, since there is generally no sign of forced entry. He probably flashes his badge whenever the opportunity presents itself, such as when paying for drinks at the local bar.

He's concerned about being caught, but so taken up by the hoopla he's created that his ego might keep him in the area even after the heat is turned up.

I had learned that a branch of the state university, which wasn't far from the murder sites, had a criminal justice department. I thought there was a good chance Search and Destroyer had taken courses there or, if not, had at least examined books on law enforcement. On our advice, police started monitoring copying machines there by making particular marks on the document glass and supplying the machines with paper bearing special watermarks. One of these watermarks on a later communication showed that he had, in fact, been hanging around the university.

I thought it was important to put as much stress on him as we could. It might be a good idea to announce that a suspect had been seen outside the Peterson or Gallagher residence cutting phone wires. The more pressure we could keep him under, the more his postoffense behavior would become apparent to those around him. Family, friends, or coworkers should be alerted to look for increased alcohol consumption, change in appearance such as weight loss, growing or shaving off a beard, general nervousness, and a preoccupation with the case, perhaps bringing it up often in conversation for no apparent reason. Just as the killings were always on his mind, so would be the search for their perpetrator. He would be both exhilarated and scared at the same time. And our job was to force his hand by forcing his behavior.

And what if he is actually a cop? I wondered to myself. This might be one of us. He could call me on another case he was working on and ask for my help and advice. I've often said so myself—they're all around us; they make us see right through them. But it's particularly damning when an offender turns out to be one who's sworn to uphold the law. It's a perversion of nature—the same sort of perversion of nature as when children precede their parents in death, a phenomenon I have seen all too often in my career.

Based on how I thought he felt about his various victims, I thought one way to bring him out would be by publicly focusing on Danny Peterson, or possibly even Frances Farrell's sons, who survived her. This could be accomplished by a newspaper or magazine story or a television feature that got the UNSUB to relate to these victims as real people. Whatever remorse, whatever misgivings, he had about his acts might then come to the surface. That's why I often liked to announce dates of memorial services or locations of graves, knowing from our research that, for a variety of reasons, offenders do return to visit their victims.

We gave the police a series of additional tips on forcing Search and Destroyer's hand—trying to bring him out into the open before he killed again. I don't want to get into too many of the specifics because they remain strategic this many years later. One thing I warned them about, especially with all the Motivation X psychologizing going on in the local media: I didn't want officials to let him be portrayed as a psychotic animal, thereby giving him an out. I thought he was more likely to kill again if he could convince himself that the acts really were beyond his control and he therefore had a psychological excuse for perpetrating them.

While we all held our collective breath, there were no more murders that matched the pattern of the Search and Destroyer. But police did receive a drawing in the mail. It was both icily clinical in style and disgustingly pornographic in content, portraying a nude woman on a bed, gagged and tightly bound, having been penetrated by a large stake. It could have been a crime-scene drawing, except that so far as we could tell, it didn't represent any actual crime. Rather, I thought, it was his fantasy conception of what he imagined his next scenario would be like. Police officers across the metropolitan area were given composite physical descriptions based on all the witness accounts and alerted as to what type of suspicious activity to be looking for, and what type of victims and MO to expect from the unknown subject.

I wish I could report that this story has a happy ending. It does not. In fact, it has no ending at all. As far as anyone could tell, after the murder of Lori Gallagher, the killer seemed to vanish. The case has never been closed, he could still be out there, and that is why I have changed the names and some of the details.

What happened? Why did he stop?

We may never know for sure. One possible explanation is that, like some other serial killers who suddenly seem to stop despite our best predictions and worst fears that they will continue, he might have been picked up for something else and sent to prison or a mental institution, never being connected with the horrible series of murders that terrified the region for so many years. He could have died in an automobile accident or been killed by a sometime accomplice or other enemy. Another possibility is that he injected himself too closely into the investigation—that he was interviewed, realized how close they were to reaching him, and got scared.

Most serial sexual predators keep going until they are stopped one way or another. But this case might have been somewhat special. This one was so visual, so laden with fantasy, so removed from any kind of real or meaningful human contact, that the fantasy itself might have been enough to keep him going, once he'd gotten a taste of the real searching and destroying that had become such an obsession to him. He may have been able to content himself with the idea that he had held the power of life and death over others, and exercised that power, and he had "outwitted" the combined forces of law enforcement, proving himself superior to them. He had been the center of media attention in ways that he never could have merited except through these flagrant acts of public outrage. In his own small and twisted mind, he had become a somebody. He still had his photographs and God knew how many drawings like the one he had sent to the police. They might have been enough for him.

Was I wrong about Search and Destroyer and that's why he was never brought to justice? I don't think so, but he's the only one who knows for sure. And I'm not even really certain that that's true, because I think, as a result of our work and research, we have more insight into his obsession than he does.

Years after all of this, there was another series of crimes that looked as if it might have had similar MO and signature elements. The media began speculating as to whether the Search and Destroyer was back. But a letter came in to one of the local media outlets, saying, in effect, "It's not me." Assuming that the letter was authentic, he was, and may still be, out there.

I begin intentionally with this cautionary tale from my early days as a profiler.

We might as well admit right here that the good guys don't always come out on top. Like medicine, what we practice isn't an exact science, and because of the stakes involved, our losses can be devastating to us, knowing that the predator is still at large, waiting to spring again. Predators come in many forms and guises, and they're all dangerous. Despite our dedication, despite our own obsessions, we don't always get them.

It's a sad truth that we don't win every battle, and we probably never will. And even for those in which we triumph, by definition we can never achieve more than a partial victory, because by the time we enlist, someone has already been victimized. It gives me some peace, however, to think that the obsession that came over me thinking about the killer of the Peterson family, of Frances Farrell and Lori Gallagher, and probably others as well . . . that that obsession stayed with me and my colleagues and helped us dedicate ourselves and fully focus on the thousands of other victims who became our clients and the thousands of other predators we helped pursue.

If the first lesson of this cautionary tale is humility on the part of those of us who go out to do battle, the second is knowledge, awareness, and some basic forethought and preparedness on all our parts— because the only total victory is when we can *prevent* these monsters from victimizing us, our family, and our friends in the first place. That isn't an exact science either, but I know it can make a huge difference.

The war never ends and we're all soldiers. But first, we have to understand the enemy and the fight we have to wage, individually and as a society. That's what we need to be thinking about.

CHAPTER TWO

THE HUNTER
AND THE HUNTED

Manipulation. Domination. Control.

These are the watchwords of all sexual predators, be they stalkers, rapists, or killers. They also have to be my watchwords, and those of my colleagues, as we try to get inside their heads to hunt them down.

The key tool we use is profiling, or, as I began calling it when I became chief of the FBI's Investigative Support Unit (which previously had been called the Behavioral Science Unit; I told people I was getting rid of the BS) at Quantico, criminal investigative analysis. This includes not only coming up with profiles of UNSUBs, but also proactive techniques for catching them, evaluation of case linkages, and then interrogation and prosecutorial strategies once an offender has been identified. But the important thing to remember is that we're not the only ones doing the profiling and analysis. The people we hunt are doing it, too; you can be sure of that.

Any sexual predator, before he's been in the business for too long, has his own preferences and learns his own techniques. He knows how to locate and identify—profile, if you will—the victim of preference, the victim of opportunity. He knows how to get inside that victim's head and create the effect he's looking for: the manipulation, the domination, the control of that individual, then the manipulation, domination, and control of the law enforcement personnel trying to neutralize him. So we've got to be able to go through the same process he does, only we've got to do it better. We're probably already dominating him—that is, the crime or crimes he's committed will be taking up most, if not all, of his conscious thought. He'll be following the media, trying to monitor the police investigation, so we've already got his attention. We've got to figure out how to manipulate the way he responds, the actions he contemplates taking, with the idea of being able to predict, and ultimately control, his next move. He's playing a game, and it's the most important thing in the world to him. We've got to be able to play that game as seriously as he does.

When I talk about playing the game, I'm not just talking about me, my fellow FBI agents, and all the dedicated police officers, detectives, and prosecutors across the country and around the world. I'm talking about you, all of you, all of us, because we're all potential prey for these guys, and we can all do something to avoid playing that role of victim, to fight back. Because it's great to be able to catch them after they've perpetrated some outrage. It's a whole lot better to be able to prevent them from doing it in the first place. But to have a shot at that, we have to understand.

This is a book about obsession: the obsession of the creatures who prey on the innocent and vulnerable, and the obsession they've engendered in people like me who've spent their careers trying to understand them and put them out of business. More specifically, it's about interpersonal violent crime and what we can do about it. And it's also about the victims themselves, and their loved ones and survivors, as they pursue their own obsession for justice and closure and peace—as they struggle, quite literally, to get their lives back. And make no mistake, when violent predators go unchecked in our society, we all become victims.

As we did in both *Mindhunter* and *Journey into Darkness,* we're going to relate some interesting stories and bring you into the heads of both the hunters and the hunted. But we want this book to be more than simply a collection of grim and fascinating case histories. While it is certainly that, we also want to show you how you can cut down the odds of victimization for yourself, your loved ones, your friends. And we also want to show that for all the bad people out there we need to neutralize, there are a lot of very good and very brave people, too, doing the work that needs to be done. We want to highlight those people and organizations whom we consider to be models for positive change, prevention, and healing. We are at war and they are our real comrades in arms.

I use the word *war* purposefully, and you might as well know right now where I'm coming from with all this. Violent, predatory crime is a scourge that has become intolerable. We either become victims of the criminal ourselves, or we become victims of fear for ourselves, our families, our children. Recently, there have been some national statistical declines in various types of violent crimes, and that's certainly welcome. But I've got to tell you, I've been in this business a long time, and I'm not terribly optimistic that this represents an ongoing trend. It won't take much—a decline in the economy, the next generation of crack babies coming of age without any realistic prospects or emotional support system—to make our society as violent as it's ever been. A lot of experts think we won't even reach the peak until between 2005 and 2010, and I wonder if the same politicians who are taking bows for the current decrease will still be around to accept the blame for what some of us already see coming. In the meantime, there's still plenty of violence and plenty of fear to go around.

If we're going to attempt to come to grips with this issue, which consistently rivals the economy and personal financial anxieties on polls of Americans' number one concern, it's only going to be by declaring outright war on the problem.

While preparing to write this book, I happened to be watching on television the debate on the 1997 Juvenile Crime Bill. I've had to testify a number of times on Capitol Hill before various committees and subcommittees concerned with law enforcement, crime, and its effects, so I was interested in hearing how the debate would be framed and which arguments—I think I've heard them all by this point—would be brought to bear, and by whom.

Some of the debaters said we need to get tougher on crime, with more prisons and stiffer sentences. Others said that this was just political posturing—that we need to spend money on social programs, and get to "the root of the problem" by attacking the foundations of poverty and social inequality. Some said the answer lies in improved education or job prospects, and that is where we should be concentrating our resources. Still others argued that the answer was early intervention with potentially problem children—to get them out of their damaging home environments and into the therapy and exposure to the positive role models they needed.

As if any of these people has *the* answer.

I say the real answer should be obvious. If we're serious about this, and not just spouting off easy, hackneyed political rhetoric, then what we need is a real war on crime. And that means you throw everything you've got at the enemy.

None of these suggestions is, or should be, mutually exclusive. Of course we have to get to the root of the problems of poverty and inequality. Of course we have to identify potential problem children and individuals and attempt to intervene before it's too late. Of course we have to give children the best educational opportunities we possibly can. Of course we have to offer better jobs and job training possibilities. And of course we need stiffer and more certain sentences so that the ones we haven't been able to help aren't free to continue their predatory ways. To hope that any one thing will work is like hoping that there will be a single cure for all cancer. It would be great if it happened, but none of the experts I know is counting on it. If you think by getting to the roots of poverty you're going to eliminate the need for prisons, that's just as naive as saying that any of us is going to feel appreciably safer or more secure if we give everyone who's been convicted of a violent crime a fifty-year sentence his first time out. In the meantime, let's see what we can do to feel more personally secure and in control.

When it comes time for sentencing, the defense attorney often asserts that despite what his client has just been convicted of doing, the defendant isn't really a bad person; he's got a good, kind, sensitive, caring, vulnerable side, too. That's what they tried to show about Timothy McVeigh during the sentencing phase of the Oklahoma City bombing trial. They showed childhood photos and had friends tell touching and funny stories; jurors heard testimony about what a loyal soldier he was from Army buddies. They tried to explain that what happened was that Mr. McVeigh was so emotionally devastated over seeing women and children burned to death in the Branch Davidian compound in Waco, Texas, that he had to vent his fury at the federal government by blowing up one of its buildings and hundreds of occupants on the anniversary of the Waco disaster.

To all of this, I say, "Wrong!" or more pointedly, "Crap!" This good, kind, sensitive, caring, vulnerable fellow coldly planned and carried out an action that predictably stole 168 innocent lives. That's what he was capable of. The other aspects of his life and personality become completely irrelevant. This is a theme we'll be coming back to again and again, as I have throughout my career in law enforcement.

We are what we think.

We are what we do.

I will concede that virtually anyone who commits murder or some other horrible or violent act can be thought of as being "mentally ill." Normal, mentally healthy people just don't do those kinds of things. I do not believe it follows, however, that such men (and occasionally women) are therefore "insane" or unable to conform their actions to the laws of society or the dictates of common morality.

Just as I do not believe that there is any one simple fix for our crime problem, it is probably also simplistic and somewhat naive to suppose that there is one single, all-encompassing psychoneurological explanation for why people commit violent crimes, particularly when they commit those violent crimes repeatedly. One school of theorists bases its ideas on the belief that violent behavior is the result of a combination of organic injuries or abnormalities in the brain, together with an abusive childhood or family life. Another theory suggests that the organic brain problems seen in certain members of such an antisocial population may actually be the result of injuries caused by reckless or foolhardy behavior, that is, the behavior may have caused the condition rather than the condition causing the behavior.

My own experience, beginning with the first organized study of serial killers and repeat violent offenders initiated back in the late 1970s when I was a young agent recently assigned to the FBI Academy in Quantico, makes me believe that virtually all of them come from abusive or otherwise severely dysfunctional backgrounds. But that doesn't explain or excuse what they do.

After all I've seen, there's no question in my mind that neglect or abuse of young children has the serious potential to produce some very psychologically messed-up people. I don't think many mental health professionals would disagree with that assessment, and all of our hearts go out to these individuals.

What I have not seen established, through any combination of logic or data, is the connection that those psychologically messed-up people are therefore *compelled* to commit violent crime. They are portrayed to us as victims of bad treatment, turning our compassion against us. But once they aggress against others, they instantly forfeit whatever claims they had to victim status. Despite a bad background or any other supposedly mitigating or explanatory factors, they choose to commit violent, predatory crime.

While a bad background doesn't make it any easier for a given antisocial individual to "go straight," we see over and over again that siblings of sexual predators and other repeat offenders turn out respectable and law-abiding. As a reaction to their early environment, many even go into the type of social work, law enforcement, or political reform that may prevent others from suffering similar experiences.

Let me repeat that, because it is one of the key philosophical underpinnings of this book and, in fact, my entire approach to crime and punishment: With the rare exception of the truly insane individual— and these types are generally caught pretty quickly as opposed to experienced and organized serial offenders—the predator, and particularly the sexual predator, commits violent acts because he *chooses* to do so. The operative word is always *choice.* That's where I stand, and if you don't agree with that, or aren't open-minded enough to let me try to convince you in this book, you may as well stop reading right now.

Those who've read *Mindhunter* or *Journey into Darkness* will recall the name Edmund Emil Kemper III. Of all the serial killers from our original study, he's probably the one who's most interested and intrigued me with the combination of his intellect, sheer physical presence, the brutality of his crimes, and the apparently genuine insight into their cause and effect and his own twisted psyche. I interviewed him at the California State Medical Facility at Vacaville. Kemper killed, mutilated, and in some cases beheaded a number of beautiful young women near the campus of the University of California at Santa Cruz in the early 1970s. Prior to that, as a fourteen-year-old, he had shot his grandparents to death while visiting them on their farm and been committed to California's Atascadero State Hospital for the criminally insane until he was twenty-one. The background of all of this is that Ed, who ended up an imposing, broad-chested man about six feet nine, had never gotten along with his mother, Clarnell, who had raised him after she and his father, Edmund Jr., had separated when Ed and his two sisters were young. Among other belittling cruelties, once the sensitive Ed reached puberty and began to grow dramatically tall, Clarnell banished him to a makeshift basement bedroom, fearing he might try to molest his sisters. It's true that Ed already had displayed some alarmingly weird behavior, including dismembering two family cats and engaging in death-ritual games with his sister Susan. It's also true that Clarnell—who by the time of Ed's murderous reign of terror had already left husband number three and was working as a secretary at U.C., Santa Cruz—showed considerably more interest in and empathy for students she met casually in her job than she did for her own son. And it's further true, as I've admitted before, that of all the serial killers and violent offenders I've had occasion to study in my career, I probably "liked" Ed the best and empathized with him more than the others because of his superior intellect, insight, and willingness to confront the monsters within him.

Having said all that, there is no doubt in my mind that Edmund Kemper picked up and killed the six young women in and around Santa Cruz as an attempt—horribly misguided though it may have been—to get back at his mother. This is certainly authenticated by the fact that he buried the head of at least one of his victims in the yard outside Clarnell's window because she'd always wanted people "to look up to her." Ed eventually did get up the nerve to bludgeon her to death in her bed, cut off her head, and feed her larynx down the garbage disposal because he was tired of the way "she'd bitched and screamed and yelled at me over so many years." Kemper told me that he had often crept into his mother's bedroom as she slept and fantasized about stabbing her with a knife or beating her to death with a hammer.

Directly after he did kill her, he called her friend Sally Hallett over for a "surprise" dinner, whereupon he clubbed and strangled and decapitated her, placed her headless body in his bed, then went to sleep in his mother's bed before setting out on a multistate car journey that ultimately ended when he contacted police from a Colorado phone booth and told them to come and get him. He'd gotten it out of his system and so was ready to call it quits. If I look into my own psyche, perhaps that's the reason for my rapport with Kemper—he stopped on his own.

Now, as much as I "understand" why Ed did what he did, this certainly does not imply that I condone or accept it as inevitable. More to the point, I do not believe, and find no evidence or suggestion, that he *had* to kill these women—that, because of his background, upbringing, and belief structure, he was *compelled* to kill them. Quite the contrary; he was organized and well-controlled. Not only did he not stage any of his crimes while a uniformed police officer was watching—a sure sign of compulsion that no serial killer in my experience or knowledge has ever displayed—he managed to drive safely through a manned guard post where cars were being examined while he had the body of one of his victims, posed as a sleeping girlfriend, in the seat beside him. He indicated to me how he took personal satisfaction in showing up at one of his parole-mandated psychiatric interviews with the severed head of fifteen-year-old Aiko Koo in the trunk of his car.

Would Ed Kemper have done the horrible things he did had he not had the bad background and family trauma? Maybe not. Does that excuse his crimes? Absolutely not, and I suspect that the bright and insightful Kemper, who expects to spend the rest of his life in confinement, would agree with that.

So let's get this straight and state it plainly: It is my belief, based on several decades of experience, study, and analysis, that the overwhelming majority of repeat sexual predators do what they do because they want to, because it gives them a satisfaction they do not achieve in any other aspect of their lives, and because it makes them feel good, regardless of the consequences to others. In that respect, the crime represents the ultimate in selfishness; the predator doesn't care what happens to his victim as long as he gets what he wants. In fact, exercising this manipulation, domination, and control—and the infliction of pain and death are for him their ultimate expressions—are the critical factors in making him feel complete and fully alive. Ed Kemper *chose* to kill those women because, for whatever reason, it fulfilled something in himself.

Are serial killers and other sexual predators mentally ill?

You could say so; it's largely a matter of definition. Certainly they're abnormal. Certainly what they do is "sick." Certainly they have a severe character disorder or defect. Certainly anyone who gets his pleasure from rape and torture and death has some fairly pronounced psychological problems. But "insanity" is a matter of definition, too. And what we rely on to test for insanity today, whether it's the traditional knowledge of the difference between right and wrong as set forth by the British M'Naghten Rule of 1843, or the more modern American Law Institute Model Penal Code Test, we're still talking about the ability to control impulses and appreciate the consequences of your actions. A lot of people don't seem to grasp the concept that you can have mental or emotional problems—even severe ones—and still be able to distinguish right from wrong and conform your behavior accordingly. In other words, *you don't have to commit violent crime.* If you commit violent crime, in virtually all cases, you do so by choice, just as any of us decide what to eat, to seek a job, to form relationships, whatever—all by choice.

A predator can be obsessed with killing, just as I can be obsessed with hunting him down. But he isn't forced to kill any more than I am forced to pursue him.

Yes, there are people who commit violent crimes because they are literally crazy, even delusional, but there aren't that many, and virtually none is a serial killer or rapist. The true crazies are not difficult to catch.

By the same token, you'll often see a claim of multiple personality disorder, or MPD, surface postarrest. William Heirens didn't kill those women; George Murman, who resided inside him, did. No one wants to take responsibility for what he's done: it's another personality that's taken over my good personality. But in every serial murder case I've consulted on in which MPD was offered as a defense, the claim was completely unfounded. First, the condition is extremely rare. Second, it begins in early childhood, generally as a defense mechanism against severe sexual or physical abuse, so there should be ample verification of the disorder's manifestations in the subject long before the commission of crime. Third, the great majority of MPD sufferers are women. And fourth, there is no psychiatric literature I know of which suggests that multiple personality disorder compels, or even predisposes, one to violence. In other words, even if you could convince me that your client suffered from MPD, that would be an incidental finding, and not the explanation for why he killed or raped.

David Berkowitz, the self-proclaimed "Son of Sam" who terrorized New York City from the summer of 1976 until he was caught as the result of a routine license-plate check during the summer of 1977, claimed in publicized letters and statements that he killed six young men and women with his .44-caliber handgun as they sat in their cars because his neighbor's three-thousand-year-old dog had commanded him to do so. Admittedly, many people commit violent crimes for reasons unfathomable to the rest of us, but that one got my bullshit detector going big time. Nothing else in Berkowitz's behavior suggested he was taking his marching orders from a dog. He had served in the Army and held a job as a postal employee in New York City. He made a trip to Texas during which he purchased a Charter Arms .44 Bulldog, a powerful weapon. He went out into the city dumps and practiced his shooting until he became reasonably proficient. And then he went out on the streets nightly, hunting for his victims of preference: young couples parked in cars on makeshift lovers' lanes, each time approaching the woman's side of the car first and firing at her.

A check of his background revealed that he had been put up for adoption as a baby but did not learn of this until he served in the military. As a child and young man he set more than two thousand fires in the Brooklyn-Queens area—some in trash cans, some in abandoned buildings—which he documented with obsessional diary entries, and would masturbate while watching the flames and the firefighters. Bringing all these people out because of something he had done was probably the only time he felt powerful and potent.

He had his first sexual encounter with a woman while serving as a soldier in Korea—with a prostitute who gave him gonorrhea. When he left the Army, he went back to New York and located his biological mother and sister in Long Beach, Long Island (as it happens, not far from where I grew up). When he finally contacted them, he was shocked and distressed to learn that they wanted nothing to do with him. It was then that his resentment and anger against women transformed into an obsession with men and women who weren't lonely and inadequate as he was, and that was when he procured the weapon that made him feel powerful and virile.

I interviewed Berkowitz in Attica State Prison when a few of my colleagues and I were conducting what became the first organized behavioral study of violent and multiple offenders. Out of this study came the book *Sexual Homicide: Patterns and Motives,* which we coauthored with Professor Ann W. Burgess of the University of Pennsylvania. More important was an approach to criminal profiling and investigative analysis that, for the first time, was based on a correlation between evidence and indicators found in and around the crime and what would be going on inside the criminal's mind at the time. Berkowitz had originally pleaded guilty and been sentenced to multiple twenty-five-years-to-life terms, but had since denied his guilt for a variety of reasons, his supposed insanity being one of them.

It will come as no surprise that it is in the nature of repeat criminals to lie as a matter of course, and the ones we interviewed, particularly the more "successful" of them, were notorious manipulators of everyone within their orbit. We had learned that if we were to get anything accurate and useful from the interviews and not merely provide a self-serving forum or entertaining diversion for a bored long-termer, we had to be totally prepared, and that meant knowing the case and the crimes at least as well as the offender himself did. This often meant slogging through hours of verbal sparring before the subject realized he couldn't con us the way he may have done with psychiatrists, the press, or even his own attorneys. This was particularly true of insanity claims.

During a long and rambling interview, Berkowitz admitted to me that while roaming the streets on the hunt, if he couldn't find a victim of opportunity that suited his preference, he would return to the site of one of his previous kills, masturbate, and relive the moment of triumph. It was the same as the Search and Destroyer's jerking off over the crime-scene photos I was sure he had.

And as soon as I heard this from David, I knew that his dog story was crap. Like the UNSUB described in the previous chapter and so many other sexual predators, he killed because it made him feel good. It let him possess women in death in a way he felt totally incapable of doing in life. His manipulation, domination, and control of his victims didn't require any verbal interchange or conversation, it didn't require bodily contact, it didn't require the taking of souvenirs such as jewelry or underwear. But it was manipulation, domination, and control just as clearly as if the crimes had had those more common elements.

When we got around to the subject of motive, Berkowitz explained to me how he had been receiving telepathic orders to kill from a three-thousand-year-old demon residing in this black Labrador retriever named Harvey, which belonged to his neighbor Sam Carr. Together with the letters full of obscure symbolism, this immediately suggested paranoid schizophrenia to much of the psychiatric community.

"Hey, David, knock off the bullshit," I said to him. "The dog had nothing to do with it."

He laughed and owned up to the hoax. It was just one more example of manipulation, domination, and control. Like Ed Kemper, the guy wasn't normal, but he knew and understood what he was doing and kept doing it.

And this is one of several reasons why, much as I'd like to believe differently, I find the hope of rehabilitation for most of these people dim to nonexistent. As we will see throughout this book, unlike burglars or bank robbers or even drug dealers, who do not necessarily *enjoy* what they do for a living—who merely want the money it brings them—sexual predators and child molesters do enjoy their crimes; in fact, many of them do not even consider them crimes. They don't want to change.

Dr. Stanton E. Samenow, the Washington, D.C.–area clinical psychologist who has probably done as much as anyone to explore, understand, and try to alter the thinking of habitual lawbreakers, challenges the very notion of rehabilitation. "Rehabilitation as it has been practiced cannot possibly be effective," he writes in his penetrating book, *Inside the Criminal Mind,* "because it is based on a total misconception. To rehabilitate is to restore to a former constructive capacity or condition. *There is nothing to which to rehabilitate a criminal.* There is no earlier condition of being responsible to which to restore him."

I'm afraid my own research and experience, as well as that of my colleagues, leads me to concur wholeheartedly with Dr. Samenow's courageous observation.

In the Investigative Support Unit at Quantico, in our work with local police, we were always trying to understand the nature of the obsession of the unknown predator.

Sometimes he communicated to us directly, as in the Search and Destroyer case, telling us just why he was doing it and how he wanted to be perceived.

Sometimes he enlightened us indirectly, giving us the clues to figure it out, as happened in Atlanta.

And sometimes, we were never sure. Those were the toughest and most agonizing cases of all. One of them nearly killed me. More about that in a moment.

But first, by the winter of 1981, Atlanta, Georgia, was gripped by a terror that had been building for a year and a half, ever since a thirteen-year-old boy named Alfred Evans had gone missing and then turned up dead three days later, in a wooded area on the west side of the city. While searching the site, police discovered another body, partially decomposed, this one belonging to fourteen-year-old Edward Smith, who had disappeared four days before Alfred. Both boys were black. Alfred had been strangled, Edward shot. By the time I got involved, there were sixteen cases, all black children, and as far as anyone could tell, the killer or killers were still active.

At that time, the FBI's profiling program was still new. It had its home at the FBI Academy in Quantico because that's where it had begun, informally at first under Behavioral Science instructors Howard Teten and Dick Ault, then gradually with more formality after the program of prison interviews with serial offenders began. I was still the only full-time profiler, and we were taken with varying degrees of seriousness, not only by the country's law enforcement agencies but within the Bureau as well. There's no question that something considered such touchy-feely voodoo could not have surfaced under the ironfisted reign of J. Edgar Hoover. We had no real operational side, so as the requests for assistance kept coming in and the caseload began to pile up, I was backed up by some of the instructors from the Behavioral Science Unit. As expert as any in the subject of rape and interpersonal violence—not just in the Bureau but the entire world of law enforcement—is Robert "Roy" Hazelwood. Now retired after a distinguished career, Roy is active nationally as a consultant.

He and I went down to Atlanta to try to figure out if the cases were actually related and what type of person or persons was responsible for the murders. To do this, we studied the victimology by going through each file and talking to as many family members and people who knew each victim as we could, visiting each neighborhood. Was there a common trait among the dead children? Then we had the Atlanta police take us to each of the body dump sites so we could start seeing things from the killer's point of view.

The predominant view in Atlanta was that some sort of Ku Klux Klan–type conspiracy was responsible for the deaths of the children, that this was an attempt at genocide against the black race. As compelling as this argument was on its face—after all, the victims were all black, and at that time, serial killers were almost exclusively white—when Roy and I really got into it, neither one of us could buy it.

First of all, the areas in which the children disappeared were overwhelmingly black. A white individual or group really would have stood out and could not have avoided notice. Yet there were no witness accounts involving white subjects. More to the point, a white supremacist group would not have operated anonymously, as this killer was doing. If a hate group such as the Klan commits a violent offense such as a lynching or other racial murder, it is supposed to be a highly symbolic act, intended to make a public statement and create an atmosphere of fear and hysteria among its intended targets. At the very least, we would expect some communication from such a group to come in to the local media taking credit for the act, just as you see after most terrorist bombings and the like, and just as we saw from the Search and Destroyer. As I said, you have to determine the nature of the obsession to determine the personality of the offender. And absent this kind of communication, Roy and I had to conclude that whoever was killing these young children, mostly boys, was doing so for other reasons.

So once we compiled our profile, we felt we were looking for a black male in his twenties who was sexually attracted to these young victims and would use some kind of ruse or come-on involving money to get them to go with him. The next question was, how would he tell us what his reasons were?

The break came on something of a fluke, a red herring, if you will. But there's a lesson in that, too, which is that no detail of a case can either be excluded outright or taken at face value. Everything must be evaluated in the larger context of the investigation.

A case generating as much media attention as the Atlanta Child Murders is bound to get more than its share of false leads and information. This, of course, is one of the reasons it's necessary to withhold certain details of the crimes and crime scenes. At one point, police in the small town of Conyers, Georgia, about twenty miles from Atlanta, got a call from a man, obviously white and a real redneck type, purporting to be the killer and promising to "kill more of these nigger kids." He specified a particular location along Sigmon Road where he said police would find the next body.

As soon as I heard the tape of this call, I was sure this was an impostor, a lowlife satisfying his own racial hatred by anonymously claiming credit for a series of crimes he did not commit. But knowing how the press was following the case, I thought it would be an excellent opportunity to test a theory.

I suggested that the police make the call public and make a great display out of looking for the body, but on the *opposite* side of the street from where he told them to look. I figured the impostor would be watching, and if police got lucky, they might be able to grab him right there. If not, he should at least call again and tell the police what idiots they are, at which point they'll have a trap and trace ready to nab this guy. And that was exactly what happened. They got him right in his own house. And I thought that would be that.

But the press had covered the Sigmon Road episode heavily, and shortly thereafter, another body *did* show up there, that of fifteen-year-old Terry Pue. Only this body showed up where the police were looking, not the side of the street the impostor had specified, which signified that our real guy was closely following the press and now wanted to show that he was superior to everyone—that he could manipulate, dominate, and control the police and press just as he had his young victims. That was the message he was giving us: he and the police were communicating with each other through the media.

The final piece of the puzzle fell into place one murder later, when twelve-year-old Patrick Baltazar's body was found along Buford Highway, strangled as Terry Pue's had been. As part of the official response, someone in the medical examiner's office announced that hair and fibers found on Patrick's body matched those found on five of the previous victims.

Then I knew: the next body is going to turn up in the Chattahoochee River, because he knows the hair and fiber evidence will be washed away by the water and he can once again prove how superior he is to all of us law enforcement jerks. And that, essentially, is what happened. Three more bodies showed up in the river. It took a while to get organized with all of the federal, state, and local law enforcement agencies involved, but Atlanta police staked out several bridges across the Chattahoochee. Nothing happened for some time, but around two-thirty in the morning on the last scheduled day of the surveillance operation, a police officer staking out the Jackson Parkway Bridge heard a splash in the water after seeing a car drive across the bridge and stop in the middle. The car turned and came back across the bridge, at which time another officer stopped it.

The driver of the car was Wayne Bertram Williams, a black male in his twenties who fit the profile perfectly. When he was arrested, hair and fiber evidence found at his house matched those of twelve of the young victims—the same twelve we had linked behaviorally to a single killer. Wayne Williams is currently serving a life sentence for murder of two of the victims.

When the UNSUB doesn't communicate with us either directly or indirectly, we have to speculate, based on our research and past experience. But unless or until we find him, we can't be sure.

The case that almost killed me was the Green River Murders, whose tally has now probably topped sixty. I left that investigation early, not because I wanted to, but because I had no choice. As readers of *Mindhunter* will recall, I collapsed in my Seattle hotel room in December of 1983 while working on the case. I was a thirty-eight-year-old victim of viral encephalitis, brought on by the tremendous stress of not only that investigation, but the 150-odd other active cases that obsessed me at the same time. I would have died in that hotel room if the two special agents I had brought along, Blaine McIlwain and Ron Walker, hadn't gotten worried when they didn't see me and broken down the door to find me. I lingered in a coma for five days, not expected to recover.

But before that, when the bodies of six young women had ended up in or near the Green River, I had done a profile of the killer. Most, if not all, of the early victims had been transients or prostitutes who gravitated to the Seattle-Tacoma corridor. A multiagency and jurisdictional task force had been formed, and the special agent in charge (or SAC as we say in the Bureau) of the Seattle Field Office came to Quantico with a package of materials on the case. As I had done with many other cases, I went up to the top floor of the library to analyze and think about the cases.

From the evidence presented to me, the UNSUB I visualized in this case was a white male in his twenties. He'd be unemployed or underemployed in some sort of blue-collar job. It was clear that he was an outdoorsman, a hunter, fisherman, or hiker who was familiar with the Green River area and knew where he was unlikely to be found. He could have thrown them off a bridge, but he took the time to carry them down to the water, to locations where it would be more difficult to find them.

Among the many details in the profile and the many factors I used in compiling it, one of the most important was the way he'd disposed of the bodies. That is, they were merely dumped, with no particular staging, no ritualistic binding or bags over the head, and no effort at respect, such as covering the body in a dignified way, as we do see with some serial offenders. What this told me was that the UNSUB had no remorse for what he was doing. In fact, I thought he was trying to humiliate the victims as he must have felt humiliated by other women in the past. He saw himself, I felt, as an avenging angel of sorts, whose duty and privilege it was to punish women for their misdeeds.

Both the Green River Killer and the Atlanta Child Murderer disposed of bodies by putting them in the river, where the water would wash away the evidence. Why, then, do I say that the Green River Killer was out to punish his victims (not specifically by inflicting pain for its own sake as a sexual sadist would, but because he felt they deserved punishment for their sins), while the killer in Atlanta had a homosexual attraction to his? There are a number of reasons, which get to the subtlety of profiling and why the process has never been effectively reproduced by computer. First, while the UNSUB may very well have been following the media coverage, there was no evidence he was playing to it or playing off of it. He sought no recognition, but at the same time, the number of cases and the level of violence of the crimes continued to escalate.

Then there is the actual selection of victims—the victimology. In Atlanta, where the victims were young black boys, we concluded that the UNSUB was a black male, which implied a certain type of relationship that we could build on. In Green River, the victims were mainly prostitutes.

Prostitutes are favorite victims of many serial killers for several reasons. First and most basic, the very nature of their work and clientele makes them extremely approachable and vulnerable. They make their living by being picked up. Second, many men, with severe self-image problems of their own, consider them "bad" or defiled or even evil, which they take as an excuse to abuse them. In several instances at Green River, the nude bodies of the victims were found with small rocks stuffed into their vaginas. I have never seen this type of thing done for sexual thrills or for any reason other than to degrade the victim.

So in his own way, I felt, the Green River Killer had told us about his obsession. But in this case, merely understanding it wasn't enough.

For one thing, this profile was general enough that it could reasonably fit a lot of men who might come into contact with the investigators. Except for the indication of familiarity with the region, these were not terribly sophisticated crimes with a unique or specialized signature. The most important use for the profile in a case like this was to structure the proactive techniques that might bring the UNSUB out into the open.

In fact, as the case dragged on and the body count rose, I became increasingly convinced that we were dealing with more than one offender. There were enough variations in location, condition of bodies, small details of the dump site, or the modus operandi, that I grouped the killings around two, then three killers. All would fit the same general profile, and all would be delivering the same sort of message.

Like the series related in the previous chapter, the Green River killings remain unsolved. For that reason, as well as the nearly deadly role the case played in my own life, it has continued to obsess me and probably always will. Someone or more likely several predators are still out there hunting.

And so are we.

CHAPTER THREE

A Tale
of Two Rapists

Imagine you're an eleven-year-old girl, drifting off to sleep. Your little sister has climbed into your bed and is already asleep as you begin to slumber. You fall into the deep, secure sleep that only comes at this age: you're old enough not to worry about monsters in the closet anymore, but still young enough to be comfortably surrounded by your favorite stuffed animals. If they're not back yet, your parents should be home soon from their party. Your grandmother has fallen asleep on the couch in the living room watching TV.

Suddenly, you're awakened by something or someone touching you. You think it's your mother, coming to kiss you good-night, but it's not. It's a strange man, who growls at you to take off your panties. You're still half-asleep, confused. *Who is he? Why is he here?* So he rips your panties off, warning that if you don't start doing what he says right away, he'll punch you hard in the face.

He raises up your nightie. He's kissing you and touching you in places and ways that hurt, but you can't get him off you, and when you beg him to stop, he tells you to shut up or he'll take you outside and hurt you more, or maybe kill your grandmother. All the while, your little sister remains innocently and obliviously asleep. *Please God she stays that way, or maybe he'll hurt her, too.*

When he's done, he gives you a towel to clean yourself up. He says if you tell anyone, he'll come back for you and he'll do even worse things to you.

You believe him; you know he's serious. And you are never the same again.

*   *   *

This sounds like something you'd expect to hear about happening in a city or suburb somewhere in the United States. In fact, it's based on an actual rape that took place in New Zealand. More shocking even than the details of this particular crime is the fact that it was just one of a series of similar assaults on young girls and women that took place over more than a decade. The offender was popularly known as the South Auckland Rapist, named for the area he terrorized from the early 1980s to 1995.

This serial rapist originally came to my attention in the fall of 1994, after two special agents in the Investigative Support Unit, Steve Mardigian and Tom Salp, came back from a conference in Australia where they did a presentation on criminal profiling. Just about whenever we're on the road for teaching or a conference, or a consultation with a local police department or task force, investigators in the area are likely to get in touch with us and ask to meet with us about their difficult, unsolved and/or active cases. Whenever we can, we try to help out.

Steve and Tom were scheduled to pass through Auckland as they traveled to Adelaide for the conference. The head of the serial rape investigation known as Operation Park—named after Manurewa district's Mountfort Park, centrally located to the rapes—was Detective Inspector John Manning. When he learned the agents would be in the area, he met with them and brought scads of material on all the cases they believed might be linked, as well as the investigation to date.

Two years later, in 1996, I was retired from the Bureau and traveling to New Zealand in connection with the release of *Mindhunter.* There, on the scene, I heard further about this case that had become the obsession of law enforcement and citizens alike. And as I learned more about the crimes of this rapist (which totaled at least fifty), I could easily see how he had captured so much attention and caused so much fear.

The rapist struck in the late-night and early-morning hours, generally breaking into homes through open windows or doors that were either unlocked or easy for him to pry open. His victims, often young girls like the one we've just described, were typically surprised in their beds, awakened by a man holding a knife to their throats. He usually covered the face of his victim or wore something to hide his own and set the scene to his liking before awakening his victims, if possible. He would unscrew lightbulbs, rip telephones out of the wall, find ways to barricade his victim or other family members who might try to help in their rooms, leave back doors open for his quick escape. On several occasions his attempted rape was thwarted when relatives in a house responded to the intended victim's surprised screams.

There were other cases in which he abducted a victim on the street, or forced her to leave her home with him, taking her on a forced march in her nightgown and bare feet and raping her outdoors. Then, too, there were instances when girls and women awoke to find a stranger in their home who just said, "Hello," if he spoke at all, and then left, never attempting to touch them. Even when the incidents did not involve rape, the intruder still terrified victims, robbing them of their sense of safety in their own homes.

The rapist could be physically brutal and emotionally cruel, especially when he encountered resistance. He punched some women, even young girls, hard enough to knock them unconscious or break teeth, sending several bleeding victims to the hospital. One young victim was left partially deaf from his blows. It's particularly upsetting to think about the injuries sustained by one victim who wore braces, which cut the inside of her mouth when the rapist hit her in the face. But the rapes were vicious even when he didn't strike his victims. He taunted many he didn't beat with threats of his return.

Yet to other victims he was apologetic, talking to them by using their names, saying good-bye or kissing them on the cheek when he left, as though they were old friends. He verbally abused most victims—even eleven-, thirteen-, and fourteen-year-olds—calling them horny bitches or asking them in vulgar terms how they liked him sexually, but he also told them they were beautiful. If you can imagine it, think of how terrifying and confusing that juxtaposition would be to a victim—especially a very young one. How do you know what to do in that case? How do you try to respond so he won't hurt or kill you? What does he want from you?

The rapist attacked young mothers while their husbands were at work, threatening to kill their children, who were often sleeping in the same room, if the mothers didn't shut up and do what he said. In one case he broke into the home of a forty-year-old single mother with a twelve-year-old daughter and a baby. First he tied up and raped the mother on her living room couch, then raped her daughter at several locations throughout the house. Both victims heard the other's cries as the rapist assaulted them but were powerless to stop him.

He also did something almost unheard of for a serial rapist: he returned to at least one of his victims and raped her a second time. Although most rapists do threaten to come back to their victims—particularly if the victim reports the crime to the police—and virtually all rape victims fear it, it is rare for offenders to actually do so. This individual assaulted his victim on her living room couch, where she'd fallen asleep, then came back about four months later and raped her in her own bed. In another instance, he returned to the home of a fifteen-year-old girl six months after he'd been thwarted in his attempted rape when the victim's mother came to her rescue. The same thing happened the second time, but in both cases the girl suffered a brutal physical attack. In one, the rapist ripped her earlobe, tearing out an earring as he beat her about her face.

Despite the unusual practice of returning to the same victim more than once, he exhibited other more predictable behaviors. We would expect this type of rapist to go back out on the hunt if he finds his efforts thwarted with his first intended victim. This type is motivated by insecurity and uses rape to confirm his masculinity in his own eyes, show himself he has power over women. If he cannot get this from one victim on a given night, he'll likely move on to another unless the risk of capture is just too great. And in fact, this rapist was known to have visited several residences on nights when he had trouble gaining access to the first or second intended victim.

Again, although this man was raised in a completely different culture, across the world from the serial offenders I'd interviewed in prison, he shared with them many of the same predictable behaviors. This only goes to show that violent repeat criminals are not merely products of a particular society or set of social values. Steve Mardigian, Tom Salp, all of us at Quantico who had studied the various rape typologies, knew what kind of man the New Zealand authorities were dealing with. His actions, his "art," gave him away. We know the motivations of men who surprise young girls in their beds, spend just enough time with them to rape them, and then get the hell out. Outwardly, they may appear to have nothing in common, but their crimes reveal that they share the same obsession.

The New Zealand rapist was also probably facilitated by the environment in which he operated, much as American criminals are typically more successful in large urban areas than small towns or exclusive neighborhoods where everyone knows or recognizes everyone else. South Auckland is the informal name for Manukau City, a suburban area of lower-cost housing, factories, and industry that comprises several districts. It is the third largest city in New Zealand, with a population approaching a quarter of a million. These factors combined to form a setting in which it is easy to get lost, to blend in. Many of the crimes took place in homes adjacent to alleyways, making for the possibility of a quick getaway.

The lower economic standard meant, too, that there were a lot of families—and a lot of potential victims—living in circumstances that made them easy prey: children whose parents worked nights and/or were separated, leaving them alone or to baby-sit at a young age; families who could not afford to fix broken windows or locks and found alternative ways to secure doors, such as by jamming a kitchen knife in the frame to hold the door shut. Some didn't even have phones, which delayed reporting the crime to police. And the rapist carefully chose the most vulnerable. One young victim had been left alone with her grandmother, who was passed out from drinking when the rape occurred. Other victims had difficult or dysfunctional home lives, with stepfathers or ex-boyfriends of their mother, possibly with histories of abuse, who now might be suspects in the rape. Perhaps for financial reasons the victim lived with an extended family in a house where so many people came and went that nobody took notice of a stranger lurking.

There was also the touchy issue of possible discrimination: about 35 percent of the population of South Auckland, including many of the victims, was either Pacific Islander or native Maori. The rapist was also described as Maori, which led to another issue later in the investigation when police, desperate for leads, began targeting young Maori men.

Many in New Zealand questioned whether the marginalized lives of the victims and the socioeconomic conditions of their environment victimized them even further. After all, if something like this had happened in a wealthier neighborhood, the local watch groups would have jumped on the case, possibly catching the serial rapist much earlier. Perhaps more victims would have come forward to the police immediately, and maybe the crimes would have been more prominent in the news sooner, some argued. Also, for a mobile serial criminal, the individual districts offered ideal stomping grounds. At first, for example, investigators in Otara didn't know about similar rapes in nearby

Mount Eden or Papatoetoe. Just as in the United States, where neighboring jurisdictions don't always have information about serious crimes committed just over their borders, incidents reported in different locations took longer to be linked.

I've consulted on many cases around the world, the Yorkshire Ripper in England being one of the better-known examples. Still, this case surprised as much as it shocked me. Not only were the individual incidents so horrible, we were talking about a rapist who operated on an incredibly wide scale: the victims could be seemingly any age, any physical description. This subject's need to dominate and control women overrode any particular preferential-victim characteristics; she just had to be a woman, and he only needed an opportunity. Like any serial rapist in our own country, I wouldn't expect this guy to stop raping until he was caught—or dead. There might be interruptions, if he happened to be incarcerated for other crimes or moved out of the area, but it wouldn't end for good until he was put away for good.

As early as March of 1989, the newspaper *Sunday News* was reporting that South Auckland police believed a serial rapist was operating in the suburb of Otara. At that time, Detective Sergeant Brett Kane of the neighboring police department in Otahuhu warned citizens that they could expect the rapes to continue until the man was caught.

This serial rapist was good at getting in and out without leaving much in the way of evidence behind. Beginning in 1990, however, it became standard police procedure in New Zealand to collect body fluids found at the scene for DNA analysis. By 1993, Detective Sergeant Dave Henwood, second-in-command in the Papakura district, was putting together rapes going back as far as 1988, linking the more recent cases by DNA and the older cases by the rapist's MO. In August of 1993, the Papakura police established Operation Park, the official special investigation into the serial rapes. The authorities' attempts to find the rapist included door-to-door interviews in the area under siege and, as a proactive technique, running an ad in a local paper, the *Manukau Courier,* asking the serial criminal to turn himself in. While laudable, I've never actually known this particular proactive technique to bear fruit. They also organized a massive leaflet drop, with information on the rapist translated into Maori and other Pacific Islander languages, which struck me as a more productive operation.

In early 1994, the Operation Park investigation was officially moved to the jurisdiction of the Manukau district, which was larger, with better resources to deal with a major case like this one. Detective Senior Sergeant Stu Mills, who'd handled some of the biggest cases in New Zealand dating back to 1970, was to lead the investigation. Henwood joined the team from Papakura and they started bringing in criminal psychology experts from around the world to consult. One expert, senior psychologist Hans Laven of the Auckland Justice Department, put together profile elements based on the rapes they'd connected to that point.

Laven observed that the rapist didn't steal money from his victims, even when there was an opportunity, which made him think the rapist had a job. One of the victims described the offender as wearing work boots, which indicated that he might be employed in one of the local factories. Since he was able to come and go as he pleased at home (evidenced by the late-night/early-morning timing of most rapes), he was either single, worked shifts, or was the dominant partner in a relationship. Laven also noted that the majority of victims were very young, and that with the older victims, the rapist had to take extra steps such as binding before he could proceed. The psychologist took this as a sign that the man they were looking for wasn't confident with adults emotionally, physically, or sexually, possibly having been abused.

I would agree with much of his assessment, especially his concern that police needed to get more detailed information from the victims about the subject's behavior—what he said and did at each step of the assault—for us to be able to draw more specific conclusions. I would have added that this subject would not only be dominant in his relationships with women, but that any relationship he had would be a strained one. In his fantasies, once he overpowers his victim, she finds she actually enjoys what he does to her. Of course, in reality, none of the young girls and women this man raped enjoyed it—in fact many spent the assault in tears—which only frustrated him more as the reality never lived up to his fantasies. So he'd keep trying again and again, trying to match up a real-life situation with his dreams.

As we see with other serial rapists, there would likely have been some triggering events—precipitating stressors, we call them—in the UNSUB's life preceding most of the rapes. I would have advised the police to look through the files for the earliest rape that matched this suspect's MO and target that area as the place he likely lived in at the time. Again, criminals tend to start out in areas where their comfort level is the highest, which generally means close to home and/or work.

It was in the early months of 1994 that police began the most controversial aspect of the proactive campaign to find the rapist: stopping men on the street who fit the physical description and asking for blood samples so that their DNA could be compared with DNA from the crime scenes. Officers set up camp at public places—libraries, parks, shopping malls—and approached slight Maori men between the ages of twenty and forty, asking for their blood. Participation, however, was said to be voluntary.

Around this time, too, the *Sunday News* offered a reward of $5,000 for information that led to the serial rapist's arrest.

Police followed up on a lead from one of the crime scenes: a shoe print left on a seat cushion the rapist used as he climbed in a kitchen window. Tracing the print to a specific boot type, then to the manufacturer and the only local supplier, police began the painstaking process of checking up on every man who'd bought that boot in the size the rapist wore in the past two years, since the tread left on the chair seemed to indicate the approximate age of the boots in question. Every time they found a guy who wore the right boots who met the physical description of the rapist, they drew his blood and added it to the samples being processed and compared with the rapist's DNA.

While this was going on, John Manning took over leadership of Operation Park and had his meeting with my Investigative Support Unit colleagues. From his research, Manning thought they were dealing with a type that has come to be called the gentleman rapist, who would fit the description I provided earlier: troubled in relationships with women, fantasizing about women enjoying being overpowered by him sexually. Steve Mardigian confirmed that this was probably the type they were looking for, although he pointed out that in the unit, we always stressed that you were dealing with individuals who might have one or more traits of some other typology. Therefore, it was necessary to focus on the individual character of this particular UNSUB. Armed with this knowledge, and more information from the conference, Manning developed a profile of the rapist, marking the first time in New Zealand history that this approach was used to help identify a serial offender.

He zeroed in on the man's likely past. The rapist covered his hands, taking precautions not to leave fingerprints behind. This, combined with the knowledge Manning had picked up that rapists often had less serious offenses in their past, made the investigator think their UNSUB had a previous record for burglary, possibly having been caught because he'd left prints at the scene. As we've shown over and over, criminals do learn from their mistakes.

The UNSUB probably also had gotten in trouble as a youth or had at least had problems in school because of behavior, so there might be a juvenile record on him. And just as in the United States, when a criminal takes his work across jurisdictions, look for a reason: maybe he moved or started a job around the same time he switched crime-scene locations.

From victim descriptions, police were pretty sure he was Maori or Pacific Islander and slight of build, which was further indicated by the small windows he'd been able to get through. He was at least five feet five or six. They estimated his age to be between twenty-five and thirty-five, since they had attributed a rape to him back in 1988.

The investigative team went through a lengthy, exhaustive, and comprehensive search, taking the physical characteristics (size, race) and age under consideration as they went through criminal records of people who'd been convicted of burglary, theft, sex-related offenses other than rape, even vehicular crimes, looking for guys who met those criteria and lived in the areas of the rapes at the right times. Detectives fine-tuned parameters over and over, generating list after list of potential suspects, collecting blood from them all until they hit pay dirt.

In the spring of 1995 one of the computer searches came up with a name: Joseph Stephenson Thompson. Thompson fit the descriptions provided by the rapist's victims. He was thirty-six years old, slim, Maori, had a record of burglary convictions dating all the way back to when he was fourteen, and had lived in several of the districts at the time the rapist had been active. In fact, there was even a record of an incident in 1984 when the police were called to a home after a woman awoke to see him next to her bed. At the time he was arrested he claimed to be a simple burglar, although in retrospect it could have been an early rape attempt.

Thompson was arrested July 15, 1995, and later pleaded guilty to 129 charges, a record in the Commonwealth. They included 29 counts of aggravated burglary, 11 counts of burglary, 6 of entering with intent, 6 of aggravated wounding, 1 count of aggravated assault, 5 of abduction, 10 of assault with intent to commit sexual violation, 46 counts of sexual violation by rape, and 15 more of sexual violation by unlawful sexual connection. The plea spared the victims a trial, but it did not satisfy the curiosity of the public and the media, who wanted to understand how anyone could do this.

In a hearing before sentencing, Thompson's defense attorney argued that he came from a background of childhood sexual abuse and neglect that, although not an excuse for his behavior, should be weighed as a mitigating factor. Thompson was said to be remorseful and offered police and researchers the opportunity to evaluate him to learn more about the psychological makeup of criminals like himself.

The prosecution brought out the horrific statistics: of Thompson's admitted forty-seven victims, half were under the age of seventeen, and only the Lord knew how many of them were psychologically scarred for life. He terrorized the victims in their own homes, beating them as well as sexually assaulting them. He planned each attack, from unscrewing lightbulbs to carrying gloves, and in later attacks began cleaning up after himself—removing evidence of the DNA he learned from the media the police were evaluating.

Thompson was sentenced to the highest penalty available in New Zealand: thirty years in prison, with at least twenty-five served before consideration of release. Although his attorney appealed the severity of the sentencing (an action that earned him death threats from the public), the sentence stood.

For his efforts, John Manning received the Queen's Police Medal. I believe he deserves that and more for taking to heart in his investigation what our research has proved time and again: no one wakes up one day and decides to be a serial rapist. There are recognizable warning signs, earlier offenses that should be seen by authorities as signposts of future danger.

When I talk about getting inside the mind of a violent offender, I'm talking about a process I've characterized as a "journey into darkness." If I allowed my personal feelings or belief system to get involved, my sense of right and wrong, my incredulity at what one so-called human being can do to another, I wouldn't be able to see the crime from the criminal's point of view and so wouldn't be able to profile him based on his obsession, the way he sees the world. It is still difficult for me and my colleagues to do, even with our forced clinical detachment and even after decades of experience, research, and practice. I can imagine, then, how horrific it must be for the victims of violent crime, who must instinctively and instantaneously go through the same process I do to profile their attackers in an attempt to survive.

So many times I have heard women talk about what they would do to outsmart and/or escape a rapist or other sexual predator. But the truth is, until it happens to you, you can't know for certain what the best course of action will be. Until you are confronted with a specific rapist in a specific situation, you don't know what type of animal you'll be dealing with; what is an appropriate response to one rapist could be deadly with another. The goal is survival, and I have tremendous respect for any rape victim who lives through the ordeal because, as hard to believe as it may seem to some, if you're alive to tell about it, you've achieved a major victory. And the rape victim doesn't have the luxury of assessing events from a distance, with the benefit of years of research: a rape victim must assess the terrifying situation as it unfolds, analyzing instinctively what to do or say to get out alive. I'm always outraged, for example, when I hear an opposing attorney or some other ex post facto commentator telling a victim from the safe remove of time and distance what he or she should have done in the heat and immediacy of a moment of life-threatening terror. Perhaps it's my own perversity that I'd like to see that individual faced with the same situation himself and see how he'd react.

In the first week of April 1984, a forty-one-year-old waitress was assaulted in her home in the Cleveland suburbs. It was early in the morning when a young, slightly built white male threatened her with a knife and forced her to perform oral sex as he fondled her breasts. He told her he wouldn't hurt her if she did what he told her to and warned her not to look at him. When it was over, he took her money and left her in the bathroom. The woman hadn't gotten a good look at him, but did note that he had one distinguishing physical characteristic: a bump or scar of some type on his penis.

It is a common reaction to the violation of being raped to consider not reporting the crime, to try to act as though it never happened and hope the horrible memories, shame, fear, and anger will fade. In addition to their own emotions, victims often balance reactions from friends, associates, coworkers, and family members in making their decision whether to report the incident. As with other violent crimes, the circle of individuals affected moves out to encompass a large group beyond the immediate victim. She may worry others won't see her the same way again or that they will blame her, making her feel even more vulnerable and insecure. On top of that, most rapists make some sort of threat of retaliation if the victim calls the police and, they assure their victims, they will find out.

This particular victim, however, had the courage to report the crime to police, which became even more important when another rape occurred one week later only two blocks away.

Just after 5:30 A.M. on the morning of April 13, 1984, mail carrier Betty Ocilka was getting ready for work when she was surprised in her kitchen by a masked man—with a stocking cap over his face—who put her in a headlock while holding a knife to her throat. When she instinctively screamed, he choked her tightly, threatening to kill her if she made any more noise. He led her at knifepoint to the living room, where he began to assault her on the couch, threatening again that while he didn't want to hurt her, he would if she fought him. A single mother (her late husband had been a Cleveland police officer who had committed suicide), she was afraid the stranger would hurt her three-year-old son if he awoke and came downstairs to investigate the strange noises during the assault.

She tried to discourage the man from raping her by telling him she was having her period, but he forced her to perform oral sex, making her swallow the ejaculate, then took all the money she had in the house—just $21 cash. As he had with the earlier victim, the rapist left her in the bathroom, warning her that he would know if she called the police and would come back for her. As soon as he left, she went to look for her son and found he wasn't in his crib. She panicked that the rapist had kidnapped him, but then she found the child in her bed. As she told James Neff, the outstanding investigative reporter whose book *Unfinished Murder* recounts the story of the Cleveland rapes, the little boy never climbed out of his crib and into her bed. So he must have heard something that frightened him and come into her bedroom for comfort. This, Neff reports, devastated her even further. Courageously, despite the intruder's warnings, she called the police right away.

As she waited for them to arrive, she made herself some coffee and drank two cups, rinsing out her mouth. Unfortunately, her instinctive effort to cleanse herself destroyed any evidence that could have been recovered.

Cleveland police detective Bob Matuszny of the Second District knew Betty Ocilka (she delivered mail in the area around headquarters), and he'd known her late husband, so he was greatly disturbed to hear of the violence committed against her. Beyond his personal sympathy for the victim, though, he was concerned because he'd investigated the rape of the waitress just one week before. He and partner Phil Parrish reviewed the police report on Ocilka's case and then went over to talk to her. There were enough similarities to warrant investigation of a possible link, but there was one point in particular they wanted to clarify: the earlier victim reported that the rapist had some sort of bump or scar on his penis and there was no mention of this type of distinguishing physical feature in the Ocilka report.

Now, this may seem like a strange characteristic to have been left out of the initial report, but it highlights one of the problems inherent in the investigation of rape cases. Rape is unlike most other types of crime in that without specialized training or experience, you're not going to be able to recognize the specific motivation of the offender and be able to identify the kind of person you're looking for. What motivates a rapist is so individual compared to that of, say, a burglar, bank robber, or car thief. If a guy robs a convenience store at gunpoint, for example, and leaves without hurting anyone once he gets his money, it's pretty clear what he's after. Although in general we know that rapists are looking to manipulate, dominate, and control others, it takes careful analysis of the rapist's behavior during the assault to figure out what type of offender he is. Behavior reflects personality, and in the case of a rapist, analyzing what he does and says tells you a lot about who he is.

As a profiler, I want to know how he controls his victim, whether he physically beats her or is apologetic about raping her, whether he gains access by conning her or by a surprise attack in the middle of the night. How does he rape her and what, if anything, does he say before, during, and after the attack? And these questions are just a broad beginning to the information we need to put together for a viable profile, which we'll get into in more detail in a later chapter.

If the officer interviewing the rape victim isn't trained to ask—or comfortable with asking—about this in detail, many victims are too traumatized, embarrassed, and frightened to think of everything. They are likely still in shock over the assault. It is not at all uncommon for victims to remember details a few days later, when their brains and bodies start to function more normally and rationally again.

In addition to having a friendly relationship with this victim, Bob Matuszny—along with his partner Phil Parrish—was among the more experienced detectives on the force. He and Parrish had grown up in the same tough neighborhood and attended the same high school. They knew what kind of information they needed to get a picture of the type of guy they were looking for.

They also asked if Betty Ocilka remembered "anything unusual about his genitals." She answered that there was "a bump or something near the end of it."

There aren't usually too many serial rapists working the same area at the same time, and the chance that two guys would be out there with noticeable bumps on their organs was even slimmer. It seemed certain one offender was responsible for both rapes.

Matuszny remembered another rape he'd worked and went back through the records of unsolved cases until he found what he was looking for: October 5, 1983, a twenty-three-year-old woman was raped in the first-floor apartment she'd just moved into—she hadn't even had time to unpack or put up curtains—just a few blocks from the recent rapes. All the crime scenes were near the wooded area of Brookside Park—presenting a rapist with an easy route to a clean get-away. And in every case police had been able to lift fingerprints from the scene, although Matuszny hadn't yet heard whether they all matched. Given the similarities and the likelihood there was just one rapist at work, Matuszny got permission from his supervisor, Lt. Robert Howell, to devote all his time to finding the serial rapist.

The first step was to check the other police districts in the city to see if the subject they now referred to as the West Side Rapist had been active elsewhere. They described the rapist's MO, as well as his distinguishing physical characteristic, and soon got reports back on two cases in the Fourth District. In the first case, which occurred just a few months earlier, on February 2, a fifty-one-year-old grandmother was assaulted by a white male who broke into her two-story home, raped her, and left her and her three-year-old granddaughter locked in the bathroom. The rapist had been able to break into the house cleanly, with no broken windows or marks left on the door or window screens. And just like the rapist in the Second District, this offender reportedly had a bump on his penis.

The next case matched the others in terms of the description of the rapist and MO, but the twenty-five-year-old victim was not willing to talk to police. Her husband was anxious to put the incident behind them, which, unfortunately, is not an uncommon reaction among spouses or partners, family members, and close friends of rape victims, who are sometimes unable to deal with their own emotions and whose only coping mechanism is to deny it ever happened. Although the victim would not cooperate in putting together the composite sketch, much less agree to testify once a suspect was brought to trial, she did describe the rapist and the assault for police: a thin white man knocked at the door, then forced his way inside at knifepoint. He told her he would not hurt her if she did what he told her to—just as the other victims had been threatened—then raped her. The victim reported that he had a bump on his penis.

With five cases now to consider, it seemed likely the police might get a break. Once they put together a composite of the rapist (and a separate composite of his sex organ), they'd be ready to get their search under way. They brought copies of a diagram of a penis to two of the victims and asked them to note where the bump was. They each picked the same area. The same victims also met with Det. Andrew Charchenko, who put together a composite sketch of the rapist's face, including his long, feathered hair. Once it was ready, the detectives brought copies to all kinds of hangout places on the West Side, posting them in bars, pizza parlors—even hair salons, since the victims described a style that was not your typical barbershop cut. All that was left, then, was to find a suspect and have him "drop trou," as it were, to see if the other sketch matched as well as the facial. Within a week or so, the same detective who'd drawn the rendering saw a man at a local restaurant-bar who looked like the drawing, wearing the same type of tennis shoes (dirty, white, with blue stripes) Betty Ocilka described. He brought the guy in for Matuszny and Parrish, whom the other detectives would soon dub the "pecker checkers." They questioned him at length. This suspect had alibis, but the detectives weren't willing to risk letting their man go. They asked to see his penis, which threw the guy until he was told it could eliminate him as a suspect.

They went to the men's room, had a look, then let him leave when they saw no bump. Soon they were working at a rate of about two suspects per week.

Around this time, the two detectives outlined the rape cases and described the rapist in a bulletin sent out to police departments in the neighboring suburbs, which also requested information on any cases with similar MOs in their jurisdictions, particularly in which there was anything unusual noted about the offender's genitals. In less than a week cases came in from three of these areas—Middleburg Heights, Parma, and Parma Heights—with a total of four unsolved rape cases. Two of the rapes, both in Parma, took place at one apartment complex: one victim was pregnant, the other was a fifty-four-year-old grandmother whose granddaughter was asleep one room over as the assault occurred. Matuszny and Parrish, together with detectives from other areas with possibly linked cases, met in Parma to exchange information, which only served to fuel their suspicions that one man was responsible for this series of rapes in the Cleveland area.

If they included three more unsolved cases that fit the MO, the total now stood at twelve. Even without an official tally, there were enough to get the attention of a city councilman, Joe Cannon. Although news of a possible serial rapist hadn't yet hit the papers or TV, people were comparing notes at neighborhood-watch-type gatherings and knew women were being raped. The pressure was on the police to catch this one, and Matuszny's commander authorized a plan for surveillance put together by Matuszny and Parrish. Extra unmarked cars would work the streets in the late-night and early-morning hours to respond quickly to reports of rape, trespassing, and the like.

Many of the cases I've worked involved extra efforts on the part of police to catch the offender in question, such as establishment of special task forces with personnel from various jurisdictions and areas of specialty, extra details set up in the affected area, coordinated efforts between police, citizens groups, the media. Every time you have a case like this, whether it's high profile in the news or not, there's tremendous pressure on the cops to come through and justify the extra expense. By June, after weeks with nothing to report, the extra surveillance was canceled. At the same time, Phil Parrish was made sergeant and assigned to a new position downtown, leaving Matuszny on his own to lead the hunt for the Cleveland rapist.

On June 23, police had reason to second-guess the call to end surveillance. Thirty-seven-year-old Marian Butler was awakened around four in the morning by a strange man moving through her apartment in Parma Heights. Just hours earlier, she and a friend had been watching the news, talking about the possible serial rapist in their midst. Although she lived on the first floor, Butler reportedly joked with her friend about what an unlikely target she would be and went to bed with the windows open to compensate for the poor air-conditioning in her building.

I've heard people wonder how women can leave their windows open at night. Interestingly, these are most often folks who have sufficient air-conditioning of their own. On a hot summer night, you weigh odds of something bad happening to you against how uncomfortable you are and how many hours of sleep you're missing. Particularly if you live in a middle-class neighborhood like Parma Heights, it's easy to understand how someone could trade a slight security risk for a cool breeze.

When Butler awoke and saw the strange man in her bedroom, she screamed. Before she could react, he was covering her mouth and threatening her in a warning that sounded a lot like the one given to the earlier victims: he had a knife that he'd use if she didn't do what he said and keep quiet. He also told her not to look at him and demanded money. Butler had recently had an operation to remove a cyst from her pelvis, and she told her attacker she was unable to have sex. As he forced her to perform oral sex, she mentally noted everything she could about him, from a description of his shoes and jacket to a bandage on his right hand, to the lingering smell of a breath mint. He accidentally turned on her bedroom light afterward, and she got a good look at his face.

He made her give him all her money, then shut her up in the bathroom, demanding she wait there until he told her she could leave. She listened as he went through her bedroom, possibly looking for valuables, and left the bathroom when she heard him leave. She called the police and gave them an impressive description of her rapist—right to the breath mints. As Neff reports, she vowed to her friend that someday she would "testify against that bastard."

Just a couple of weeks later the rapist struck again, this time assaulting a twenty-three-year-old mother as her three-week-old baby slept next to her on the couch. Her description of the rapist matched what other victims had said about their thin, dark-haired, slight assailant. He even wore the same clothing: jeans and a black jacket that stopped at his waist. His behavior was also consistent: he cut her telephone cord, woke her up by fondling her, and threatened her with a knife, telling her to do as he said and he wouldn't harm her baby. As with Butler, when this victim complained she was physically unable to have sex with him (she'd just given birth to her son weeks earlier), he forced oral sex, which gave her the opportunity to observe the distinguishing bump on his penis.

It had to be incredibly frustrating for Detective Matuszny that this rapist who'd stayed out of sight during the extensive surveillance campaign went back to work as soon as the detail was called off. At least this time, however, they got some evidence: he'd left a Marlboro cigarette behind, which might yield saliva, which in turn could provide his blood type. And one neighbor had seen a man matching the physical description of the rapist cut through the neighborhood.

Matuszny turned to Quantico for help, having heard about our services from one of his bosses who had taken courses at the FBI Academy. The detective sent us information on seventeen rapes. Blaine McIlwain, one of the two guys who'd broken down my hotel-room door and rescued me in Seattle, became the point of contact at the Investigative Support Unit. He was still fairly new at this, but very talented. I trusted his instincts and had found him to be a quick study. We met and discussed the cases as he worked up each part of the profile.

Since the first rapes took place in the area near the zoo, we felt the police should be looking for a guy who probably lived within walking distance. He would have gone through his own surveillance to choose victims who would be easiest to control, such as those with young children they needed to protect, or women he knew would be alone when he struck. The early-morning timing of the rapes indicated the rapist probably didn't hold a day job. If he had a steady job at all, which was doubtful, it would be some kind of menial position that did not involve much contact with the public. As with many of these offenders, he would alternate between deep feelings of inadequacy and insecurity (using the rapes to boost his perception of his own sexuality), and grandiosity, plus pride in his new, infamous identity as the West Side Rapist. For this reason, he would probably collect newspaper articles about the rapes.

Because of his feelings of inadequacy, any social relationships would be with much younger or less sophisticated women. In general, though, our profile maintained, he'd be a loner. There was probably a dominant female in his life with whom he might still live, such as a mother or aunt or other female relative. Conflict with this woman puts him under stress and causes him to question his masculinity, which is part of why he feels the need to rape and dominate his female victims. It is also likely that he collects pornography, and he might keep a diary of his offenses, a record of all the women he's spied on, as well as his actual rape victims, almost like a collection, as if he now owned them. He would have a record for related crimes as a juvenile, such as voyeurism, breaking and entering, theft of fetish-type souvenirs such as jewelry or lingerie. He'd be the type to own a motorcycle or a dark, older vehicle in poor running condition.

A number of the victims had noted how clean he was, so we thought there was a good chance he worked in a capacity that required cleanliness, such as food preparation, hospital work, or something of the sort.

In addition to collecting media accounts of his work, his postoffense behavior would include exaggerated elements of his normal behavior. For example, if he used drugs or alcohol before, he would be drinking more, or abusing drugs. Blaine noted, too, that if he was a religiously observant person, to cope with the stress he would probably have become even more religious.

On July 26, the rapist struck again, cutting his way through a window screen in the living room of another Parma Heights apartment to awaken its twenty-seven-year-old resident and rape her at knifepoint. Then on August 17, a sixty-year-old woman from the same area was sexually molested by a man who also gained access to her apartment as she slept.

The rapist continued his pace. In the early-morning hours of September 14, 1984, twenty-three-year-old Karen Holztrager became his latest victim. The pretty mother of three small boys had heard of the previous crimes and tried to take steps to secure her family's first-story apartment, calling their landlord and getting him to promise to fix several of the windows that would not lock. With her husband working nights, she kept the windows closed; in just a few weeks they were to move farther outside the city, into a home of their own.

Holztrager was awakened by a strange man sitting on her bed. He produced a knife and told her he'd seen that her kids were fast asleep and closed her bedroom door; they wouldn't awaken or be hurt as long as she cooperated. Before he raped her, he asked if she knew him, saying, "Well, I know you. I've been watching you."

After the assault, he demanded all her money and left her in the bathroom, with the warning that if she called the police, he'd come back for her and her children. Despite his threats, she did call police and provided a description that corresponded with the others, except for what he was wearing.

Over the next year, Det. Bob Matuszny continued to work the case, updating bulletins and passing them around the different districts, following up on leads. But there was no break. At the same time, a new centralized Sex Crimes Unit was established at police headquarters downtown. Instead of having detectives from the individual districts work sex crimes in their area, all were to be investigated by this special unit, led by Lt. Lucie J. Duvall, one of the highest-ranking women in the Cleveland Police Department and the first female officer to command a vice squad there.

Matuszny knew from the next case on, all future acts of the West Side Rapist would be worked out of the new Sex Crimes Unit, but he had no interest in transferring downtown. Fortunately, one of the detectives from the Second District, who was also a friend of his, did transfer there. Ed Gray was at work in the new unit just a few weeks when he and his partner responded to a rape in the West Side that sounded just like the cases he knew Bob Matuszny had been working on: a young white man fitting the earlier descriptions of the West Side Rapist—including the bump on his penis—broke in on the victim just after her boyfriend had left for work. He then forced her to perform oral sex at knifepoint.

If a case isn't solved within the first few days, there is always a chance it will go stale once it cools off. I've seen a lot of investigations languish over time as responsibilities are reassigned, people retire or get transferred, and there's little continuity. But Ed Gray did not let that happen. He called Bob and invited him to go along as he and his new partner, rookie Andrea Zbydniewski, known as Zeb, went to interview the victim. It's not easy to share turf you've been working for years, let alone turn it over to someone else, but it's classy and professional to get the information out to people with the authority to help while not turning your back on it entirely. It became apparent to all three of them that this was likely the work of the same man.

About a month later, with two detectives already looking for reassignment elsewhere, and with the tally up to twenty-four in the West Side Rapist investigation, the new Sex Crimes Unit needed help. Duvall requested the temporary reassignment of Detective Matuszny. The bad news for him was he'd be working downtown without a partner. The good news was he still had an opportunity to nail this guy he'd been hunting for so long.

Looking for any new leads, Matuszny sent information on the rapist's description and MO to police departments all around the country, asking in return for information on any similar rapes out there. This is the type of thing that I'd like to see computerized on a national level, as the FBI has been trying to do with its VICAP (Violent Criminal Apprehension Program) for more than a dozen years. With proper funding and a mandatory case-reporting requirement from local investigators, each department would have at its fingertips the kind of information Matuszny had to jump through hoops even to look for.

Although the response was tremendous in terms of the volume of return teletypes and phone calls, nothing fit. He went back to following up further on local cases—the latest rape in particular—with one change in his investigating process: his new supervisor, Lieutenant Duvall, told him he was not to inspect any more suspect penises. By November, his report on the most recent case finished and with no new leads, Matuszny reluctantly knew it was time to pack it in and move on to other challenges. He then requested transfer back to the Second District and out of the Sex Crimes Unit, a transfer that was approved.

Just one month later, early in the morning of December 13, 1985, the rapist hit again, breaking into a home and assaulting a woman in the shower, raping her at knifepoint while forcing her to tell him she loved him, as if following a script. After terrorizing her and threatening to come back to kill her if she called the police, he warned her to look out for the hot curling iron she'd left warming up in the bathroom, as though he were concerned that after all he'd done to her, she'd be hurt accidentally.

With this new case, Ed Gray and Andrea Zbydniewski were back on the investigation, although they were also busy with the rest of their caseload of child abuse and other rapes. This time, however, they might have a lead: a newspaper delivery boy had seen a man lurking around the area about a month earlier. The man had worn a ski mask, which he took off so he could smoke. The boy helped police work up a new composite, which looked a lot like the previous sketch of the West Side Rapist. He was also able to describe the UNSUB's clothing. Gray and Zbydniewski circulated the new drawing, which led to more leads, but none of them panned out. In early February 1986, the police released a full-color sketch to the media and offered a $2,000 reward.

In late May, after months of apparent restraint, the rapist struck again, breaking into a first-floor apartment in North Olmsted just before five o'clock in the morning, surprising and raping one of the two young women who lived there while the other wasn't home. North Olmsted was outside the jurisdiction of the Sex Crimes Unit. Investigating Detective Frank Viola had met with Matuszny two years before, and he recognized the MO of the West Side Rapist. In addition to branching out into potentially new territory, the subject seemed to be growing more sophisticated, as this victim related that he forced her to swallow his semen so it couldn't show up as evidence. But the police were able to lift a partial fingerprint from a windowsill.

August 1986 saw an interesting development. A suspect was arrested in Arkansas. He'd previously lived on the West Side, not far from several of the rapes, and had left town after the composite sketch of the rapist appeared in the news. Arrested on an unrelated warrant, he came to the attention of authorities because of his resemblance to the well-publicized composite. Although he did match the physical description of the rapist, he spoke with a Latino accent, which hadn't been mentioned by any of the victims. He also had an alibi for most of the rapes and had another physical characteristic to support his claims of innocence: much of the time in question he'd spent with a broken foot, and none of the victims had mentioned a cast.

After a year of frustration, no leads, and theories that perhaps the rapist had moved out of the area (or maybe the latest victims hadn't reported their assaults), there was another potential development. As she sipped her morning coffee in the kitchen, Betty Ocilka heard a sound outside her window and noticed a shadow suggestive of a man's head. Ever ready with the gun she'd kept handy since her own attack, she pulled back the curtain to reveal a man standing there. Startled, she screamed, firing a shot at him as he ran away.

At the time, Matuszny and Gray thought it highly unlikely that it was the rapist, back for another look. This was not the first time Ocilka had called them, convinced she'd seen her rapist. After what she'd been through, it was understandable that she could still be traumatized by the assault.

But Gray had had enough. He asked Lieutenant Duvall for a transfer, which she turned down. In November of 1987, Police Chief Howard Rudolph—who lived near several of the West Side Rapist's victims—expanded the responsibility and authority of the Scientific Investigations Unit, hoping that better handling of evidence would assist in case closure. Gray transferred to the unit.

After several months without a new case, the rapist kept the police busy during the holidays. On the morning of November 18, he entered the apartment of a twenty-two-year-old woman who'd left the door open as she went to start a load of wash in the laundry room. Holding a knife to her throat, he forced her to perform oral sex, then raped her vaginally. After ejaculating on her stomach, he wiped off the evidence and threatened to return and kill her if she contacted the police, part of the West Side Rapist's standard MO.

A few weeks later, he assaulted a twenty-seven-year-old woman in her fiancé's home—just two blocks away from the home of the chief of police. As she wrapped Christmas presents and waited for her fiancé to come home, the rapist surprised her, grabbing her by the hair and clamping a hand over her mouth. She fought back with the scissors she'd been using for the gifts and screamed. Faced with a victim who fought back aggressively, the rapist grew more violent, punching her in the face over and over as he grabbed the scissors away from her. Then, threatening her with the scissors, he demanded money. She told him she only had $2 in her purse. He said he knew that but wanted whatever was in the house. Then he led her to the back door and told her to open it, presumably so he wouldn't leave fingerprints behind. When she had trouble opening it, he forced her to undress, using the scissors to cut off her bra. He saw she was having her period and forced her to perform oral sex. Then, as Neff reports, he threatened, "If you call the police, you won't have a Christmas."

As 1988 began, the police were at a loss and pressure from the public continued to grow. In early March the rapist struck again. At first a woman just noticed him outside her first-floor apartment. She called the police, who found marks on the front door as though someone had been trying to pry it open. Then a few nights later, the same woman was awakened by a man in her bedroom, who she first thought was her boyfriend. But then he climbed on top of her and threatened her with a knife. He cut her nightgown with his knife, then raped her.

It seems crazy that the rapist would return to a scene where he'd been thwarted by police just days earlier. Actually, though, this behavior is predictable of serial offenders, who grow more cocky with each "successful" venture. Much like other types of criminals who send letters to police or the media taking credit for their crimes, this rapist wanted to show the authorities he could outsmart them. They knew where he operated, but he could still get by them and take what he wanted. This type takes pride in his work, and ultimately it is this pride that, we hope, will lead to his downfall. Some, as we've already noted, even write letters.

One night during the summer of 1988, the rapist's cockiness led him to make the kind of mistake the police were waiting for. After breaking into an apartment and raping the woman inside, the daughter of a Cleveland detective, he stole the victim's bank card. Before he left, he demanded her password for the card and her telephone number. Then he made his usual threats about not calling the police.

This time, in addition to a victim-witness, the police had a lead. The card had been used at an ATM about five o'clock in the morning. A security camera had captured the transaction. The only problem was that between the rapist's efforts to hide behind sunglasses and the poor resolution of the blurry, dark picture, it didn't provide more than the composite sketch the police already had. All they could see was the lower part of his face, long, wavy hair, a cigarette, and the collar of a jeans jacket.

The Sex Crimes Unit immediately released the photo. The local TV networks featured the story, providing a phone number for tips. The first strong lead came quickly. A woman called that night to report that she knew who the man in the photo was, knew where he worked, knew he owned a pair of sunglasses just like the ones in the photo, and provided his name. Police discovered that he lived near several of the rape locations; he worked near others. Armed with a search warrant, detectives waited anxiously until their suspect returned from work to arrest him. With support from the chief of police and Assistant County Prosecutor Tim McGinty, police then organized a lineup, but the West Side Rapist's latest victim did not see her assailant there. The suspect was released—although they did get some hair samples so they could compare his DNA against evidence left at any future crime scene.

In November, a young woman was awakened in the early morning by unusual sounds in her apartment. Looking around, she saw a man masturbating outside her living room window, and he'd already removed the screen! She called the police immediately—her father was a captain on the force—but the man was gone by the time they got there. Since his behavior and description matched that of the West Side Rapist, police stepped up patrols of the neighborhood.

Even with the added security, one Saturday toward the end of the month the young woman was awakened by a man on top of her, holding a knife to her face. He called her by name and asked why she'd called the police, telling her she would not be hurt if she did what he instructed. She got a quick look at his face, covered by a nylon stocking, before he warned her to look away. He raped her, ejaculating on her stomach, then used her blanket to wipe up the evidence. Along with her money, he took her bank card and demanded her password. As he left, he warned he'd come back and murder her if she contacted the police again. She tried to call police immediately but found he'd cut the phone line, so she drove to her father's police precinct.

Everyone was terribly frustrated that this guy had struck again— hell, not only did police have warning this time, the victim's father was a cop! But the bank card offered a ray of hope. Sure enough, when sex crimes checked with the bank, they learned the card was used minutes after the rape and the transaction had been captured on camera. Because it took shots in three-second intervals, the police had a series of photos to review: the first was an outline of a long-haired man with a newspaper; the next showed him using the paper to block his face before he held the paper directly over the camera. After a few black photos, the last shot showed the man walking away from the camera: a look at his back as he walked to his car.

It didn't seem a tremendous breakthrough, but Vic Kovacic, head of the Scientific Investigations Unit, thought perhaps they could use the technology at their disposal to get more out of it than originally appeared. The unit had a computer designed to analyze evidence such as photos, and it could clarify the image. They scanned in the picture and had the computer blow up the image, enhancing it to the point where they were able to identify the car in the photo by its right rear panel. According to their reference books, it was a dark Chevrolet Monte Carlo, model year 1975 or 1976. There was even visible damage that could further identify the vehicle. Soon the entire force had a description of the car, which, I was glad to hear, was consistent with our profile.

After years of hunting this guy, the police finally had something solid to work with. Yet we must never forget to factor in the element of luck. It can work to the advantage of the criminal. But it can work for us, too. On December 21, 1988, Vic Kovacic got lucky. After weeks of driving around the West Side looking for the suspect vehicle in his spare time, he stumbled upon it. The lot of a restaurant he was going to was full, so he had to park in front of an apartment building next door. That was where he saw it: maroon Monte Carlo with the same rusted fender and pushed-in bumper shown in the bank photo. He took down the plate number and rushed back to his office.

Computer records said it was registered to a Ronnie Shelton, twenty-seven years of age, five feet eight and 138 pounds, matching the physical description of the rapist. Further checks revealed Shelton had a criminal record that included an arrest for voyeurism—behavior consistent with rape. Finally, Kovacic compared fingerprints taken from Shelton following an arrest in 1985 for theft with prints from several rapes. It was a clean match.

Their first stop was Shelton's parents' house, where his father told them he hadn't seen Ronnie and didn't know where they could find him. Following up at the apartment building where Kovacic spotted Shelton's car, police learned a friend of Shelton's was being evicted that day. Ronnie had stayed with him and, presumably, was helping him move. What police didn't know was that the real reason he was returning was to get his own stuff out, having had a falling out with the guy as he'd had with many other former friends.

Around 7 P.M., Shelton returned to the apartment, driven in another friend's car. Although the two detectives didn't notice him at first in the strange car, Shelton spotted them, but mistook them for buddies of the guy being evicted, brought in to make sure Ronnie didn't cause any trouble. Fearing for his safety since the guy had called the police on him before following their argument, Shelton had his friend drive to a pay phone where *he* called the police to ask for an escort into the apartment.

Waiting for his escort, Shelton saw the guy come out of the apartment and stepped out of his friend's car, at which point he was identified by the officers who were actually there to arrest him. Just as they got him against the car to cuff him, the police escort called to the scene by Shelton did arrive, without being advised of the arrest. It was a tense moment for the arresting detectives as they identified themselves to the uniforms. A slight battle raged over who'd arrest Shelton: whether it was a sex-crimes collar or the Second District's, based on jurisdiction. Eventually, the ones from sex crimes took him in and retrieved his car from his parents' house. In the car they found such items as sunglasses, a switchblade, binoculars, and women's jewelry.

Once he was left alone in jail, Shelton connected the zippers from several prison-issue jumpsuits and attempted to hang himself from the top bar in his cell. It wasn't strong enough to support his weight, though, and he was placed on suicide watch.

Was it a genuine suicide attempt? Captured, Shelton could no longer manipulate, dominate, and control. It was his turn to have it all done to him. Every element of his life would be regulated by others. He wouldn't even have control over the food he ate, when he ate, what he wore. Suicide would have been his ultimate act of control; he would have denied police the opportunity to try him and cheated his victims out of the chance to confront him and put him away for good. That's why we see many of these types attempt suicide once caught, and why I often recommend automatic suicide watch.

Detective Zbydniewski was the first to interview him. In the first session, he didn't admit to anything but drug use and hinted at credit card theft. Trying a different tack, the detective asked if he'd been abused as a child, and he answered not sexually, although he'd been beaten. She tried showing him the pictures from the bank surveillance camera. He appeared distressed to see himself on film but regained composure and refused to talk further—although he didn't yet ask for an attorney.

A few days later he had his lawyer. Christmas Eve, Jerry Milano, an attorney with a lengthy record of criminal defense, was asked by Maria Shelton to help her brother.

In the meantime, police worked to see how many of the unsolved rapes could be linked to Shelton. His fingerprints were matched with latents from four rape scenes. To get the others, Assistant County Prosecutor Tim McGinty turned to Bob Matuszny, figuring he was not only familiar with the case but already had a rapport with many of the victims. McGinty warned him there wasn't budget for the overtime

Matuszny would probably put in, but he was sufficiently obsessed with finally getting his man that he'd put in all the time on his own.

McGinty's first step was to get the suspect to submit to a photograph of his genitals so they could resolve the issue of the bump. Some victims of the West Side Rapist reported the bump, others didn't. The prosecutor needed to clear up this discrepancy. They also began the task of finding victims and getting them in to try to identify Shelton from a lineup. But many of the traumatized victims had left the area years ago. The prosecutor's office asked local papers and TV stations not to publish a photo of Shelton, explaining the defense would be able to argue later that any positive IDs had been corrupted by the media coverage. The media showed tremendous restraint.

In addition to the original cases Matuszny worked, the police rechecked cases handled by Gray and Zbydniewski and cases referred to them by Special Agent John Dunn of the FBI's Cleveland Field Office, who sent unsolved cases from the suburbs that matched the West Side Rapist's. At that point, the total of possibly linked cases was approaching forty.

One of the first victims called in to identify her assailant was Karen Holztrager, who easily zeroed in on two of the five men in the lineup. Detectives asked each man to speak language the offender had used during the rape, and Holztrager made her choice—the wrong guy. As she was leaving, she told the police that she knew she had the wrong man but was too afraid to identify the real offender.

Shelton had been arrested for the rape that led to his identification through the bank surveillance camera. Two weeks later McGinty got grand jury indictments on five more cases where fingerprints at the crime scene matched Shelton's.

In the interest of leaving nothing to chance, the prosecutor continued looking into Shelton's previous record, checking with former girl-friends, everything down to traffic violations. Good prosecutors believe in knowing the opposition, and McGinty was a firm believer in being prepared. One of his concerns was that Shelton's lawyer would go for an insanity defense, which, if successful, could keep him out of prison.

Searching Shelton's past, McGinty learned about a suicide attempt in 1986 at the apartment of a former girlfriend. This led to a psychologist who had treated him back then, Ross Santamaria, and to the former girlfriend. Santamaria reported he found Shelton not insane but manipulative—an assessment he would testify to. The former girlfriend then provided information that not only backed up what the psychologist had said but gave McGinty even more than he'd imagined.

She filled in the details of Shelton's violent personality, describing how he'd beaten her and how his temper caused him to get into fights. She told of crimes he had committed against her, from stealing her credit cards to rape and attempted murder. Although she was willing to testify, she was embarrassed to admit her involvement with Shelton. Even her parents didn't know the depths to which he took her, and she wanted to keep it that way. She tried to explain that at times Shelton was completely charming, which made it difficult for her to leave him. Most important, though, she cleared up one of the big mysteries of the case: in the spring of 1986, she paid for a doctor to remove Ronnie's genital warts.

James Neff describes McGinty's surprise, almost perplexed amusement, when she reported how popular Ronnie could be with women. With his long, effeminate hairstyle and overdone appearance, McGinty couldn't fathom what women saw in Shelton.

From what this woman said, Ronnie Shelton fit a classic profile for this type of rapist: inadequate personality, trouble holding down a job, ongoing conflict with parents and girlfriends, insecurity about his sexuality (he hated when people teased him about his hair, neat appearance, or small stature, especially if they called him "fag"). It's as if these offenders are walking a tightrope, charming enough to win over any woman one minute, desperately needing to control and assert their masculinity the next. It doesn't mean they have a split personality; it just means they are capable of controlling their insecurities and impulses when it serves them. When they want or need something, they can behave appropriately to get it, which is how so many rapists have active consensual sexual relationships at the same time that they assault other women.

McGinty and the police were still having trouble gaining ground on more than the original five rapes for which they had Shelton's fingerprints. They were convinced he was responsible for at least twenty-three, but needed some way to tie him to the others. In several instances, physical evidence taken from the crime scene was contaminated, or nothing was collected at all. And in some cases Shelton fit the description given by the victim in her statement, but she was unable to pick him out of a lineup.

The prosecution and the police talked to John Dunn again, and he recommended they get in touch with me, figuring I might be able to tie them together behaviorally. Though I think McGinty was skeptical at first, he must have thought it was worth a try. The catch was that it would be the first time this type of expert-witness testimony would be introduced in an Ohio courtroom.

McGinty's team was preparing a 230-count indictment, the largest in county history. Jerry Milano announced publicly that his client would plead insanity and at most would serve only fifteen years before he'd be eligible for parole, regardless of any possible sentence. McGinty argued that Ohio law needed to be changed, that there should be no way for a serial rapist to get parole so quickly. He also convinced Shelton's ex-girlfriend to testify about his behavior, including her rape, to help counter the insanity argument.

As Neff quotes McGinty:

"I want to show a jury that he's a son of a bitch twenty-four hours a day, not just at six in the morning. . . . I want to show that he raped her, abused her, gave her VD, took her credit cards. . . . I want to show little Ronnie's manipulative behavior. We can argue that that's how he was able to get whatever doctor he hired to say that he was nuts. Plus we need her to show that he could get laid. She shows that he had normal sexual outlets. That means he raped for thrills. It'll show the rapes were crimes of violence."

In the meantime, as I went through the materials myself, I couldn't help but see the similarities between the different cases. Elements of his modus operandi were consistent: the targeting of first-floor apartments with easy escape routes, timing the events typically in the early-morning hours when the victim would be alone or with dependent children nearby, surprising the victim, threatening her with a knife or other sharp object at the scene. But more than that, the rapist's signature—the things he does that are not necessary to the perpetration of the crime but that he needs for his emotional satisfaction—was also consistent. For example, in many instances he either masturbated before the victim or pulled out while raping her to ejaculate on her. This indicated to me that his motivation was power, he wanted to symbolize his total domination of these victims. This ritualistic behavior was consistent throughout the series and indicated to me that all the rapes had been committed by one man, to which I would gladly testify.

Along with my testimony, McGinty had Dr. Michael Knowlan, the court-assigned psychiatrist who interviewed Shelton for nearly eight hours over the course of eight days. The defense based its case on the argument that Shelton had suffered brain damage when he fractured his skull in 1983 in a fall from a ladder while working in construction. And in an interview with Cuyahoga County court-clinic social worker Rita Haynes, Shelton had mentioned that during the series of rapes, he felt as though he was "protected" from police by a shield. After his meetings with Shelton, however, Knowlan decided that the defendant was, in fact, sane. He was a substance abuser with an antisocial personality, but this did not "constitute a mental disease or defect," and Shelton could certainly distinguish between right and wrong.

Knowlan also noted that Shelton told him he thought about raping women "fifty times per month, yet he only committed approximately fifteen rapes. The fact that the defendant had thoughts about raping, but did not act on some occasions, suggests that he had some ability to refrain from committing rapes."

To address these arguments, the defense lined up forensic psychiatrist Dr. Emanuel Tanay. He'd worked with Milano before in the case of defendant Michael Levine, accused of the aggravated murder of successful Cleveland businessman Julius Kravitz. In his sixties with gray hair and an elegant European accent, Tanay had the experience that comes from testifying in hundreds of cases, including those of Ted Bundy and Jack Ruby. After meeting with Shelton, Tanay concluded that even though Shelton had told Knowlan he hadn't raped as many times as he'd felt like raping someone, he was still compelled to rape, and that "efforts to resist compulsive behavior are the very characteristic of a compulsion."

As the trial date drew closer, Judge Richard McMonagle expected a plea agreement to be worked out between the two sides, since, as Milano had pointed out, Ohio law had a cap on sentences for rape. McGinty, however, kept adding charges and was determined to go to trial. It was a gamble, but McGinty felt all the victims should be represented with charges—which wouldn't happen if he agreed to a plea—so they would all have an opportunity to give input before the parole board and try to keep Shelton locked up as long as possible. And in the larger frame, McGinty hoped the sentencing rules would be recognized as ludicrous once people understood the atrocity and magnitude of the rapist's crimes and that they would provide ammunition for changing the sentencing laws. After all, those of us who'd studied the subject knew that fifteen years on ice is not likely to cool the obsession whose life's work, as it were, had been rape.

McGinty used a new tactic in preparation. Since the victims held the key to the case, he felt he needed to make sure they were all ready to testify, that as terrified as many of them still were, they'd be able to reach a jury with their story and not be destroyed by the other side. He met with Carla Kole, a social worker with the court's Witness and Victim Service, a group that acted as part of the court system to provide counseling and support for witnesses and victims of crime. Together, they invited all the victims of the cases going to trial—thirty in all—with their husbands or boyfriends if they wanted, to come together to get ready emotionally for what they were about to face in court. They discussed everything from how to preserve their privacy, to what a sentence might be if Shelton was found guilty, to a discussion of plea bargaining, even how to deal with the family of the accused, since Shelton's ex-girlfriend complained that his sister had been following her around. McGinty even asked what they felt a good sentence would be.

Jury selection began September 11, 1989, and it was a media frenzy. At McGinty's urging, all thirty victims showed up at the courthouse every day, even if they had to wait outside because they hadn't testified yet. Ronnie Shelton's family—his parents and sister, Maria—were also in attendance.

Initially, Milano tried to keep the victims from testifying, arguing that since Shelton admitted to the rapes, the only issue left was his sanity. Milano argued it would save both time and money if the jury heard only the experts on that point, but the judge decided to let the victims have their say.

The judge did, however, inform jurors that if they found Shelton not guilty by reason of insanity, he would not just go free; he'd be sent to a penal institution where his sanity could be reviewed every six months and that he could possibly remain there for the rest of his life. It concerned the prosecution that jurors who would otherwise be afraid to vote him insane might see this as a good way to admit they weren't sure, but still have the relief of knowing he'd be put away.

I met with McGinty on September 18, the night before he planned to call me to the stand to close his case. I could tell that even though he appreciated the report I'd sent him, he was still concerned about how effective I would be on the stand. Especially after days of dramatic, moving testimony from the women who were Shelton's victims, I'm sure he didn't want to close with someone whose credibility could be shaken in any way. Over dinner, we went back and forth until I could tell he was loosening up, feeling better about putting me on. I'm glad he didn't focus on the fact that even though I believed in what I was saying, what I did was still new enough that if something happened and I bombed, it would have repercussions beyond even the thirty women and their families counting on him. But even with that pressure, I felt confident because, to me, the links between cases were so strong that I knew I could get the jury to understand. McGinty needed me to establish and point out the links because even though Milano didn't contest Shelton's guilt, he could have come back later and asked for a dismissal of any charges McGinty hadn't been able to prove. In a sense, for the jury, I had to place Shelton at those rapes where he'd left no prints or other physical evidence.

I wanted my testimony to be an educational experience for the jury, to get them to understand how and why these various crimes were linked and why it was overwhelmingly evident that one individual had committed all of them. The most important thing I had to get across was the signature aspect, how it was related to, and how it differed from, the better understood modus operandi.

MO is what an offender has to do to accomplish a crime. It's learned behavior and gets modified and perfected as the criminal gets better and better at what he does. For example, a bank robber's accomplice might realize after one or two jobs that he ought to leave the getaway car's motor running during the robbery. This would be an aspect of modus operandi. The signature, on the other hand, is something the offender has to do to fulfill himself emotionally. It's not needed to successfully accomplish the crime, but it is the reason he undertakes the particular crime in the first place.

To get this point across, I cited an example I'd used many times before in my teaching at the Academy, and it, too, involves bank robbery. I worked on two cases, with two different offenders working in two different states, yet both did a similar thing during the robbery. In a case in Grand Rapids, Michigan, the robber made everyone in the bank undress—take off everything—and stay that way until he had left with the money. In another case in Texas, the bank robber also made his victims undress, with one variation: he posed them in degrading sexual positions and then took photographs of them.

Now, what is the difference between these two similar actions? I asked rhetorically. The difference is that to a trained analyst, the first case is an example of MO, while the second is an example of signature.

In the Michigan case, the robber had everyone strip to make them uncomfortable and embarrassed so they would not look up at him and be able to make a positive ID later on. Also, once he escaped, they would be preoccupied with getting redressed before calling the police or reacting in any other way. There would be a lot of confusion before they could get sufficiently organized to pursue him. So this MO greatly helped the offender accomplish his goal of robbing money from that bank.

In the Texas case, having everyone strip so he could take pictures of them had nothing to do with accomplishing the robbery; in fact, quite the opposite, it slowed him down and made him easier to pursue. But it was something he felt a need to do for his own emotional satisfaction and completeness. This is a signature—something that is special (possibly even unique) to that particular offender.

Another example of signature would be the serial bomber I profiled who spray-painted the insides of his devices black. This had nothing to do with how effective the bomb would be; it was just something he did for his own reasons.

In the case of a sexual predator, we can speak about signature and MO in a wider context than merely the crime itself. For some types, the courtship—wine, soft music, intimate lighting, and candles— might be an MO to lure the victim into his control. For other types, a quick blitz-style attack from behind might accomplish the same purpose. Once each predator has the victim in his control, whether it's through a fancy dinner or a knock on the head, then he is free to exercise his obsession, to introduce his own signature.

And a signature could be almost anything—a burglar who urinates on the floor at the crime scene to show his arrogance and contempt, a sexual sadist who tortures his victim in a particular way, another vicious predator who videotapes his rape-murders so he can relive them again and again—all of these are signatures I've seen in numerous variations throughout my career.

Shelton used the same types of degrading language with most of his victims. He raped them in the same degrading manner. "The underlying theme in this case is not sex," I testified. "The underlying theme is anger, is this power. And the method of his sexual assault—masturbating on the victim, performing vaginal sex, withdrawing, ejaculating on the victim's stomach, or masturbating over the victim, masturbating between the victim's breasts—it tells you this is total domination of the victim."

I went on to explain that "these elements of this particular crime are very, very unique—in fact, so unique that there's no hesitation of saying that you have one person operating in Cleveland, Ohio, who's perpetrating these particular crimes in this cluster of cases here. You have one person."

In addition to explaining the signature link, I also testified that Ronnie Shelton was what we call a "power assertive" rapist, which is one of the rarer types. Only one in ten rapists fits his style. We'll get into the different types more in the next chapter, but suffice it to say at this point that compared to, say, the so-called gentleman rapist, who is often apologetic about raping his victim, Shelton represents an uncommon group. His motivation was anger, power, the quest to manipulate, dominate, control, and degrade these women. I would have been shocked to see two rapists fitting this description, with this particular signature, operating in the same area at the same time.

I explained that Shelton was like a predator in the animal kingdom: he didn't need to rape every night, but he was always out on the hunt, looking for victims of opportunity. In fact, although it wasn't part of my testimony, Shelton had been arrested several times for voyeurism, which would be consistent with his hunting, getting ready for his next assault.

I clarified that it was not surprising to hear that Shelton had been in consensual sexual relationships during the period when he was raping his victims, because that's actually common with this type of offender. Often, there's a problem in that relationship that's the precipitating stressor to his crimes and is the underlying motivator. He can't confront the woman with whom he's really having problems—the wife or girlfriend or whatever—so he takes all that anger out on a victim of opportunity. As I also said in my written report to McGinty, I testified that the way he raped these women, all showed his need to dominate them. I closed by saying that in the more than five thousand cases I'd worked on, the majority of which had been rapes or rape-murders, I found the power-assertive elements of his crimes unique to the point that I was certain he was responsible for all the rapes presented.

Had I ever heard the term "compulsive rape syndrome?" McGinty asked me on the stand.

"No, sir," I replied.

Now I have to confess that what happened next is one of my favorite memories from providing expert-witness testimony. I was still on the stand when Jerry Milano got up to cross-examine me. But instead of beginning his questioning, he asked permission to approach the bench for a sidebar. I couldn't hear what he, Judge McMonagle, and Tim McGinty were saying, but I did notice the judge shaking his head and McGinty smiling broadly. Milano moved to have my testimony stricken from the record, but Judge McMonagle ruled that it could stand. He then called for a brief recess.

As the court was clearing and I was stepping down from the witness stand, McGinty came over to me and related that, during the sidebar, Milano had muttered something to the effect of, "What the fuck am I gonna ask this guy? This guy's worked more cases than One-A-Day vitamins!" A little later, while I was waiting in the corridor outside for the trial to resume, I could hear Milano on the phone to his office, expressing essentially the same sentiment.

When court resumed, I took my place on the stand. Judge McMonagle looked to Milano and said, "Your witness."

"I have no questions for this witness, Your Honor," he replied.

As part of his testimony, Dr. Tanay played a tape of an interview with Shelton, which included the tearful defendant talking about his miserable family life, among other things. Under cross, in hours of back-and-forth argument between the prosecutor and the witness, McGinty stressed that Tanay's opinion had been formed after just one hour of examination, and that it was possible that Shelton had lied to him. In redirect, Tanay argued that such lying would be consistent with his diagnosis, however.

The strongest argument on the defense side came when Dr. Tanay focused on the head injury that had left Shelton unconscious for three days. The doctor argued that since the rapes began after that, Shelton's rape impulses may have broken loose as a result of that injury.

Though it didn't come out until after the trial, in a journalistic tour de force, James Neff identified an unsolved rape with similar characteristics that had taken place five years before the injury. Sure enough, when Neff got detectives to investigate, the UNSUB's prints matched Shelton's.

After all was said and done, the jury went off to deliberate, coming back with a verdict in four days that must have been an agonizing wait for the victims. Before the verdict was announced, they all clapped for McGinty as he entered the courtroom to hear it read: guilty of 49 rapes and 200 criminal counts in total.

Judge McMonagle then made history with his sentence. He imposed the maximum sentence for each crime committed against each victim, ranging from ten to twenty-five years, to be served consecutively in actual time, meaning no possibility of parole until he'd served the full sentence, the longest sentence in the history of Ohio— 3,198 years. The night of the sentence, the victims held a victory party, where they burned Ronnie Shelton in effigy.

What I found most fascinating about Ronnie Shelton was the issue of victim choice. I knew from the victim statements that his primary goal was to dominate and degrade these women. I knew from my interviews with serial offenders and my research into their backgrounds that the victims often represented some woman he actually hated but felt powerless to act out against. Think of someone like Ed Kemper, who vented his rage on young college students before he was finally able to get rid of his mother.

Ronnie Shelton's preferential victim was simply female. As I looked across the courtroom at those thirty women, I was shocked that the only observable characteristic they had in common was race: they had different color hair, body types, styles of dress. They were a variety of ages, with occupations ranging from student to mother, Avon lady, office worker, and waitress, to name but a few. The woman could have been eighteen or eighty, I observed, as long as she lived in a place with a window or door he could penetrate. And despite their different styles, the same was true for Joseph Stephenson Thompson, half a world away.

Shelton and Thompson share other characteristics, too, that we in law enforcement need to take to heart. To begin with, in both cases, authorities basically knew whom they were looking for all along, they just didn't have his name. Both bore a striking resemblance to profile elements developed by the FBI and local investigators. Each committed his crimes in a geographic comfort zone, especially the early offenses. Shelton most often operated near his parents' home, a girl-friend's house, his job, or someplace in between. Thompson stayed close to his current and former residences, or someplace on his way to work. As profiled, Shelton did not have a regular job and had trouble keeping one, feeling he was too good to be working for someone else in a subservient capacity. Similarly, as had been predicted, Thompson worked in a local factory. Both men had troubled or volatile relation-ships with the women in their lives and were the dominant party in on-again, off-again relationships with women who were typically younger and/or dependent in some way. Shelton had an extremely conflicted relationship with his mother—described by him as domi-neering and inappropriate in her behavior toward him—and with his sister, whom he seemed to want to control.

Although they fit profiles in other ways as well, the most striking ele-ment in both cases is also the most disturbing one from a law enforce-ment perspective. It had been noted that the UNSUB in each case likely had a previous criminal record dating back to juvenile offenses. Not only did this turn out to be true, but with each there were numer-ous missed opportunities—times during the investigation when the authorities almost had their man but didn't realize it. I'm saying this not to criticize the fine men and women who work long hours at a some-times tedious, often dangerous job. Rather, I think we need to look hard at these cases and educate ourselves so we can pull something useful from these experiences and give the hardworking officers and detectives the kind of help and support they need and deserve.

Prior to his ultimate arrest, Thompson was picked up by the police for a variety of offenses that should have set off warning buzzers. In addition to the collar in April 1984 when he was discovered in a woman's bedroom and claimed to be a burglar, he was arrested and even served time on other charges, and he was picked up on drug charges as well as numerous driving offenses. We know that sex offenders often have prior records of non-sex-related crimes, and that burglary is a common precursor to rape. Certainly, if someone is arrested for burglary while a series of rapes is being investigated, that person should be evaluated as a suspect for the rapes as well.

Within the police organization, too, different departments need to communicate with one another. In September 1990, Thompson was arrested for dangerous driving in a car that was described a week later on TV when the program *Crimewatch* featured the vehicle in its coverage of a recent rape. The traffic cop who'd stopped him never made the connection, which was a tremendous embarrassment to the force when this mistake was later realized.

Shelton had his share of lucky breaks, too. In late spring of 1985, a woman called the police after spotting him hanging around first-floor apartment windows. When questioned at the scene, Shelton said he was trying to find an address and thought he had it wrong. The officer checked him out and found no outstanding warrants and so let him go.

This pattern repeated itself several times over the next few years, as Shelton was arrested for voyeurism and other related offenses. In February 1987 he was arrested for criminal trespass after someone saw him—in a ski mask—standing outside a neighbor's apartment window. He told police he was looking for a lost dog; the cop never made the connection between this and the serial rapist they were looking for. Later that year, Shelton was even called in for questioning after police tracked him in connection with a Peeping Tom report. At the time, Shelton was convinced they had him, but it turned out they were looking for a suspect in a burglary in that area. They knew that the burglary UNSUB had cut himself on a window, and when Shelton's hands came up clean and undamaged, they let him go. In December 1988, he was arrested for voyeurism in the middle of the West Side Rapist's stomping grounds, with several rings of master keys to an apartment building in his pocket. Still, he was charged only with the minor offense and let out on bond the same day.

These are only some of the more egregious examples of times *somebody* should have been suspicious. We're talking about mostly sex-related offenses, in the vicinity of numerous crime scenes, and a guy who looks a hell of a lot like the composite drawing the police had been updating and circulating for years.

Even Shelton was surprised the police let him go so easily. He couldn't believe they didn't know that peeping was how he found his future victims.

Finally, in some ways, Shelton represents a shortcoming of the criminal justice system. In 1982, he and a girlfriend had staged a fake robbery at a money exchange in Colorado, where he was living at the time. He ended up with a fine and a suspended sentence and moved back to

Ohio. The whole time he was committing these rapes, destroying lives, he was on probation.

Before we condemn his probation officer, though, it should be noted that the guy was distrustful of Shelton and did his best to get him off the streets, but simply didn't have the power or authority to do more than he did, which was get him arrested for violation of probation in 1986 (following an assault conviction related to a fight at a bar). The officer also wrote to the authorities in Colorado to inform them that Shelton was in violation of his probation agreement; aside from the arrest, Shelton didn't have steady employment, hadn't sent full restitution out to Colorado for the robbery, and kept changing addresses, among other violations. The officer requested that Colorado extradite him and lock him up. The answer came back within days: Colorado didn't want him, he was Ohio's headache now.

Shelton's story and Thompson's confirm something we've got to get across to those in the criminal justice system. It is that, in many cases, early crimes are a harbinger of future, more serious violence. When we see someone with a long arrest record for voyeurism or breaking and entering, we should consider him a likely candidate for future rape—if he hasn't done so already. We know that many of the juvenile offenders of today become more violent adult offenders tomorrow.

Between the two of them, Shelton and Thompson admitted to raping more than seventy women and young girls. Who knows how many others they victimized—women who were just too afraid to report the crime. We owe it to all of them and to future victims to learn from these cases so that the next time we can spare potential victims the pain and suffering these people went through.

CHAPTER FOUR

The Dimensions
of Rape

I've seen the look in the eyes often enough to know right away what it means.

Most often it'll be when I'm giving a speech or part of a seminar or other public presentation. It happened several times when I was out on the road in connection with the publication of *Journey into Darkness*.

Just as we're finishing up, she'll make her way to the front of the room and say something to the effect of, "Mr. Douglas, I wonder if I could talk to you a moment."

"Sure," I'll reply. There might still be a number of people around me, some wanting to follow up on things I've said during my presentation, others posing the single question I'm asked most often—How can I get into behavioral profiling?

"Why don't you wait until everyone else is gone?" I'll suggest. "Then we'll have some time to talk."

She waits patiently until the last of the crowd drifts off. Then she tells me her story.

It could be someone she knew well, or a total stranger. It could have happened in a public park or when she came home unexpectedly and surprised a burglar. It could have been a mild-mannered individual who apologized for everything he was doing to her and kept asking for reassurance that he wasn't hurting her, or it could have been a man who tortured her simply to hear her scream and beg for her life. He could have driven up beside her in the mall parking lot as she was walking to her car and pulled her into the back of his windowless van, or he could have been a guy she'd been dating for the last six months. She could have been twelve when it happened to her, or she could have been sixty-eight. The common denominators are that a man did it to her, he did it to her against her will, and her life has not been the same—indeed, in some ways, she feels her life has not been her own—since then.

Sometimes, if the rapist hasn't been caught, I can suggest proactive strategies for identifying him or somehow getting him to come forward. Other times, when the offender has been tried and convicted, I'm asked to explain what it is that motivates a man do this to an innocent woman. And then sometimes, I can only listen and offer my sympathy, joining my outrage with hers. Whatever the case, I'm no longer surprised when women want to talk with me about these horrible experiences. Traditionally, sexual assault has been the one vastly underreported crime because people didn't want to talk about it, partly because sexual assault is the one crime in which the victim usually has been evaluated for complicity in her own victimization. With the advent of the women's movement and vigorous legal advocacy by people such as Linda Fairstein, head of the New York County District Attorney's Office Sex Crimes Unit, this is beginning to change. But not nearly fast enough.

This increasing awareness, and the public outrage that goes with it, is a positive and hopeful trend. There's another trend I've noticed that isn't nearly so positive from a personal security standpoint, however understandable and well-intentioned it may be. And that is to lump all rapes and sexual assaults together—to say, in effect, rape is rape and every one is just as damaging.

Yes, absolutely all rape is horrible and each sexual assault leaves its victim, her partner, friends, and loved ones devastated. I've spent enough time on rape cases and with rape victims to know this to be true. But I've also learned something else: we do a grave disservice to all victims and potential victims if we don't take the time and care to distinguish between the various established types of rapes and rapists. It may seem more sympathetic and caring to proclaim, for instance, that date rape is the same as stranger rape, but that just isn't true: so much depends on the circumstances of the assault. To assert that a date rape not involving a weapon and that does not cause the victim to fear for her life is the same as a stranger-abduction rape at knife- or gun-point where the victim is brutally beaten oversimplifies the situation and hinders our ability to defend against both crimes and their different types of perpetrators.

There are certain things that all sexual assaults share. But what they don't share is, in some ways, even more important if we are to learn prevention strategies from them and help victims recover from their individual traumas.

Those of us at the FBI's National Center for the Analysis of Violent Crime (NCAVC) at Quantico—the umbrella organization that encompassed my Investigative Support Unit—have studied rape extensively enough to devise specific categories and subcategories. Much of this was based on pioneering work that had come before, including research by Dr. Ann Burgess, as well as my colleagues Special Agents Roy Hazelwood and Ken Lanning. In 1992, after more than ten years of investigation and study, these categories, along with similar breakdowns of homicide and arson, were organized into the *Crime Classification Manual,* a standard system for investigating and classifying violent crimes, which I wrote along with Profs. Ann W. and Allen Burgess and former Special Agent Robert Ressler. An understanding of these categories won't help the potential rapist become better at his particular obsession any more than it would make an addict who robs convenience stores for drug money turn to extortion or some other means for funding. But it could help the rest of us avoid him or, if we can't, increase the odds in our favor. I say "we" because in one way or another, this is a crime that affects all of us.

In our research, we reviewed case files, victim statements, police reports and court testimony, school reports and psychiatric evaluations, parole and probation records, and records of family and developmental history. After all the analysis, we broke rapists down into four basic types: the power-reassurance rapist, the exploitative rapist, the anger rapist, and the sadistic rapist. We also broke down the crime of rape into more than fifty subgroups. Over the years, different researchers have assigned their own labels to the typologies but the behavior is so consistent within each that the types should be recognizable regardless of what we call them. What do we mean by each of these types of offenders?

The Power-Reassurance Rapist feels himself to be very inadequate, not the type with whom women would voluntarily become involved. So he compensates for these feelings of male inadequacy by forcing women to have sex with him. All the while, as the designation suggests, he is looking for reassurance of his own power and potency. This type has sometimes been referred to as the gentleman rapist, or even classified as an "unselfish" rapist, in large part because his offenses, while traumatic, are usually less physically damaging to his victim than those of the other types of offenders. Although they certainly do not all behave this way, some may apologize during their assault or ask their victim if he's hurting her—a question that serves his need for reassurance more than it expresses a genuine concern for her. The kind terms *gentleman* and *unselfish* therefore are really only applicable within the context of the full spectrum of rapist types out there.

This type tends to be a loner who fantasizes that his victim is actually enjoying the experience and might even fall in love with him as a result. He may even contact the victim after the attack and ask her to go out with him. Of course, the reality of the rape can't live up to his fantasies: instead of winning over his reluctant lover, he's terrorized, hurt, and angered an innocent person, and most rapists of this type will admit that they don't enjoy the sex with their victims. The experience, then, will not satisfy his underlying obsession and he will have to try again with another woman.

Not surprisingly, victims of choice are generally about the same age or younger and usually of the same race as the perpetrator. If he dates at all, the women will be younger and less sophisticated than he; this is the only way he can feel equal. Because of his feelings of inadequacy, he gains control by surprise; he doesn't have the self-confidence or skills to con his way into a victim's apartment smoothly and is more likely to break in in the middle of the night, for example. When we delve into this type's past, we generally see a history of various unusual or bizarre masturbatory fantasies and often voyeurism, exhibitionism, cross-dressing, and/or obscene phone calls. He frequents adult bookstores or movies and collects pornography. If he has a specific sexual dysfunction, it is likely to involve premature ejaculation, which would be exhibited in consensual relationships he may have and which he would report as a problem (from his point of view only) in his rapes.

He probably prefers the night and operates within his own residential or work area—in other words, within a very prescribed comfort zone—and usually travels to the crime scene on foot. If he is a serial offender, this is particularly true of his first offenses. He uses a weapon of opportunity, often something he finds at the crime scene, his patterns of crime are generally consistent, and the entire act, from the time he overpowers his victim until the time he leaves, is relatively brief, sometimes as little as five or ten minutes. He won't use profanity or try to demean or humiliate his victim to the extent that the other types will, but may require her to recite a "script" in which she praises his lovemaking or expresses desire for him.

He might cover the victim's eyes or mask his own features both for the self-preservation motive of preventing identification as well as the possibility that he knows he should be ashamed of his actions. He is timid and will do whatever the victim allows him to. Rather than tear off her clothes or force her to strip, he may only expose the parts of the victim's body he intends to assault. He is apt to keep a journal, news clippings, or some other record of his assaults to reassure himself of his potency, and for the same reason he may take souvenirs, often pieces of the victim's underwear. Afterward, he may feel guilty or remorseful. But unless this is a "one off," who tries it, doesn't like it, and decides never to do it again, he *will* do it again. He will keep raping until he is caught or stopped in some other way, such as being killed or seriously injured in another crime or other unrelated incident.

He lives alone or with parents or in some other type of dependent relationship. His mother probably was—or is—domineering. He's employed below his ability level in a job that doesn't require a lot of contact with the public. While this is the least physically dangerous type of rapist, if he's successful over a series of attacks, his confidence can be boosted and he may become more physically aggressive.

Joseph Thompson, the South Auckland rapist, was of the power-reassurance classification, and if you're unfortunate enough to come in contact with a rapist, it's the type you're most likely to encounter.

The Exploitative Rapist is a more impulsive predator. His crimes are more the result of seizing an opportunity that presents itself rather than of fantasizing ahead of time about what the act is going to be like. He might approach the potential victim with a ruse or con, or it could be a direct, overpowering blitz-style attack. Unlike the power-reassurance rapist, this type will not appear concerned with the victim's welfare. He is selfish—verbally, physically, and sexually. He may suffer some form of sexual dysfunction, and if he does, it will be just as apparent with his wife, girlfriend, or any other consenting partner as it will be with a victim of force. Sexual dysfunction often centers around retarded ejaculation or difficulty in reaching climax at all. Victims of preference will tend to be around his own age. He is on the prowl for a victim of opportunity, and this could take place in a bar or a neighborhood he's targeted. Once he has a woman in his control, his only real concern is getting her to submit sexually to him. That is the real thrill for him—the sex act is satisfying as an act of domination and control rather than as providing what we think of as sexual gratification. Once he's forced her submission, as far as he is concerned, the experience is over. But during that encounter, he can be expected to inflict multiple assaults on the victim. Anal assaults are common. Masks or attempts at disguising or hiding his face are uncommon. With this type of offender, there will often be an interval between rapes—a day, a month, six months—until he once again goes on the hunt, but unlike the power-reassurance rapist, he won't try to maintain any contact with or come back to a victim once he has left her, although he often threatens to return if she reports the assault to police.

This type will be very body-conscious. He will want a macho reputation, to be known as a man's man, and therefore is likely to have some physically oriented employment. He's very interested in sports. His vehicle will reflect that image, too. In some regions of the country, it would be a Corvette or some muscle car; in others, it might be a pickup well-equipped for hunting. He does not take well to criticism or authority. He probably didn't do well in high school or go on to college. Not surprisingly, if he is married, he will have a history of cheating on his wife and paying scant attention to his children. When we look into the background of offenders like this, we often find that his father treated his mother the same way he treats women.

Ronnie Shelton was an exploitative rapist. Next to the power-reassurance rapist, this type is the most common, although it still represents only one of every ten rapists.

The Anger Rapist is just what the name implies. Also referred to as the anger-retaliatory rapist, his sexual assault is a displaced expression of the rage and anger within him. For this type, the victim represents the person, or group of people, the offender hates. This could be a mother, a wife, or a girlfriend, or even women in general if the guy feels a grudge against them. The point is, this person's motivation doesn't have to be rooted in an actual or legitimate wrong perpetrated against him. It would not be unusual for this type to have an ongoing relationship with a woman. And because he is driven by rage, the consequences of the anger rapist's attack can be anything from verbal abuse to a severe beating to murder, though since his conscious or subconscious intention is to get the anger out of his system, this type usually will not kill.

His attacks will be episodic, not at any predictable intervals, triggered by precipitating stressors involving the woman or women to whom his rage is actually directed. In almost all cases, the displacement means that he will not attack that person. He may even attack someone else he knows, using weapons of opportunity such as kitchen knives, or even just his fists if he's strong enough. Because he wants not just to overpower but to humiliate his target, there could be anal sex followed by oral sex, he will use a great deal of profanity, and the context of the behavior will be intention to degrade, such as ejaculating on the victim's face or clothing.

As readers of our previous book *Journey into Darkness* will remember, the late Timothy Spencer (executed in 1994) was an anger rapist. This type is far less common than either of the previous two, possibly as little as 5 percent of total rapists.

The Sadistic Rapist is, in many ways, the most dangerous sexual predator of all. The purpose of his attack is to live out his sadistic sexual fantasies on the unwilling victim. With this type, sexual fantasy and aggression merge, which is why he's also referred to as an anger-excitation rapist. Aggression and sadistic fantasy feed on each other, so as the level of aggression rises, so does his level of arousal. His aggression is not anger-based as it is with the previous category. In fact, he can be quite charming and seductive as he lures his intended prey into his web. He is completely self-centered. The only thing he cares about is his own pleasure and satisfaction. He simply gets off on hurting people, on having them in his power. Therefore, with this type we'll see various forms of mental and physical torture, and the physical torture may be directed particularly at sexually significant parts of the body such as mouth, breasts, genitals, buttocks, and rectum. His weapon of choice is often a knife because it is so intimidating and causes mental anguish. He will often cut or tear off the victim's clothing because he figures she will not need it anymore after he has finished with her.

Depending on his preferences, there may be a lot of sex, probably highly perverse in nature, or even none. He could, for example, prefer to penetrate with a sharp object rather than with his penis. His language will be commanding and degrading, but impersonal. The victim is merely there as an actress in his self-scripted drama, and her role is to show fear and respond to pain. There is, therefore, often a victim of preference, symbolic to him in some way, be she old or young, white, black, or Asian, slim or full-figured, black-haired or blond, redhead or brunette.

The sadistic rapist anticipates his crime, in fact has perfected his MO over his criminal career. As his fantasy evolves and he gains more experience with different victims, he will take more time planning for successive crimes. He brings his weapon with him and may have a torture kit made up, including pliers or other sharp instruments, whips, manacles, needles, whatever he needs to fulfill his fantasy. Since his assault unfolds over a long time, he will have a place to which he can take his victim where he knows he will not be disturbed. This might be an obscure cabin in the woods or a specially outfitted and sound-proofed van. He may tell the victim that if she does what he tells her to, he won't hurt her any further or he'll let her go, but this is only a ruse to control her and get her to cooperate. Because his satisfaction lies in tormenting and dominating his victim, he may take photographs or record the scene as it is unfolding on either audio- or videotape. For the same reason, he may also take souvenirs to help him relive the experience whenever he wants and demonstrate to himself that he "owns" the victim. These souvenirs might include jewelry, items either of clothing or underwear, or even body parts.

The attack will tend to be highly symbolic. There will be no remorse because the rapist has totally depersonalized his victim; he doesn't even think of her as a human being. This is the type of rape that most often ends in murder. In fact, killing the victim may be an integral part of the sadistic fantasy scenario. He may continue to engage in activity with the body after death. It is generally impossible to play on his sympathy, because he has none. He wants his victim to suffer. The only instance in which he might relent is if the victim can somehow break through the depersonalization and get him to regard her as an individual. I have known this to occur, for example, one time when a woman stated that her husband had cancer. It happened that the rapist's own brother was battling cancer, and so he let her go. Another time, a sadistic rapist told me that one of his victims reminded him of his mother, and so he released her. Unfortunately, this is an uncommon scenario with the sexual sadist.

The sadistic type is usually white, with above-normal intelligence, and may be college-educated with a good middle-class job. He will have a dominant personality and collect bondage and sadomasochistic pornography. He may also collect related items, such as knives, guns, or Nazi memorabilia, and read military, law enforcement, or survivalist literature. He may have a large attack-type dog such as a German shepherd, Doberman, or rottweiler. Because of his intelligence and planning, he will be difficult to apprehend.

The late Steven Pennell (executed in 1992), the so-called I-40, Killer, in Delaware, who picked up prostitutes along Interstate 40, then raped, tortured, and murdered them in the back of his specially equipped van, was a sadistic rapist. This is the least common variety.

As we all know, human nature is not exact, and not every rapist is cooperative enough to fit neatly into one of these four categories. There is often a mixed presentation, with elements of one classification grafting onto the general description of another, which is why it is so difficult to give specific advice on how to react to a sexual criminal, particularly under the acute stress of the attack itself. But in the great majority of cases, one category will dominate, and our reaction should be molded around the understanding of what motivates that type of rapist and what he is after.

Even with the areas of overlap or crossover, it is tremendously helpful to understand the type of offender we're dealing with in each case. The point of classification is to provide potential victims—and investigators if it comes to that—with an understanding of the rapist's individual obsession. Motive is a tough call in most rape cases, compared to those in neater, easier-to-define crimes, such as burglary, for example. If a potential victim understands an assailant's motive—what he's after—she may be able to defuse him or otherwise deal with the situation before he has the opportunity to harm her. And if we in law enforcement understand our UNSUB's obsession, we may recognize what type of beast we're dealing with and be able to tailor our investigation, prosecution, and sentencing accordingly.

Linda Fairstein has been a New York City prosecutor since 1972.

Since 1976, she has been chief of the Sex Crimes Unit of the District Attorney's Office. She is also an accomplished author, both of the highly respected *Sexual Violence: Our War Against Rape* and two well-received crime novels. Her personal obsession has led to meaningful changes in rules, procedure, police and public attitudes toward sexual assault, and greater confidence in the ability of the legal system to render justice. Her own journey from a suburban childhood to college and a prestigious law school to urban hero in a relentless job that is admittedly not for the squeamish is a saga of dawning awareness of the dimensions of rape and what it has done to us as a society.

Like most of us who deal with rape, she credits the women's movement with focusing attention at a time when nobody else seemed interested. But one thing that disturbed her was the common claim that rape was actually a crime of violence, and that it wasn't about sex. She notes, "That bothered me, because I'd handled every other kind of assault and it's different. It's not beating someone over the head with the baseball bat. It's not using hands and fists. There is a sexual element to this that isn't part of any other crime, and that can't be denied. It's very much the piece of the crime that the victim doesn't want to happen or is afraid of. And so to me, it was about the one weapon that this type of offender had that other offenders don't use and victims don't want used against them."

What Fairstein came up with, and it's as good a thumbnail analysis as any I've heard, is that rape is a crime of violence in which sex is the weapon. That's what distinguishes it from every other violent crime, and that is at the heart of what makes it so traumatic and so difficult to prosecute effectively. For example, we've already noted that sexual assault is the one violent crime in which there is often widespread speculation about whether the victim somehow contributed to her predicament. Did she lead him on? Was she "asking for it" with what she said . . . how she was acting . . . what she was wearing . . . or not wearing?

It may not be the wisest move in the world to carry thousands of dollars in cash on a city street, but do we say that someone who does is asking to be robbed? Do we say that someone who drives a shiny new Ferrari is asking to be carjacked? Do we say that because he was rich and famous and talented, John Lennon was asking to be murdered?

Fairstein agrees that the first line of defense is to understand the enemy.

"People have very mythical stereotypes about these crimes and who the offenders are, and who the victims are," she states. "And that's true both in the acquaintance category and in the stranger category. People tend not to be interested in understanding this better until it happens to someone near and dear to them, or to themselves. And then they get a very quick education."

She recently spoke at a public forum about a serial rapist still at large who'd committed more than thirteen rapes on the Upper East Side, one of the safest neighborhoods in Manhattan. The most recent crime took place in a building in which his picture was posted in the lobby. The victim went right through the door without noticing or bothering to lock it behind her or wait for it to close. And he just followed her in.

Was this victim "asking for it"? Definitely not. Could more awareness regarding potential predators and greater prudence on her part have cut down the odds of her becoming a victim? Definitely so. Sometimes, even the rapists themselves warn us to be more careful.

It really shouldn't surprise us that there are so many different types of rapists. Think of all the different reasons why people become doctors or lawyers or policemen, or burglars, for that matter. At the Investigative Support Unit, one of our guiding principles is that behavior reflects personality. And this is true whether we're talking about the behavior of children in a preschool setting, trying to imagine from watching them who and what they will grow to be, or analyzing the behavior of an UNSUB while investigating a sexual assault. Teachers and other people who spend a lot of time around children become good at assessing their strengths, weaknesses, interests, and trouble areas. My colleagues and I make much the same assessments; our area of focus just happens to be adults with much darker drives.

And we are not the only ones who differentiate between the rapist typologies. Sexual predators themselves make distinctions. Men who prey on children have traditionally occupied the lowest rung in the criminal pecking order. A sadistic monster who beats a woman to death, mutilates and sexually violates her corpse, may view the behavior of a child molester as "sick" even as he justifies his own actions in his mind.

We had a case one time of a man who came to the aid of a woman he observed being beaten by another man trying to subdue and rape her. When the rescuer was later arrested for a series of sexual assaults of his own, the police who interrogated him expressed confusion over why he would rape women himself but save one victim from another attacker. This offended the man, who couldn't believe they would compare his assaults to the attempted rape he thwarted. In his mind, since he controlled his victims by threatening and intimidating them, he had nothing in common with a man who would physically hurt a woman by beating her. The fact that he traumatized, terrorized, and sexually violated a series of victims seemed apparently lost on him.

Serial rapist Ronnie Shelton was often abusive in relationships with the various women in his life. At his trial, one former girlfriend testified both to his violent side and to an incident when he raped her. Still, Shelton expressed pride in his perception that he treated women well, whether it was reminding his sister or a girlfriend to lock her doors and windows, defending a woman from a drunk or brutal boyfriend in one of the nightclubs he frequented, or pulling over to help a damsel in distress stranded on the side of the road. According to James Neff, Shelton treasured a note sent to him that read, in part, "I just wanted to thank you for helping me the other day. If you hadn't stopped, I don't know what I'd have done. If more men were like you, we'd all be a lot safer."

Shelton often acted in ways that seem on the surface to be entirely contradictory to his rapist behavior, except that the underlying motivation is consistent. Whether raping or protecting a woman, he was in control of the situation—asserting his masculinity, beefing up his strong side to suppress his feelings of insecurity and inadequacy. His "good behavior" probably helped him self-justify those times when he was abusive; the women or some other outside force must have caused the situation. His girlfriend must have done something to provoke him or a rape victim's husband should not have left her home alone and defenseless.

Just as there are differences in rapists, there are similarities, too, and that is what allows us to type them. Once we have an idea of the type we're dealing with, we can provide a description of his postoffense behavior and the other profile elements we hope will help investigators. I know from years of interviewing offenders and studying their work that much as they like to believe they are unique, with few exceptions they have similar general motivations that are expressed in similar fashions. So I know, for example, that regardless of where in the country a rape takes place, similar crimes, committed for similar reasons, indicate similar types of criminals at work.

In investigating rapes, the biggest clue to what type of rapist we're dealing with is his behavior. *Behavior reflects personality.* In addition to the crime-scene indicators, physical evidence, and victimology, with sexual assaults we often have a vital source of information that we don't get with other types of crime, such as murder or some robberies. And that is a live victim who experienced the crime firsthand and can tell us what was done and said. I'm not only talking about the information people normally think of, such as physical characteristics, a description of the vehicle the suspect drove, and the like, but the even more important behavioral clues the offender inadvertently provides during the commission of the crime. These are the pieces that will lead us to his motivation—his obsession—which in turn will point to his overall typology and the personality traits and characteristics that commonly apply.

Returning to our burglar analogy for a moment, junkies desperate for drug money break into homes differently than professional cat burglars. Although on the surface the primary need served is obtaining money, the underlying motivations—as well as the skill level and the desperation level—are different, which can be seen in the way they rob. If we accept that the main motive for rape is not primarily sex, but has more to do with aggression and power, our only real clue to the sex offender's motivation and personality is the way he conducts his crime.

With sexual assault, the key areas we need to look at are the verbal, sexual, and physical behaviors of the rapist. In analyzing the verbal cues, obvious clues to the UNSUB's identity would be any accent he might have or unique colloquialisms he may use. But we can often get information that's just as telling from a less obvious source: the things he says or forces his victim to say. A rapist who makes his victim tell him she wants him and loves him is looking to get something different out of the encounter than one who uses a high degree of profanity, calling his victim a slut, bitch, or whore. And both differ from one who forces his victim to beg for her life. The first offender has emotional needs centered around his inadequacy, more of a power-reassurance type, whereas the second is much more concerned with making sure he humiliates his victim, letting her know she's worthless to him. The last is a sadistic type, who enjoys seeing and hearing the fear and pain he's causing. Although all have a need to control, the points of departure in their words (and the ones they script for their victims) are like signposts providing different directions for investigators to follow as they hunt for their suspect.

Similarly, the types of sexual acts and their sequencing provide insight into the rapist's motivation. A power-reassurance rapist is more likely to kiss his victim, fondle her, shift positions during vaginal penetration or perform cunnilingus as though to please her. An anger rapist more interested in punishing his victim may incorporate anal penetration, although, depending on how and when in the assault it occurs, this could also indicate another type of rapist's interest in experimentation. Forced oral sex after anal penetration, as mentioned earlier, usually indicates an offender who wants to degrade or humiliate his victim. Finally, anal sex may indicate that the rapist has spent some time in jail—particularly if the victim describes him as having a muscular, well-developed upper body.

The amount of physical force used to accomplish the rape also tells us a lot about our UNSUB. Just as his word choice can provide clues to everything from his education level and background to his underlying desires from the assault, his actions betray his personality. As rapists themselves have observed, there is a difference between a guy who launches a blitz-style attack against an unsuspecting victim, beating her senseless before attempting a sexual act, someone who uses threats to get his victim to submit, and someone else who can initially charm his prey into his sphere of control. Again, these differ widely from one who inflicts pain in discrete acts of torture, looking his victim in the eyes as she realizes that there's nothing she can do or say—no act of compliance—to get him to stop to save herself.

If an offender does grow violent in the course of a rape, it's important to know when. Did he seem calm and in control until his victim refused to do something, at which point he grew physically abusive? And if the victim complied with the rapist's demands, for example, why did he beat her anyway? The motives of each can range from a need to punish his victim—who may represent another person, the true focus of his anger—to the operational need to keep his victim under control throughout the assault, to the desire to dominate a victim so completely he dictates her pain and suffering, her very life and death. In each of those cases, we're dealing with different personality types, men who would be described in completely different terms by their neighbors, coworkers, and friends.

Even acts as simple as taking something from the victim reveal aspects of the UNSUB's nature and lifestyle: leaving with the victim's cash serves completely different needs than robbing a victim of her underwear or driver's license. The power-reassurance type has even been known to return stolen objects.

As with other types of crime, we also analyze the rapist's behavior to gain insight into his level of criminal sophistication. An UNSUB who instructs his victim not to look at him but doesn't actually wear a disguise, for example, is operating on more of a novice level than one who cleans up after ejaculating in or on a victim so as not to leave evidence. One who brings his own rope to tie up his victim, delaying her discovery or escape, giving himself more time to get away safely, is more sophisticated than one who comes to the scene with nothing and simply wings it.

Roy Hazelwood has made a career-long study of sex crimes and their offenders. Getting the right behavioral information from the victim is so critical that he developed a list of questions investigating officers should ask to elicit details ranging from the way the offender approached and gained control over the victim to the level of physical force involved, whether and how she resisted, and other vital information.

Just as we can use these typologies to help us zero in on characteristics and traits of UNSUBs, we have developed useful strategies to get these guys off the streets based on type. We know, for example, that the power-reassurance rapist's fantasies of a continued, loving relationship with his victim can lead to his undoing. Police have had success with simply tracing calls to the victim's home over the next few weeks—or watching her house and mailbox to see if he returns to drop off a note or some token of affection, such as flowers, stuffed animals, or other items that real lovers exchange. Other times, the victims have been able to construct a ruse to lead this type of assailant right to the authorities: making a date with him where the offender can be arrested as soon as he shows up.

There are also general investigative techniques that are applicable regardless of which type of rapist we're dealing with. As Ronnie Shelton's multiple arrests for voyeurism and Joseph Thompson's for burglary illustrate, often enough, so-called nuisance crimes and nonviolent offenses are warnings of much more serious, dangerous offenses to follow. Clearly, an adult burglar arrested coming out of a home with cash and jewelry should be recognized as having a different agenda than a teenaged one arrested with stolen panties in his pocket. While the first might seem a more dangerous intruder and the second merely a Peeping Tom with a common fetish, all things being equal, I'm going to be more concerned about that teenager, in terms of potential for violence and trauma. Certainly there are a lot more Peeping Toms out there than serial rapists, so a simple fetish does not always lead to violent crime, but a man arrested for voyeurism today may well evolve into a rapist in the future, when merely watching women through a window and masturbating as he fantasizes about them no longer satisfies him.

In case after case we've been able to chart the progression: a person with fantasies of dominating women may start out by collecting pornography depicting bondage or even draw restraints on models in lingerie ads. As his need to express his desires grows, he may purchase rope—a completely nonsexual item to most people—and masturbate as he holds it and imagines what he could do with it. (These are the types of items I'd include in a search warrant once a suspect's been identified in connection with a sadistic rape, for example.)

I don't want to give the impression here that I believe pornography causes otherwise okay people to commit sexual crime—I don't, any more than I believe that violent movies or television shows cause otherwise okay people to rob banks or blow up airplanes. There is absolutely no evidence or data to support either assertion. But I do know from my extensive interviews with offenders of all types that for men who already have the disposition, collecting pornography, particularly bondage and sadomasochistic pornography, is an indication, a symptom, if you will, of their particular dangerous obsession. And while I'm on the subject, I certainly do not blame violence in the media for violence in real life, but I do believe that the constant exposure of children and teens—not to mention adults—to depictions of violence has to have the cumulative effect of desensitizing all of us to the horrors we see visited around us. I would much rather have my children see a program that portrays violence as it really is—quick, senseless, revolting—than one that pretties it up and glorifies it for the sake of making some movie star look heroic.

After the pornography phase, the next step may be for the subject to start following women home, fueling his fantasy with actual potential objects for his desire. He's committed no crime, nobody may even be cognizant of his actions, but whether he's consciously aware of it or not, with each step he gets more and more comfortable with the idea of acting out his desires, until someday he's ready to do it.

Many times, these men will hire prostitutes to act out their inner desires, which is why police often turn to them when investigating serial sexual offenses with an unusual fantasy component. Often, too, sex offenders have consenting relationships with girlfriends or even wives, and elements of their sexual fantasies—and areas of sexual dysfunction—are apparent in these relationships.

The offender's behavior before, during, and after a sexual assault not only reveals his underlying motives and fantasies, but also provides a valuable clue to his intelligence. The ability to construct and carry out complex scenarios, requiring a great deal of planning, clearly indicates an offender with a higher intellectual level. That's not to say they're rocket scientists—we grade criminals on a curve.

You can see how everything an offender does and says in the commission of a sex crime can be used against him in terms of focusing the investigation. And you can see how difficult it would be for him to disguise these elements, which is why I say we're not giving away any secrets here. Especially in the realm of sexual offenses, where obsessions are so complex, individual, and personal, there simply would be no impetus for the offender to act any other way. If the aspect of his life that provides him his greatest satisfaction is rape, and he only gets satisfaction in rape by humiliating his victim, then he would be no more motivated to change the way he acts with his victim than he would be to stop assaulting women altogether. And if he will stop because he reads this and recognizes the truth in it—that he rapes because he's a pathetic little nobody and nothing else makes him feel important—then great; I'll even refund him the price of the book.

But unfortunately, I don't think I'm going to be shelling out much money on that offer. The sexual predator commits his individual crimes in the way he does because it is what he must do to satisfy himself. It's who and what he is—the proverbial case of the leopard not being able to change his spots. To change, he must reorient his thinking.

Because they can't disguise their obsession as they commit their crime, sexual offenders also can't hide their inherent dangerousness—the likelihood that they will repeat offenses and/or grow increasingly more violent. A lot of people in the mental health profession and even in probation, parole, and other fields of law enforcement will tell you that violent behavior cannot be predicted. What they're really saying, though, is that *they* can't predict it. In fact, without being cocky, simply stating the result of years of research and experience, plenty of us can make those predictions with a high degree of confidence.

Linda Fairstein agrees: "I do think that the behavior, with people who are trained in this field, is predictable. I mean, a good cop who's done this work, or any colleague of mine, can study the case histories and the defendants' backgrounds and tell you almost to a certainty which ones will be back and which ones won't. And that's the sad fact of it."

People often ask me if a good profiler can observe a troublesome child and predict whether he's likely to grow up as a violent threat to those around him. I reply, "Sure we can, but so can any good elementary-school teacher." It's not magic; it's merely a question of careful observation and applying accumulated experience and data. In 1983, a study conducted on sixteen sexually sadistic offenders found that while the core fantasy was fully developed by age sixteen, it took a number of years after that to be encapsulated into the crime that led to the first arrest.

I would add to this the declaration that once someone has committed a serious crime, the best predictor of future violence is the way that crime was perpetrated, because it gives us insight into what the offender's motivations and fantasies are—and how he may evolve. Ask Linda Fairstein or any other good prosecutor who's seen as many cases as she has and they'll tell you the same thing.

And this is particularly true with respect to sexual predators. In the vast majority of cases, once someone has developed the obsession that leads him to commit rape, child molestation, and other heinous sexual crimes, it is going to be very difficult, if not absolutely impossible, to turn him around.

Dr. Stanton Samenow knows whereof he speaks. While most psychiatrists and psychologists have come to their views either from reading and training or whatever bias they held when they entered the profession, Samenow came by his the hard way—by intensively studying the offenders themselves. From a psychologist's frame of reference, he did much the same thing that I did from a criminologist's. Joining the late psychiatrist Dr. Samuel Yochelson, who had already been working with hard-core offenders for nine years, Samenow undertook a pioneering study of violent criminals at St. Elizabeth's Hospital in Washington, D.C.

Samenow went into the profession believing he could help all of his criminal patients go straight by providing them with the insight necessary to understand their backgrounds, psyches, and why they turned to a life of crime. "Instead of criminals with no insight," he recalls, "we had criminals *with* insight. They were still antisocial. What I was doing made no difference at all. In fact, if they didn't have enough excuses for crime earlier, perhaps what I was doing was inadvertently giving them more."

It was this extensive firsthand experience that made Samenow abandon his earlier views. "I had to throw them away, lead sacred theoretical cows to pasture and slaughter," he states. The first chapter of the first book of his monumental three-volume study with Yochelson, *The Criminal Personality,* is entitled "The Reluctant Converts."

"It doesn't refer to the criminals," Samenow comments. "It refers to Dr. Yochelson first and later to me, and how reluctantly we gave up what we had been trained in, learned, and practiced. It just didn't square with what was emerging over and over again. We were dealing with people who were far more victimizers than they were victims of any background or system: people who had made choices, rather than being hapless victims of adverse environments."

What has Samenow's clinical experience taught him about predicting a sexual predator's future path?

"If you've worked with sex offenders—people who have committed these offenses again and again and again—you know that we do not in psychiatry and psychology have a way to change sexual orientation. People who molest kids, for example, they've done it and they've done it and they've done it and they haven't been caught for a fraction of what they've done. To turn these people back into the community knowing that we have nothing to offer them that is going to ensure the safety of kids is unconscionable."

Samenow doesn't believe that castration—physical or chemical—provides much of a solution, either. I agree with this premise. Most of the European studies that point to castration's effectiveness in preventing repeat rapes and child molestations involve candidates who "self-selected" for the "treatment"; that is, these were people who specifically wanted help, always the first necessity for change. For years I've been saying that if rape is often a crime of anger, and you cut off an individual's balls against his will, you're going to end up with one angry individual.

Samenow says it in a somewhat different way: "There's no exception. Every person I've ever interviewed who's been convicted of rape has committed other sorts of crimes. It may be property crimes, it may be nonsexual assaults. The issue is not only the sex crime itself. It is the mind of this kind of person. It is the person who seeks conquest of other people. Rape is an avenue for conquest; obviously it's a sex crime. But to say that if you castrate a person, this is going to alter the entire criminal personality of this predatory individual, I don't think there's any evidence for that."

We know from our research that certain behaviors can be seen as stepping-stone offenses, working up to rape. Ronnie Shelton's career is a perfect example of this. There were warning signs in his life much earlier, even, than his arrests for voyeurism in the late 1980s.

In 1978, when he was sixteen, Shelton approached a twenty-nine-year-old next-door neighbor he had admired and fantasized about, knocking on her door and essentially asking her outright for sex. When she rebuffed his adolescent sexual advances, he pulled a handgun (belonging to his father) and tried to control her by hitting her with the butt of the gun. When she tried fighting back, reaching for a hammer lying nearby, he took it and hit her head to subdue her. She tricked him into believing she was having a heart attack and was able to get away from him, although he fired two shots after her as she ran from her home.

Shelton pleaded guilty to attempted rape and was sent to a medium-security institution for juvenile offenders with psychological problems. He spent eight months at the Training Center for Youth in Columbus, Ohio, and was released to return home and enroll back in high school.

It is obvious, looking back to that original offense, that Ronnie Shelton learned from his experience—not to avoid doing it again, only to do it better and more effectively. For one thing, he figured out the direct approach didn't work for him, which I believe led to his decision (consciously or not) to use a surprise approach in his later, adult attacks. This gave him control from the outset, rendering him more powerful than his victims before, during, and after the assaults, which was much more satisfying for him. Like most "successful" repeat offenders, he also moved on to strangers, limiting his risk of identification and capture should something go wrong.

We can also take lessons from Shelton's early crime. Without pointing fingers, it has to seem to most people that a young man who could bludgeon his next-door neighbor in an aborted rape attempt is a potential future threat. He's already proven himself highly dangerous once—and that was just an occasion when he was caught. There were others, and on a statistical basis, I would expect there to have been more than an equal number of incidents in which he wasn't caught. Whether he received therapy or not during his institutionalization, the manner of the crime indicates the young man had a lot of anger and not a lot of self-control—a dangerous combination. So at the least, any later offenses should be viewed in the context of this earlier crime—committed as a juvenile or not. Events as simple as barroom brawls should be seen as warning signs that he's still violent, just as suicide attempts, domestic violence against family members and girlfriends, as well as the "nuisance crimes" for which he'd been arrested, all needed to be viewed as part of a dangerous "big picture"—a life in complete disarray, a chronic, proven violent offender—rather than as isolated incidents.

This is an ongoing problem throughout the criminal justice system. It drove me crazy during and after the O. J. Simpson trial, for instance, to hear first defense attorneys and, later, jurors proclaiming that this was a trial for murder, not domestic abuse. The implication was that the defendant's established record toward his wife was not relevant to the question at hand. Come on, people! Do you think someone just wakes up one morning and thinks to himself, "Today I begin my career as a violent criminal"? There is usually an escalation, whether we're talking about a Peeping Tom who evolves into a rapist or a wife-batterer who evolves into a murderer. Patterns of behavior cannot be ignored.

Like Ronnie Shelton in Cleveland, Joseph Thompson in New Zealand started getting in trouble with the law early, at an even younger age. At ten, he was arrested for stealing a watch; the Children's Court placed him under supervision. His family life was one of disruption, poverty, and neglect. He was moved repeatedly between relatives, all of whom had more children than they could comfortably feed and house, or lifestyles not conducive to raising children. At twelve, Thompson and a brother—two of the twelve children born to his mother and father, not including siblings conceived in his parents' other relationships—were picked up by a social worker as they loitered in the street. Their mother finally came for them after the Department of Social Welfare advertised in the local news for the parents to claim the boys. From that point on, Thompson became an accomplished thief and was arrested as a young teenager in connection with a series of robberies. He joined a gang and was arrested for offenses ranging from car theft to drunk driving. By his early twenties, he'd graduated to violence, fighting in public after getting drunk. His twelve-year string of rapes began as many single rapes do, when a burglar—someone with a lot of practice getting in and out of homes unseen—saw an exciting opportunity present itself, tried something new, and found he liked it and could get away with it.

During my prison interviews of serial offenders, I talked to another sexual predator whose career started early. Monte Rissell—at home in the Richmond Penitentiary when I met with him—started raping and murdering women as a teenager after spending his earlier years in trouble for offenses ranging from writing obscenities on the walls at school to using drugs, even shooting a cousin with a BB gun. By the time he was twelve, he was stealing cars and committing burglary. As detailed in *Mindhunter*, Rissell committed his first rape-murder as a high school student following a precipitating stressor. Upset over losing his girlfriend, he drank some beer, smoked some marijuana, and when an opportunity presented itself—in this case, a prostitute who came home late one night, alone in the parking area of the apartment complex where she and Rissell both lived—he raped and murdered her. He went on to rape and kill four more women in the Alexandria, Virginia, area before his arrest.

Each of these rapists came from a less-than-ideal upbringing. In addition to Thompson's background of poverty, neglect, and reported sexual and physical abuse, Shelton described years of physical abuse at the hands of his parents, and Rissell claimed that when his parents divorced, if he'd been allowed to live with his father, rather than his mother, he would have grown up to be a lawyer instead of a rapist and murderer.

I think that's stretching things a bit. After all, consider how many other children with equally difficult beginnings do not choose to become violent offenders. But I would assert that the various points where they got into trouble—and the escalation of behavior from the initial simpler offenses to more aggressive, daring, and/or violent acts—indicated they were moving in that direction and that some form of intervention was necessary.

All of the offenders described up to now have been members of the highly dangerous class of sexual predators—they get whatever satisfaction they derive from their crimes from the hunt and chase, rather than the sexual elements. Their offenses fit a pattern of victimizing that occurs over and over. Whatever their obsession, the rape experience for them never quite lives up to their needs and expectations, so they continue to hunt and victimize, always looking for the one that will be different, that will finally satisfy them. Of course, if they did find their "ideal" situation—where the thrill of the hunt and the total domination of the victim completely fulfills them—they would still only be sated for a time, after which they'd be out on the hunt again, looking for another experience just as good as the last one. This is, after all, what they do in life; this is their obsession, and they will want to repeat it. Simply reliving it in their minds will not be enough to last a lifetime. Compound this with the high this insignificant, underemployed, self-doubting loser gets from outwitting the system, and you can see why the pattern is repeated.

Dr. Park Dietz of Newport Beach, California, is among the leading forensic psychiatrists in the United States. Our paths and careers have intersected continually. He has been a longtime consultant to my unit at Quantico, and he readily admits that he has learned a lot from watching us work, too. Dietz explains it this way:

"What the predator discovers when he actually commits the [initial] offense is that, first of all, it wasn't as good as he expected it to be. Secondly, that it wasn't as difficult to get away as he expected it to be. And because of those two things that he learns, he thinks, 'Well, here's what I'll have to do to improve and make it better. And why not, since I didn't get caught that time.' Hence, he goes on to the second one, adding a few things that he thinks will improve it. Unfortunately for him, and for us, it's never as good as he expects it to be because it can't really match the fantasy. He never gains as much control as he imagines he will have."

When a predator realizes, after each successive experience, that his fantasy hasn't been completely fulfilled, rather than look for another outlet—a productive, legal one—he gets more frustrated and (depending on the type of predator) even angrier. This is why we often see an escalation of violence in an UNSUB's series of crimes. And this is why I say that until a predator is locked up, dies, or grows too old and feeble to commit his crime of choice, he will not stop.

But it's important here to get one thing straight: not every rapist is a true sexual predator. There are some offenders who commit rape as a result of a combination of precipitating stressors, emotional catalysts often fueled by drugs or alcohol, and situational factors. This is not to say this type can't help himself or shouldn't be punished for his crime—I think I've made myself clear on both of those points. But this type of person is not someone who would necessarily make sexual assault a career choice, and this is what makes him the only type of rapist for whom I believe there is any hope of true rehabilitation. He was functioning before the crime, and he may be able to pull his life back together and avoid the combination of factors that led to the problem.

But we have to look at the total picture to make this determination. This type of subject does not have a history of violent assaults. Instead, this one event represents the bottom of a downward spiral in his life: perhaps he's lost his job and his wife is pregnant, or maybe his wife or girlfriend left him. The offense is not planned and the victim is usually one of opportunity, such as a neighbor. A scenario might be that the guy starts drinking heavily, depressed over his job and/or women problems, and goes next door to talk to a sympathetic friend. His buddy isn't home, but the man's girlfriend—who's always been friendly and seems to care about her neighbor's troubles—is home, and she's alone. The subject continues drinking, starts behaving inappropriately, one thing leads to another in his mind, and he takes advantage of the situation and assaults the woman. Analysis of his behavior shows him to be a power-reassurance rapist, and he displays genuine remorse for his offense. If, on the other hand, the analysis shows him to be an anger or sadistic type, the assumption has to be that he has a potential for continued predatory violence.

His postoffense behavior is critical to an assessment of whether he will be able to turn his life back around. If the rape was truly more situational than anything else, he will turn himself in or readily admit his crime, shaken himself by the event and by the scope of his problems. This behavior is completely opposite from what a career rapist does. If, in contrast, the subject runs out postoffense to establish an alibi, lies in the police interview, never admits the crime, and never shows remorse, then my hope for his future dims considerably.

Says Linda Fairstein, "I don't think every rapist is a sexual predator. I think stranger serial rapists certainly are. I think pedophiles are in that category. Both of those tend, once they do their act successfully, to repeat them over and over again. I have certainly had the date-rape offender who assaults once in a particular situation and will probably never offend again. Some of these people respond well to either incarceration, because they never want to be back and they learn from it, or from rehabilitation as it exists. But the category that we are calling predators, I think there is no known form of rehabilitation that works. I have seen no model of it that works in any degree as well as the people who are running it claim it works."

I bring up this last type of rapist not to confuse the issue but to point out why it is so complicated to try to render definitive advice about what to do to avoid rape in any given situation and what to do with convicted rapists. Each case needs to be looked at individually, and every person who has the potential to rape (or rape again) must be evaluated in light of his previous history and behavior.

Says Fairstein, "I've had scores of cases in the predator category where, for ten years, a guy has been a burglar without exhibiting any sexual assault tendencies. And then he hits on an apartment in which a woman's alone and vulnerable and rapes her and likes it and begins to pick that up as part of his criminal behavior."

The burglar who rapes once because it's easy and convenient, while despicable, doesn't worry me nearly so much as the type Fairstein just described who falls into it accidentally, but keeps on doing it. The key word here is *pattern*.

And this attention to patterns of behavior applies across the board. Children who start out as troublemakers need to be recognized so that they receive intervention early enough to foster development in a more positive direction. Juveniles and young adults who've established a violent pattern of behavior must be seen as the danger to society they are, regardless of their age, and treated appropriately to protect their potential future victims. And once a crime has been committed, everyone in the criminal justice system—from the cop who takes the victim statement to prosecutors, to psychiatrists who make evaluations for the court, to juries and judges—needs to look carefully at the details of the crime, the behavior of the offender. What is the real likelihood this could happen again?

Without being too paranoid, all law-abiding citizens need to do some profiling of their own. You can't necessarily stop a sexual predator in his tracks, but you can lessen the chances that you will be his victim. By this, I certainly don't mean that victims of sexual assault have done anything wrong or anything to deserve what happens to them. I do mean, though, that sometimes good common sense can be an invaluable commodity, even if it seems at times to be inconvenient.

Is it worth going out of your way nine times needlessly if the tenth time saves you from a bad situation? Every individual has to do her own math, weigh the trade-offs for herself, but for myself and those I care about, I'd never want to be vulnerable in a situation that could have been avoided with a little planning.

You can bet that the bad guys are planning, and it only has to happen once.

CHAPTER FIVE

WHAT ACTUALLY HAPPENED IN CENTRAL PARK?

Rapes are not always easy to detect. By that I don't mean that sexual offenders are good at covering up their crimes; I mean that a crime that appears on its surface to be a rape—even a rape "gone bad"—can actually be something else. A classic example of this was Linda Fairstein's so-called Preppie Murder case in the late 1980s.

My unit at Quantico got involved in that one through a somewhat unusual route. Fairstein had seen an article on us in the *New York Times* a couple of months before, about how we came up with behavioral profiles of unknown offenders. So she called us to say, "We've got exactly the reverse situation. We know who the killer is, but we don't have a motive. Can you try and reverse the process for me? We don't have to prove motive in court, but everybody's going to be asking why he did it, and it'll be easier to get a conviction if we can explain it to them."

What had happened was this:

Around 6:00 A.M. on the morning of Tuesday, August 26, 1986, a mutual funds trader named Pat Reilly was riding her bike for exercise in Central Park. Behind the Metropolitan Museum of Art, she stopped when she noticed an apparently female figure lying on the grass. At first she thought it was someone sleeping, perhaps a homeless person. But when she got closer, she realized it was a young woman, her denim jacket and shirt pushed up around the top of her chest, her skirt bunched around her waist. Below that, she was naked. She wasn't moving or breathing. Reilly called 911 from the nearest phone, and an NYPD patrol car arrived at the scene a few minutes later.

The first officers on-scene quickly examined the woman and realized she was dead. They called for detectives. By now a crowd of onlookers was forming at the stone wall at the edge of the park.

"When the police found her body in Central Park connected to nothing and nobody, the first thing they believed was that she had been killed somewhere else and deposited in the park," Fairstein explains. Parks, woods, and rivers are always favorite body-dumping sites for killers. Maybe she was a prostitute, judging from the time of night the crime must have happened. Prostitutes are always vulnerable. A stranger could have picked her up, killed her, dumped her there.

But in this case, the officers had misinterpreted the physical evidence. "They missed one-half of the crime scene," says Fairstein. "Her underwear was some distance away under a tree." When we analyzed the case, we agreed that this was where she had died.

Normally in this type of situation, identifying the victim is a major issue. But this time it wasn't. The woman was carrying an ID. Her name was Jennifer Dawn Levin. She was eighteen years old, five feet eight inches tall, 120 pounds, dark-haired, and beautiful. The medical examiner determined that she had been strangled.

Her parents were notified, always the single toughest part, emotionally, of any homicide case. They had divorced when Jennifer was only a small child, and she had gone with her mother to live in California, before coming back to Long Island some years later. When she was fourteen, she had left her mother's house in Long Island and gone to live a more exciting life in Manhattan with her well-to-do father and his second wife.

Jennifer's father told detectives she had been out with friends the previous night and mentioned the ones he knew about. Those friends mentioned other friends, and before long, the police had a pretty complete narrative of where Jennifer Levin had been the previous night, when she'd been there, and whom she'd been with. Detectives did not tell any of the people they interviewed that their friend was dead, only that she was missing. The last person they could determine who had seen her alive was Robert Chambers, a good-looking twenty-year-old with whom Jennifer had been very taken.

Two detectives went to the apartment on the Upper East Side where Chambers lived with his mother, wanting to know where he and Jennifer had gone after they were seen together leaving a bar called Dorrian's Red Hand on Second Avenue at Eighty-fourth Street, how long he could account for her whereabouts, and if he knew whom she was with after she left him. He agreed to go to the Central Park precinct with the detectives to tell them whatever he knew. As with Jennifer's other friends, they didn't tell Robert that she was dead.

One odd thing the detectives noticed was that Chambers's face was scratched in several places. When they asked, he told them his cat had done it accidentally while he was playing with her, tossing her in the air. They were suspicious, but at that point, there was no reason to disbelieve him.

Det. Mickey McEntee questioned Chambers in the interrogation room after first Mirandizing him. Chambers told McEntee that even though several of Jennifer's friends had seen her walk out of Dorrian's with him about four-thirty in the morning, they'd parted company as soon as they went out the door. She had gone to buy cigarettes at the deli across the street and he'd gone home, stopping on the way to get some doughnuts at a shop at Eighty-sixth Street and Lexington Avenue.

In addition to the scratches on his face, the detectives noticed some cuts on his fingers. That was easily explainable, too, Chambers said. He had been sanding a floor for a woman upstairs in his building and the sanding machine had gotten away from him. Throughout the encounter with the police, Chambers was polite, cooperative, and confident.

Two other detectives took over the questioning—John Lafferty and Lt. Jack Doyle, commander of Manhattan North Homicide. Chambers stuck by his story. Then McEntee came back in with another Manhattan North detective named Martin Gill. It was Gill's last day on the job. The next day he was retiring from the force.

Gill got Chambers to repeat the story about how they'd parted company outside of Dorrian's, he for doughnuts, she for cigarettes. Only Gill had had time to get some information from several of the friends, and one bit was crucial. By the time he talked to Chambers, he knew that Jennifer Levin didn't smoke. That was the first crack in the dam.

Okay, then maybe she hadn't actually gone to buy cigarettes, Chambers revised. Maybe they'd actually walked together for a while before they parted, from Second Avenue to Lexington, when she got into a cab. Gill then confronted Chambers about the scratches, asserting that the medical examiner would be able to tell the difference between feline scratches and human scratches. The first thing they would do was examine the cat.

Okay, well, actually, Chambers admitted, the cat had been declawed for apartment life. Jennifer had scratched him after a spat as he was about to go into the doughnut shop (which was an admission that they'd been together longer than he'd said, even in his amended story). Gill claimed he knew someone who worked the late shift at the doughnut shop and he'd remember any lovers' quarrel vociferous enough to produce deep scratches.

Did he say Eighty-sixth and Lex? Chambers backtracked again; he meant the doughnut shop at Eighty-sixth and Park. But that was enough. The other detectives returned to the room to have it all out. When they asked him to take off his shirt, they saw deep scratches on his torso as well. Chambers admitted that he and Jennifer had walked to Central Park together. A few minutes after revealing this, he confessed that he'd killed her. But it was an accident, an accident she'd provoked during an episode of the wild and rough sex he claimed she liked so much and in which he became a hapless participant.

Now there are several ways we can go with such a case at this point. One way is to believe the subject that it really was an accident and get all the corroborating details. Another way is to assume he took her into the park for no good—that is, with the idea of raping her, and that the sexual assault had degenerated into a killing. And a third way is to figure that what we were dealing with was not a sexual assault at all, but an outright murder. So what would have had to happen for that to be the case?

One of the critical aspects in any profile or behaviorally based criminal investigative analysis is victimology. What was the victim like? Was she high risk or low? How would she have reacted? What kind of behavior would her responses have provoked in the subject?

From all accounts, Jennifer Levin was a bright, popular, precocious girl, often the center of attention, who relished the exciting social life of Manhattan. By the time she was seventeen, she and her girlfriends were frequenting the East Side bars. After graduating from high school, she was planning to go to art school. She was popular with boys, but Fairstein's meticulous investigators found absolutely no evidence of Chambers's claim that she liked "rough sex."

"She was absolutely not wild at all," says Fairstein, based on her in-depth research. "She was never a discipline problem. And very loving, very much a family kid. She had a lot of friends and she liked being with people."

She had met Robert at Dorrian's the previous fall and was taken with his dark good looks, his commanding six-foot-five height, and intrigued by his mystique and the somewhat shady past her friends warned her about. He was said to make a practice of stealing things from the homes to which he was invited for parties. When word got back to Jennifer through another friend that Robert thought she was really good-looking, she was thrilled. They had their first sexual encounter shortly thereafter and had sex together periodically throughout the winter, spring, and summer.

What was Chambers's side of what happened in the early-morning hours of August 26?

He said that Jennifer had actually been pursuing him that evening but that he was involved with another young woman who interested him more, and it happened that there was some truth to that. It's what he claimed the scratching incident was about. According to several accounts, Jennifer had seemed upset that she was apparently more interested in him than he was in her. The roguish Robert was always being seen surrounded by other attractive young women, she knew he was sleeping with at least some of them, and when she saw him in a public setting, he was often aloof or wouldn't even acknowledge her presence. She didn't appreciate being trifled with and wanted a clearing of the air. So she went to Dorrian's on the night of August 25 to have it out with him. According to people who were there that night, the two of them talked intently for quite a while, and whatever the nature of the conversation, they did end up leaving the bar together.

After they left Dorrian's, Jennifer and Robert went into the park, where they'd agreed to have sex. So the first thing we have to accept is, however the crime might have seemed, this was not a rape, and this is an important point to establish.

According to Chambers, they had picked the spot under the tree, near Park Drive and the obelisk, away from potential prying eyes. She told him she was going some distance off to pee. When she returned, she was apparently carrying her panties, because she surprised Robert from behind and bound his wrists together with them, immobilizing him. He'd been leaning back on his hands, so they were convenient to her.

Remember what we're talking about here: a five-foot-eight girl "overpowering" a six-foot-five guy and, in an instant, efficiently tying him so tightly with her cotton underpants that he couldn't get his hands free.

This allowed her to initiate the rough sex she'd been relishing. She opened his pants and began stroking his penis. At one point, according to Chambers, she squeezed his testicles and kept squeezing them harder and harder until he couldn't stand the pain. This gave him enough strength finally to break free of his wrist bindings and reach up forcefully to pull her off him. He grabbed her around the head or neck and flipped her over him and onto the ground. In the process, he must have struck his own neck with the edge of his watch, which accounted for one of his more telling bruises. He told her to get up, that the sex was over and it was time to go home, but she didn't respond. That was when he realized he must have accidentally killed her.

He staggered away in a daze, eventually coming to rest seated on the stone wall where he waited for someone to find the body and report it. In fact, videos taken by several onlookers later revealed Chambers among the crowd when the police had come to investigate.

Of the several problems with this story, not the least was the idea that this young woman could so easily physically dominate this big, strong guy. But there were even bigger problems, the most important of which was that the wounds on Jennifer Levin's body did not even closely correspond to what Robert Chambers said had happened. Then there was the actual manner of death, which the ME determined to be strangulation, and for which her neck bore the marks. Chambers denied having put those marks there, perhaps implying that his victim previously had engaged in some kind of autoerotic asphyxiation games.

But again, fate, in the form of irrefutable visual evidence, intervened. Just hours before her death, Jennifer and two girlfriends were photographed, posing joyfully with their arms around each other's shoulders. It is a beautiful picture, made almost unbearably poignant by the events of a few hours later. Each girl seems to be reveling in the others' company and happily looking off into the bright future each had a right to expect. Jennifer is seen wearing the same denim jacket in which she was later found. With the scoop-neck top she was wearing in the photo, it is abundantly clear that her neck and upper chest are completely unmarked.

From that moment when the photo was taken until she disappeared with Chambers, Jennifer's whereabouts can be completely accounted for, so there is no chance the injuries occurred before her encounter with him.

Finally, the discrepancies in Chambers's story bring up an advantage we investigators have on our side. Crimes are committed in the heat of the moment, and it is difficult, even for the cleverest or most experienced offender, to make physical evidence fit a story and logic he imposes after the fact. If you "stage" a crime scene—that is, try to make it look like some other event took place, such as a man killing his wife and staging it to look like a robbery gone bad—you're giving us an awful lot of behavioral evidence to work with. And the more you show us, even in an attempt to mislead us, the more you're going to point to your own crime and profile.

Chambers told detectives that Jennifer must have choked when he flipped her off him and onto the ground. But perhaps he hadn't seen as many strangulation murder cases as they had. Because anyone who's handled a few and talked to the medical examiner knows that you don't normally asphyxiate in a split second; you have to keep hard pressure on the air passage for some considerable period of time. The marks on her neck clearly demonstrated *repeated* applications of force rather than any sort of single blow.

While there were these distinct marks on Jennifer's neck, there were no ligature marks on Robert's wrists, which we certainly would have expected to see had he been bound as tightly as he said he was and broken free with so much force that the resulting action was enough to kill her.

"There was a broken bone in one of his fingers," Fairstein recalls, "which our orthopedic man testified was what's called a boxer's fracture, because it results from a glancing blow that breaks the finger. And there were bite marks on his hands from where we believe he had covered her mouth. And in typical asphyxial fashion, there were scratches of her own on her neck, from where she was trying to free herself."

Unmistakable conclusion: There is no way Jennifer Levin could have died in the manner Robert Chambers described. In the various detectives' opinions, in Linda Fairstein's opinion, in my opinion, Chambers could only have killed intentionally. Intent can be formed virtually instantaneously, and whether he planned to kill her earlier in the evening (which I doubt) or a moment before he did it, he did it on purpose.

Forensic evidence notwithstanding, the one consistency throughout Chambers's account is that he was the victim—that Jennifer Levin died accidentally as a result of her own actions and aggression toward him. So if he claims to be a victim, we said, let's do some victimology on him, just as we would investigate any other victim in a case brought to us. Linda Fairstein wants to know why he did it. Okay, let's analyze his background and try to figure it out.

On the surface, Robert Chambers had it all. He was tall and handsome, well-spoken, magnetic to women, and apparently sufficiently well-off financially to travel in sophisticated and elite circles. He went to prep schools, including Choate, giving rise to the moniker that would haunt Linda Fairstein throughout the trial and the long months of preparation. But the real story was far from the surface one. He may have once technically been a preppie, but he didn't graduate from Choate. In fact, he never did well there and dropped out fairly soon after he arrived. And while his father had a steady, respectable job, the Chambers family was not rich, so he was decidedly less well-off than most of the people he liked to hang around with.

Robert therefore supplemented his income by stealing, mainly from the houses of his friends' parents when he was invited to parties. Jennifer Levin wasn't the only one to be warned about his practice. The word went out that you never left Robert alone at a party, because something would always be missing. He was thrown out of one school for helping to steal a teacher's purse and lost a summer job his mother had gotten him working on a wealthy friend's yacht for stealing cases of liquor. After finally making it out of high school, he took courses at Boston University, but didn't do well there either and was expelled for stealing a credit card. Then in September of 1985, he enrolled at Hunter College in New York, but attended classes only rarely, continued to steal, and continued another pattern already well established—taking illegal drugs.

As Fairstein puts it, "He was running in a crowd where he didn't have the money to keep up with these other kids and began using drugs. He was the bad-boy connection. He would do the burglaries and get the money to get coke for the other kids who wanted it, so they wouldn't rat him out."

What was his attraction for Jennifer? Certainly there was the physical aspect, the intriguing fact that he was so popular with other girls, but there was more to it than that, Fairstein believes. "She was a very good kid, and one of the things she saw in Robert was wanting to get him off drugs. She drank, she liked to have a good time. She was a very vibrant, vivacious kid. But she didn't do drugs. And one of the things that she was trying to do that may have backfired that night was to save him—in the big sense. I mean, she thought she could do him a big favor and get him off drugs, without having any sense of how far gone he was. This was not an amateur job."

Nor did Jennifer apparently comprehend the depth of his rage and animosity. Fairstein explains, "He had gone to the bar that night to see somebody else, with whom he had a fight because Jennifer was hanging out, expressing her interest in him that night. And the girl he had come to meet ended up throwing her packet of condoms at him and saying, 'Use these with her! I'm leaving.' So he was angry at Jennifer for having thwarted that."

Fairstein also believes her investigation supports a strong anti-Semitic bias on the part of the Waspy Robert toward the Jewish Jennifer. "I think he didn't like her. I think he didn't like anything about her, in part because she was Jewish. But as his friends described it, he would rather have sex with someone. It was better than going home and masturbating. He was willing to have a quick sexual encounter with her and then leave her, but he didn't want to wake up to have her in his home in the morning, or go to where she was staying that night, at a girlfriend's house, and have to wake up with her. And that's why, I think, they went to the park."

Whenever we profile an UNSUB in a crime of this nature, we always look for precipitating stressors—some factor or factors that help send the subject off the deep end. Certainly the argument with the other woman who threw the condoms in his face could have set off a volatile person like Robert. But there is usually something even deeper and more fundamental, something that affects an individual's basic security or self-image that will help explain the ultimate crime. And we found that, too.

He had been living at home with his mother. He didn't have a job. He was doing drugs, definitely on the skids, and his mother had given him an ultimatum: get a job or get out. The night of August 25, all of the other kids in the bar were celebrating going back to school, Jennifer included. And Robert had no place to go and nothing to do, other than to steal to support his drug use.

Another telling aspect of the crime is the way the body was found, with the shirt pushed up above the breasts and the skirt bunched around the waist. This is quite typical of staging when the perpetrator wants investigators to think it was a sexual assault by a stranger. We have seen this over and over again in cases of domestic homicide in which a husband murders his wife but then tries to make it look as if an intruder has broken in and sexually ravaged her. In effect, it is what an inexperienced offender thinks a rape is supposed to look like, and when this sort of staging occurs, it is likely an individual who knew the victim.

When we add it all up, Robert Chambers does not make a good candidate for victim. So what made him do it? What made him kill Jennifer Levin behind the Metropolitan Museum of Art, early on the morning of August 26, 1986? The fact is, there are no clear-cut and easy answers. What there is, instead, is a certain personality type, a certain personal history, a certain relationship between two people, a certain set of general and immediate stressors, and then something happening in the mind of one individual that suddenly focuses all of the negative elements and brings them explosively to the surface.

We know, for instance, that he had been drinking heavy amounts of both tequila and beer that night. Investigators were told, though they were never able to prove, that he had also been using both marijuana and cocaine at the same time. Forensically, there was no evidence of seminal fluid on Jennifer's body, clothing, or anywhere else at the scene, nor is there any evidence of condom use. We can interpret all of this to mean that because of his impaired state, he wasn't able to perform. And with a guy as vain about his image as Chambers, this might have brought his anger and frustration to the boiling point.

When we hear confessions or other suspect statements, we try to figure out what they are really telling us, much as an actor might search for the "subtext" in the dialogue he's delivering. Keep in mind the kind of arrogant, controlling, generally predatory personality that Robert Chambers represents. So when he says that Jennifer enjoyed rough sex, what he might actually have been saying is that she liked to control the situation, which, for someone like Chambers, would have been an untenable affront to his masculinity. And then, if, in fact, he couldn't get it up, the danger level could have reached critical mass quickly.

Linda Fairstein says, "I think what might have happened was that she taunted him about that and he ended up striking her. First, because she had the marks that not only suggested a blow to the mouth and a blow to the eye, but that she then tried to get away from him."

There were two distinct parts to the crime scene: the area where Jennifer's underwear was lying and the area where her body was discovered. What we believe happened is that the actual attempt at sex took place at the first location, and that she extricated herself and tried to run away from him. He took off after her and caught up with her before she reached the roadway, which is where he strangled her and where she died. The autopsy photographs showed bruises and lacerations all over Jennifer's face. Her eyes are bruised shut. There are cuts around her mouth. There are petechial hemorrhages under her eyes, which are a hallmark of strangulation. There are also contusions covering her hips, thighs, knees, even ankles. Where the hipbone juts out on the right side, the area has been rubbed completely raw. None of this is consistent with Chambers's story of her being on top of him and his throwing her off. Moreover, while his chest was covered with her nail marks where she tried to fight him off, and her nails were, in fact, all jaggedly broken, his back was completely clear, bearing none of the abrasions we would expect to find if he'd been on his back, struggling on the grass as he described.

He claimed that an abrasion on his neck was caused when he reached up to pull her off him and inadvertently hit himself with his own heavy metal watchband. While this makes no sense in the context of the wound pattern, when I looked at the autopsy photos, I noted an impression on her neck that, to me, was clearly made by Chambers's watch. He must have ground it into her neck by pressing on her throat with his wrist and forearm. This is a compression wound, not one caused by blunt-force trauma. Also, the autopsy revealed that the delicate hyoid bone in the neck was not broken, which is more consistent with this type of compression asphyxiation than it is with simple manual strangulation. Just looking at this photograph, I could visualize the struggle.

From all the evidence, it was clear to me that this young woman must have fought heroically before she was finally subdued.

The case had caused a media sensation in New York, which reached a fevered pitch as Chambers approached trial. Of course, there had to be a news handle, and with a guy as good-looking and "interesting" as Robert Chambers, that handle became almost inevitable: the Preppie Murder.

"The greatest disservice the media has ever done me was dubbing him the Preppie Murderer," says Fairstein. "In fact, he was a drug-addicted burglar who had been thrown out of every school he'd gone to. But to describe him that way in the press wouldn't have been nearly as sexy. So that's what we were fighting—the public perception that this clean-cut, nice kid had snapped in the park that night."

This is another thing that we see commonly in the trials of sexual predators. By the time he's in court, he's so clean-cut and innocent looking that the jury says, "This nice young man couldn't possibly have done that." It's why we recommend that the prosecution try to introduce his booking photo, to show what he actually looked like the night of the crime.

The trial lasted thirteen weeks, during which time Robert Chambers did not take the stand, allowing Fairstein no opportunity to show the jury what this man was really like.

Chambers was defended by Jack Litman, a distinguished criminal-trial attorney with many years of experience. Fairstein is still outraged about the way she feels he tried to drag the victim's reputation through the mud in an attempt to win sympathy for his client. Unfortunately, this is all too common, virtually a standard technique in rape trials. But thanks to people like Fairstein, it's starting to change; judges and juries won't accept it nearly as readily.

Everyone is entitled to a vigorous defense, but neither Fairstein nor I can quite stomach the perceived need to revictimize someone who has already experienced the worst from the hands of the man now being given every conceivable benefit of the doubt. "You know, that's one of the things that I will never understand," Fairstein comments, "how you do something like that to another human being, no less somebody who's dead and can't defend herself. But that was one of the ugliest things about the defense in this case. And they didn't just let it be there. They pursued it so aggressively."

Fairstein's summation lasted for four hours, during which time she reviewed every aspect of the case and all the evidence that indicated Chambers had acted deliberately rather than as the result of a momentary, instinctual action. The jury stayed out for nine days, apparently unable to figure out what to make of the sympathetic preppie Chambers's pleas of self-defense—in other words, how this young woman much smaller and weaker than him had managed to disable him with her underpants and so brutalized him that he was completely beyond himself and killed her by accident. When both sides faced the likely prospect that they'd have a mistrial on their hands and have to go through the entire ordeal again, they started talking. After consulting with Jennifer's parents, Fairstein agreed to a plea bargain, reducing the charge of second-degree murder to first-degree manslaughter, which carried a lighter sentence of five to fifteen years. It was not the total victory she sought, but she was willing to do whatever she had to to keep him away from society.

"We had obviously played every card we had the first time, so it doesn't generally get better."

As we've made clear, I consider Robert Chambers a murderer, not a rapist, and not someone who killed for the sheer sexual pleasure of it. As such, interestingly, he may be less of a threat as a repeat offender than if he were a serial rapist. But I think the threat is still great. He is a predator, and his criminal record for non-sex-related crimes shows a complete contempt for the rules by which normal people live. If he gets out of prison and finds himself in a similarly stressful situation as the early morning of August 26, 1986, it would not surprise me if his anger would surface explosively and he could react exactly the same way again. For this reason, as well as the fact that I don't consider ten or fifteen years sufficient punishment for willfully taking the life of an innocent young woman, I, for one, don't want to see him back out on the street.

Fortunately, it doesn't look as if this is going to be a problem for a while. He's been incarcerated in several prison facilities throughout New York State and is not exactly racking up a stellar record. Fairstein reports that he's been sanctioned a number of times for possessing drugs. As of this writing, he is in the Greenhaven Correctional Facility in Dutchess County, where he was caught with a stash of heroin in a deodorant can.

As Fairstein comments, "He has come up for parole several times and it's been denied. He's doing more to keep himself in jail than I ever could, which is fine with me."

Looking at Robert Chambers from the outside, it is easy to see him as Jennifer must have in order for her to be drawn to him. If you could get him off drugs and break his other bad habits (such as stealing), you'd be left with a good-looking guy, educated in all the best schools (at least, for as long as he could stay in one) and well-connected socially. The problem is, of course, that this was not a spoiled toddler who only needed loving, firm "training" to improve his behavior. Robert Chambers was a grown man who'd established a pattern of criminal behavior and chronic substance abuse. In some ways, he can be compared to Ted Bundy, who was also good-looking and even better "on paper," but who was nonetheless irredeemably flawed in terms of character and conscience. Whatever else you are or do, if you intentionally assault or kill women for the sheer pleasure and satisfaction of it, you are a monster who has to be removed from society.

As it did the Chambers murder case, the dichotomy between the well-dressed, attractive gentleman in the courtroom and the vicious, violent offender at the crime scene haunts many rape trials. Even where there is ample physical evidence connecting an offender to an obviously forced encounter, jurors sometimes confess they had trouble convicting the defendant because he didn't look like someone who would have to resort to rape to get a woman. It just doesn't make sense to them. Maybe he is a successful professional—a dentist or lawyer, perhaps. Other times he is more like Robert Chambers, someone with a criminal record for burglary, for example. But he seems so attractive on the surface that the juror may not understand the dynamics leading to rape. The situation is even more confusing when it is a case of acquaintance, rather than stranger, rape. And this is amplified further still in cases in which the defendant has a wife or girlfriend—with whom he has a consensual sexual relationship—who loyally sits behind him all throughout the trial.

He doesn't look like he needs to rape to get a woman.

What we need to keep in mind, however, is that rape is primarily not driven by the goal to have sex, but to control and dominate a woman, whether to reaffirm the offender's masculinity, assuage his anger, or satisfy a more complicated fantasy. The sexual act is secondary. To the extent that we can't get that across to juries or the public, we haven't lived up to our responsibility to the victim.

One case that brought together many of the difficulties involved in acquaintance-rape trials where the defendant is a handsome, popular member of the community was that of Alex Kelly. Unlike Chambers, Kelly was not a killer. But he was tried and convicted of rape after an eight-year run from the law that cost his parents $140,000 in posted

130

bond and took him through fifteen countries, including Japan, Greece, and Sweden.

In February of 1986, Kelly was a popular eighteen-year-old senior at Darien High School, in the wealthy Connecticut suburb of New York. Cocaptain of the school's wrestling team, clean-cut and handsome, he looked like the kind of guy most high school girls would love to go out with. On February 10, he attended a party at a friend's house following a school basketball game. As the night wore on, one of the girls began looking for a ride home. She was with a group of friends on break from St. Mary's High School, a nearby all-girl Catholic school. She had turned sixteen just five days earlier and was anxious to make curfew. Alex Kelly offered to drive her home in his girlfriend's Jeep.

As they headed through a light snowfall and came to a stop sign, Kelly tried to kiss her. She resisted his advances. When they got to her house, he didn't stop but drove instead into a cul-de-sac. In this secluded setting, according to her testimony years later, "He grabbed my throat with his left hand. He squeezed as hard as he could. He told me that I was going to make love to him or he was going to kill me."

Kelly pushed down the backseat, forced the girl into the back, told her to take off her clothes, and then raped her. She was a virgin and was left bleeding from the assault, staining the carpet of the Jeep. After threatening to assault her again and kill her if she reported the rape, Kelly dropped her off at her house, where she immediately told her sister and parents. They took her to a doctor and the police the next day. In addition to her emotional state, police noted bruises on the girl's chest, neck, back, and buttocks.

Just four days later, a seventeen-year-old girl from the nearby community of Stamford came forward with a claim that she had been assaulted. She provided details strikingly similar to the first case: she was attacked while being driven home from a party. Kelly was charged with both crimes and was scheduled to appear in court on February 18, 1987. But he was a no-show, marking the beginning of eight years on the run.

From what authorities were able to piece together, though, he led a much more comfortable existence than the average international fugitive. In fact, he seemed to have adjusted nicely to a lifestyle of skiing, sailing, and other sports and even set up housekeeping in Sweden with a pretty, blond girlfriend.

By early 1995, however, with the authorities getting closer and reportedly threatening to arrest his parents if he did not turn himself in, and with his passport about to expire, he turned himself in in Switzerland. From there he was extradited to face the charges in Connecticut. He returned in May to what looked like a hero's welcome. His parents' house was decorated with balloons, and he greeted the flock of reporters waiting for him with smiles and waves, commenting, "I'm happy to be back." As he awaited trial, he spent his time riding his mountain bike around town, going out first with his Swedish girlfriend (rumored to be his fiancée), then, after she left, with a local woman, Amy Molitor, who'd been his girlfriend in high school. It was in her Jeep that the first alleged assault took place. All in all, his life back home was pretty normal, but for the electronic monitor worn around his right ankle to make sure he didn't violate the 9 P.M. to 6 A.M. curfew the court had imposed.

The trial on the first charge took place later that year, and it was ugly. For his defense, Kelly and his parents enlisted the help of Thomas P. Puccio, a high-profile attorney who first entered the public spotlight as the federal prosecutor who won convictions against several congressmen in the Abscam scandal (many remember the videotapes showing corrupt politicians pocketing money). His notoriety grew as he switched sides and successfully defended Claus von Bulow, acquitted of attempting to murder his socialite wife. With a reputation as someone who hated to lose, Puccio was quoted in a December 1996 profile in the *New York Times* as saying, "There's the real world and the world of the courtroom. What matters is: What is the government going to prove? Not: What actually happened?" In connection with the Kelly case, he stated, "This is going to be a direct attack on her credibility." That's what we're up against, folks.

Puccio also told a reporter he felt a special bond with Kelly's parents because his own son had died in an automobile accident while he had been teaching the young man how to drive. Thus, he could clearly empathize with the fear of losing a son. I wonder if he could also empathize with the fear of having a daughter raped and brutalized.

Back to the subject of credibility, Kelly's explanation for his flight, made to ABC News upon his return to the States, was simply, "I was scared. I ran."

As promised, Thomas Puccio worked the accuser, attacking her credibility of ten years ago and criticizing her later demeanor in court.

He complained about the "dressed to kill" attire and hairstyles of the victim and her family members, which I find interesting coming from a man who certainly made sure his client showed up well-dressed every day with his concerned family and then fiancée in tow. Consider, too, that while Alex Kelly was off windsurfing and skiing and bumming through Europe, his victim grew up, earned a college degree, married, and got a job as a sales representative for a pharmaceutical company. Certainly, dressing well and fixing her hair was more in keeping with her career and lifestyle than Kelly's at the time of the trial.

I don't want to comment on this particular trial because I wasn't in the courtroom. But I have been present at enough rape trials to say in general that these kinds of defense techniques make me sick. And I'm not the only one.

"Very often during deliberations," Linda Fairstein comments, "you're all just hanging out together. Nobody else is there but your team and their team, and so you talk. And the usual overture is my opponent coming over and saying, 'Gee, you know, I was really sorry to do that to her but . . .'

"And that's usually the first point at which I lose it. If I know that it's been a disingenuous and fabricated defense, I will flat out say—sometimes with foul language and sometimes more politely—that I simply don't accept the apology, don't believe it, and don't respect it. I have sat there for two hours asking, 'How do you do that to another human being who has already been victimized?' To this day, I have not had a satisfactory response from anybody who's ever said anything other than, 'He's entitled to a good defense.' That still, to me, doesn't mean a *dishonest* defense. And I don't understand on a human level how you do that in a public forum to another human being."

Alex Kelly's victim had been a sixteen-year-old virgin at the time of the assault, hadn't known him before that night, but needed a ride. Before the basketball game and at the party afterward, kids had been playing "quarters," a drinking game involving pitching quarters into glasses of beer. Puccio tried to use this to his client's advantage, asserting that the victim might have been drunk, but prosecutor Bruce Hudock brought in seven witnesses to testify that she was not intoxicated. The defense also tried arguing that the sex had been consensual. In the end, after five days of deliberation, the jury of six (split evenly between male and female jurors) deadlocked, with four ready to convict and two holdouts, resulting in a hung jury. Not willing to give up, Hudock boldly tried the case again the next summer before moving on to the second case against Kelly. This time, Hudock won a conviction after eight and a half hours of deliberation. Kelly was sentenced to the maximum of twenty years, suspended after sixteen served, and was fined $10,000. At the time of this writing, the trial on the second rape charge had not yet begun.

Immediately after his disappearance, people following the well-publicized case tried to interpret his flight. Was this a sure sign of guilt or was he truly a frightened teenager—high school student and champion wrestler—terrified of getting in trouble for something he didn't do? As in the Chambers case, Alex Kelly appeared to be a "preppie" kid from a well-off family. How—and why—could he be responsible for something as horrible as rape?

In fact, the two offenders had much in common. Like Chambers, Kelly's background was not quite as pristine as it seemed. Although he grew up in a wealthy community, his family didn't truly fit in: his father was a plumber and his mother worked as a travel agent. They did well with real estate investments but did not enjoy the standard of living of many in Darien, leaving Kelly trying to keep up in wealthy circles. Also like Chambers, and like many of the rapists I've described, Kelly committed a series of other lesser crimes before and after the rape. As early as 1983, he was burglarizing homes in his neighborhood with friends. Following an arrest in May of 1984, he was charged with nine counts of burglary and turned in his accomplices. Sentenced to thirty-five months, he ended up serving just sixty-eight days in the Bridgeport Correctional Facility before later returning to high school, ostensibly rehabilitated. The next year, back in school and reportedly doing well, Kelly was arrested again, for a fight after a hockey game. Then came the rape accusations in 1986.

Just as Kelly's pattern of criminal behavior started early, there was a pattern of denial or ignored accountability. What I find particularly appalling is that in this case rather than intervene to try to alter their son's behavior, when Kelly's parents learned of trouble, their response was to bail him out. Even if they believed him innocent, how could they in good conscience stand by as he fled the country rather than face the charges? And even if they did not know about his intentions or help him flee, photos have been published of Kelly, his Swedish girlfriend, and his father on vacation in Europe, and of his parents visiting the girl-friend's parents in their home.

Some in the Darien community forgive the Kellys, feeling sorry for the hardworking parents who have—in their eyes—tried to do the best for their family. Besides, they've already lost one son. In 1991, Alex's older brother, Chris, died of a drug overdose. I can feel sympathy for their loss but find rather incredible Joe Kelly's assertion that his son "was one brave kid to do what he did—right or wrong." When criticized that he and his wife possibly aided their son's escape, warning him in Sweden that authorities were getting close, Joe challenged one accuser to say he'd turn his own son in, given the same set of circumstances.

In an incident in the summer of 1996, Kelly—wearing his electronic monitor—caused a scene in a local bar. After insisting to some women that he hadn't committed rape ten years earlier, he harassed them with obscene words and gestures until police were called. According to that police report, "Kelly was thoroughly uncooperative and appeared to be alcohol-impaired."

And in September of that year—while presumably on his best behavior prior to trial—Kelly got himself into more trouble with the law. Driving home with girlfriend Amy Molitor one night, trying to make curfew, he was clocked at exceeding the speed limit in a 30 mph zone by 25 mph. When police tried to stop him, he reportedly sped off, wrecking Molitor's sports car and leaving her injured at the scene. When police found him at home, he denied any involvement in the accident but turned himself in a couple of days later when police issued a warrant for his arrest. He pleaded not guilty to charges of evading responsibility in a serious accident, interfering with an officer, and speeding. According to the police report, officers "detected a strong odor of alcoholic beverage on Kelly's breath." The police officer also noted that Kelly—whose girlfriend was left bleeding, with broken ribs, upside down in a flipped car—appeared unmoved as he denied knowledge of the accident.

If you think back to my earlier description of the type of rapists who can be rehabilitated, a key factor was whether they took responsibility for their actions and were genuinely remorseful. Following his conviction in connection with the first rape charge, as he was led off in hand-cuffs, sobbing, Kelly cried out, "I'm not guilty! I'm not guilty! I'm not guilty!" He looked over to the jury and pleaded, "God, I didn't do this.

Why are you doing this to me?" It sounds a lot like Robert Chambers playing the victim in Jennifer Levin's murder, and it also sounds like Ronnie Shelton blaming his victim or her husband for his sexual assault.

At Kelly's sentencing, defense attorney Puccio argued for leniency, painting a picture of Kelly's life as "eight years of fear, deprivation of a normal life." Excuse me? Somehow this doesn't square with Kelly's own words in letters he sent his parents from Europe, stating, "I would like to live like this forever." It wasn't until his sentencing that Kelly said he was sorry for what happened, but even then he couched it in terms that were comfortable to him, terms that made it sound as if it were a misunderstanding, rather than a brutal rape: "I never meant to hurt her. . . . I realize now that I did hurt her. I'm sorry. I wish there was something I could do to take the pain away from her."

The woman who brought the case against him sounded much more responsible and courageous as she came forward for the first time in public following the conviction. Adrienne Bak Ortolano said all that she'd gone through over the past decade and more, seeking justice, would be worth it if her case helped other women come forward: "The most important thing to me is that people know that I'm not ashamed of who I am. I am a rape survivor. I don't have anything to hide." Ms. Ortolano is the real hero of his entire tragic episode, and all of us in law enforcement ought to be proud of her and grateful for her resolute bravery.

The other hero, of course, is the prosecution team that worked so diligently to get a guy like Alex Kelly off the street. There's an emotional toll to this kind of work, too, and I have nothing but admiration for people like Linda Fairstein who can fight the good fight year in and year out. And she's had many cases to try in the years since she sought justice for Jennifer Levin.

But after all the work and all the emotional commitment, after all of the involvement with Jennifer's family and friends, what does Fairstein take away from that tragic case?

"The vision for me is Jennifer being after Robert that night, leaving the bar with him at four or four-thirty in the morning, walking with him from Second Avenue, to Third . . . Lex . . . Park . . . Madison . . . Fifth. And what I keep wanting as I relive it is getting to the corner of Eighty-sixth and Fifth and putting her in a taxi and getting her safely home. 'Don't go into the park with him!' I hear myself saying.

"It's the classic situation. And by this I don't mean I'm blaming the victim, which was done more than enough by the defense. But she was playing with fire. He was so intoxicated and angry that night—I don't know to what extent she knew that—but under any circumstances, I couldn't imagine what had transpired between them being a pleasant, loving experience."

There must have been so many warning signs that night.

"For me, despite the fact that we made clear it was a murder in the context of consensual sex, the Chambers case is very much part of the acquaintance-rape problem. The fact that seventy percent or more of this kind of crime happens between individuals who know each other surprises a lot of people. The lesson is how to make judgments about the people you think you know. Because mistakes in judgment that we make can lead to being victimized—fatally, in some cases."

Alex Kelly's victims, too, made a simple judgment call—out of naïveté, driven by the need to get home so they wouldn't get in trouble with their parents—that turned out to be the wrong call. They figured, as many of us do, that someone invited to a party by our friends, or even our friends' friends, must be okay. It happens to older, more experienced, and less trusting people every day: the forty-six-year-old woman whose car breaks down and a familiar face from the neighborhood offers her a ride; the fifty-eight-year-old who lets the deliveryman in to use the phone.

As Linda Fairstein sadly sums up, "There are so many people in whom we place our trust and we are betrayed because we placed it wrongly. And Jennifer is the most tragic extreme of that."

CHAPTER SIX

THE SURVIVOR'S JOURNEY

On March 25, 1931, on an eighty-car freight train passing through Alabama on its way to Memphis, Tennessee, a fight broke out between some blacks and whites. They were all in their teens—except one who was twenty—and all had hopped the train as hoboes, the older ones looking to find work in one of the towns along the way, a common practice in the Depression years. The blacks "won" the fight, largely through force of numbers, and ended up tossing their white adversaries off the train. When the train made a stop in Paint Rock, Alabama, a sheriff's posse was waiting and arrested nine of the blacks, which essentially represented the number they could catch and control. Apparently, as the white losers of the fight had walked back along the railroad tracks, they were fearful of being picked up for vagrancy so they told the authorities they had been attacked and thrown off the train by this pack of Negroes to deflect attention from their own situation.

Things only got more complicated from there. On the train, sheriff's deputies also found two white women dressed in overalls. They were Victoria Price, nineteen, and her seventeen-year-old friend Ruby Bates. Afraid they were about to be arrested for vagrancy or worse, the young women stated that they had been gang-raped by twelve black men, including all of the nine who had just been arrested. Price said that the other three must have jumped off the train before it pulled into Paint Rock.

The defendants hadn't even all known each other before they were rounded up. Of the nine, only four were traveling together: eighteen-year-old Haywood Patterson, his nineteen-year-old friend Andrew

Wright (both from Chattanooga), Wright's brother Leroy, and Leroy's friend Eugene Williams, both thirteen. They were taken to the jail in the nearby town of Scottsboro, where, that night, they were nearly lynched by an outraged citizenry. So began the story of perhaps the most notorious case of false allegation of rape in American history.

The trial of the nine "Scottsboro Boys," as they soon became known throughout the nation, began less than two weeks later. Victoria Price, who had already been married twice, testified that she and Ruby Bates had each been raped six times on the floor of a freight car. Both women had been given medical examinations, which did indicate that both had had sexual intercourse, but not recently enough to have happened while they were on the train. Also, there were no wounds, bruises, or other marks on either woman's body corresponding to the force they claimed had been used in assaulting them. After a three-day trial, all but one of the nine Scottsboro boys were sentenced to death; the youngest was sentenced to life in prison. The trial transcript records the prosecutor summing up to the all-white jury with the words, "Guilty or not, let's get rid of these niggers."

The Scottsboro case quickly became a national and international cause célèbre. Organizations as diverse as the NAACP and the American Communist Party became involved. So did such celebrities as Albert Einstein and writers Theodore Dreiser and Thomas Mann. Ruby Bates recanted her testimony. So egregious was the lack of fairness and due process in the trial that the Supreme Court granted a new trial. This time, in April of 1933, at a courthouse in Decatur, Alabama, the nine were defended by an experienced New York trial lawyer named Samuel Leibowitz, who put on the stand Bates's boyfriend, Lester Carter, who had accompanied her on the train ride and also denied that a rape had taken place. This time the prosecution's summation to another all-white jury included the exhortation, "Show them that Alabama justice can't be bought and sold with Jew money from New York!"

Again the verdict was guilty for all defendants. But this time, the judge was an incredibly courageous man named James E. Horton, who overturned the verdict, declaring that he had heard nothing during the trial that pointed to the guilt of the defendants. In the next election, Judge Horton was overwhelmingly defeated.

In a third trial with a new judge and jury, the Scottsboro Boys were again found guilty, and again the case found its way to the Supreme Court, which ruled that the systematic exclusion of blacks from juries was grounds for reversal. In the fourth trial, in 1937, four of the defendants were found not guilty and the other five were convicted in a behind-the-scenes deal wherein the Northerners agreed to stop protesting and stay out of it if Southern authorities would gradually and quietly release the five from prison. But by the time the last defendant, Andrew Wright, was actually freed in 1950, the nine Scottsboro Boys had served a total of more than a hundred years in custody for a crime they not only did not commit, but that never happened in the first place!

In the Scottsboro case, a charge of rape became not only a weapon for one human being to use against another, but a metaphor for the entire bleak state of race relations in the American South of the 1930s and 1940s. And it pointed up a perception and fear that had already been prominent for centuries: that any woman could accuse any man of sexually assaulting her and it would be her word against his. The resulting conclusion, that false allegations might be plentiful and the credibility of the accusing woman could always be suspect, continues to haunt some rape cases even today.

Recently, not too far from where I live, a woman charged that she was abducted from the parking area of a fashionable suburban shopping mall one afternoon, carjacked some distance away, raped, and returned to the mall. The story was covered heavily in the local media that same evening. Since I am always warning women, beginning with my own family members, about being careful and alert in shopping mall parking lots, this story grabbed my interest and I began looking into it.

Understand that I do not enter into the analysis of any crime—rape included—with any particular bias. To do my job effectively, I must be as objective at the outset as I can be. But with this case, as soon as I started thinking about the facts as they were reported, a couple of things didn't square. To begin, whenever we analyze a violent crime in my unit, we evaluate whether the victim is high risk, low risk, or somewhere in between for this particular incident. Despite the fact that this woman was alone, her situation struck me as low risk. The crime occurred during the afternoon, when the parking structure was well-populated. I knew there were security guards patrolling the area. She said she did not know her attacker, so what made her his specific target? They drove away in her own car, yet this mall is accessible only by car or bus, so how did he get there? Did an accomplice drop him off? The victim said there was no evidence of anyone else helping him. Did he take a bus with the idea that he would rob or rape someone, but then give her back her car, walk over to the bus stop, and wait for the bus while police would undoubtedly be combing the area for a man of his description? And they'd surely have his description, since the victim said he'd made no attempt to disguise himself.

All things considered, the facts just didn't add up or correspond to any combination of the rapist typologies my colleagues and I had developed over the years. This doesn't mean the crime did not happen; it just means you have to investigate scrupulously to see why a particular scenario or detail is out of the ordinary.

As it turned out, this case was later proven a false allegation, a complete fabrication. The motive? The likely one would have been to shake down the shopping mall for damages resulting from negligent security. But in this particular case, it was a simple, misguided plea for attention from a woman who felt lonely and out of place.

Why was this case so easy to crack? The main reason is that the alleged victim constructed her story to conform to what she thought an abduction-rape by a stranger would be like. She ran into the same problems offenders encounter when they try to stage a crime scene: she didn't have enough experience or common sense to realize that the police have seen enough of the real thing to be able to detect her amateurish attempts at deceiving them.

In point of fact, false allegations are relatively rare, estimated to be about 5 percent of all reported rapes, which corresponds to the statistic for the false reporting of other types of crime in general. But rape false reports are destructive in vast disproportion to their numbers. First, because anytime someone is intentionally accused of a crime he did not commit, the collective sense of fairness and justice is perverted. Second, the small number of false allegations call into question the veracity of the overwhelming number of genuine claims. And third, that 5 percent figure is somewhat inflated by the fact that rape is a vastly underreported crime to begin with—as all the "silent victims" I've met at public appearances and received mail from attest.

For trained investigators and prosecutors, there are ways of cutting through bogus accusations to the truth. It's worthwhile examining them both to underscore that these lies are difficult to sustain—and if you're caught, the false report is a crime in itself—and to stress that the cases good detectives and district attorneys bring to trial are legitimate.

What are some of the more common motives behind false rape allegations? Extortion, as we originally suspected in the shopping mall case, is clearly one of them, or similarly attempting to blackmail a politician, a celebrity, or a wealthy person. Another motive is retribution—wanting to get back at someone and destroy his reputation. A woman might falsely allege rape to explain her presence where she shouldn't have been, such as with a man other than her husband. A variation of this is lying to avoid punishment—from the law or parents or other authorities—for having broken curfew, for example, or to explain away sex with a boy you've been forbidden to see.

These false allegations are all pretty unusual, and the only reason we're considering them here is because of the effect they have on true allegations. What we do see more often, and what is more complex to deal with, is an essentially true story that has been exaggerated or embellished, often for a similar set of motives.

Linda Fairstein tells the story of a sixteen-year-old high school student who actually was raped, but not under the circumstances she initially claimed. She reported that she had come in to Washington Square Park in Manhattan from her home in the suburbs for an afternoon rally staged by some NYU students in support of the legalization of marijuana. From there she was abducted at knifepoint by a homeless man, who forced her onto the subway, to the Upper West Side, where he then took her to his "home" among a large outcropping of rocks in Riverside Park. That was where he assaulted her, still threatening her with the knife. A uniformed police officer found her wandering around dazed, with her clothing dirty and torn. She identified her attacker, who was picked up almost immediately at the site of the attack. He did not deny that he had had sex with her, but claimed it was consensual and that he and she were actually friends—a common defense.

The medical examination indicated that the young woman had indeed had sexual intercourse and that it had been brutal. There was enough terror in her rendition and a sufficient level of detail to make Fairstein's associate believe that she had been raped in a life-threatening situation.

But as with the story of the woman at the suburban shopping mall, certain things were troublesome. For one, the abduction would have to have taken place in broad daylight, in a crowded park with a lot of police present. When the stated purpose of the rally has to do with marijuana, how difficult is it to figure out that in addition to all the uniforms, there are going to be a bunch of undercover cops hanging around, too? Are you going to take a chance on abducting someone at knifepoint in that setting when it would be so much easier in any number of venues just a few blocks away? Then there is the subway ride, which covered a hundred city blocks. Because of the concerns for violence, New York subway trains are pretty well patrolled. What are the chances no officer or passenger would notice anything unusual during the entire trip uptown?

Fairstein decided to question the victim herself. She told the young woman they all believed she had been raped, but if any part of her story was shown to be untrue, even a part that seemed inconsequential to her, it would undermine the entire account in the jury's mind and the rapist would end up looking like the victim.

Then it came out. Not surprisingly, her parents were against her attending this rally. She had met the defendant there, and over several hours, they had struck up an acquaintanceship. He told her he had some marijuana stashed at his place uptown, and if she accompanied him there, he'd give her some and they could share the profits from selling the rest. He promised to get her back to Grand Central Station in time for her train back home. So she left the park with him voluntarily, got on the subway with him voluntarily, and went into Riverside Park with him voluntarily. Once they were amidst the large rocks, away from other people for the first time, she saw the knife. He threatened her with it for the next hour as he brutalized her.

Unquestionably, this young woman had been the victim of a violent sex crime. Underlying her entire fabricated story was the fear of her parents' reaction—that she would lose their trust and they would severely punish or restrict her because of her actual behavior and poor judgment. If she could convince them that she hadn't done anything "wrong," that everything that had happened was forced upon her, then the only thing they could blame her for was going to the rally in the first place.

Fairstein tried to convince her that her mother and father were overwhelmingly relieved she was alive and safe, that any punishment they might impose would be meaningless compared to what she'd already suffered. Fairstein also told her client she would break the news of what had actually happened to them and make sure there were no lasting recriminations.

Don't think it is just naive teenagers hoping to avoid their parents' anger who get themselves into these kinds of situations. We've seen more than one case of a mature man and woman, having an affair in a hotel room, being accosted by an intruder who then ties up the man and rapes the woman. You can imagine the impulse to fabricate extra details to that story to get yourself where you need to be with your spouse—or your children. But like a totally false allegation, it is likely to blow up in the face of the perpetrator, and at the worst possible moment.

As Fairstein says, "Nobody gets to lie and have us just gloss over it. All of that gets turned over to the defense, and she will have to explain it. Most of the time it is explicable: 'I lied because I thought I'd be punished by my mother.' 'I thought the cops wouldn't believe me.' 'I thought if I admitted I was a prostitute, nobody would investigate the case or care.' "

The key here is that a good investigator or prosecutor has to make sure he or she is on top of the situation, getting the full story but not losing that vital link of trust with the victim. There are various methods of accomplishing this.

"How I convince them to tell me the truth can be gentle or not," Fairstein explains. "Some people respond and get the point quickly. Some need to be pounded on that there's one person in that courtroom who knows more about the situation than I do, and that—believe me—this is the last place they want me to find out about it, because then they're out of there. The three factors [in why victims mislead] are generally alcohol, drugs, or consensual foreplay. Minimize or lie about one of those things, and if the defendant tells a more credible story and I hear it for the first time in the courtroom, you can be sure that the jury will react accordingly. I will be my clients' advocate if I know everything that went on and believe that a crime was committed. But if they hold anything back from me, they will not get what they're looking for. Then I explain what perjury is and I explain what happens if they lie under oath. I will prosecute for that. Then something that they have been the victim of turns out to be more painful for them if they can't deal with the whole truth."

As we saw with Robert Chambers, a defendant can change his story as many times as he wants, but if we want to put guys like him away, the victim must be held to a higher standard of truth, regardless of the trauma she's gone through. It's a sad fact, but one we've got to deal with.

As a society, we have to get to the point where rape victims are unafraid to come forward with their stories—even if certain details make them seem less than the ideal of virtue. And we have to make sure they know that our aim is not to judge them for being raped, but to get at the truth so we can seek justice for them and protection for the rest of us. Because until we start to recognize that even imperfect citizens (which includes just about all of us) have the right to say no, we will never be sure how many dangerous, repeat sexual predators we're keeping out on the street and on the hunt, whom we might have had a chance to put away for good.

There is a reason that conquering armies have used rape throughout history to vanquish their enemies. To borrow Linda Fairstein's definition again and broaden it to suit a much larger scale: mass rape is a crime in which sex is the tool used to exert dominance and control over defeated "victim" populations. Even with all the technological and scientific breakthroughs in chemical, biological, and nuclear weapons of mass destruction, the systematic rape of women—wives, daughters, grandmothers—can be counted on to be tremendously destructive, demoralizing, and debilitating to one's enemies in a way the others simply can't. We saw this thousands of years ago and we see it today. And the process epitomizes how a soldier must dehumanize his enemies to be able to destroy them. As individual victims of a serial rapist often represent the true target the offender is unable to lash out at directly (his mother, perhaps, or wife), victims of wartime atrocities are mere symbols of the society under attack.

When we hear of these war crimes we are universally outraged: the horror, shame, and depravity of the act transcends cultural, religious, or political differences. All civilized people condemn the aggressors and feel for the victims, whether the crimes take place between ethnic factions in Bosnia, warring tribes in Zaire, or virtually anyplace in between. What has always been perplexing to me, then, is how this outrage is muted when it hits much closer to home and on a much more personal level. When a woman is raped in the United States today—maybe the soccer mom next door, or the teenager who baby-sits your kids, or a prostitute who works not far from your office (although it seems like worlds away)—reactions can be mixed. Although in this case, the sexual assault involves a similar motivation on the perpetrator's side—the drive to dominate and conquer transcends any sexual pleasure he may seek—the context of the event seems more difficult for us to digest, and more difficult even for the victim to process.

This explains, in part, why far, far more frequent than cases of either false reporting or false allegation is the outright lack of reporting of rape. There are many reasons for this disturbing phenomenon, occasionally having to do with the victim's fear that the rapist will return to assault her again (as Ronnie Shelton threatened to do as part of his modus operandi), although we can assure rape victims that this happens very, very rarely with rapes by strangers.

But the primary reason is the victims' perception of their community's reaction. And by community, I include all of us—everyone from her spouse, lover, or boyfriend, to the police, health care workers, attorneys, judges, juries, media, and the public at large.

Consider the plight of a young woman in her early thirties. She has a decent job in a support position at a law firm that specializes in real estate transactions. One of the firm's clients is an attractive doctor in his early forties, never married, who asks the woman out. On their third date, thrilled that this polite, handsome, charming, successful man is interested in her, she goes back to his place after dinner and a night of dancing. They share a bottle of wine and she feels as if there's nothing they can't talk and joke about. In fact, she may be falling in love with him. She'd like to spend the rest of the night talking, lying in his arms. It's too early to have sex, though, she feels, both because she'd prefer to wait until they've known each other longer and because she doesn't want him to think she's too fast. Everything he's done and said up to now makes her believe he cares for her, too, and that he'll be sensitive to her feelings.

As it turns out, it doesn't matter what she wants. Around three in the morning his kisses grow more insistent. She tells him to wait, but he holds her hands up over her head and won't stop. She can't move. She starts crying, begging him to get off her, listen to her, let them talk about this. Is it suddenly a bad dream? But it's too late.

He never threatened to kill her, never held a knife to her throat. He simply overpowered her physically. Afterward, he may be nice, telling her he enjoyed being with her, which is both confusing and alarming to her. Or he may be mean, warning her that nobody will believe her if she says anything. "It's your word against mine. Look at the two of us—who do you think people will believe?" In either event, he's obviously finished with her when he lets her pull her clothes together and go home.

On the surface—to us—it's an easy call: report the bastard. But put yourself in the shoes of the victim. She feels incredibly betrayed, hurt, and ashamed about what happened. How could she have so misjudged him? Were there any subtle clues she could have missed somewhere along the line? What may frighten her further is the idea that if she had it all to do again, she can't think of anything that would have set off warning buzzers in her mind; he was such a gentleman up to that point, and he seemed so trustworthy. She starts questioning her instincts.

She may be afraid that if she tells the police that she'd been drinking—not drunk, but drinking—they won't believe the rest of her story. Aside from the presence of sperm, there may be no physical evidence to back her up. After all, it's not as if he beat her. And this guy's a successful professional. He could get any woman. Why would he need to rape her? Her self-confidence—never at a real high level before—has been shattered by this event, and she can imagine jurors thinking she was lucky to get him in the first place.

In this case, too, he's a client of her boss's. She could lose her job. In fact, she could lose everything, since even her family may not be supportive. Her mother doesn't understand why she isn't married yet—to her, this guy is a perfect catch. In the end, after the humiliation she can imagine in dealings with everyone from her family members and friends to the police, to her coworkers, she'd still have to go through a trial where it would be, as he said, her word against his. He's handsome, successful, not someone you'd imagine to be a rapist. Besides, she heard what people said about the woman who accused Mike Tyson before he was eventually convicted of her rape: What was she doing in his room late at night? As though it were her fault.

The issue becomes even grayer when no physical force is used, but threats and intimidation make the victim comply. If, for example, a rapist says he has a gun or a knife and isn't afraid to use it, but the victim doesn't see it, it may be harder for her to get others to understand the level of fear she felt facing her attacker. Again, until we've walked in her shoes, none of us can be sure how we'd react in such a situation. People reach different levels of intimidation at different points, and if you have reason to fear for your life, then simply living through a sexual assault is a successful outcome. Not seeing a weapon doesn't guarantee there isn't one, any more than it guarantees the offender won't resort to physical violence to control his victim if he feels he needs to.

With so many elements subject to postassault interpretation (and second-guessing), it's not hard to imagine why some perfectly nice, honest women still think twice about reporting a sexual assault. It's not right. She didn't deserve what happened to her any more than he deserves to get away with it. Unfortunately, it happens. And if you move farther down the spectrum from the "ideal" rape victim—a virtuous virgin raped by a stranger on her way home from church one Sunday, whose assailant is witnessed and arrested at the scene by a uniformed patrol cop—it's even easier to see why rape is underreported. There are still a lot of people who believe it is impossible for a prostitute to be raped, or for a woman to be raped by a man she's previously had consensual sex with—say, an ex-husband or former boyfriend. This may sound ridiculous to the enlightened readers I like to believe make up my audience, but consider this frightening statistic: more than half of six thousand adolescents, aged eleven to fourteen, in an American Medical Association survey voiced their opinion that there were some circumstances under which rape is acceptable, such as if the male and female had dated six months or longer or if he'd spent considerable money on her.

Where does this come from? Have we really raised our children to think this way? Is this what we want? Should our sons *and* daughters truly think that at times it is socially acceptable to ignore someone else's feelings and will about her own mind, soul, and body?

Dr. Ann Wolbert Burgess, professor of psychiatric mental-health nursing at the University of Pennsylvania, has been my colleague and frequent partner in the study of crime ever since we collaborated on the serial-offender study in the late 1970s. She has always been extremely supportive of me and my work, encouraging me in publishing and broadening our research. Among her many fields of expertise, she's one of the nation's leading and most sensitive experts on sexual assaults and rape victimology. More than anyone else, she has shaped my views on the subject and influenced the direction I went in hunting sexual predators. In 1972 at Boston City Hospital, Ann founded one of the nation's first hospital-based crisis-intervention programs for rape victims and served as chair of the first advisory council to the National Center for the Prevention and Control of Rape at the National Institute of Mental Health. Since then, she's served in numerous official capacities for the attorney general, the surgeon general, and Congress.

Ann makes the point that "society's perception of rape is strongly influenced by a puzzling mixture of prejudice, credence, and voyeuristic curiosity." Her research has led her to believe that whatever our past experience is, it tends to color the way we react. For example, if a rookie cop handling his first rape appears too sympathetic or sensitive to his fellow officers and they ridicule him for it, he's likely to harden himself the next time around and not give the victim the sort of response she needs and deserves. By the same token, if his first case turns out to be a false allegation, he may be prone—either consciously or subconsciously—to discount or be dubious about subsequent claims.

As part of their recovery from the "rape trauma syndrome" some victims suffer postassault, Ann always stresses the need for both police officers and prosecutors to recognize how their behavior with the victim affects, in her words, "not only an immediate and long-term ability to deal with the event, but also her willingness to assist in a prosecution." Just as people who've lived through other types of traumatic events can develop post–traumatic stress disorder (PTSD), there is a similar syndrome particular to rape victims that should be understood by those who come in contact with them postassault. The effects can be short-term and/or long-term and can range from sleep and eating disturbances to the development of phobias—e.g., a new obsession with security and/or a fear of being alone. Recognizing this, the first people to come in contact with a victim postassault have an opportunity to set the stage, through their behavior and reactions, for an easier or harder recovery for that victim—and for a willing or hesitant witness.

While investigators can usually recognize false elements in a report fairly quickly, the extent to which an honest victim will be traumatized by her assault (and the way this will manifest itself) is much harder to assess. And there's no single, standard, or "appropriate" victim response to rape, which is why many police officers and investigators are uncomfortable with it. Ann Burgess describes two general types of immediate reactions we see from women who've just been sexually assaulted: expressive and guarded. Some victims may exhibit both responses during an interview, depending on how long it goes on, who is conducting it, and whether it is broken up into more than one session. For example, a victim might be expressive with a police officer immediately after the rape, but then guarded the next day talking to a detective at the precinct.

Although the raw emotions exhibited by expressive types make some investigators uncomfortable, guarded types are more difficult for most investigators, some of whom interpret silence as withholding information or details. In fact, this is often an attempt on the victim's part to maintain control of herself after an event in which control has been completely taken away.

And just as the rape victim often feels she's lost control of her life, the crime can reach out and affect the very relationships she'll need to get through her ordeal, compromising her ability to resume a "normal life" further. As Burgess and my FBI Academy colleague Roy Hazelwood write in their book, *Practical Aspects of Rape Investigation: A Multidisciplinary Approach,* "Rape can precipitate a crisis not only for the victim, but for family, friend and others in her network. Police officers and attorneys very likely will have to deal with these family members and some understanding of the impact the rape has on their lives may help to create a more cooperative victim and partner."

The issues for victims and the people emotionally close to them can become complex and problematic. Does a husband or lover view the victim as an individual he loves who has been badly hurt and is still suffering, or as an extension of himself—a "possession" that has now lost some of its value? Does he view the rape as something that happened to the victim, or does he feel she somehow brought it on herself? Does he blame the assailant for doing this terrible thing to her or himself for not being able to protect her or stop it? How will they deal with the ordeal of the investigation and the trial, particularly if it is at all publicized?

Many men will feel as if they themselves have been victims, and in some ways they are. I've often said that each violent crime has a long string of victims. But they must not forget who the primary victim is. A man might feel that the woman should have fought harder or resisted more intensively, and it's important to deal with this particular notion right away. Any woman who emerges from a sexual attack alive should be recognized for her courage and resourcefulness, and no one should ever second-guess her tactics in handling the crisis. What any of us might think with the luxury of twenty-twenty hindsight—and from the safe distance of one who was not there, facing a determined assailant—is meaningless except in terms of how it helps us to deal with the next one. The critical thing is that she survived, and that is something she accomplished on her own.

When a man questions the way his wife or girlfriend handled the assault, it may be a symptom of his own embarrassment or helplessness or guilt in the situation. Another manifestation of embarrassment or emotional confusion is to lose physical desire for the woman, another circumstance that may require immediate counseling.

A more positive response is when the victim's partner wants to "get the guy who did it." This can be one of the healthier attitudes we see because it may encourage the woman to report the crime. On the other hand, if she had been hesitant and just does so because of his urging, without coming to grips with her own emotional issues, the relationship can be made more difficult and filled with trauma.

These problems are not merely limited to "traditional" sexual assaults. Burgess and Hazelwood cite the case of a homosexual rape of a man whose wife felt he should have been able to fend off the attack, and of a woman whose lesbian partner was hurt and angry that she had had sex with a man, even though it was against her will.

Any of these reactions can obviously hamper a victim's ability to rebound emotionally from her assault—a process that may be already complicated by recovery from sometimes severe physical injuries. But here's one thing upon which virtually all the experts agree: that the more support the victim gets from those close to her, the smoother or easier her recovery. The problems arise when people have unrealistic expectations or may project their own needs over those of the victim's.

A husband may express his frustration that his wife hasn't "gotten over it" yet. I've seen the same thing happen many times to the families of murder victims. Well meaning but ignorant and insensitive friends, relatives or even casual acquaintances and total strangers counsel that they will not "feel better" or "have closure," or whatever, until they can put this horrible event behind them and "get on with their lives." Pardon me, but this is a load of crap. Time will make the pain less acute, but telling a victim or survivor to get on with his or her life is the same as questioning the value of the murdered loved one or—in the case of rape—her life before the attack.

Well-intentioned though he may be, and with her best interests at heart, the husband may now be ready for her to have more good days than bad, not be fearful in strange situations or when left alone, and to show more interest and vigor in making love to him. But it's a vicious circle: the more pressure he puts on her, the harder it will be for her to come to grips with what's happened to her. Just like the survivors of other violent crimes, rape victims go through a grieving process, missing the more carefree life they've lost. And again like survivors of other crimes, everyone grieves in different ways and at different paces. It is completely insensitive for anyone to set what he or she believes is a reasonable time frame for someone else's recovery. Like veterans of a war, survivors of sexual assault run the gamut from those who adapt fairly well quickly to others who suffer long-term physical and emotional symptoms recognized as part of the larger rape trauma syndrome.

We shouldn't lose sight of the good news, though, which is that many victims of sexual assault do fully "recover." This is not to suggest that they ever forget what happened to them, any more than the murder victim's survivor ever removes that person from the heart, but they are able to put it behind them enough to function normally again and accomplish what they want in their lives. Like getting out of the assault alive, recovery is a process that calls on all the resources and courage a survivor has, and this should be recognized by those she counts on to support her over the short and long term.

Investigators, prosecutors, jurors, and the rest of us also have to understand that rape victims in the immediate aftermath of the crisis may not react with all of their normal faculties. If you've ever suffered a life-altering trauma—the sudden death of a loved one, a serious and/or physically debilitating automobile accident—then you know that it takes a while for your head to clear and your heartbeat to return to normal. And there may always be things that make you start, that trigger an actual physical reaction, as long as years after the event. For a rape victim, this temporary disconnect from normal processing capabilities can lead to delays in reporting, which can ultimately affect a successful prosecution.

What we recommend when a victim does come forward after some delay is not to berate her for not reporting it right away, telling her what a problem this is going to be, but to have the investigator get her to explain what it was that finally allowed her to reach this point and make the difficult decision to report. This tells you a lot about where the victim is coming from and makes her a better witness later on.

One of the things we cannot stress enough is the importance of having specially trained and experienced, professional law enforcement personnel involved, who employ established standard methods of information and evidence gathering. Physical evidence has been lost by untrained officers and crime-scene technicians who, in a laudable and understandable effort to be sympathetic to the victim, allow her to change clothing or wash herself before giving a statement or going to the hospital—or even offer a good stiff drink to help calm the nerves of a victim of an oral sexual assault! If there is no semen on the victim or elsewhere at the scene, an inexperienced investigator may think this means there was no sexual assault, that the victim is not being truthful, particularly if she reports having been raped several times over the course of the attack. But as we've noted, difficulty or failure to ejaculate is not uncommon among rapists, and it's a detail that might actually give us information to go on in our investigation.

This is what I always make a point of to investigators: In addition to getting a physical description of the rapist, what he was wearing, any disguise, any weapon he might have carried or other implement he brought with him, the type of car he drove, etc., etc., it is vitally important to assimilate as much information on his *behavior* as possible. What did he say during the attack? What, if anything, did he make his victim say during the attack? How did he attempt to control her? What did he do to her physically? What did he do to her—or force her to do to him—sexually, and what was the order of sexual acts? How long did he take? What was his demeanor? Many law enforcement agencies find it useful to rely on queries like those in the questionnaire Roy Hazelwood designed when we were both working at Quantico. These more specific questions elicit the type of behavioral information we need to develop a useful profile of the unknown rapist. Specially trained and sympathetic law enforcement personnel will know how to ask these types of questions. I liken it to the process I use in profiling offenders, when I evaluate the crime scene from the victim's perspective. The interviewer, too, needs to "walk in the shoes of the victim," do some victimology, and understand how to relate to her.

To give an idea of how important this can be, some victims may not know or recognize the proper terminology for different types of sexual assault and may inadvertently provide incorrect information. You can't automatically assume *sodomy* means the same thing to everyone, or that everyone has even heard the word before. A skilled interviewer will recognize how to phrase questions and will similarly know to clarify when colloquialisms are used to make sure the information gathered is accurate. Elderly victims may not know how to describe what happened to them or may be too embarrassed to admit certain sex acts occurred, simply because "in their day" people didn't have oral sex and it is seen as perverted and humiliating, for example. At every step, the interviewer needs to make sure the victim understands why the question is being asked, and why a complete answer, however discomforting, is so important.

Even though it is painful for the victim to relive the experience in such detail, a thorough interview may actually prove therapeutic. First off, through simple actions such as asking the victim if she'd like to be addressed as Ms. So-and-so, rather than immediately using the more familiar first name, the interviewer gives the victim some control over her situation. A skilled interviewer will balance the emotional needs of the victim with the need to gather pertinent information and will be able to work toward a more comfortable outcome for her. And by making the victimized woman a "partner" in the process, we not only get more useful information for our investigation, but we may help her regain some of the control over her life that was taken from her in the assault—she can help us nail the guy who did this to her.

A sensitive but critical issue is convincing the victim to get proper medical attention. This is important both for her own health and the "health" of the case. Fairstein says, "Whether or not she decides to finish formal reporting at that point is less important than documenting what's in and on her body immediately, because you can't go back and retrieve that."

After this consideration, Fairstein continues, "You have to make sure she can get the accurate answers about what the process involves for her. How many times will she have to tell her story? Who will she have to see? Do her parents or her husband or her children have to be told about what happened? Is the guy likely to be found? Whether it's an acquaintance or a stranger rape, how much about her personal history is going to be explored in the case? Most of these things are questions that can be answered at the time she first comes into contact with a police officer. It's bigger than any victim can deal with in the first moments after the attack, and there are ways to help her through it that the police officer who responds has to be able to deal with."

While the investigator needs to be sensitive to the victim's physical and emotional welfare, keeping in mind that his or her behavior is largely going to affect not only the disposition of the case but the woman's overall mental health, this is equally true of medical professionals. As strange as it may be for a profession that seems to have a specialty for everything, only recently have medical personnel been trained specifically to handle sexual assault—that is, how to treat the emotional and physical problems of the victim while at the same time effectively gathering and preserving crucial evidence. This is one area where we have seen improvement, though, as standard kits have been developed (and used more universally) to gather evidence of sexual assault.

And there are many complicated issues here, too. What is the legal definition of rape operative in the particular jurisdiction? Is the emergency room physician required as a matter of law to report to the police any injuries consistent with the crime of rape, or does he need the written consent of the patient to do so? How should the medical records reflect the physical condition of the patient without reaching conclusions that should be left to a jury?

A victim in an emergency room may have to tell her story several times to several different types of people, after she's already told the first investigating officers, which may greatly upset her and make her feel even more victimized. Like the police officer with his side of the case, before the physical exam takes place, the doctor or nurse should explain everything that is to be done, so the patient won't feel even more vulnerable and out of control. This is especially true for any part of the exam that may be physically uncomfortable, since she may already be in considerable pain. Depending on the age of the victim and her level of sexual experience, this may be the first gynecological exam she's ever had—a procedure that can be frightening enough when done on an elective basis in a considerably less fragile and battered emotional and physical state.

"One problem," says Fairstein, "is that some ER doctors don't feel that treating a rape victim is a medical problem, that collecting evidence in the emergency room is not something that a doctor should do, that if her life doesn't need to be saved, it's not an ER problem. We confront this regularly, and I lecture about it in every hospital in the city that'll have me.

"The medical piece of it is, she has not only had the trauma of the rape, but she's possibly been exposed to sexually transmitted diseases, possible pregnancy, and certainly now, exposure to HIV infection, which is a very serious problem that many victims don't think about in surviving the attack but which becomes critical right afterward."

The medical professionals who treat a victim with dignity, according her privacy and respect, can help her take an important step forward. I've heard of cases to the contrary, however, that do a tremendous disservice to the sexual assault survivors and to the medical profession. I used to tell my people that all of us professionals need to "watch our mouths."

A woman lying on a gurney or examination table, who's already been victimized by one stranger that day, certainly doesn't need to hear an orderly or nurse walking by her door (or the curtain temporarily separating her from the rest of the ER) announce to a physician coming on duty, "That's the rape victim." There can be a tendency to see the victim first as a walking crime scene and then as a human being who's been wronged, and we need to remember to address both of those truths.

After the initial encounter with the victim, the investigator has to begin putting together the pieces of the puzzle and figuring out how to hunt down the offender and bring him to justice. From the outset, acquaintance-rape cases are handled differently than stranger assaults. The immediate advantage in investigating an acquaintance rape is that you already know the identity of the alleged assailant. In trial preparation, in addition to confronting any issues that will arise in the credibility war between defendant and accuser in court, it's critical that the prosecution team understand what the story is from the alleged rapist's perspective. By this, I don't mean just keeping up with the latest version of events as told by a Robert Chambers type. Instead, I mean that if his claim will be that sex was consensual, what happened between the two of them that either led him to believe that or could provide support to his story in the eyes of a jury? If, say, the woman returned his kisses and eagerly took part in the interplay, he may not have interpreted that how she meant it. A more extreme instance would be if the victim went along with oral sex but didn't want vaginal penetration out of fear of pregnancy. Members of a jury, however, may need to be educated, and the prosecution needs to be prepared to handle consensual (or seemingly consensual) acts leading up to the sexual assault. Linda Fairstein notes, too, that anything unusual about the situation will need to be dealt with up-front—even at jury selection—because jurors often will not be able to respond beyond their own frames of reference.

Fairstein says, "You will get, for example, the victim who will describe what most of us in the business would call a dysfunctional offender, who will maintain an erection and penetrate and remove himself for a period of three, four, five hours while she's bound during a burglary in her apartment. And you will find people who will say, 'Not possible. She's lying. You can't do it for that long,' based on their own personal experience and not understanding the pathology of some of these offenders.

"People who come to the jury box with stereotypes, with biases, with prejudices, will incorporate those. And you don't get those out, necessarily, in jury selection. I mean, it isn't until somebody's waved the tiger-striped bikini panties in front of her that a juror says, 'I buy white, cotton Carter's underwear, and a woman who wears underwear like that must be . . .' It's that kind of thing."

Fairstein had another case in which she found one of the jurors having to be convinced that a man and a woman could have sex standing up, otherwise the victim's story would not be believed.

In the case of stranger rapes, an important consideration is to determine whether or not this rape is part of a pattern—that is: Are we dealing with a repeat or serial offender? It deeply frustrates those of us in law enforcement and the criminal justice system when we see cases where a paroled offender—often convicted of a previous sex crime—returns to the system again after committing an assault even more violent than the last. In fact, recently released prisoners are often an ideal pool of suspects in a stranger rape, as we saw in the Timothy Spencer case in Virginia, recounted in *Journey into Darkness*.

Assessing whether a stranger rape is actually part of a series is a subject about which I often offered court testimony when I was with the Investigative Support Unit.

The impediment to an investigator's seeing cases as related is referred to as linkage blindness, and it can happen for a number of reasons. One is associating crimes only by location, when a particular UNSUB may, in fact, have a number of comfort zones. Maybe he lives in one part of the metropolitan area and works in another. Maybe his girlfriend or another family member lives somewhere else. And, of course, when you shift law enforcement jurisdictions, such as when an UNSUB leaves one city and moves to another, linkage is particularly difficult.

Another cause of linkage blindness is depending too heavily on MO to the exclusion of other factors. If an UNSUB uses a knife in one crime and then a gun in another, or if he jimmies a window open at one location but comes right through the front door at another, we can clearly see that the modus operandi in each case was different. That doesn't necessarily mean it's two different guys. Remember, MO is learned behavior and it evolves based on experience. Maybe he didn't feel comfortable using the knife and so he decided to try a gun, knowing he wouldn't have to get as close or exercise as tight control to subdue a potential victim. Maybe he realized that breaking through windows was too risky and left too much evidence, so he began surveilling locations where the door was unlocked or unsuspecting women would answer a knock without looking to see who it was first.

It's also important to remember that while MO isn't the most reliable indicator, it can also evolve into signature, at which point it will become a more standard part of the presentation and give us more behavioral evidence to work with. A good example of this would be an offender who brings cords or ropes with him, which he uses to control his victim. He sees this is an effective method, so he continues to employ it in subsequent rapes. But then during one of them, he realizes he's getting a charge out of seeing the woman choking under the ligature or gasping for breath, and erotic asphyxiation becomes part of his signature. If that happens, we could expect to see some variation of that in subsequent crimes.

Of course, there can also be a tendency to look for patterns where none exist, particularly if an area is experiencing an upswing in the number of reported assaults. But because of what we know about all varieties of rapists, most rapes by strangers should be considered as potentially part of a series unless there is strong indication to the contrary. And, as I think we've seen from earlier chapters, a pattern of behavior may not mean that a rapist has committed earlier rapes per se.

Look at the Peeping Toms and burglars arrested in the area and see if descriptions match.

What used to be particularly frustrating about rape cases was the uneven treatment of the victim's personal life and past versus what the jury (and often the press) got to hear about the defendant's history. The numbers would probably be appalling if we were able to assess how many rapes are unreported because a victim (or her husband or parents or other influences in her life) did not want to deal with being dragged through the mud. Think of the "rough sex" claim that haunted the memory of Jennifer Levin in the Robert Chambers trial, even though there was no shred of evidence to support it, together with the fact that the jury was never allowed to hear about Chambers's genuine criminal past.

Fortunately, we have seen some substantial improvement in the way rape is prosecuted, thanks in large measure to people like Linda Fairstein and so many other dedicated individuals who decided to specialize in what for so long was an unpopular backwater of criminal law.

"The big surprise for most people is that the criminal justice system works at all and that it can work," Fairstein states. "I'm a real optimist about it because I started doing this at a time when it didn't work at all and there were corroboration requirements [someone else had to testify as a witness or be able to verify that the rape had taken place], and most women had to be turned away by me at the door. It's amazing, but that's the way it was."

Rape shield laws offer the victim protection from some of the ugliest forms of attack by preventing the introduction of information about her past or what she was wearing that has nothing to do with the crime committed against her. And we may finally be getting to the point where most juries just won't accept the tired defense strategies that attempt to sully the reputation of the victim to make the defendant look like an altar boy.

"The stranger-rape defense nowadays is generally very gentle on the victim," Fairstein observes. "It doesn't have to impugn her reliability, her personality, or her lifestyle at all. It can just say, 'You're right, I believe you, this is a terrible thing that happened to you, Ms. Smith. But this is the wrong guy. My guy didn't do it.' And I can respect that as a defense strategy. I can get angry or not at the level of the attack, but I can respect that kind of defense."

The rape shield laws are just one area where education of the public about an unfair, discriminatory, unwarranted, and damaging practice led to change. We should see this as an encouragement that other problem areas in the prosecution, conviction, and sentencing of sexual offenders will be addressed in the not-too-distant future. Sometimes evolution in thinking and awareness results from publicity surrounding circumstances that simple common sense tells us are wrong.

Some inappropriate reactions are so blatant as to be all but unbelievable. I am reminded of a 1989 case in which a woman claimed to be abducted at knifepoint from the parking lot of a restaurant in Fort Lauderdale, Florida, and raped repeatedly. The alleged victim, a twenty-two-year-old woman, was reportedly dressed in a tank top and lace miniskirt with no underwear. The jury ruled the defendant not guilty because they felt she had solicited the sexual act.

"We all feel she asked for it the way she was dressed," the jury foreman told *Time* magazine.

Whether this victim's mode of dress was wise or not under the circumstances, what is it going to take to get some people to realize that women do not *ask* to be raped? Never, ever. By definition, it is impossible. Yes means yes, no means no, and there is little ambiguity possible between these two responses.

Equally outrageous is a case of Fairstein's. "There's one judge I had a terrible experience with," she recalls. "He'd been on the bench a long time and had a relatively good reputation and was supposed to be a nice guy. We were trying the case of a forcible rape of a twenty-five-year-old woman. She had the mental development of a six- or seven-year-old, and when the time came for sentencing, the judge announced that he was going to give the minimum sentence because the rape could not have impacted her the same way it would a 'normal' person, because she was retarded. And secondly, she had previously been the victim of physical child abuse and neglect, so he said this was just one more incident.

"I took on the judge and I made statements out of court to the press that these were medieval views he had expressed. He took me to the disciplinary committee of the bar for my remarks about him, but he was not successful."

First of all, the notion that an offender's punishment should be less severe because he took advantage of a mentally handicapped person is preposterous on its face. Would the judge have given a lighter sentence to a man who raped a wheelchair-bound woman on the grounds that since she couldn't get around as well as an able-bodied person, the assault wouldn't have the same impact on her life? If a blind woman was raped, would His Honor have concluded that since she couldn't see the knife or gun, she wouldn't have had the same fear as a sighted victim? Last time I checked, the phrase "Equal Justice Under Law" was still carved above the front door of the Supreme Court.

As demoralizing as these specific incidents are, there is reason for optimism. There are signs that the tide is turning. From the establishment of more local, community rape crisis centers to "Take Back the Night" rallies, to rock concerts held, in part, to benefit organizations that support sexual-assault victims, to the rape shield laws that make it much more difficult for the defense to try to make the victim's personal history a part of the case, the emphasis is slowly moving to represent the rights of the victim at least as well as the rights of the victimizer, which is only fair.

It will never be easy, though. As should be clear by now, any discussion of the prosecution of rape and sexual assault is going to be full of good-news/bad-news situations. Beyond emphasizing that no one "asks for it," it's time for us to recognize that no one ever *deserves* to be raped and no sexual assault should go unpunished.

Finally, I'd like to close this chapter by addressing sexual-assault survivors directly. Whether you've already been through the system or you're a "silent victim" like the many I've come to know, you may not feel particularly courageous or heroic. But I believe you are those things and more to have gotten through your ordeal as it happened and to be getting through each day since. I am not surprised that you have been able to overcome the experience (even if you are still working through it), but I do marvel at it and we should all respect your strength. One thing I have learned from violent-crime victims in general, and sexual-assault victims in particular, is that survivors all heal in their own way and at their own pace. It is never easy, but you should know that the burden does not have to overwhelm you.

As Linda Fairstein says, "Getting control back is the first step. I am a big believer in the fact that most rape victims recover from the crime. They don't ever forget that the crime occurred, but most recover very well. And how they recover has to do with how they are responded to personally by people close to them, and for those who choose to enter the criminal justice system, by how the criminal justice system responds."

If you have not kept silent about your assault, and if you are not getting the support you need from family or friends, it's not because your experience doesn't warrant their concern. It may be that they need help to confront their own feelings and fears and learn how to deal with them. But please don't let your loved ones' guilt, shame, misunderstanding, or simple awkward silence affect your recovery. And if you have been a silent victim, know that you only have to keep your secret as long as you want to.

Some people can get through it on their own. But for others, there are rape crisis centers where you can meet other survivors of sexual assault—people who've been there and know what you're going through. If you feel uncomfortable contacting someone face-to-face or by phone, as a first step there is a vast array of resources available on the internet—Web sites for national organizations established for victims that can provide general information and refer you to local support. Or just start in your phone book. We'll talk more about survivor support in the next chapter.

Just as no one deserves to be assaulted, no one needs to go through the process of reclaiming her life alone. God bless you and those who make the journey with you.

CHAPTER SEVEN

KATIE'S STORY

"I'm sorry you have to belong to a group like this. I'm sorry you qualify for a group like this. But I'm glad that you've come together to help each other through caring and sharing. And everything that I know about homicide, I learned from a homicide survivor."

These are the words Carroll Ann Ellis uses to open the biweekly meeting of the homicide support group in Fairfax County, Virginia, outside of Washington, D.C. The term *homicide survivor* may appear, at first, to be an oxymoron; by definition of the crime, the victim does not survive. Yet this seeming contradiction highlights what is probably the simplest and, at the same time, most profound concept in the entire field of criminology and law enforcement: Each crime, no matter how specifically directed at a single individual, leaves many victims and many deep scars. And murder, or any form of homicide—the taking of a human life by another human being—leaves the most victims and the deepest scars of all.

Carroll Ellis is director of the Victim-Witness Unit, which is within the Criminal Investigations Bureau of the Fairfax County Police Department. Tall and attractive, with a striking bearing and commanding presence, Carroll would seem at first glance to be the proverbial fish out of water—a civilian in a police world, a woman in a man's world, a black in a white suburban world. And yet many people credit her with making it possible for them to continue their lives. Paradoxically, she has a deep and robust laugh, which comes easily, as if bearing witness to all the tragedy she has seen has made her value more preciously moments of levity and humor.

She can also be sardonic, as when describing the banality of people who just don't understand: "How do you balance your life with the woman next door whose tulips just aren't as brilliant as they were last year? You just say to them, 'This is what I do' or 'Let me tell you what *my* day was like.' We call that 'slapping them around a little bit,' and it can be fun because of the reaction you know you're going to get."

But Carroll's real concern is with the people who *do* understand, who can't help but understand because of what they have had to endure.

Jack and Trudy Collins lost their beautiful, blond, nineteen-year-old daughter, Suzanne, to a vicious sexual predator in July of 1985. It was a life and a case we recounted in detail in *Journey into Darkness:* how the spunky and adventurous young woman enlisted in the Marine Corps, excelled and proved herself throughout the rigorous basic training at Parris Island, South Carolina, then went to the Memphis Naval Air Station outside Millington, Tennessee, for avionics training, with the hope of becoming among the first women Marine aviators. Late in the evening of July 11, 1985, while jogging alone on the base, Suzanne Collins was attacked, beaten, abducted, horribly sexually tortured, and murdered in a public park in Millington by Sedley Alley, a twenty-nine-year-old, six-foot-four, 220-pound laborer for an air-conditioning installation company whose wife was enlisted personnel on the naval base. Alley is currently on Tennessee's death row, where he has been for more than a decade as his seemingly endless appeals churn through the system.

After I worked on the prosecutorial phase of the case and meeting and spending time with the Collinses during the trial, we became good friends. They also became dedicated advocates for victims' rights, speaking around the country, including at congressional committees and the FBI Academy. At the time of the murder, Jack, a retired foreign service officer, and Trudy lived in Fairfax County, which was where Suzanne and her brother, Stephen, had gone to high school. The Collinses were there at the beginning of the homicide-victim support program in 1990 and 1991, and what they have to say about Carroll Ellis and her staff is typical of the reactions I've heard.

"It may sound somewhat trite these days, but Carroll shows true compassion and empathy," Jack comments. "She was a marvelous guide for us through the jungle of emotions we were all dealing with. It's strange, but after a while, our hearts went out to her. Here we were unburdening ourselves of this incredible pain, and Carroll would go home from these sessions taking all of our pain on herself. And you can't pay a person enough to make her want to do this kind of work. What she did was strictly out of love for all of us."

"She let us shed any guilt we might have felt about being angry," states Trudy Collins. "We had been feeling not only was there no light at the end of the tunnel, but no end of the tunnel. She urged us to express ourselves, so we were no longer bottled up, no longer buried under a rockslide of grief and sorrow with no way out."

Adds Jack, "There was never a moment of awkwardness with Carroll, no hesitation. She's become a member of the family."

Carroll feels the same way. "I have learned more from those people than I've learned from any other experience that I know of. I've learned how to live because of these people. I learned about true courage. And I've learned what real strength is and what real guts are all about, because these people go on. For others who would say, 'Get over it, stop bellyaching and quit whining,' they haven't a clue, because these survivors get up every morning of their lives and they shower and they get dressed and they go out and, as the expression goes, they take on the world. But they take on the world with such a heavy heart and such a burden to their lives that most people who have not experienced it have no idea. You simply don't take a shower and wash it away. It doesn't go away."

To look through the files of the Victim-Witness Unit, to read through their newsletter, to attend one of their support groups, is to be confronted by the enormity of evil, by what one human being is capable of doing to another. But also of what other human beings are capable of doing to say, "We acknowledge your pain. We can't make it go away, but at least we want to respond to it. We want to try to do something for you, and for that vague concept of justice, which is so hard to define or fully achieve but which is at the basis of everything we need to be to live in a society. Because if we're serious about our constitutional rights, the most basic of which are life, liberty, and the pursuit of happiness, then we must acknowledge the impossibility of all three without the concomitant pursuit of justice."

The job descriptions of the members of the Victim-Witness Unit are as varied and changing as the needs of the individuals they serve. At the heart of the issue for most, though, is that vague and often elusive quest for justice, however they define the term.

"I think when people first come to the criminal justice system as innocents—the very first time having become victims—they do have a reasonable expectation that there will be justice . . . until they get involved in this cumbersome, complex process and begin to realize that there are so many pitfalls and so many tentacles and so many 'ifs,' they become skeptical. They become frightened and they feel betrayed because things don't run smoothly, and sometimes there is no justice."

The Victim-Witness Unit is set up to be the friend and advocate of victims and survivors, whatever it takes. An equally important function is to prepare witnesses for the experience of trial testimony. It's a hugely positive trend that is definitely on the upswing around the country, and we should not be satisfied until every jurisdiction has such an effective unit. Another significant aspect of the program in Fairfax County, Virginia, is that unlike many around the country that are tied in to the district attorney's office, Ellis's unit is a creature of the police department. The reason this is such a fundamental consideration is that it allows victim coordinators to become involved literally as soon as the first officer on the scene calls in and the detectives arrive to begin investigating and interviewing potential witnesses. In the case of a rape or murder, this can often prevent or minimize major problems down the line, both in terms of the emotional well-being of survivors and willing, well-prepared witnesses who have had the system demystified for them and are not as afraid of what they might face.

Carroll Ellis's closest associate in the unit, as well as one of her best friends in life, is victim coordinator Sandra S. Witt, universally known as Sandy. At a first meeting, she might seem in many ways to be Carroll's opposite number. They are both mothers—Carroll of a son in college, Sandy of two young daughters and a son. But Sandy— younger, shorter, white, and a faster, more intense, admittedly opinionated talker—is a pretty, former Air Force brat whose family ended up in the area for high school. She stayed through college and a degree in criminal justice at the George Mason University in Fairfax, with the intention of becoming a parole officer. Instead, she became an intelligence analyst for the Drug Enforcement Administration. She heard about the Fairfax Victim-Witness Unit, thought it sounded interesting, and signed on.

Carroll comes from a more traditional background, the daughter of a carpenter-cabinetmaker father and a schoolteacher and reading-specialist mother. She was born in New Orleans and lived for a while in New York City while her mother cared for Carroll's grandmother, who was dying of cancer. Then, in search of work, her family moved to what is now the tough urban community of Gary, Indiana. But in those days, she reminisced, "It was middle America, straight out of *Leave It to Beaver.*"

She majored in psychology at Central State University in Ohio. "My master's degree is in psychology and counseling from Marymount University. But I always believed that I could help people and make a difference. It was something that I was always drawn to. I grew up in a time and an era and in a family where it was very important to give something back. There was always volunteer work through scouting, Sunday school, church efforts, civic organizations. My parents were involved in those kind of activities, and it just was the natural thing that I would also care about community and family and people in general."

Before coming to Virginia, Carroll was a social worker in Chicago, a probation officer in San Francisco and then just over the Golden Gate in Marin County, a teacher in Germany, and a volunteer worker with domestic-violence victims. Her husband, Claude, is a retired Army colonel, now the head of his own firm, and she has two brothers. Her older brother is a former high school principal who is now a college professor, and her younger brother is a television news anchorman in Detroit.

Neither background, however, prepared Carroll or Sandy for what they would face in their work.

They both began within a month of each other in 1990, hired by the director, Joyce Williams. The unit, then known as the Victim-Witness Assistance Program, or V-WAP, was just getting off the ground, having been in existence since 1986. County and police officials thought it sounded like a good idea, but no one quite knew what to do with it. One of the main defined functions was to provide escorts to court and baby-sitting service to mothers who had no place to leave their kids on trial days.

"We were shortcutting and dead-ending people without extending counseling services and reaching out beyond and looking at what we could do to expand services and resources," Carroll recalls. "How can we meet the unbelievable needs that we were finding out there? Essentially, what we were passing off was ourselves as baby-sitters—which we didn't qualify to do, because we weren't licensed to provide child care, but were doing it anyway, while one of us would take a mother to court and sit there and hold her hand or keep her apprised of the docket, upcoming hearings, and provide support throughout the trial. I couldn't spend my life doing that. That wasn't enough for me. And that's why I knew that some changes had to be made. You've got to make assessments, then go in and provide services and tailor them specifically to the needs you find. You've got to go face-to-face with people and bring them in. Over a period of time, we began to change the unit."

The first thing they tried to get across was that their work could not be quantified by time. Sandy says, "We'd get questions like, 'Why did you spend an entire hour with that family just to explain our services?' And the answer is, 'Because you have to! I might have to spend twenty hours with them if that's what it takes.' That's a lot of what Carroll taught me, of how to spend the quality time with the clients that we're working with. *Getting in the moment with people.* Really understanding what their experience is all about. I don't see how any victim-service program can be effective without understanding the victim's experience to some extent, without getting in the moment with those people."

Just as our studies show that predatory offenders have a particular triggering experience that moves their obsession beyond the realm of perverse fantasy and into reality, it's also true that many of the good people on the other side can point to a specific trigger that turned their vague ideas into concrete reality. For Sandy Witt, it was coming in contact with the mother of a college freshman by the name of Meredith Mergler.

"It's so hard to look back because my whole understanding is so different now than what it was then," Sandy says. "But I tell you, I can sit here and close my eyes and remember certain victims or discussions I had with certain people and feelings that I had of being handicapped because there was nothing else I had to offer them. And one of those I remember is this lady, Mary Alice Mergler. Mary Alice's daughter, Meredith, was murdered down at Virginia Tech, where she was a student. She was missing for sixteen months before they found her body in the bottom of a well about twenty miles from campus. She was murdered by a guy named John David Lafon, who's now been convicted.

"Mary Alice used to call down to the detectives every Tuesday, and then she would call me. And she would be on the phone with me for hours and hours. But what was going on then was that I would get off the phone with her, and a second later the next person would call and it would be another homicide case. And it would be very much the same conversation that I had just had. And I was getting into a rut, of having these days where I was coming in and I was on the phone with people—maybe three clients a day. They were talking to me because they needed so much. I was starting to realize that I didn't have a proper understanding of the enormity of what's been left behind. All of those crime victims had really specific, special reactions and needs. And you have to understand each one of them before you can really get in there with people and help."

In the late fall of 1990, the crisis hit for Sandy and Carroll. And that crisis began them on the journey that ultimately led to one of the model victims' programs in the country.

"I was supposed to be working the homicides and Carroll was supposed to be working rapes and child sex cases," Sandy explains. "And suddenly we got hit with a whole slew of homicide cases in a row. Like five of them in about three weeks. That was when Destiny's case hit."

Destiny's case.

Even today, there is a peculiar haunting cadence to the words around the Victim-Witness Unit offices—as if they have the power, which they do, to conjure up both the unbelievable depths of horror of which some human beings are capable . . . and the soaring heroic heights to which some other human beings may ascend in the everyday conduct of their lives.

"That's the one case that started me on the path," says Carroll.

On September 17, 1990, she and Sandy had been with the unit about three months when they got word of the most horrific crime they had ever heard of. Destiny Ann Souza, known as Dee, eight years old, dark-blond-haired, and cute as a button, was found by her thirty-one-year-old pregnant mother, Kathleen, known to everyone as Katie. Destiny had been beaten to death in the basement of the town house she and her mother shared in the Newington Forest section of Fairfax County.

Seven years later, Katie sits with her new husband, Steven Hanley, retired as a sergeant major after twenty-eight years in the Marine Corps, in the living room of another town house in adjoining Loudoun County, remembering those horrible events with a clarity and courage that is almost transfixing. The room itself is an arrangement of poignant images: a stained-glass panel of Shakespeare's "Seven Ages of Man," a replica of Degas's statuette of a little girl ballerina. Then there are the toys: Winnie the Pooh and Barney and a bike with training wheels. The animals belong to two-year-old Casey, the bike to six-year-old Tyler, born months after his sister's death. Studio-quality portraits of Dee and Katie—a beautiful child and a beautiful mother—hang on the wall above the staircase.

Katie Souza was a single mother, divorced from Destiny's father. She was an acquisition analyst for TRW, where she still works. Destiny, a responsible girl who had just started the third grade, who was as much concerned with taking care of her mother as in being cared for by her, would come home after school, let herself in, go to the bathroom, then immediately call Katie at work. On the afternoon of September 17, Katie received no such call. She then called the house, but got no answer. She let some time go by and called again, but still nothing.

"I went to my boss and said, 'Something's not right there. I have to go home.'"

"Hey, by all means, go," he replied.

"So I get home and I think I unlocked the door, or it was unlocked—I'm not really sure. And I go upstairs because I hear the TV is on. I see her book bag there, but the key's not there attached to the book bag as it should be. I see that she had started her homework, she'd taken off her school clothes, hung them up on the outside of the closet door. Then I went into my bedroom, and I'm noticing that there's a drawer open in my nightstand and a drawer open in my chest of drawers, with stuff hanging from it and down on the floor."

Katie went back downstairs and called the school secretary, Cynda Roberts, to ask if Destiny had missed the school bus.

"I'm talking to Cynda, and all of a sudden I looked over my left shoulder and there was this light coming from the basement. I said, 'Cynda, let me call you back.' Then I went down the stairs, rounded the corner, and looked down. And she's lying right there; I mean, I could barely get by her."

The basement had been outfitted with a sofa, love seat, television, and two dressers, where Katie's sister, Rebecca Hall, known as Becky, and her boyfriend, Rob Miller, had been staying until recently. Almost trancelike, Katie did not notice that paneling had been broken, lights had been smashed, and the blood on the floor and furniture. She was moving as if in slow motion.

Destiny was dressed in a T-shirt, shorts, and tennis shoes. She was lying on her side, facing toward the dressers.

"I rolled her over, her hair was a mess, and I saw her left eye was black-and-blue and bulged out. And blood was coming out of her mouth. I started slapping her on either side of her cheeks, yelling, 'Destiny, come on, come to!'"

But nothing happened. Katie ran upstairs and called 911. The emergency operator led her through CPR while help was dispatched.

"I went running back downstairs and opened up her mouth. There was a hole in her teeth like a perfect circle. I started doing CPR, but I didn't know if I was doing it right; all I was hearing was gurgling. I lifted her shirt up to see if her chest rose as I blew in, and it was all blotchy brown under her skin, and I realized she had internal bleeding."

The rescue squad arrived, barreled down the basement stairs, and brought Destiny up where they could work on her. They put in IV lines and a breathing apparatus. As they took her out on the front lawn, then to the helicopter that would medevac her to Fairfax Hospital, Katie didn't even realize she had Destiny's blood on her mouth from her efforts to breathe life into her daughter.

"I just kept saying, 'You know, I hope she comes to. When she does, we'll find out who did this to her and I'll take care of it.'"

But Destiny never did come to.

"I'm sorry to have to tell you this . . . ," the doctor said bleakly.

"We go into this room; it's like a viewing room—a small table and lamp and a bed up against the wall. A police officer standing guard. They had a sheet up to her neck and her hands were resting on top, wrapped in plastic bags. They wouldn't allow me to get too close. I felt like I was in a funeral home already. Nobody would let me alone with her."

In shock, Katie let herself be carried along on the tide of confusion and grief.

"Some friends from work decided that I had to come stay with them, that I should not be home alone. So they took over my life and had me stay at their place, helped me arrange the funeral. I had other people from work coming over to help me pick out the dress and stuff."

But before she could even leave the hospital, she received an even greater shock.

The detectives took her aside to ask questions. For reasons Katie did not at first comprehend, they all seemed to center around the significance of the basement as the murder site.

"Why would Destiny have been down in the basement?" one of the detectives asked.

"She wouldn't have been," Katie replied. "She hated the basement."

Not only that, the basement door was kept locked and Destiny couldn't have gotten in on her own because the handle didn't work. But the investigators kept hearkening back to the significance of the basement.

"And I said, 'Look, you know what it is? A couple of weeks ago my sister, Becky, and her boyfriend lived down there. That's the only significance of the basement. What are you getting at here?'"

Later that night, the police called Katie at her friends' house and told her they had arrested Becky's boyfriend, Rob Miller, at a nearby McDonald's restaurant where he had just begun working, on charges of murdering Destiny.

Katie couldn't believe it. Becky had dominated that relationship. Katie thought Rob was so wimpy she couldn't imagine him hurting anyone. She had even had to referee in disagreements that sprang up between Rob and Becky, since he didn't seem capable of standing up to someone his own age.

But homicide detective William "Bill" Whildin knew that the suspect list for this particular crime would be extremely limited. "Homicide investigations open quickly," Whildin explains. "We try to keep it focused. In this case, it looked like it wasn't a stranger; it was someone she knew. So then you say, 'Well, who was it?' It wasn't Katie. Was it Katie's sister? It could have been, but we didn't think so—too violent, too much of a physical aspect. So then you get to Rob.

"There are certain types of murders and there are certain ways people are killed, and they give you clues," Whildin observes. "This type of homicide, it was an overkill from the very beginning. It was brutal. The girl was killed and just smashed in every part of her body. Now, either he went into some rage because of something she said to him, or there was something else more to it that put him in a rage.

"He was really disheveled that night. He looked almost a little confused, like he had a lot on his mind. But he wasn't drunk and he didn't appear to be on any narcotics or anything. You could see he was nervous. You could see he was hiding something. He started off by saying he didn't know anything about it, but then once we pressured him, I think that he felt relieved he could just say it was an accident, and if we would buy that, then he wouldn't be in as much trouble as he was convinced he was going to be in."

Before long, Whildin and fellow detective Thomas J. Lyons would have a confession. Rob had returned to the house and apparently gotten into an argument with Destiny. He said she was "being smart" with him and "mouthing off." He had picked up a wooden jewelry box and struck her with it. He was afraid she'd tell her mother and knew he had to somehow keep her quiet.

"After I hit her," Miller told the detectives, "something had to be done."

But hitting her hard enough with this box to do serious injury? There had to be more to the story. "And that's what I was trying to determine," says Whildin. "Why would he do it? So she mouthed off to him, maybe he would have slapped her for it and maybe slapped her again. But it was more than that, and that's what we were trying to get out."

Sandy Witt began calling Katie Souza within days of Destiny's funeral, to offer whatever services or comfort she could. She tried calling several times each day, but never got any response, perhaps because Katie was still with her friends. Then Carroll Ellis gave it a try and happened to get through to her.

Carroll introduced herself, then said, "I'm sorry, I've heard the disturbing news and I can't tell you how sorry I am that your daughter has been murdered. I'm from the Victim-Witness Unit. We're within the police department and our role is to provide supportive services to you. And I'd like to be able to come over and talk with you if I may."

Katie agreed and Carroll made an appointment to visit her at her friends' house in Vienna, which was across the county from Katie's own home, but near police headquarters in Fairfax City.

"When I saw her, she looked like a young Candice Bergen," Carroll remembers. "A beautiful blonde with deep green eyes, very athletic-looking. She was in the home alone and she was about four months pregnant by a man with whom she was no longer associated. I walked in and she opened her arms to me, and I believe that this was the moment of my actually walking into this business, with no return, because she made me feel her pain. It was so apparent; it was hanging in that room. You could see it . . . feel it . . . taste it . . . smell it. It was there. Death was there. She cried and cried. And once that was over, we sat down together. Her grief was so overwhelming, you couldn't help being touched by the pain she was experiencing and the fact that there was no need for words. It was like, 'Welcome to my world,' and I had no choice other than to be a part of her world."

Tears still come to Carroll's eyes as she recalls that first meeting with Katie. "All of my professional reserve or veneer—gone . . . gone . . . gone. Because my job was to be there to provide professional services, and what do you say, what do you do, how do you do it, in the face of someone whose only child has been beaten to death? This is a little girl. This is an eight-year-old child who was beaten to death. Where do you even begin to make sense of that or to put that together?"

Katie told Carroll that she wanted to see the crime-scene and autopsy photos of Destiny. She wanted to see the medical examiner's report on what had actually happened to her. Carroll was determined to do for her anything she requested, but asked her if she was sure about this, that seeing that material could be even more upsetting.

"She said to me, 'I want to see everything. This is my daughter. Nothing worse can happen to me. The worst thing that can ever happen to me has already happened.'

"And then I remember her telling me how she went to the mortuary in the days before the funeral and she insisted on seeing her child's body. And she went over every inch of that little girl's body because it was her baby and because she wanted to see and she wanted to know how she had been hurt and where she had been hurt. I can conjure up a vision of that even to this day, in terms of the pietà, Christ and Mary and going to the tomb, and the wrapping of the wounds and the pierce in the side. I still see in my mind this Madonna with child in this private moment, seeing her child's wounds with her own eyes."

The funeral home was called Money and King, a well-established and respected one right on the main street of Vienna. They had strongly resisted Katie's request and tried to talk her out of it, offering the excuse that they had just received the body and hadn't had time to prepare it yet. Her friend Richard, the husband of the friend she was staying with, also urged her not to go through with it.

"Don't tell me what I can and cannot handle," Katie snapped. "I want to see her. Bring her out."

So they wheeled out the naked body, covered only in a sheet, from the refrigerated storage where it was being kept and into a viewing room for Katie.

"I wanted to see what was done to her," Katie says.

With the funeral director standing next to her and Richard standing back behind her in case she needed him, Katie began examining Dee's body, inch by inch.

"We went from head to toe. And the funeral director told me that there was a barrette that had been lodged in her skull. He showed me her ear, he showed me her teeth and her mouth and all the bruising. I looked at her fingernails. He didn't want me bringing the sheet down, afraid of what I'd see. And I said, 'I don't care what I'll see. I have to know.'

"So I pulled the sheet down. And the thing that amazed me the most was when I got down to the arches of her feet. I said to myself, 'My God, how in the world could he have bruised the arches of her feet?' Because she had had sneakers on. What in the world could he have done? And I was just amazed by it."

From his own perspective, Bill Whildin confirms everything Katie saw and felt that day. "At the medical examiner's office, we couldn't figure out what the little dot-dot-dot dot-dot-dot marking was on her head. And it was where the plastic barrette she was wearing had been driven with such force that it crushed down into her skull, leaving those indentations.

"At the crime scene, over on the wall where the light switch was, there was a portion of the wall that was broken in—pushed in. And it had a little yellow mark on it. And we couldn't figure out at first what the yellow mark was from. Destiny was doing her homework and she had put the yellow Number Two pencil behind her ear. And he had picked her up and threw her into the wall. Her head went into that wall. And that little yellow Number Two pencil left an impression in the drywall. We put that together.

"How do you summarize for a jury or a judge the violence that he did?" Whildin poses. "How do you summarize in words the emotions that Katie had when she came home and found her daughter lying there? Those are the things that I physically see. I can close my eyes and see that, it leaves such a lasting impression."

Katie stayed with Destiny's body in that room in the funeral home for about forty-five minutes, trying to understand, trying to take the little girl's pain onto herself.

Days later, Carroll sat with her, enduring her chain-smoking and seeming addiction to diet Pepsi, just listening.

"She was very, very persistent," Katie says. "If she hadn't have been, I wouldn't be here today."

To begin with, Carroll just listened. Then she asked Katie what she wanted, and after Katie told her about her visit to the funeral home, Katie said she wanted to see the autopsy report, to talk to the emergency room doctor, to know, step by agonizing step, exactly what had happened. Had Dee cried out for her? Had she ever regained consciousness? Where had she actually died—in the basement or in the emergency room or on the trip between the two? All the individual nuances; she just had to know as much as she could from whoever might have information or clues.

"Are you sure?" Carroll asked quietly.

Katie was sure. So Carroll made it happen. She called the medical examiner, who expressed predictable skepticism at the request. "This is a very determined person," Carroll explained, "and this is how she processes information. This is what's going to help her."

Katie recalls that the resulting session was probably emotionally harder on the doctor than it was on her. "I was in shock. For me, basically, it was as if I was dealing with another individual. But this was the way I had to get through it."

There was a lot to get through and no obvious way to do it. "I went to Carroll and I said, 'There's no place for me to go. There are no experts out there on how to deal with people like me.' There were no experts out there to help the survivors get through it. There were no experts out there to help the siblings or the children of the people who had been hurt or killed."

So Carroll Ellis became an expert.

Katie and Carroll saw a lot of each other in the weeks and months that followed. "I could call her day or night," says Katie. "We walked through the system together. She saw my outlook and what I needed to get me through it, and she's now experienced other survivors' needs and knows that everyone's different. And when I approach new people that are now going through it, I say to them that whatever they're feeling is valid and they've got to deal with that."

Katie was shocked and appalled to find out what many victims come to realize—that she had little, if any, official standing in the system. "I called the prosecutor and asked him when he wanted to talk to me. He said, 'Why do we need to talk? This is a case of Robert Miller against the state.' If I had it to do over again, I think I'd hire my own lawyer to look out for Destiny's interests—to protect the integrity of the system."

Carroll admits she was driven, too: "I took it home and I involved my entire family at that point. At that time my son was in high school. I couldn't sleep and my husband, Claude, became very much aware of what I was going through. I kept thinking, 'If I'm not in there providing this help and doing something, who will?' She had my beeper number; she had my home telephone number. I was there for her anytime she needed to call. She was a smoker, she still is, and we had hard and fast rules about smoking in the police cars. But I let her smoke in the car, because for me, it was, whatever gets you through the night. If that puff on that cigarette is going to give you some kind of comfort and relief, then smoke on."

One of Carroll's primary concerns was to make sure that Katie received proper medical care. She was four months pregnant and Carroll became worried that, along with all the cigarettes and caffeine from the diet Pepsi, Katie wasn't sleeping, eating, or gaining weight. And as their relationship developed, as Carroll accompanied her to various doctors' appointments and counseling sessions and legal interviews, Carroll did become bolder in trying to tell Katie how to take care of herself. For her part, Katie says that two things saved her life that year, curbed her impulses toward self-destructive behavior. One was the knowledge that if she destroyed herself, she would be killing her unborn child. The other was Carroll's intervention in her life, and she readily acknowledges that the two were related.

"I know that if I had not been pregnant when my daughter died, I probably would have been in the bars every single night. I know that I would have ended up in the gutters or I would have committed suicide. I know that's what would have happened to me."

It was at least in part the realization of what her behavior would have meant that saved her life. "Rather than my own health or safety, I was more afraid that if I killed myself, what made me any better than Rob Miller? I would have been killing my own baby, and God would have looked down on me for that."

"We had quite a bit of arm wrestling back and forth on various issues," Carroll admits. "During those days, she was priority in my caseload, so that whatever was going on, when Katie called, everything stopped because I believed that she needed that kind of protection and service from me."

Carroll spent hours just listening to Katie talk about Destiny: about her joys of being a mother and her frustrations over Destiny's lifelong struggle with a learning disability that made it difficult for her, despite her intelligence, to read and write. *Destiny* was not a name Katie selected capriciously or happened on by chance. She had had nine miscarriages, and when this little baby survived, she considered it a gift from God, the reason she now understood she had been put on earth. Even now she is grateful for the eight years they got to spend together.

Among the issues Carroll helped Katie sort out was her sense of guilt at not being there at the moment her child needed her most. This is a common reaction among parents of violent crime victims. "I should have been there," Katie kept saying. "I just absolutely felt horrible that she had to go through the pain that she went through and that I wasn't there to protect her. And if I had come home while it was going on, he'd have been the one lying in the morgue, because there would have been no stopping me!"

Throughout the process, Carroll had to face her own reactions to the horror she was seeing. "That was another big issue for Sandy and me, that we always avoided saying 'I understand" and 'I know.' Because unless you've been through it yourself, you *can't* really know or understand, but I felt some of it. And that was that the aftermath of homicide was something very, very different from the reaction to any other kind of death experience. It was shocking. It was sudden. It was unnecessary and uncalled for. It was unjust. It was as though there were no place else to go, no way to hide. It was the end of something very important in her life—stability, normalcy, call it what you will. But her life would never be the same again and I knew that. I knew that as sure as I was sitting there."

It would be difficult to imagine a sadder or more traumatic scenario. As the mother of one of Destiny's schoolmates said, "Destiny did everything that you tell your children to do. She didn't let a stranger into the house. She came right home after school. It's the worst possible situation to try and explain to your children. They don't understand how this could happen to one of their own."

Katie showed Carroll photos of Destiny lying in her coffin, photos that would eventually become part of the victim impact statement. Despite advice against it, Katie had insisted on an open casket at the funeral, and the body was positioned so that most of the damage did not show. She told Carroll of her discussions with the principal of Destiny's school over whether her classmates should be allowed or encouraged to attend the funeral. Katie firmly stated her opinion that, like adults, children mourn and handle grief in individual ways, and that, therefore, those who wanted to come would be welcomed, and those who were uncomfortable about it should be allowed to say good-bye in their own way. She asked the parents of those who did want to attend to let them come up to the casket, but first to explain that Dee would not look exactly the same as when they had last seen her: that her face would be a little fatter, that there would be some black-and-blue marks around one eye and on her arm; and that if they wanted to touch her, that was fine, but that they should probably touch her cheek, because Katie knew it would feel the most lifelike to them. And if there was anything they wanted to bring her, Dee would like that very much, too. By the time the casket was finally closed for good, it was completely packed with gifts and mementos. "Stuffed the whole way up around her," Katie remembered, "so that the only thing that was showing was her face."

She reminisced, "I remember Destiny always coming to me and saying, 'Mommy, so-and-so—he's picking on me,' or, 'He lifted my shirt up,' or, 'He pulled my hair,' or this, that, or the other thing. And I'd say, 'Dee, that's because you're beautiful and they like you. That's just a first- or second-grader's way of showing you. They don't even know they like you; they just do it.' And when I saw all those little boys at the funeral, just crying their eyes out, I said to Dee, 'I told you so. I told you that these little boys liked you a lot. Do you believe me now?'"

Principal Robert Holderbaum and his school reacted sensitively and impressively, arranging counseling for both students and parents. It was an agonizing time for area parents in general. The community was still reeling from the murder of ten-year-old Rosie Gordon and the disappearance of five-year-old Melissa Brannen, both of whose cases my unit worked on. As their own memorial, Destiny's classmates insisted that her desk remain unoccupied for the rest of the school year.

Carroll and Sandy committed themselves to making sure there was a place in the system for each victim to turn to, whenever and for whatever that victim felt he or she needed. "With one victim, we may spend five minutes in a phone call," Sandy comments, "and somebody else we may spend literally hundreds and hundreds of hours. It's very complicated when you're looking for funding and you're trying to explain to people who don't understand that it's a very long, complicated process to provide assistance to victims. You can't really come up with an agreeable definition of what success is in this business, or what mental health or mental stability is after something like this has happened.

"The goal is to stabilize people and get them to a *new* normal level of functioning, and try to explain to them that whole process, that they're not going to be who they were before. And part of being able to do that is getting them to deal with what's happened to them. The thing is that you don't quit. You continue going with them as long as it takes."

Of course, this is never a simple process, nor was it with Katie. "Not from day one was anything simple with Katie Souza," Carroll declares. "And it still isn't. She's still a compelling person in terms of all the complexities in her life, that generally date back to her early childhood. Lots of old baggage has come to the forefront."

Once Katie had gotten beyond her initial need to know, as well as dealing with the guilt, there still remained the overwhelming task of making sense out of the tragedy, which meant nothing less than confronting the entire weight of her own harrowing past and her relationship with her family. It was a task that easily could have destroyed a weaker or less determined person.

Katie grew up in Lancaster, Pennsylvania. "We moved from place to place to place. My mother was an alcoholic, and she was in and out of mental hospitals, trying to commit suicide. So we lived out of our suitcases, from grandmother to grandmother to aunt, to wherever. I never had a sense of belonging. I came from a household where we had sexual, physical, and emotional abuse."

She was about six when her father left for the first time, though he came back from time to time, such as during her mother's hospitalizations. She reports that she and her brother, Ted, were never close with him, but that the younger sister, Becky, always seemed his favorite. When Katie was in ninth grade, she told her father she wanted to leave. He told her to go ahead. Despite her mother's neglect, Katie, the middle child, tried to keep the household functioning, making sure her brother and sister were properly clothed and fed, carrying heavy bags eight blocks from the grocery store, cooking, cleaning, doing the washing. By the time she was sixteen, she couldn't take it anymore and left home. By that time, Ted, who was two years older, had already been in a foster home.

She eventually went to live with her aunt, her mother's sister, and for the first time in her life felt a sense of normalcy and belonging. It was there that she was given the first birthday party she had ever had.

She joined the Air Force after high school, where she became a maintenance analyst, then developed a specialty in contracts. She stayed in the service ten and a half years altogether. While she was stationed overseas, she married a man, but quickly fell back into feelings of emotional neglect that continually tore at the fragile fabric of her self-esteem and confidence.

But the question we ask over and over again in these situations is, Why would a woman who has been through this before voluntarily place herself back in the same role? After all, she was bright and extremely attractive, with a solid job and a promising future. Katie's answer is realistic and insightful:

"It's something that happens and you don't even realize it. You're a magnet. It's like going into a bar and having a billboard on your back that says, 'I'm a victim.' I mean, of all the men, that's what I was attracted to. I could say that my ex-husband was good-looking. He had control of the situation. He was very possessive of me and, hey, gee, nobody else was when I was growing up, or fought for me. And I mistook that for the wrong thing."

Ultimately, Katie decided she needed to leave the marriage. They had been living in California and she picked up, took her daughter, and moved to upstate New York to be as far away from him as possible. Then she moved to Virginia.

Unfortunately, not everyone has Katie Souza's courage.

The one thing that fulfilled her life, that gave her meaning and direction, was being a mother, and Destiny was a delightful infant and child. Within months of her birth, Destiny's father was largely out of the picture, so it was just the two of them. They did everything together—ice-skating, roller-skating, camping. They camped out overnight in the parking lot of the Capital Center arena to get good seats for a Janet Jackson concert. When Destiny was still a baby, wherever Katie went outside of work, she took her along. She didn't like the idea of baby-sitters and felt that if there were places she couldn't take Dee, she didn't need to be there herself. It was the first time in Katie's life that she'd ever experienced unconditional love.

Destiny was two years old when Katie finalized her divorce. The child came up behind her when she found out, patted her on the back, and said, "Don't worry, Mommy. It'll be okay. I'll take care of you." Katie's heart nearly broke when she heard that. It was as if the little girl had become her, desperately trying to hold a family together and take care of everyone else.

Destiny adored Katie's brother, Ted. As soon as they would get to his house, Dee would run upstairs with him to his computer room. Katie didn't discourage the bond, but it made her extremely nervous. She remembered him sexually abusing her as a child. So whenever Dee was with Uncle Ted, Katie would nervously keep her eyes and ears peeled for any sign. When they would leave, she would question the child at length to see if anything had happened. Destiny was confused by the questioning. Eventually Katie told her the truth. As far as she could tell, nothing ever happened between Ted and Dee. But because of her own background, Katie was always nervous and cautious with Destiny, as well as other young children, around men.

"I was strict with her and wouldn't let her run around the neighborhood by herself because I was always afraid that some of the things that happened to me might happen to her. I was pretty possessive, and as she got older, I tried to explain why."

In the early-morning hours of a Friday in May of 1990, Ted was talking to his wife on the telephone. Ted had a history of drug and alcohol abuse, and they were having problems in the marriage, too. She heard the sound of a shotgun blast. But he'd missed. So he tried again. This time he was successful. He'd tried to kill himself the week before with pills, but had failed. When he woke up, he'd been extremely upset about it.

He was supposed to come down to visit Katie the day he killed himself, to try to straighten things out. She had done her share of drugs, and now that she'd cleaned up her act, she thought she wanted to try to help him. She couldn't bear to tell Destiny that her beloved uncle Ted had taken his own life, so she just said that he had died. Dee insisted on going to the funeral, where she held her head in her hands and cried inconsolably.

Meanwhile, Katie's sister, Becky Hall, was living up in Pennsylvania. She'd been discharged from the Navy. She had a child and was on welfare. Katie had spent most of her life trying to protect Becky, and she didn't feel she could stop now. In fact, when things had been really bad when they were children, either she or Ted would try to get Becky out of the house so she wouldn't know what was going on. Now, Becky had a baby girl of her own, and Katie wanted to get her sister off welfare, so she invited her and the baby to come live with her in Virginia until they could get back on their feet.

Katie also knew from her own experience and reactions how easy it would be for Becky to fall in with the wrong person. She'd already been married twice, and some of the men in her life had been ex-cons. In Katie's words, "After a while I began asking her, 'What are you doing, waiting outside the jail for these guys to come out on probation?' And she laughed, because it was true—anything from robbery to people that were doing bombs. She hung out with bikers, she was in a very bad group."

This was already the second time that Katie had come up to get Becky, and after talking to her mother, Katie was concerned about Becky's emotional state.

About two and a half months after Becky and the baby moved in with Katie and Destiny, Becky got a call from her boyfriend in Pennsylvania, Robert Miller. He told her he was having trouble up there and couldn't take it any longer; he had to get out of town for a while; he needed a break. As she listened, Becky repeated the litany of complaints to her older sister.

Katie said to her, "You act like you're waiting for me to make a decision or something."

Becky replied, "Well, yeah. He's on the phone."

Katie had met the tall, thin, wavy-blond-haired Miller a couple of times, and he was always polite and deferential to her, even calling her "ma'am." Her impression was that Rob was a step up from some of the men Becky had been associated with. So Katie said okay, he could move in. "Because I pretty much gave in to whatever Becky wanted.

Becky and Rob lived in the basement of Katie's rented town house in Newington. This was summertime. Becky had a job, but Rob didn't, so Katie asked him if he would look after Destiny during the day until she went back to school in the fall. The polite and quiet Rob had no problem with that. Meanwhile, Katie had arranged day care for Stephanie.

The arrangement seemed to work. Rob took Dee places like the swimming pool during the day and they became pals. Katie actually felt sorry for him because of the nasty way she thought Becky was treating him. In fact, Katie thought it had driven him to drink.

When he was supposed to be baby-sitting, she would come home to find a bottle of liquor broken on the floor and Rob cleaning it up, explaining that he or Destiny had knocked it over. Only after this happened several times did she realize that it was his way of covering the fact that he was actually emptying the bottles, drink by drink. Then he stopped trying to hide it. Several times she came home to find Rob passed out and Destiny fending for herself. Katie attributed the drinking to the aggravation he was getting from Becky and tried to talk to her about it several times, but she wouldn't listen.

As we discussed in *Journey into Darkness,* we've got to teach our children—of whatever age—to be "profilers" of adult behavior so they can know whom to trust and whom not to trust, whom to listen to and whom to rely on if they get lost or need any kind of help or assistance. If a child has confidence in these skills, and the security of knowing that his or her parents and other important adults are supportive and understanding, then that child is far less likely to become a victim.

As Katie perceived it at the time, the main conflict was with her sister. If they got into an argument at the dinner table, Becky would storm off, taking Stephanie with her. Becky would borrow the car, which Katie would let her do, but then remind her, "Okay, but Dee needs to go to ballet practice," or, "She has gymnastics. If you need the car for work, can you do me a favor and go take her there?" Katie later found out Becky wasn't always taking Dee.

Ultimately, Katie came to believe that Becky felt that Destiny had replaced her in her older sister's love and affections and that Katie's love of Destiny represented an abandonment of her, an abandonment similar to when Katie had left home as a teenager, then joined the Air Force, thereby—in Becky's mind—not taking care of her any longer.

"At one point my sister came downstairs when we were living in the town house and she was all upset. I said, 'What's wrong with you?'

"She answered, 'You've got to do something about your daughter. I'm sick and tired of what she's been doing.'

"I said, 'What are you talking about?'

"And she said, 'Well, come here.'

"So she takes me up to the bathroom. She had just gotten finished with a shower and shows me where it says, 'I hate you Becky,' on the mirror. Well, my sister apparently did not know Dee could barely write, and when she wrote, it was backward and upside down. So when I looked at the mirror and saw this plain writing, I started laughing. And she said, 'What's so funny?'

"Destiny had been right at my side the whole time and I told Becky, 'You're setting my daughter up. It would just please you to no end if you stood there and watched me spank her.'

"'Well, after what she did . . . ,' Becky said.

"I said, 'But you don't understand something.' And then I told her.

"She said, 'Are you calling me a liar?'

"I said, 'Yeah.' And so things got worse."

The strain continued to build all the way around. Eventually, after a petty argument between the two sisters, Becky decided she'd had enough and announced that she and Stephanie and Rob were clearing out.

For his part, Rob said he was happy where he was, but it was Katie's impression that Becky called the shots in that relationship. They went to the next-door neighbors and told her Katie had kicked them out. The neighbors, with whom Katie is still friends even though both have moved, kindly agreed to take in Becky and Rob. During the next several days, Rob would return to Katie's house frequently to pick up various belongings and supplies. Katie told him to take whatever they needed. In the next few days they moved again, this time into Becky's boss's house, about two miles away.

On the morning of September 17, 1990, Katie awoke with severe stomach cramps, which she attributed to her pregnancy. She was in the bathroom when the phone rang. Destiny answered it and told her mother it was Rob.

"Well, tell him I'm in the bathroom right now," she replied. "Can he call back in ten minutes?" He said okay.

An hour went by. She had to get into the shower so she wouldn't be late for work. Sure enough, that was when Rob called back. Destiny came running into the bathroom and said to Katie through the shower curtain, "Mommy, Rob called again. He said that you're not supposed to hide from him anymore or he's gonna make you pay for it. Quit avoiding him or he's gonna make you pay for it."

What was that all about? Katie wondered. He had never talked to her that way before. He couldn't stand up to an adult; anyway, they'd never had a disagreement. In a way, they were emotional allies when things got rough with her sister. Katie couldn't figure it out.

That morning represents Katie's final memory of Destiny.

"While I was doing my hair, she was doing her hair at the same time. And I was telling her how gorgeous she was and how she was going to make all the little boys jealous at school, and she was giggling. And I gave her a kiss and she went downstairs and I said, 'Don't forget your book bag.' She said, 'I won't,' and I said, 'I love you,' and she said, 'I love you, too, Mommy.' And she left.

"And that was the one memory that I guess I hold on to the most: the giggle . . . when we were doing our hair together. And that it wasn't a bad morning or a rushed morning. It was a good morning."

When the police told her Rob was the killer, just hours after Destiny had died, Katie was still in shock. Her first reaction was disbelief. Det. Bill Whildin, now an investigating social worker with the county's Child Protective Services, came to visit her. He kept pressing, sensitively but firmly, on anything she could tell him about the relationship between Rob and Becky.

"What are you getting at?" she wanted to know.

Whildin explains, "Things were adding up. There was something about Rob. His relationship with his girlfriend was a little funny; not the best. That's giving us little clues about his personality."

In his confession, Miller told police that Destiny had found him in the house and threatened to tell her mom. He couldn't let that happen. He admitted picking up a heavy jewelry box and hitting her on the side of the head with it as she was walking away. Whildin questioned him about whether he had been sexually involved with Destiny and posed a scenario that had her finally threatening to tell her mother about his molestation or improper attention—if true, would be why he had killed her with such rage.

"When we confronted him with the possible sexual end of it, he became very agitated, very upset, very angry that we would even say that," Whildin recalls. "When I said, 'Rob, I think you sexually molested her and she was going to tell her mother that day,' he jumped. He stood right up, right out of that chair. So he was real agitated and he wouldn't sit still and he wouldn't let us keep prodding that way." He denied the allegation.

Later, when Katie was cleaning the basement, she found pornographic books wedged into the cushions of the love seat and sofa. She called Whildin, who came by and picked them up from her.

Between the day of the murder and the funeral, Becky did not communicate with Katie.

Despite the tension between them, Katie could hardly believe that she received so little support from her own sister. "And that was it for me. As far as I was concerned, she couldn't have been my sister."

Becky moved back to Pennsylvania, where their father saw to her needs. When Katie asked him why he hadn't looked out for her the same way, she remembers him saying, "You didn't need me. You've always been the strong one. She needs me because she's always been the weaker one."

"And I said, 'Well, even the ones who have their heads on straight still need love, need to know you're there.' "

Katie's mother lived another two years after Destiny's death. She went to the hospital one evening with pneumonia and died, alone, the next morning. "My mother and I weren't very close," Katie comments. "I often asked myself, if we had met on the street, would she ever have been my friend? But I did vow to myself that if she ever became ill or couldn't make it, that I would take her in and take care of her. So there wasn't hatred for my mother; there were no feelings. And it felt bad because I could go up to my aunt and give her a hug and a kiss, and my poor mother would be standing there and that would make me feel so guilty, but I just couldn't go over and do it. But had I known she was ill, I might have gone up there. No one told me."

Before her mother's death, Katie had continued to maintain some relationship with her, but she couldn't do that with her father. "He felt sorry for Becky, the fact that she had to raise a daughter on her own now. He specifically said that to me, and I said, 'Well, at least she has a daughter to raise.'

"In fact, probably about three or four days after it happened, he said I had to get on with my life, to put this behind me. He still to this day cannot understand why I'm having emotional ups and downs.

"I met with my dad a couple of times and I said to myself, 'I can't be part of this family anymore.' So I shut myself off from that side, except for my aunt, who was the one I had lived with when I was fifteen. To this day, my father doesn't understand . . . never had and probably never will."

Less than a month after Destiny's funeral, Becky filed suit against Katie for Rob Miller's possessions, which she claimed should be valued at about $7,000. Included in the two-page enumeration of "Household Goods Detained at Kathleen S. Souza'a House Without Permission" was one "handmade jewelry box" valued at $20.

Stunned and angry, Katie countersued, stating that Becky and Rob had used her credit cards and checkbook, leaving her $17,000 in debt. Ultimately, she had to file for bankruptcy.

"My father said, 'How can you do this to your sister?'"

The case against Katie was dismissed.

When Katie moved, she refused to give her father or Becky her new address.

The last time she saw Becky was when their mother died. "She acted as if I'd just seen her last week. She was there with another ex-con. She was living with this character."

After the funeral, Becky and Katie had to go back to the house to deal with their mother's possessions. "All I wanted," Katie recalls, "was my mother's books, so I could figure out who she was, because based on what people read, you can kind of figure out something about them."

There were only a few other things she wanted. "Her religious medals, because she had converted to Catholicism when she quit drinking and had changed her life and I knew that was very important to her. From the kitchen, I wanted her cutting board, and the one pan that we used to get hit with all the time."

We asked if that was because it symbolized finally taking control, of not allowing others to beat or abuse her any longer.

She thought about this a moment, then smiled and shook her head. "No, I had just done a lot of cooking with it over the years."

Carroll Ellis and the entire Victim-Witness Unit stood by Katie as Rob Miller's trial approached. The case was highly publicized because of the age and innocence of the victim and the sheer brutality of the crime. This wasn't the kind of thing that was supposed to happen in peaceful, upscale Fairfax County, Virginia. District Attorney Robert Horan said it was the most brutal attack on a child he had seen in his twenty-five years as a prosecutor.

Before the trial began, though, in February 1991, Rob Miller pled guilty. Carroll, Sandy, and Katie all had several theories about this, most having to do with trying to avoid the death penalty.

Katie and Carroll were relieved in one sense, but in another, they felt Destiny had been cheated out of the chance to make her killer pay the ultimate price for his actions. And without a trial, none of the vital answers Katie had sought for her own closure would be forthcoming.

Virginia is one of the states that allows victims or survivors to submit an impact statement to the court prior to sentencing. I think this is a critical step forward in the area of victims' rights. The defense gets to bring up every mitigating factor they can think of, from childhood attention deficit disorder to what a wonderful adult the convicted killer's been (except for that one unfortunate incident, of course). It only stands to reason that the truly innocent party should have the right to tell the court what this person's actions have meant.

Carroll Ellis worked extensively with Katie to craft a proper victim-impact statement. She came over to Katie's house and the two spent long hours getting it in order. One of Carroll's strongest memories of that time was Katie's showing her the photograph of Destiny lying in her coffin before the funeral.

They talked about Katie's relationship with this only child, after waiting through the anguish and disappointment of so many miscarriages. Katie was back living in her own house now, and this was the first time Carroll had been there.

"The house was immaculate," she recalls. "A light, bright place where you would find a single mom and her little eight-year-old daughter living. Katie was then, and is now, the kind of mom who buys marvelous, wonderful things for her kids: the right clothing, the right toys, and lots of them. And everything is always kept perfectly. So here she is in this delightful-looking place, but for the fact that her daughter has been murdered down on the lower level. She took me down there and raised the rug to show me the bloodstains. It was a new experience for me. I wanted to be strong for her and I didn't want to offend her—whatever it was she wanted to show me, to be attentive to it. And I did it."

It was a little later that Carroll realized how serious Katie's emotional condition was at that time.

"She called me one day, and she said she just didn't know what to do. She was never in a position that she didn't know what to do. She was always in total control over what to do and how to do it. And I think saying to me that she was not, that was a key for her—being able to admit that fact to someone and not have that person either condemn her or take advantage of her."

Destiny's father, who was living in California, sent his own victim impact statement. Perhaps most touchingly, so did Destiny's classmates at Newington Forest Elementary School. Katie and Carroll worked with the principal, who felt the school should do something in this extraordinary situation. The children had been grieving, and it was only fair that they should have their say, just like the other victims, that they should have some resolution and closure, too.

In Virginia, victim impact statements are presented in writing. This is fine for some people and some situations, but I would prefer the victim or survivor had the opportunity to stand up in open court and let the full emotional weight of her statement ring forth. In any event, though, Katie came up with an eloquent statement, several pages in length, chronicling her loss and the difference in her life. She included two photographs: Destiny as she had been, full of life and laughter and love, then Destiny in her casket. The effect, to Carroll at least, was devastating. The thrust of the message was "Why?" Why did you kill her? What could she possibly have done to provoke you? Carroll feels that Katie set a standard from which the courts could not retreat.

Fairfax County Circuit Court judge Johanna Fitzpatrick sentenced Robert A. Miller to life in prison for first-degree murder, which in Virginia at the time meant he would be eligible for parole in thirteen years—on July 7, 2003, to be exact. The sentence exceeded the recommended guidelines, which would have called for a maximum of sixty years (which, of course, means a lot less in real life). The judge rejected a defense plea for leniency based on the assertion that Miller had been drinking and therefore had lowered inhibitions. Assuming (which I do not) that Destiny had "mouthed off" to him, how much do a 170-pound man's inhibitions have to be lowered before he'll fracture an eight-year-old girl's skull, rupture her lung and liver, and stomp on her back in an attempt to break her spine? And then tell me whether, regardless of his motive, regardless of his subsequent behavior in prison, you ever want this man near your children. I can tell you I don't want him near mine.

Carroll and Katie were both in the courtroom, and they heard Judge Fitzpatrick cite Katie's moving and powerful impact statement, then turn to the defendant and say that this mother wanted to know why. She asked him directly if he had any response to her. He did not.

On September 17, 1990, an adorable and loving little girl named Destiny "Dee" Souza was found by her mother, Katie, in the basement of their house in Fairfax County, Virginia. She was eight years old and had been beaten to death. Katie's sister's boyfriend, Robert Miller, was convicted of the murder. (Photo by Katie Souza Hanley)

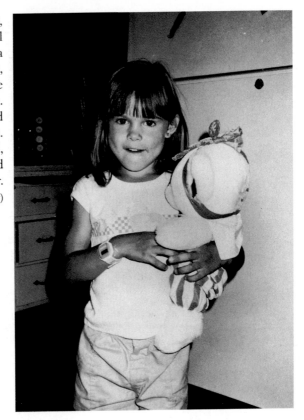

Katie Souza in happier times. Since Dee's death she has struggled heroically to put her life in order and fight for victims' rights. (Photo by Keith Souza)

Carroll Ann Ellis, director of the Fairfax County Police Department Victim-Witness Unit. Many survivors credit her with literally saving their lives.
(Photo by Mark Olshaker)

Sandy Witt, Fairfax County victim coordinator. She says, "There are no time limits in what we do. It's a 24-7-365. Whatever it takes, we'll be there for them."
(Photo by Mark Olshaker)

Stephanie and Jeni Schmidt. Practically from the day she was born, Jeni looked up to and idolized her big sister. At the sentencing hearing of Stephanie's killer—Jeni confronted him with what he had robbed her of.

(Photo by Gene Schmidt)

Stephanie Schmidt was a beautiful young woman, beloved by her family and many, many friends. The quote under her photo in her senior class yearbook said, "A day without laughter is a wasted day."

(Photo by Gene Schmidt)

$1,000.00 REWARD

**FOR INFORMATION LEADING TO THE ARREST OF DONALD GIDEON
WANTED FOR PAROLE VIOLATION
AND QUESTIONING IN THE DISAPPEARANCE OF STEPHANIE SCHMIDT**

Donald R. Gideon

DONALD R. GIDEON

**31 years old
5' 7" 150 LBS**
Hair Color: Brown
Eye Color: Brown
Date of Birth: 2/18/62
Warrant #   37793

Stephanie Schmidt

*Gideon was last seen offering Stephanie a ride in a 1974 faded blue Ford PU
bearing KS FQV-633, from Bootleggers Bar & Grill, Pittsburg, KS.*

IF YOU HAVE ANY INFORMATION, PLEASE CALL
Pittsburg, Kansas Police Department: 1-316-231-1700
Kansas City Crime Commission: 1-816 474-TIPS (Call Collect)

This flyer was widely distributed after Stephanie disappeared and Donald Gideon left town. He turned himself in weeks later in Florida after the case was featured on *America's Most Wanted*. Gideon, who was paroled after serving half his sentence for a previous violent sexual attack, pled guilty to Stephanie's murder and led authorities to her body. (Flyer by Peggy and Gene Schmidt)

The authors visit the Schmidt family at their home in Leawood, Kansas. From left to right: John Douglas, Gene Schmidt, Peggy Schmidt, Jeni Schmidt, Mark Olshaker. (Photo by Carolyn C. Olshaker)

July 6, 1997. Two days after what would have been Stephanie's twenty-fourth birthday, friends and family gathered at the Schmidts' house for a celebration of the Supreme Court victory in *Kansas v. Hendricks,* a case that challenged a key provision in the Stephanie Schmidt Sexual Predator Law. Kansas attorney general Carla Stoval reminisces with Gene, Jeni, and Peggy before cutting the cake. (Photo by Mark Olshaker)

In honor of the Supreme Court decision, Carla Stoval presented the Schmidts with a handmade angel doll with blond curly hair like Stephanie's. The doll is holding a heart, upon which is written the date of the high court's ruling and the phrase "Stephanie Smiled." (Photo by Gene Schmidt)

The pit in the cellar of Gary Heidnik's Philadelphia house where he placed his female victims. On one occasion he filled the pit with water and electrocuted one of them. (Photo courtesy of the Philadelphia Police Department)

Gary Heidnik, bright enough to amass a stock market fortune from his military disability pension, abducted women and kept them as slaves in the basement of his house in Philadelphia. (Corbis-Bettmann)

Theodore "Ted" Bundy,
shortly before his execution
at the Florida State
Penitentiary at Starke.
(Photo courtesy of the FBI)

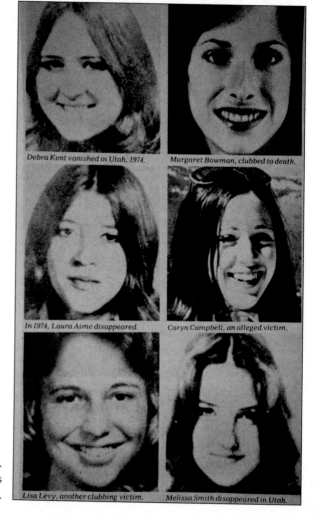

Debra Kent vanished in Utah, 1974.

Margaret Bowman, clubbed to death.

In 1974, Laura Aime disappeared.

Caryn Campbell, an alleged victim.

Lisa Levy, another clubbing victim.

Melissa Smith disappeared in Utah.

Some of Ted Bundy's victims.
His "preference" in victims
is obvious.

Worden's Hardware Store in Plainfield, Wisconsin, where Edward Gein shot Mrs. Bernice Worden before taking her corpse to his farm. (Photo courtesy of the Waushara County, Wisconsin, Sheriff's Department)

The bloody marks on the floor of the store where Mrs. Worden was dragged. (Photo courtesy of the Waushara County, Wisconsin, Sheriff's Department)

Authorities found a hatbox in Gein's farmhouse in which he kept the "face masks" he had fashioned from the skin of some of his victims. (Photo courtesy of the Waushara County, Wisconsin, Sheriff's Department)

Edward Gein, the so-called "Butcher of Plainfield," served as a model for both *Psycho* and *The Silence of the Lambs.* (Corbis-Bettmann)

The last-known picture of Jennifer Levin (far right) taken with two friends at Dorrian's Red Hand on the night of her murder. Note, as Linda Fairstein did, that this photograph shows no bruising or other marks on her neck.
(Photo courtesy of the New York County District Attorney's Office)

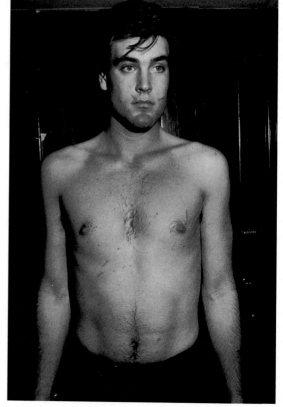

Jennifer Levin's killer, Robert Chambers. This photo shows the scratches and wounds Jennifer made in trying to defend herself from his attack.
(Photo courtesy of the New York County District Attorney's Office)

It is now part of the Victim-Witness Unit's responsibility to track him (he was moved from a Virginia prison to one in Pennsylvania) and keep Katie informed of his progress toward parole. Katie and Carroll will both do whatever they can to see that he is never free to prey on innocent children again.

I wish more judges, mental health professionals, and parole boards understood as well as Katie. I wish fewer of them were strongly swayed by such considerations as "good behavior" in prison, which is relatively meaningless as an indicator of future violence compared to the details of their previous crimes. As we've indicated in this and previous books, a lot of these guys do fairly well in the structured, restrictive prison environment, then pick up where they left off as soon as they're let out. My personal preference for killers like Robert Miller is that they be safely put away six feet underground. Short of that, it is unthinkable to take a chance on letting someone like this out on the street again until he's physically too old to prey on others.

Dr. Stanton Samenow, who is as realistic as anyone I know on the subject, clearly states that there is no hope for a criminal turning himself around until he honestly admits, and believes, that there is a problem with the way he thinks.

I've often said that each violent crime claims many, many victims. Carroll Ellis thinks of it as a rock thrown in the water, with rippling waves that go on and on and finally out into the community as a whole. In the case of Destiny Souza, one of those victims wasn't even alive yet at the time of her death, but the impact upon him was tremendous nonetheless. Tyler was born just days after Rob Miller pleaded guilty to murdering Destiny. This turned out to be an overwhelmingly stressful event for Katie, and she was dismayed that she didn't feel a strong emotional connection with Tyler.

"It was as if I was a little girl who'd had a doll for eight years. That doll got lost and they tried to replace it with another one. That's the way I felt when he was born. When they brought him to me the first time and put him on my belly, it felt like an alien. I said, 'Get him off of me.'

"I could not bond with him. It took probably a year and a half or two years. I took care of his physical and medical needs, but I kept an emotional distance."

In spite of this, Katie was self-objective enough to acknowledge that had the baby been a girl, it would have been even worse for her. It would have seemed a cosmic joke, of one baby replacing another. Katie worked hard to overcome her problems regarding the new arrival, and she readily confesses that attending to his needs made her realize that she had to go on living and functioning, that she couldn't give in to despair.

Having worked through those agonizing months, though, Katie realized that Tyler could give her something she hadn't had since that one horrible afternoon: joy.

One year after the murder, on September 17, 1991, Katie went back to Newington Forest Elementary for a memorial service in honor of Destiny. With six-month-old Tyler smiling in Katie's arms, a plaque was dedicated and helium-filled balloons, each with a message written on it by a student or teacher, were released into the air.

Katie also wrote a poem, published in the fall 1992 issue of the Victim-Witness Unit newsletter, *Sharing and Caring,* which sums up a mother's love and loss as well as anything I've seen. It is entitled, simply, "Destiny."

The most I miss you is late at night
When I want you there to hold me tight.
I think of your tender finger tips
And when you reach my soul with your loving kiss.

Then as I retire myself to bed
And as on my pillow I lay my head,
I turn away and start to cry,
And I think of you when you said goodbye.
Knowing we're apart just makes me blue;
Every time I close my eyes I think of you.

So sweetheart since you have gone away,
I have thought of you both night and day.
To me you will always be a part
And I will always hold you in my heart.

I love you for all eternity . . . Mom

No homicide victim story ever has a happy ending. Katie knows she will never be as she was. But this story is at least happier than might have seemed possible a few years before. Katie is remarried to a sensitive, devoted, and caring husband. She has a handsome, charming son and a lovely baby daughter named Casey.

Finally, she felt ready and comfortable with a serious male relationship. "A lot of it has to do with self-esteem," she observes. "I would never allow myself to get serious because I was afraid of getting right back into the old pattern again. And until I lived with me and was happy with me and was independent and knew that I didn't need anybody or anything else other than my child, and felt strong that way, I wouldn't repeat the pattern. You've got to figure out who you are first."

Katie Hanley finally knows who she is. So does Steven Hanley. In fact, he probably understands his wife as well as anyone—her needs, her strengths, her fears. Even though they haven't been married long, they've known each other for many years. They met when Steven was stationed with Katie's uncle. He used to baby-sit for Destiny and his sons—one two years older and the other two years younger—played with her. He was overseas when she was killed. Katie's uncle called to tell him.

"When I first met Katie," he states, "one of the things that struck me was her independence. I mean, she didn't need anybody; she didn't need anything. She always had everything together. But after we got together, I realized it was a wall and that was for everybody else. Inside the wall, there's a very hurt kid who lives there and doesn't understand why things occur the way they do."

Steven has two teenaged sons from his first marriage, and when they fight or argue with each other or pick on six-year-old Tyler, as normal teenagers do, Katie has trouble dealing with it because of her own background—because her experience tells her, despite Steven's reassurance, that any kind of argument leads to serious violence and long-term emotional hurt.

Tyler is proud of his progress in karate. As of this writing, he had just graduated from novice blue belt to upper blue belt, and he expects to work all the way up to black belt. At one class, he was named Student of the Month. In the car on the way home, Katie was singing his praises, telling him how much he had accomplished. But when they got home, she thought he just "didn't seem right."

She asked him, "What's wrong, honey?"—at which point he broke down and cried.

"Mommy," he said, "I wish Dee Dee was there. I'm so mad at Rob for what he did, that he took my sister away from me."

Though she had never actively talked about Destiny around Tyler, Katie had always sensed that the spirit of the sister he'd never met was always with him. As soon as he could speak, he would point to pictures of Destiny on the wall and say, "Dee Dee."

"My son is very, very sensitive and always brings her up."

"Honey, she's there," she told him. "Through all the important times of your life and through all the sad times. Through times that we couldn't even possibly imagine." She fears, though, as Tyler gets older, Dee will become less his spiritual companion and more simply a vague memory of loss. "The other day he said to me, 'I wish she could've been here for this.'"

Katie reports that Tyler is just as good and loving with his baby sister, Casey, as she's sure Dee would have been with him.

In the months after the funeral, Katie visited Destiny's grave frequently. She hated to think of her little girl lying in the cold winter ground, wanted to be there with her and was concerned that the grass be cut regularly and the area well-tended. She was touched when Dee's school friends would visit. Sometimes they would leave flowers or even some of their trick-or-treat candy. One little boy who remembered Dee's rock collection left a colorful rock on which he'd painted, "I miss you."

But Katie hasn't been back to the grave in the last four years, even though she planned to and even has a collection of things she's meant to bring out. She even bought the plot right next to Destiny's so that she could be with her daughter forever.

She's not sure exactly why she's been unable to go back, but she thinks it has something to do with a dawning realization for her that that is not really where Destiny is. "And basically, anything I've ever had to say to her, I've said before I got there."

Everybody deals with it in his or her own way.

Katie faces her emotional challenges with the rare heroism she has faced all of the other adversities life has thrown her way. "I have my good days and my bad days. It takes me by surprise when they happen, and sometimes I don't realize it's sneaking up on me until it does, and then it's like I should have seen it coming," she says.

Perhaps as a result, Katie has few specific memories of Destiny, which she thinks may be a way of protecting her system from emotional overload. "There are a lot of things I just don't know about her that I wish I did," she says. "But in another way, I'm kind of glad that I don't because it would probably eat at me even more."

She pauses, then adds, "I just wish I did have a moment with her again."

Carroll was always amazed that despite Katie's volatile personality and controlling manner, she displayed little raw anger, even toward God.

Katie replied, "Some people are very angry and have a lot of hatred, blame God, what have you. But how can I be angry or hate Him? This was not God's doing; this was Rob Miller's doing."

In prison, Miller actually put Katie on his visitors list, thinking she would want to come to see him. But she was not interested.

"If I ever did meet up with Rob," she says, "and I've thought a lot about having a meeting, the only question I would ask is, 'Why?'"

CHAPTER EIGHT

FOR THE VICTIMS

"Why?" is a question they grapple with over and over in the meetings of the homicide survivors support group.

It is one that is ultimately unanswerable in any way that makes human, moral sense, and one that has so many other questions agonizingly buried within it, perhaps the most sublime of which is, Where was God the day Meredith Mergler was murdered . . . or Dana Ireland . . . or Robin Anderson . . . or Tommy Neu . . . or Rosie Gordon . . . or Laurene Johnson . . . or Suzanne Collins . . . or Destiny Souza . . . or any of the others—so many others that the enumeration of their names would require many pages of this text.

Various members or veterans of the group might offer differing possibilities. Jack Collins, whose brave and lovely nineteen-year-old daughter died at the hands of one of the most horrifying and sadistic murderers I have ever had to deal with, is a devoutly religious man. He would tell you that the most significant gift God has given man is free will, and that once it is given, He cannot, or chooses not to, take it away. This is not an indication of indifference, Jack believes; God is always present, even at the moments of horror. He was there weeping and agonizing over Suzanne's pain. Yet He cannot stay the hand or stop the bullet. But then, afterward, He is forever available as a source of empathy, compassion, and strength. Jack, a tireless champion of the victims' rights movement and advocate of judicial reform, will also tell you that even with his strong faith, he and his wife, Trudy, have ached in sadness for Suzanne's loss every single day since July of 1985.

Carroll Ellis would say, simply, "I'm angry with God from time to time, and I would love to talk to Him about it. Because if you're talking to a mother whose eight-year-old is gone because of mankind's inhumanity to man, I need an answer that lasts a little longer and does a little more than what I've come up with."

What both Jack's and Carroll's beliefs underscore for me, though, is that power of choice. We can debate and deliberate about where it came from, but all of my research with repeat offenders has led me to the same conclusion about the free will to commit—or not to commit—violent crime.

The Fairfax survivors support group was begun a year after Destiny Souza's murder, as a means of providing a "safe and trusting place where survivors are free to express their feelings."

Katie Souza, who had been serving as a consultant to the unit in defining what their long-range plans should be, was one of the first members. Carroll remembers, "She had a specific agenda of what she wanted to get from the group, in terms of something that would help her toward resolution of all of her feelings of anger and guilt at not being able to do anything for her daughter."

So the group became a journey of sorts, with every member searching for individual goals, but with the support and companionship of other people who truly could know what they were going through. There was no attempt at one-upmanship; they each came to the table with the realization, as Carroll put it, that "nobody's ice is any colder than anybody else's. It isn't a matter of, it's worse if you lose a child or a parent or a spouse or whomever. Death is death, and homicide is homicide. I don't care who was murdered. It doesn't matter; it shouldn't have happened."

The other two original consultants were Mary Alice Mergler and Lucy Bhatia, whose eighteen-year-old son, Vinay, the second of five boys, was murdered on September 9, 1989, while voluntarily working an extra late shift at his job. His killer, George Wiggins, now known as Raheed Muhammed, was convicted of first-degree murder in March of 1990 and sentenced to life in prison. He will be eligible for parole in July of 2002.

"What we effectively said to these three," Carroll recalls, "was, 'Listen, we're strangers in a strange land. We don't know what we're dealing with. Teach us. Tell us what it is that we need to know in order to be able to help you. And if backing off or closing the door and getting out of here is what will help you most, we'll do that, too. But right now, tell us what we need to know to be effective.' And they did.

That's why I say that everything I know about homicide, I learned from a homicide survivor."

What she and Sandy learned specifically was that there was no special place, no focus, no gathering point, for victims of homicide to come and openly talk with each other about how they felt, and that people in the mental health professions needed to realize how lacking they were in the provisions of special services. As Carroll put it, "Homicide was an underserved crime category."

The people who were doing anything at that point were largely the families themselves. Roberta Roper, whose daughter Stephanie had been horribly murdered, was spearheading the effort in Maryland and created the Stephanie Roper Foundation. Lula Redmond was doing something similar in Florida, and we were seeing the emergence of effective groups such as Parents of Murdered Children. But the official, system response was generally slow and hesitant.

Carroll's own chief goal is to bring comfort and solace to her clients, who also become her friends. But she would be the first to admit that she seldom maintains a professional detachment from the subject of violent crime. She understands well that it can destroy the spirit, even when it doesn't destroy the body. Her anger, her outrage, come through loud and clear, as when she speaks about a recent case that has come to her:

"A typical situation," she tells us, "we had a rape the other weekend of a forty-six-year-old Vietnamese woman. She's raised two kids, she's got a job, she's got a town house. She's a good citizen; she's living her life. Then somebody came into her town house in the middle of the night and put a knife to her throat and raped her and sodomized her. That angers me. That makes me so mad. He had no right! How dare he! She didn't invite him in, she didn't ask for it, she didn't want it. And how dare he do that to her? I'm angered as a citizen. I'm angered as a woman. I'm angered because what are we doing with the likes of him and how can we catch him and what can we do with him once we do catch him? You can't imagine the times that we've spent together as a staff conjuring up things to do to those people who would hurt all the good people. Part of your reaction comes out as raw anger and part of it comes out as hurt. You're hurt so deeply because other people are hurt and afraid and vulnerable, and you know that, but for the grace of God, there go I."

But her most righteous indignation is reserved for homicide, for those monsters who feel it is their right to take the gift of another life simply because they feel like it.

"We had the case of a man who was murdered down there at the University of Virginia. He was a doctor. He was working on some kind of cure for a disease and was well into his research. He had gone down for a game or something, was eating in one of those little restaurants right in front of the campus, and some guy who'd had a bad day with his live-in, or whomever he was associated with, came in and took his life. And I can't get over the insult of that: that this was a worthless good-for-nothing who did that because he was having a bad day! He had no job. He had nothing. But yet he took the life of a man who was making a difference for so many people in this world. Senseless, unnecessary, cruel . . . for a man of that stature who had made such a contribution to lose his life at the hands of a worthless son of a gun. He insulted this human being by deciding on his own that he would take this life. He made the decision that he would do this. And what he's left behind is unbelievable. It's a miserable way to leave this life, at the hands of this worthless person."

The support group began meeting in 1991, to deal with, in Carroll's words, "the complicated grief associated with homicide." Those present could vent, rage, cry, or laugh, all in the presence of other people who shared a similar journey. In fact, the only guideline was not to be rude or intentionally hurtful.

Additionally, they also invited as guests the people members would be dealing with as they worked their way through the system—police officers, district attorneys (known as Commonwealth attorneys in Virginia), judges, and even defense attorneys. At the request of some of the members, they once even invited a psychic.

Having guests was a two-way street. The visitors could give group members some sense of what they did, and they, in turn, would get some education and appreciation for what victims and survivors went through. To gain trust, and to make sure everyone was candid and straightforward, it was also established early on that everything said in the meetings would be considered privileged and confidential.

From the outset, Carroll and Sandy strove to deal with both the immediate and long-range problems of the group members—how were they feeling, what were they going through, how were they dealing with their lives on a day-to-day basis? But what they missed by doing this—and it is so obvious to them in retrospect—was that this was not the main concern of the members themselves. As Carroll and Sandy were focused on them and their needs, they were focused on their murdered loved one: what he or she went through, how afraid were they, what were they thinking and feeling. All of the things Katie Souza had taught them.

"What we realized," Sandy admits, "is that we were dealing with the aftermath of the homicide. The survivors needed to deal with the event itself before they could go on and integrate it into their lives." As a result, they started facing the same hard, cruel issues that Katie had taken upon herself. In a sense, it is the same type of victimology that my colleagues and I practice when we develop a profile or analyze a particular crime: What actually happened between victim and offender at the scene? And neither we as profilers nor the survivors themselves can move on until we deal with that issue.

Since the beginning, the group has met on alternate Wednesdays. As a result, alternate Thursdays can be bad days for Carroll and Sandy. "You're exhausted, drained from the meeting," Sandy explains, "and a lot of times what happens is the people who don't want to talk Wednesday night, they'll call you first thing the next morning."

And inevitably, the stress and anguish take their toll. "I don't think you can live around this kind of pain and not suffer some yourself," says Sandy. "Part of my coping mechanism—because I don't want to go home and talk to my husband and make him completely insane—is that we spend a great deal of time debriefing each other."

Sandy's husband, Paul, has always been extremely supportive of her work and accommodating of her schedule in terms of taking care of the children. When the homicide support group first started, roughly around the time their daughter Emily was born, the sessions would often go well into the night. Sandy notes, "When we got done, when the last person finally dragged him or herself out, we were numb and needed to talk to each other. So we would talk about each case and go over what we could do, and commiserate, and cry, and we really needed that time before we made the trek to our homes and families."

And Sandy adds, "If you're a fake, if you aren't sincere, they'll smell you out in a second."

Carroll calls it "coming from your gut. And that's pretty much how

I view life and how I view the work that we do. And if your gut tells you something—if you feel something so strongly there—then you have to be honest about that and react to your feelings about it."

Carroll and Sandy coined an unofficial slogan for the work of the Victim-Witness Unit, which could work equally well for other aspects of this business: "It's not easy, it's not simple, it's not fun, and it's not for everyone."

By the same token, I can tell you from personal experience as the father of three that you can't be involved with this kind of work without having it affect your perceptions of your own children's safety and well-being. Sandy and Paul have two girls and a boy, ages five to eleven, with the nine-year-old boy in the middle. "On the one hand," she says, "I want them to have the freedom they need to learn to be independent. But seeing what I've seen, it scares the hell out of me. I think that my perceptions of what I'm afraid of change as each one of them gets older and moves into a different area of life."

She admits, "It's hard because I'm very controlling of them, I know, in terms of needing to know where they are and what they're doing, much more so than parents of some of their friends. When I get home, I have to concentrate on stepping back and trying to be a mom and not this person who I am here at work."

It is particularly hard when Sandy thinks of Kimberly Moyer, one of her early, intense cases, though more appropriate words come to mind, such as *client* and *friend*. Kim Moyer's infant son, Christopher, was killed in 1992 by a day care provider. It was June; he would have been a year old in October. Sandy had just come back from maternity leave from her third child a week or so before it happened.

She recalls, "Carroll and I went to see the Moyers at their house up in the mountains. And this young family was about the same age as me and my husband, and all I could remember thinking at the time was, 'These people were doing everything right. They're professional, they waited for children until they could give them the best of life, they moved out here to give their lives a better quality. And all of a sudden . . . they get the worst news that you can ever bring to someone's door.'

"I felt as if Kim brought me to my knees. She was breast-feeding at the time; I was breast-feeding. I would think about how her milk was drying up because of the fact that her baby's been ripped from her. They had had a lot of trouble having children. Then they had a little girl and they hadn't expected to be able to have this son. I'm here with this woman whose baby was killed in day care. And I started to question my own values, like, God, maybe I shouldn't be here. Maybe I should be home with my baby. All of those things started working, and professionally, in my own mind, it was a turning point for me right there. I decided that the only way I could emotionally cope with continuing to work in this job was to really begin to understand that this is a calling, but that it was also a job, that I had to learn to turn it off when I went home."

With that self-examination, Sandy was able to commit emotionally for, as she puts it, the long haul. Kim Moyer has channeled her grief into impressive good works, including child advocacy and lobbying for compensation for victims. But like the others, her agony can never be fully erased. She wrote a searing and poignant letter to the editor in Christopher's name, which was printed in the fall 1992 issue of *Sharing and Caring,* the survivors group newsletter. It talks about what would have been and what now will not, all from the perspective of her murdered child. And without a doubt, Kim Moyer speaks for every bereaved parent.

I want to stress the importance of the victim-witness unit being part of the police department—specifically the Criminal Investigations Bureau, or CIB—rather than the district attorney's office, as these units are in many other jurisdictions that even have them. Carroll calls it "being in the belly of the whale." In jurisdictions where the unit is part of the DA's office, it can be weeks or months—in fact, sometimes not until the case is ready to go to trial—before the victim or witness has any contact with a coordinator or counselor. By then, the emotional wounds may be even deeper, at least in part because there has been no one to try to heal them.

What makes the Fairfax County program work so effectively, and why it should be a model for other programs throughout the country, is the human relationships. That's what it's all about—between police and the unit, between the unit and their clients, between the unit members themselves.

As Carroll notes, "If we've had any success and if there is anything novel in our program, it has developed out of the relationship that Sandy and I had shared in working together, and the shared commitment to what we've done, over seven years, really. Dealing with homicide, it was something very special that happened to us, that evolved between us, and we clung together. It was as though we had entered a dark forest and we were groping along together."

The strength of the unit was, and is, that it could give each survivor the individualized service, attention, and support that he or she needed. But when the homicide survivors support group began, Carroll and Sandy soon learned that some things were common virtually throughout the group membership, and Katie Souza's experience and observations turned out to be accurate guidelines to this.

They wanted to know how, when, and why. Specifically, they all wanted to know about the last harrowing moments of their loved one's life. Sometimes those answers are forthcoming. Sometimes there is no way to obtain them. And when that is the case, the support group has to deal with that, as well.

But they also learned something profound in the process. As Carroll put it, "I have since come to learn that homicide survivors are so much stronger than I am and most people are—that they don't need that kind of smothering and protection. They need information so that they can process it and go forth and do what it is that they must do as they move along the path."

While no one's ice is any colder than anyone else's, there are many nuances that come under discussion in group meetings. For example, how is it different if a child has been murdered than an eighty-five-year-old man or woman? This was something the group had to get past, and they did.

"They had to," Sandy comments. "I mean, that's part of the education process, too. You've earned a place at the table because of this horrible thing that's happened. But beyond that, if it's your brother or my father or her daughter, we're all grieving and we're all on a journey."

When Carroll and Sandy began the homicide victims support group, most of the killings in the county were relationship murders: people in the same family, or who otherwise knew each other. Sometimes these were domestic arguments that got out of control. Sometimes they were just as horrifyingly tragic in a different way. Sandy had to deal with a Cambodian woman refugee married to a Vietnamese man. She had been a survivor of one of the notorious Cambodian political prison camps. She was mentally unstable, delusional, kept hearing voices. She strangled her two children, ages two and four—

and left them in a closet. Later, she hanged herself in the hospital mental ward where she'd been taken.

Another woman was stabbed thirteen times on her doorstep by her estranged husband. She had a court restraining order against him. We'll talk about the issues surrounding restraining orders in the next chapter.

As time went on, while the percentage of acquaintance and domestic homicides remained high in the county, they were seeing a lot of different types of scenarios, including the particularly fearsome stranger murders. As the Washington suburbs became more culturally diverse, so did the patterns of homicide.

Regardless of whether the murder has been committed by an acquaintance, a family member, or a total stranger, one of the most painful things for Carroll and Sandy to experience—in fact, for all of the "veterans" of the support group—was the acute pain they saw and felt just about anytime someone new came in.

Through their own experience and the writing and research of other experts, the victim coordinators came to recognize several distinct psychological stages following victimization.

The first is referred to as the *impact* stage, also as the shock, acute, or immediate stage. This can last for hours, days, or even weeks, during which the victim is still reeling from the event, feeling numb or paralyzed, unable to make decisions. He or she will be extremely vulnerable and easily confused, possibly extremely lonely, helpless, or in despair. Coping with anything challenging may seem all but impossible. Some people manifest this stage by feelings of withdrawal or detachment. Others may refuse to believe what has happened. Still others will react understandably with out-and-out horror.

The *recoil* stage will be associated with anger, severe depression, resentment, even denial. Great mood swings are likely and can be triggered by small and insignificant stressors. There may be uncontrollable crying, feelings of rejection, loss of identity or self-respect. The victim can experience insomnia or nightmares, or a cycling between the two. She may go back and forth between blaming others and blaming herself for what has happened to her loved one, which means she is likely to take on the baggage of unwarranted guilt. And this is the time when the big question of "Why?" is likely to keep intruding into a corner of every waking moment.

A poignant example from Sandy:

"Kim Moyer called me one day about four months after her son was murdered. She had pulled over on the side of the road and she was sobbing, that crying we all know so well. That place where people, I think, are really raging inside, grappling with the decision about whether they're going to continue to live or whether they're just going to die. She said to me, 'It just finally hit me. The reality just finally hit me that he's gone.' Who else could she call to be able to say that? And I had to be able to stay on the line and understand her and be able to tell her that she wasn't going crazy."

But because of people like Sandy Witt, the individual struggle and journey does continue.

The *resolution* stage is the one in which the victim-survivor gains some perspective and begins to integrate the experience into daily life. He realizes he and life will never be the same as they were before, but they can both go forward. The anger, the rage, the fear, might still be there, but they can, with time, diminish in intensity, and emotional energy can now be directed toward other activities and other people. I have found with some of the most heroic survivors—Jack and Trudy Collins and Katie Hanley certainly among them—that their murdered loved one becomes a virtual presence in their daily lives; they can talk about her and think about her for what she was and what she still means to them, not merely as an unfortunate murder victim. Katie talks to her son, Tyler, about Destiny and how happy she would have been participating in all the events of his life. Jack and Trudy have taken to going out to dinner each year to celebrate Suzanne's birthday. This final phase may be years in coming, and it may take more years to evolve. The important point is that the loved one is never forgotten, but remembered in a richer and fuller way.

Another way to state it is through the four stages outlined by psychologist William Worden, upon which the group also relies: adjustment to the shock; accepting the reality of the loss; working through or "leaning into" the pain and adjusting to a world where the loved one no longer exists; and finally, bridging the gap back to community.

The message here is a tough but hopeful one: you will forever be changed, but with love and help and courage, you'll be able to deal with it, and your loved one will always be with you and a part of you.

None of this is to suggest that there won't be setbacks along the way and reversions to previous feelings; there probably will be. I know from my own experience how many times I've been out with my kids, say, near a river or in a park and I'll have a flashback to a scene similar to the setting we're in, and I'll visualize what it was like when a body was pulled from the water or taken from under a tree. Imagine how much more intense this feeling must be for the families of victims of these violent crimes. What we're talking about is nothing less than post–traumatic stress disorder, a medical and psychological condition whose manifestations have been well studied in wartime. And as I've said, this is a war, too. We shouldn't be surprised to see similar symptoms.

"It's always so difficult," says Sandy, "to watch it with a new person in the group and to just know I've heard this before and how it has to evolve, to know where she's going, to hear something like, 'It just hurts so much!' or 'Why does it hurt so much?' It's almost a rite of passage you have to go through. But the group will embrace you and help you through it."

And share their own journeys.

John and Louise Ireland were among the first to begin coming to support group meetings, and they still come. They were already into middle age, retired from the Army and living in Springfield, Virginia, when Dana Marie arrived, after a somewhat unexpected pregnancy, on December 12, 1968. Their daughter Sandy was already practically grown.

From the beginning, Dana was a beautiful, special child, sweet and gentle and loving, but with a strong independent streak and capable of standing up for herself when the situation demanded. She had a close and warm relationship with both John and Louise, who took to this second round of parenthood with a newfound enthusiasm and delight. Dana also had many friends and adored animals, often bringing home strays. She released her pet hamster because she couldn't stand to see it caged up. When she got older, she made a habit of stopping her car on the highway if she saw a wounded creature.

Always a good student both at West Springfield High School and then at George Mason University, Dana was also a gifted athlete, into soccer and hiking, surfing and scuba diving. When she got out of college, she began searching for her life's work, which she knew would be an adventure. With her sister, Sandy, whom she idolized, she had traveled throughout the South Pacific and was strongly considering joining the Peace Corps. Everyone who knew Dana described her as a joy.

It was while she and her parents were visiting Sandy and her husband, Jim, for the holidays at their home in Kapoho, Hawaii, that Dana

Ireland died. It was Christmas Eve, 1991. She was cycling along a rural road near Hilo when she was spotted by some men in a car. They ran into her to knock her down, then abducted her, raped her, and when they were finished with her, left her to die along the roadside. She was discovered by a passing motorist, who called for help. It took the ambulance so long to arrive that Dana bled to death from her injuries. She was twenty-three years old.

"John and Louise were living the American dream, and then without warning, these demons came along and their entire world was turned upside down," says Sandy. In fact, they had been model citizens, living the good life after working hard for many years to earn it. Suddenly, though, everything was wrong. Their beloved Dana had died, they were not getting answers as to why, there had been no arrest, and as far as they could tell, not nearly enough was being done in working the case.

So John, in his late sixties, transformed himself for the sake of his daughter and the other innocents like her. He became an activist, an investigator, a lobbyist. He became the modern equivalent of an Old Testament prophet, demanding truth, honor, and justice. His sense of mission was fierce and inspiring. He flew back to Hawaii and made repeated trips after that, all at his own expense, pressuring the media and the police to do something. He secured legal assistance. He filed a suit against the county where the crime had occurred for negligence in not coming to Dana's aid sooner after emergency services were called. He demanded to see the governor, who met with him and heard his grievances. As Sandy says, "He demanded that the case be kept alive."

But John's work and passion went far beyond Dana's case. He lobbied the Hawaiian state legislature for victims' rights and raised the sensibility of the entire state. Among the things he was more or less directly responsible for were items as diverse as the use of victim impact statements in sentencing violent offenders and the installation of emergency telephones at remote locations like the one where Dana was attacked. In Washington, he pursued a similar path to that of his fellow support group member Jack Collins, going up to Capitol Hill, knocking on doors, testifying before Congress on victims' rights legislation, and demanding to be heard. His message was always the same: we desperately need to change our laws. He was one of the key advisers on the Department of Justice–funded project on impact statements, "A Victim's Right to Speak."

At the same time, John and Louise also set up the Dana Ireland Memorial Scholarship Fund at Dana's alma mater, George Mason University, for residents of Virginia or Hawaii who are the children, spouse, or sibling of a homicide victim. It was originally funded with proceeds from the settlement of their civil suit. John, an avid golfer, also staged yearly golf tournaments to benefit the scholarship fund. Like Jack and Trudy Collins's establishment of the Suzanne Marie Collins Perpetual Scholarship for the children of foreign service personnel, as Suzanne herself was, John and Louise's endowment for Dana is a beautiful living memorial to an extraordinary young woman, and the achievements of its recipients will grace Dana's memory long into the future.

But it was in the survivors support group that they felt comfortable venting their true feelings—feelings of grief, of anger, of frustration by the appalling lack of closure. Only in the past month since we write this has there finally been an indictment in the case, and I believe that would not have happened at all had it not been for John's efforts. Victims themselves should not have to be responsible for this, but the effort and dedication put forth by John and Louise and an increasing number of others across the country signal a new and, to my mind, positive trend. Victims are demanding justice and saying, in effect, "We are not vigilantes; we will not take the law into our own hands. But we will watch you and follow you and help you, and if you do not take our interests to heart, we will hold your feet to the fire and we will not go away."

Perhaps most impressive of all is the Irelands' connection with others in similar situations. Sandy reports that they are always extremely supportive, particularly of "new" people who have just recently experienced the horror. They counsel, they go to trials and hearings with them, they share the power of their consolation and their anger.

And that is one of the things that has impressed us most about this group, and Carroll and Sandy as well. They are, by turns, compassionate, nurturing, spiritual, philosophical, practical. But they have not lost their anger or their outrage. They understand human frailty and human heroism, and regardless of what has happened to them, they have not given up on the notion that if we are to have a civilized society, there are certain absolute standards that we must demand and we must never turn away from them.

The loss represented by this group spans the entire continuum of life, from the Moyers' infant son to Katie Souza's eight-year-old to the

Collinses' nineteen-year-old to the Irelands' young adult, all the way up to Audrey Webb's mother.

Laurene Dekle Johnson was eighty-five when she was stabbed to death in her home in the Buckhead section of Atlanta on May 27, 1991. When Audrey couldn't get her on the phone for several hours, she became concerned and called her mother's neighbor and close friend, Jeanette Cox, who called another neighbor, Nadine Shank. Both Jeanette and Nadine had known Laurene since the 1930s. A third neighbor, Mike Wheeler, and Mrs. Shank found Mrs. Johnson's body on her bathroom floor. Laurene died a year to the day after her husband, John Wesley Johnson, had passed away from a heart attack. At that time, they had been married for sixty-one years.

Police charged twenty-two-year-old Terry Dale Redd, whom Laurene had hired to do yard work, with murder and robbery. He confessed to Atlanta police in early June when confronted with the thumbprint he had left on a vase in the house, as well as other physical evidence. He subsequently pleaded not guilty, claiming his confession was coerced. But after that, another witness emerged who testified how Redd had described to him the same evening how he had committed the crime.

Audrey Webb and her husband, Dick, had both been extremely close to Laurene. They were devastated, overwhelmed by her murder. What kind of monster could stab an eighty-five-year-old woman twenty times?

After repeated delays, trial was finally scheduled for March 1993. The assistant district attorney handling the case assured the Webbs that it was such an open-and-shut case that a guilty verdict was inevitable. As a result, the Webbs feel he was not adequately prepared.

"It was a travesty of incredible ineptitude on his part," they wrote in an open letter to their friends. "He was ill-prepared and yet so arrogant and cocksure he had a guilty verdict in the bag, no matter what happened."

But on Tuesday, March 30, 1993, the Fulton County jury found Redd not guilty. To the Webbs, to Mrs. Cox and Mrs. Shanks, to the prosecutor's office, to the Fairfax Victim-Witness Unit, and to all of the members of the support group who had been following the investigation, the evidence, and the trial so closely, the verdict was an inexplicable shock—nothing short of a revictimization of this gentle lady and her adoring daughter and son-in-law. It seemed, in fact, nothing short of jury nullification of a just and fair outcome to this case.

When one juror granted an interview and said that questions about the confession and whether it had been coerced played a part in the acquittal, Atlanta police chief Eldrin Bell declared, "I'm outraged. The credibility of our homicide squad has not, to my knowledge, ever been placed in question."

Even Redd's attorney, Robert Maxwell, told the *Atlanta Journal and Constitution* that he was "really surprised" at the verdict because the evidence "was overwhelming against him."

Dick Webb wrote an eight-page letter to the prosecutor, expressing his and Audrey's anguish and anger over the result. He cited all the things he and his wife had done to help the case along, including noting the out-of-place decanter on which Redd's fingerprint was found, which became a crucial piece of evidence. And Dick Webb decried all of the mistakes of strategy and oversights he felt the prosecution had made during the trial.

I was not there, so I cannot form an independent judgment of that. But I have reviewed some of the evidence, and whether the jury was confused or simply did not want to convict, it does appear to have been a serious miscarriage of justice. Dealing with the possibility that justice might be miscarried was not something the Fairfax Victim-Witness Unit had spent much time contemplating until the Johnson verdict.

Sandy says, "We were just completely blown away and felt extremely irresponsible in not having sat down with Audrey and saying, 'What do you think you'll feel if this happens?' You have to accept the fact that we don't have a perfect justice system."

As devastated as they were, as deep and pervasive as the pain was, and is, the Webbs did not let this ruin their lives, which are active and full. They continue coming to group meetings, at this point mainly so they can support others who need their guidance and perspective and can learn from their experience. Not only was Audrey's mother a professional at a time when fewer women were, she was also a generous, giving, and loving person, and Audrey and Dick have certainly been honoring her memory by doing the same.

"What we need more of in this country," Dick wrote, "is a clearer vision of what is the truth and what is the reality. The more passion we as a people have for truth, the closer we will come to better justice for defendants and victims and security for society as a whole."

When offenders do admit guilt, or when the admission is thrust upon them by overwhelming evidence and a perceptive jury, another issue can emerge, and that issue is forgiveness. It is one that understandably comes up over and over again in victim-survivor circles. My own view is that, given the individual circumstances, it is sometimes possible to forgive a violent offender. Personally, though, I find it difficult to think of forgiving a murderer. As I stated in *Journey into Darkness,* the only one truly capable of forgiving the killer is the murder victim herself, and by the very nature of the crime, that is not going to happen in this world. Yet forgiveness must be a case-by-case issue and an individual decision. Some survivors may be able to move forward better if they offer it. Others need to see final justice executed before they can even consider it, and I have equal respect for both points of view.

As Carroll says of the group, "This table includes many people who are located at varying places along the road to recovery. Forgiveness may be the way to go for some, but it may not be for others."

Carroll has defined the meaning and purpose of the homicide support group in terms of four initiatives, as she calls them.

"The group allows us to make victims safer. We can't make people absolutely safe; that's a myth, but we can help to make them safer.

"We stress the importance of holding the abuser or murderer accountable for his actions and give people in the group the opportunity to work toward making that happen.

"We work for prevention and protection for people within our communities." The unit makes it clear to victims that they have a legal right to know when someone who has harmed them is about to be released from prison or his legal or correctional status changes in some other way.

"And perhaps most vital of all is that we allow people to come together to talk about how important it is to honor the memory of those loved ones who have gone on, and remember them in a positive and meaningful way. We want to ensure that victims don't die in vain and work together toward efforts to ensure that we never forget the loved one, that we never forget what happened or how it happened, but that we always glorify their memory."

One of the ways this is done is through physical reminders. In some sessions, people are asked to bring in something that belonged to the loved one and talk about it. John and Louise Ireland brought in a tile bearing Dana's handprint as a little girl.

"When he walked in with that," says Carroll, "you could have scraped me off the floor."

Kathleen Spencer, whose young son was beaten to death, brought in a little wooden box with her son's important things in it. "And she went through that box and pulled out every one of those things," Carroll remembers. "They were the last things he had."

I remember visiting Jack and Trudy Collins in their home in North Carolina. Trudy brought out all the family relics—baby albums, photographs, report cards, the works. And then she showed us an envelope containing a lock of Suzanne's wispy golden baby hair from the first time Trudy cut it. And then Jack brought out the black-and-white hat (or cover, in military parlance) that Suzanne had worn so proudly with her Marine dress uniform. The juxtaposition of the two will be forever seared in my memory.

The survivors group session ends with the "feeling round," in which Sandy asks each participant for a one-word description of how they feel. Words you are likely to hear are *sad, happy, hurt, angry, coping, impatient, confused, bewildered.* Carroll says, "My word is almost always *inspired,* because I find tremendous inspiration in the journey these people are making and the courage with which they do it. We find that this final round helps people to go out into the night after what is almost always an extremely emotional and intense session."

As Sandy puts it, "The criminal justice system is not structured for emotions; it's structured for law." It might therefore seem difficult for an emotion-centered group such as the Victim-Witness Unit to fit in with a group of hard-ass detectives, and in a very real sense, it was.

Says Carroll, "Law enforcement is a male-dominated profession, and in order to be a cop it is expected that you will be tough and gung ho and aggressive. The sheer nature of the job itself requires that you be that way. And it's very much like the military, that there are just certain gates that you have to go through and conduct yourself in a certain way."

In other words, they had to earn their place at the table.

"In 1990," Carroll recalls, "we worked with specific detectives on specific cases and we found a mixed bag. We found those people who understood how to use us and used us effectively, and we found others unwilling to use us at all.

"Sandy and I each approached the challenge in our own way. I used my experience and my ability to work with people. I'd be polite and courteous and not intrusive and call up and say, 'This is Carroll Ellis. I have a case and I need some information,' or, 'What can I do to help you?' Eventually it won over some people who responded to that. I've since changed because I have become a little more policelike in my way of dealing with people, and I do that now with confidence as a result of the police experience.

"From the beginning, Sandy came in and demanded, because that's her personality. She's tenacious, and in some instances it worked because police officers looked at her and saw her style and recognized that it was something they could respect. There were others who were offended by that. Where did she get off? She's gutsy and she's elbowing her way to the table and she doesn't have a place here."

But gradually, as the old guard retired and the new generation saw what the unit could do, things turned around.

"When you get hard-core homicide cops calling a civilian woman out to a scene and feeling that you're not going to get in the way and that you're going to be okay, then you've been accepted," says Carroll.

Fairfax County chief of police M. Douglas Scott puts it plainly: "It's their ability to deal with the victims, to set them at ease, that may or may not lead to the ultimate solving of a crime."

He explains, "I think that over time law enforcement has recognized that we need to be conscious of the impact the crime has on the victim, and that not only is it psychological, but also the way that they're dealt with by law enforcement may influence greatly their cooperation in the case. Because the bottom line is, if you are very cynical and if you are very hardened, the victim is going to pick up on that right from the outset and that level of cooperation is going to evaporate.

"I think that at the point that the unit came into the department, there was a void, and it was recognized by the detectives. They had huge caseloads, they were being torn in many directions, and the ability to have somebody else step in and do things like transportation to and from court, witness preparation, housing alternatives, these were things that traditionally the law enforcement officer just would not or could not do. After the unit was established and we began seeing results, then it was a very tight connection, and it has remained so."

If something like this is going to work, though, there has to be an understanding that everyone is working in the same direction and on the same team. I've seen too many investigations go sour when this doesn't happen. "We consider ourselves law enforcement personnel in this unit," Carroll explains. "And one of the important criteria for being a member of this staff is that you understand the police experience and respect it. Now, that understanding doesn't happen immediately unless you've come out of that kind of background, so we place heavy emphasis on staff growing and developing the police experience, which for me is a group of dedicated people who have chosen to do something special with their lives in keeping and protecting the public trust. Unless a new worker in this unit understands how fiercely police officers feel about what it is they do, they'll never make that adjustment. They've got to understand that—that it's very important, all these codes and all these laws and all these protocols that have to be lived with. We've got to walk within the guidelines on everything that we do."

Homicide detective Robert "Bob" Murphy began working with Carroll and the unit when he worked sex crimes. He sees them as advocates for victims and witnesses, representing their interests throughout the system. "They are there for that person. When they started, suddenly we found ourselves with a person we could hand the victim off to while we continued working on the case."

Det. Dick Cline, also in homicide and another veteran of the Sex Crimes Unit, adds, "Before they came along, as a detective you had to wear several different hats, one of which was a social worker's, trying to put the victim at ease and explain the system and get her ready for what she's going to experience. A lot of victims thought they were being victimized again. They've been a very big help to us."

When he has a large case with a lot of witnesses, Cline will use the unit to organize witnesses and get them ready to give statements while he pursues the immediate investigation. Detectives like Dick regard Carroll's team as partners in their investigative work.

One of the most important functions involving any potential witness is preparing him or her for trial. Bob Murphy says that the Victim-Witness Unit has largely been able to take over that function from the detectives, freeing them up to work with the prosecutors in preparing the physical case.

Homicide detective Dennis Harris says, "Communication is the key. Victims want to help themselves, and if you let them know, 'I can't do this without you and so I need your help here,' most times they'll respond to that. Once they understand why things are being done the way they are, they want to help and they'll start working with you that much harder." This is a point Carroll stresses over and over again: victims need, are entitled to, and can process all of the important information about the case.

A member of the unit will go with the victim or survivor to court appearances. Sometimes, in a murder case when there are no family or close friends, they will go anyway, just to make sure the dead person is represented. "I can remember in years gone by," Carroll says, "where there was nobody else and Sandy or I would go to court and say, 'We're here for that person.' Nobody else cared, or there were no family members. We would take that as a serious mission. And we would go to those sentencings and we were very much a part of any hearing."

Or, if there is a survivor or loved one in the courtroom, the victim coordinator will take it upon herself simply to act as an emotional buffer or bodyguard, which in this case is almost like being a physical protector. I can't tell you how many times I've been in court when they bring in the defendant, he glares over at the victim or her family, and the look is one of contempt, rage, wounded innocence, or, sometimes worst of all, indifference. If the survivor has someone there with her to give her strength and support, it can make a world of difference.

Another need may be even more basic. Violent crime can mean a new set of expenses—some direct, some indirect. These can include funeral and burial costs, medical care, and psychological and physical therapy, even things as basic as bus or taxi fares to get to court or child care during hearings or trials. The Victim-Witness Unit can not only help out with these costs, but also aid the victim in securing grants for the larger expenses and financial losses he or she might suffer.

Aside from the homicide support group, there is another more general crime-victim support group, which Sandy runs. The unit also supports the department's Child Sex Crimes Unit in the delicate task of preparing youthful victims to be witnesses. In this they work closely with both detectives and prosecutors so that the child and the parents will become comfortable with the process and what they might face. Among the issues are ones as basic as making sure the child understands that it is the defendant, not the child, who is on trial. The victim coordinator will always praise the child for her courage, reassure her of her safety, and let her talk openly about her feelings and fears.

The unit has developed a checklist of things that children have said they find frightening. Together with the child, the coordinator will fill out the form, putting check marks under the three headings: Really Afraid, Sort of Afraid, Not At All Afraid. The categories covered are such concerns as going into the courtroom; the judge in black robes; promising to tell the truth; seeing the defendant (the person who did the wrong thing); sitting on the witness stand; talking into a microphone; saying words about the private parts of the body; being a child in an adult place. Once the coordinator has homed in on the fears, she can work with the child witness to allay them before the trial and before the child feels she has been revictimized by the system.

The next step is another list they came up with, entitled "What Would You Do If," that includes such issues as someone asks you a question that you don't understand; you feel angry or sad and start to cry; the attorneys start to argue with each other; someone in the courtroom looks mean; and even, you need to use the bathroom or you feel like you're going to be sick. Under each of eleven scenarios there are three possible answers, and the coordinator will go over each one and discuss which is the best response under the circumstances.

Not only does this practice produce better witnesses and, therefore, better justice, it also goes a long way toward assuring that these innocents are not damaged any further and, in fact, feel that they have had a positive role in seeing justice served.

As desensitized as we are to violent crime these days, there is a tendency almost to discount the significance of anything short of murder or rape. That is, until you've experienced it yourself. Then your perspective changes pretty quickly and you realize the value of the support the unit offers.

"I could call you if you had had a gun stuck at your head," says Sandy, "and I could talk to you and offer our services. And the first thing you might say to me is, 'Oh, I'm fine. Thank you very much for calling.' But if I dug deep enough with you and held you on the phone long enough, I would know that you were scared shitless at that moment and you could probably tell me that you were thinking about how you were never going to see your wife or kids again. That changes you. I want to make you understand that that's why we're here, and I know it's not going to happen if I just fire off a letter that says, 'We're here if you think you need us.'"

The fact of the matter is that any encounter with violence or potential violence makes us feel violated and vulnerable. It perverts our sense of the natural and logical order of things, of basic fairness and benevolence. And once they are gone, it is not easy to reclaim feelings of security and stability in our lives.

Well-meaning friends might tell us how lucky we were, that "it could have been a lot worse"; we might have been killed or seriously injured. But that is just the point. Once we experience firsthand how capricious life can be in this context, we may begin to brood upon how tenuously we are connected to everything we love and hold valuable, how fragile is our sense of control. This is one of the many things the violent criminal steals from us.

When Sandy talks about "getting in the moment" with the victim, what she means is being able to understand just what the crime meant to him or her. Maybe this rape was the worst thing she could imagine, the worst thing that could have happened to her, a kind of death or worse. Or maybe she feels lucky to be alive, that she survived the ordeal. Both of these reactions are completely understandable, completely valid. But each requires a different response from Sandy or her associates, and that can only be achieved by getting in that moment.

By its very nature, the unit is most often dealing with the effects of violent crime. But there is one area in which they have taken large strides to prevent it from happening in the first place, and that is in the area of domestic violence.

As Carroll says, "Fortunately for us here in Fairfax County, we have an aggressive policy that our police officers will go out and arrest the guy doing the abusing and cart him off to jail—not that they may arrest, but that they *shall* arrest the primary aggressor in a domestic violence incident and also accompany a woman to get an emergency protective order, where indicated."

The centerpiece of the program, funded by a grant won by the unit, is Someplace Safe, a physical safe haven for domestic violence victims that is available on an emergency basis, twenty-four hours a day. Says Carroll, "If we have a tragic situation where a woman has nowhere to go, we're taking her to Someplace Safe."

And the service reaches out to those not in immediate need of alternate housing. Members of the unit are available by page around the clock. Certain high-risk victims are given pendants with electronic transmitters to contact police instantly. Virginia "Genny" Struyk, one of the original members of the unit, coordinates the program.

Stalking is another area in which the unit hopes to prevent crime, rather than having to deal solely with its effects. "In the past it was one of those gray areas where you're not sure how to proceed," Carroll comments. "But from this office, we have encouraged victims to report every single instance where they have been aware that somebody is stalking them. We've been very supportive in working out safe plans and how to avoid threatening situations. We have aggressively sought help through our various local police stations. Basically, a victim can call us or come to our office and say, 'I need help,' and we will help them."

For Carroll and Sandy and the rest of the staff, this kind of proactive work helps balance out the emotional toll of the type of horror they are unable to prevent.

"There's so much you can't do," says Sandy. "The can'ts are easier to list than the cans. You can't bring back the dead. You can't give rape victims their previous happiness and security back. You can't heal the limbs that have been broken or severed. You can't give a molested child back his innocence. If you're a little old widow and you've been the victim of a burglary, we can't restore this little bit of a sense of security you had left in the world that now is just completely gone. There's so much of that. For me, I have to go back to that idea of being in the moment. What can I provide? I can provide whatever limited understanding I have of what their experience is. You know, there aren't a lot of people who will come to you and say, 'I am yours anytime you need me. You can call me day or night,' and mean it."

The program is so highly regarded that Carroll and others are continually being called on to speak to other groups, such as police academies and state crime commissions, and to help other victim-witness programs throughout the country get established and set up good working relationships with their respective police departments.

Much of what the unit does may seem routine and obvious, but we have only to look to jurisdictions where nothing like this is available to see how vital and unroutine it really is. I recently read a newspaper interview with the mother of a homicide victim who, many months after the murder, had heard nothing from the investigating detective and had not even been able to get her son's watch back. All of her calls went unanswered. This woman felt completely cut off and removed from the investigative and judicial processes, and her grief and anxiety were only being compounded. She could not possibly begin her journey toward closure and some semblance of livable life.

Now I happen to have worked with the police department in question on several occasions throughout my career at Quantico. It's a good and conscientious department in a city with a number of high concentrations of violence, which means they're overworked and underfunded, and I know from my contacts that morale is not what it should be or once was. Can I countenance or condone the way this mother has been treated? Of course not. But I can understand that an investigator with the kind of unsolved caseload this detective is working under is going to have to put public outreach low on his list of priorities. If this woman had a victim's advocate working with her, to meet with people and run interference when necessary, she could get the information and simple human kindness she so desperately needs, and the entire system would be better off, particularly when this case is ready to go to trial.

Ultimately, as Sandy says, the job is to "empower victims to become survivors."

And one of the ways you empower is by remembering, as Carroll always stresses, by keeping the victims alive through honoring their memory. That is why, during National Crime Victims' Rights Week each April, the unit holds a "Candlelight Vigil of Courage, Hope and Remembrance" in which victims' names are read off one by one. There are speakers and the entire community is invited to participate.

At the ceremony held on April 13, 1997, Jack Collins spoke about what it meant to be a survivor and how you go on living your life. Two gifted young women, Christy Brzonkala and Aisha Barber, read a powerful poem they had written entitled "Silent No More." And Martha Bazan, the mother of a homicide victim, spoke for mothers and fathers throughout the world who have suffered terrible losses when she read the English version of a poem she had originally written in Spanish. She called it "Remembering Tony."

As Carroll says, "Real healing comes when you can take those memories and transport them to another place, removed from the sordid and horrible and painful way that the loved ones left, and deal with the legacy. And then that person lives on forever."

CHAPTER NINE

STALKING

When I joined the Bureau in 1970, you wouldn't have seen stalking listed as a category, even in a criminology textbook. In those days, there was no single, encompassing term for the set of behaviors we now recognize as menacing rather than annoying, and more dangerous than what was then generally lumped under the heading of simple harassment. The first U.S. antistalking law wasn't enacted until twenty years later, in 1990, when California passed landmark legislation. And it is only in the last few years that other states have adopted their own laws to address the crime.

Legal definitions vary from state to state, but, to borrow language from a model statute developed by the National Criminal Justice Association, working with the National Institute of Justice and the National Victim Center, among other groups, the basic message is this: a stalker is someone who engages "in a course of conduct that would place a reasonable person in fear for (his or her) safety, and that the stalker intended and did, in fact, place the victim in such fear."

Depending on the stalker, this conduct can range from overtly aggressive behavior, such as the abduction and murder of the victim's pet or threats in letters, to repeatedly calling someone, say, every hour on the hour all day long, asking for a date. The key is that the behavior is repeated over time, establishing the type of pattern Stanton Samenow has defined so well, and creates fear in the victim.

These days, we hear of so many frightening examples: A woman claims to be comedian and *Late Show* host David Letterman's wife and has been arrested living with her son in Letterman's home while he was away, driving his Porsche. A man is shot and wounded by pop star and actress Madonna's bodyguards as he breaks onto the grounds of her home, screaming his intention to "marry the bitch or slit her throat." Even the word *stalking* itself has become such a natural part of our lexicon that it was used to describe the paparazzi's treatment of the late Princess Diana, likening the way they followed her everywhere, clearly causing her emotional distress, to a hunter stalking his prey.

The National Institute of Justice reported that in the twenty years preceding 1989, we'd seen as many public figures assaulted by people with mental disorders as there had been in the 175 years before that. Is it because today's media makes celebrities seem more accessible? Or could it be that a generally more mobile society and cheaper, faster transportation have made it easier for obsessive fans to get to their targets? Or is it as simple as the possibility that there are just more mentally ill people out there, as funding for state hospitals and de-institutionalization policies have put more potential stalkers out on the streets? While I don't disagree with any of these suppositions, I believe stalking behavior has probably existed in one form or another for as long as there have been humans on the planet. I don't think it's that we've only recently seen this phenomenon so much as that it wasn't organized under an umbrella heading in the past. The same laws that will make it easier for a victim to prosecute a stalking offender will also allow law enforcement to track the incidence of the crime more effectively.

The National Victim Center, headquartered in Arlington, Virginia, a nonprofit organization founded over a decade ago to advance the rights and interests of victims of all types of crime, is one group that has focused on advancing the cause of stalking victims, from providing counseling to legislative advocacy in support of antistalking laws, even assisting with prosecution and litigation. The Center estimates that up to two hundred thousand people are being stalked in this country at any moment, and that one out of every twenty women will be the target of a stalker at some point in her life. They are not alone in their frightening assessment. Dr. Park Dietz, probably the preeminent forensic psychiatrist practicing today, who consulted with my unit at Quantico and worked on the case of obsessed fan/would-be assassin John Hinckley Jr., has also stated his finding that about 5 percent of all women in the United States will likely be victimized by the unwanted and persistent attention of a man at some point in their life. Linda Fairstein—for whom stalking is not a specialty per se—still sees around ten cases each year and suspects that that number is artificially low, as many victims are either too scared to report the crime or unsure there are laws to help them.

When most of us hear the term *stalking,* we think of the well-publicized cases involving celebrities. And it seems there are new examples of that every day. But the statistics indicate it's a far larger problem than that. Plenty of cases involve ordinary citizens, most of which are actually part of a larger pattern of domestic violence. In many cases, the victim already had a restraining order filed against her stalker, ostensibly to protect her from the man who ultimately hunted her down.

There are also instances where a victim is stalked by someone with whom she never had a relationship—maybe someone she never previously met. Indeed, even as this book is being written, such a case is in the news near where I live.

It started innocently enough. A twenty-one-year-old college social-work major was courteous to a fellow employee at the large department store where she had a part-time job. The coworker, described by the victim as a loner who was shunned by and alienated from others on the job, read quite a bit more into her simple kindness than she ever intended. He began sending her E-mail messages and giving her gifts, behaviors that she did not reciprocate. She began noticing him in places she didn't expect, such as outside her home, where he left a note and a cookie for her on her car. This note was neither romantic nor threatening, but it was entirely inappropriate. It thanked her "for being supportive" of him at work, which seemed to imply she'd done more for him—or at least said more to him—than she had. She'd shown him the same degree of friendliness and courtesy she did every other acquaintance and stranger she met.

When she left her job in July 1997, he showed up at her college. At that point, she contacted the police and filed a harassment complaint. Just about two weeks later, he appeared at her house one morning and abducted her at gunpoint, according to numerous neighbors who witnessed the woman being handcuffed and forced into a car by a man holding a gun. The neighbors flooded 911 operators with desperate calls, shocked that something like that could happen in such a quiet, upper-middle-class neighborhood.

In another neighborhood, folks were equally shocked that the hometown boy who shoveled snow for them in the winter and apparently never gave them cause to worry would do such a thing. One was quoted in disbelief, "I saw him just the other day and he looked happy and said hello to me." Of course, he may have been happy because he was planning the abduction that would finally unite him with his true love. It was later learned that he had purchased the handcuffs and gun in the month before the harassment report was filed.

As required by law, police had warned the suspect after that report was filed that he could be facing charges. At that time, the suspect said he would leave the woman alone, a response that at least some members of the police department must have recalled as they issued a description of the man and his vehicle after the apparent kidnapping. Local FBI agents also began search efforts. Tracing a phone call from the victim to her family made about eight hours after she disappeared, and using information on ATM card activity, law enforcement agencies tracked the pair to a nearby state, where they issued an alert for all officers to be on the lookout for the vehicle. Police spotted it early the next morning in a parking lot, where the suspect had apparently pulled over to catch some rest. They saw him taking a nap in the backseat as the woman sat in the front passenger seat, handcuffed to the seat-belt strap. The doors were unlocked and police were able to break in, free the woman, and arrest the suspect without a struggle. Almost nineteen hours after the ordeal began, it came to a much more positive end than many had predicted. In addition to a 9 mm Glock handgun, police found a knife in the suspect's possession.

Although the woman was physically unharmed and reported that her captor tried to comfort and reassure her that he was not going to hurt her as he drove seemingly without a plan, I believe her to be a lucky young woman, under the circumstances. At some point, it would have become clear to this guy that his fantasy of life with her—whatever details he'd imagined—would not come true. Instead of "coming around," growing to love him back, she would remain a frightened captive. And as we've seen over and over again, when reality doesn't live up to the fantasy, that can be when a victim faces the greatest danger.

Fortunately, not only was she found before any physical harm came to her, her alleged abductor crossed state lines, meaning he now faces a federal kidnapping charge as well as state charges both of kidnapping and first-degree assault. The federal charge alone could land him a life sentence. This may sound harsh to some who would feel sympathy for the confused young man; even the victim's own mother told the *Washing-*

ton Post, "He's a victim of society. We're talking about a sick young man who needs help and hasn't gotten it. Now he's going to spend maybe the rest of his life in jail." But one thing we have learned is that many obsessive personality types don't lose interest, and they pose an ever-growing threat to the objects of their obsessions. Some victims have been stalked by the same offender for decades. The stalker may focus his attention on someone new (which solves the original victim's problem but means a life of terror and uncertainty for the new target), or he may die, but he rarely gives up the obsessive behavior altogether—particularly when he's gone as far as abducting a victim. Behavior based on fantasy—regardless of the type of crime in which it manifests itself—has an overwhelming tendency to escalate rather than wind down.

Even today, with new laws in place and greater public awareness, we still have difficulty dealing with the crime, in large measure because we're talking about a crime that is defined by often subtle actions on the part of the offender and is often only witnessed by the victim. Sometimes there are obvious warning signs: a series of threatening letters or messages left on an answering machine tape. Other times there may be no overt clues that a crime has occurred. Unlike other categories of crime, with stalking we find no money missing from a purse, no fingerprints on the steering wheel of a stolen car, and (in the cases that turn out well) no dead body at a crime scene. A stalker's weapons of choice can be items normally not considered menacing, such as a phone that rings too often, or gifts left on a doorstep or office desk. But as we see, these can be just the prelude to a harrowing future moment when more traditional weapons (guns, knives) will be employed.

Particularly frightening and confusing for the stalking victim is that she often recognizes that something is not right long before those around her, sometimes including law enforcement. David Beatty, an attorney with extensive legislative experience who is acting executive director of the National Victim Center, points out that even though the legal definitions of stalking vary from state to state, one thing that remains constant in the experience of victims is that "stalking begins *before* the legal definition kicks in. . . . You can be harassing and you can be threatening before your actions reach the level of the legal definition." What's so bad about having an admirer, secret or otherwise, leaving gifts for you? How can you really expect the police to consider a bouquet of roses with a love note attached threatening?

What antistalking groups, many of which are founded by former and current victims of stalkers, emphasize is that a pattern of this unwanted and unwarranted behavior does create fear and stress in the recipient, who realizes both that it is not normal, socially acceptable behavior in its context, and that it can be a precursor to violence. Acts and words that seem harmless today may turn lethal down the road, which is a message that is only just now starting to be heard and understood.

Like acquaintance rape, stalking is also disturbing because we like to believe we can pick dangerous people out in a crowd: we can recognize the bad guys and steer clear and we'll be safe. But by their very nature and success, sexual predators often look just like us; they don't look like ogres. Unfortunately, in some ways it is harder to develop a general profile of a stalker than it is a rapist or murderer. They can come from any background, any walk of life, and their behavior can accelerate from seemingly "normal" to deadly quickly. The majority of stalkers are men, and in most cases (75 to 80 percent, according to the National Victim Center), a male offender stalks a female victim. Most stalkers are in their late teens and early twenties, up to their forties, and of above-average intelligence. It will come as no surprise that they are typically lonely people, often socially withdrawn, and may have a closer relationship with their television set (providing a rich source for their fantasy life) than with other human beings. Some have never had a close personal relationship, never had sex, and have no immediate prospects of either.

The generic profile elements stop there, however, and you can see that it's not all that limiting or illuminating a description. Part of the reason it's difficult to assign characteristics to stalkers is that this is still such a newly defined crime category with much research yet to be done. But it is also because stalkers really do run the gamut from the clinically psychotic to otherwise fully functioning, successful, and well-respected members of our communities. As with other crimes, their choice of victim—from a famous celebrity who doesn't even know they exist to a former lover—and the different types of stalking behavior they engage in give us clues as to what sort of individual we're dealing with in a given case. And although specific behaviors and characteristics exhibited by stalkers vary widely, we start out by placing them into one of two broad categories: so-called love-obsession stalkers, whose victims are people they don't really know, and simple obsession stalkers, who focus their attention on people they know and with whom they might have had a previous relationship, rather than on complete strangers. Since simple obsession stalking is so closely tied to issues of domestic violence, we'll deal with that crime separately in the next chapter.

The love-obsession variety are what most people think of upon hearing the word *stalker*, since their cases often get the sensational press coverage. This type fixates on a celebrity, although they have been known to develop obsessions with ordinary, nonfamous people as well, perhaps a teller at the bank, a favorite waitress, a coworker, or simply someone who smiled as they walked by in the mall. The key is that the victim has no real relationship with the stalker; they could be casual acquaintances or not have met at all. And just as a movie star or popular singer has done nothing to invite this person into his or her personal life, all you have to do to become the object of a love-obsession stalker is be at the wrong place at the wrong time.

With the obsessions I "must" maintain in my work, I try not to obsess about the safety of my loved ones, yet, I have to tell you, stalking poses a threat that I find deeply disturbing. We all caution our kids from a tender age against perverts and various types of strangers, but this is a crime that, I admit, is difficult to protect them from or adequately explain, even as adults. My daughters are both young women now—old enough and with good enough judgment that I don't have to be concerned they'll get in a car with a man they don't know or put themselves in other obviously vulnerable situations. But I'm almost tempted to advise them against being true to their warm and friendly natures: Don't talk to that man behind you in the supermarket line. Don't say, "Excuse me," and smile at that guy you bumped into on your way to the bathroom at the movies; maybe you're the only woman who's paid any attention to him his whole life. One misplaced smile could be enough for someone to start building an entire fantasy world around you. Because for this type of offender, that—or even less—may be all he needs. Park Dietz has described the first case of this nature he dealt with, "a man who was launched on a mission by a waitress who served him a cup of coffee. . . . Obviously not the sort of thing you can guard against."

What's perhaps even more chilling is that some of these offenders are so inadequate that they build their fantasies around children. I've seen cases where a young man in his late teens or early twenties fixates on a little girl who lives on his block, watching her from a parked car as she waits for the school bus, approaching her to talk as she rides her bicycle, leaving notes for her, even scolding or berating her if he catches her talking to a little boy. As hard as it is for an adult woman to deal with the strain and fear of a stalking experience, it is even more devastating for a child who not only doesn't understand why this is happening to her but may get to the point where she doesn't remember what it's like not to live in fear that "the bad man" is going to get her.

As with other types of crime, I believe different stalkers act out differently depending on their motivation, or as David Beatty puts it, depending on where their wiring went bad. Experts may assign their own labels to the different types, as we saw with the rapist typologies, but all tend to break them down into the same general groupings, and all are related to motivation and behavior.

Behavior reflects personality.

Gavin de Becker, who founded his own security firm in the Los Angeles area, is one of the leading experts on threat assessment and stalking; he has often worked with us in the Investigative Support Unit. Not only does he have extensive experience with his own clients, he's done the hard research to back what he says. He has developed impressive computer models to evaluate the seriousness and dangerousness of various threat situations. Gavin uses motivation as a way to categorize different types of stalkers who pursue celebrities.

"Attachment seekers" are motivated by the desire to form a relationship with the individual they stalk. "Identity seekers" are looking for fame themselves, and the recognition they can attain through their acts. "Rejection based" stalkers may be attachment seekers gone bad, stalkers who are looking either for revenge for their perceived rejection by the celebrity or to change the star's mind about them. These are the most dangerous type, more likely than the others to harm or kill their prey. Finally, "delusion based" stalkers think there is a force (sometimes God) leading them to fulfill some mission. These are the hardest to treat and the least predictable.

Park Dietz similarly describes the different types of so-called romantic stalkers. Of those who obsess about people they don't know—including celebrity stalkers—Park states that they range from the truly delusional to those who become pathologically dependent on a love object who would never be interested in them—someone completely unattainable.

Though delusional stalkers represent the majority of those who pursue the rich and famous (estimates go as high as 90 percent), they are in the minority (between one-fifth and one-quarter) of all stalking cases. This is good news for the average citizen who might be stalked someday, but bad news for celebrities because these pursuers can be highly unpredictable and dangerous. They often suffer from some mental disorder, such as schizophrenia, paranoia, and/or erotomania, a psychiatric condition wherein the stalker actually believes the object of his obsession returns the desire and wants to pursue the relationship. Their mental illness also makes them difficult to treat or rehabilitate. Think of David Letterman's stalker: in her mind, she was his wife and had good reason to move into his home and drive his car.

Socially inadequate and often incapable of forming personal relationships in the real world, many stalkers create a fantasy life with their love object. They script it out and expect the other person (who may be completely unaware that the stalker exists until some form of contact is made) to act accordingly.

The love-obsession stalkers who are not delusional nonetheless operate with a heavy dose of fantasy as well. For a man who believes that some woman is his destiny, who sees the two of them as halves of the same whole, incomplete without each other, the fantasy relationship is critical to his sense of self. He likely doesn't have much in the way of self-image, particularly if he's lacking other relationships in his life. If he's someone whose neighbors would describe as a loner or a loser, who doesn't seem to have any friends, he's going to invest heavily in his relationship with this woman—his victim. It may take years for him to adequately prove his love and win her over (or wear her down), but someday, he is confident, she will be glad he kept trying. Rather than taking rejection as a sign he should leave her alone and move on with his life, he sees this as an indication that he has to step up his efforts.

To some degree, this belief is supported by messages he gets from movies and television. Think of all the movies in which boy meets girl, boy pursues girl, girl rejects boy, boy persists and eventually triumphs, and they presumably live happily ever after. In some ways, this type of stalking is another criminal symptom of a society that doesn't get the message that when a woman says no, she means no.

The danger develops in many cases when the stalker does not get what he wants from the victim. Desperate for the relationship of his dreams, if the object of his affection does not respond positively, the offender may turn to intimidation and threatening behavior to get the response he seeks. Failing this, he may turn to violence.

For some, the violence is simply an acting out of their frustration, while others make the conscious decision that if they cannot have the positive relationship they want, they would rather have negative attention than none at all. David Beatty describes how one action, and its corresponding frustration, leads to the next. Take the example he gives of a stalker who calls his victim every hour on the hour to ask for a date. Beatty notes that anyone "could reasonably believe that that behavior is so erratic—it is so inappropriate—that it is dangerous. If someone's willing to go that far, if someone cannot take no for an answer, they are on a spiraling track to the next act." In the offender's mind, says Beatty, "If you care about me . . . because you fear me, that's still care. . . . I'm having an impact on someone who is larger-than-life for me."

The larger-than-life persona of the victim may be a projection of the stalker's own inadequacy, as in the case of a man who stalks a coworker, or it can be a function of the victim's fame. In some cases, as much as he desires a relationship with his victim, the stalker is driven more by the celebrity of the victim and his need to tap into greatness and importance so lacking in his own life. As Gavin de Becker observes, "We've seen many people seek to prove their love through public acts of violence. When all else failed to give them the identity they hoped a relationship would bring, the handgun would be sure to do it." This was the motivation behind most of the early public-figure stalking cases, from obsessed fans of celebrities to political assassins.

As modern serial murder usually begins with Jack the Ripper (although many of my colleagues and I feel it goes a lot further back than that), the case considered the first recorded celebrity-stalking shooting in history is that by Ruth Steinhagen, an obsessed fan of Chicago Cubs baseball player Eddie Waitkus, who shot Waitkus in his room at the Edgewater Beach Hotel in 1949 (a scene on which parts of the movie *The Natural* were loosely based). As with other fans of celebrities, Steinhagen devoted tremendous energy to her obsession, collecting memorabilia, going to his games, studying Lithuanian out of respect for his heritage, even setting a place for him at her dinner table at times. Yet after she shot him (he survived and recovered), she was frustrated by the lack of attention she got. She waited for people to swarm her. Instead, as she woefully described, "Nobody seemed to want me much. I could've walked right out of that place and nobody would have come after me." Rather than elevate her status and importance as she sought, after all the buildup and the excitement of finally seeing Waitkus face-to-face, shooting him simply highlighted her own insignificance.

In the years following the Waitkus murder attempt, political assassinations occurred with greater frequency than celebrity murder, though stalking was probably still common.

I've spent a lot of time interviewing and studying assassins (and would-be assassins), including Sirhan Sirhan, James Earl Ray, and Arthur Bremer, who shot Alabama governor and then–presidential candidate George Wallace in a parking lot in Maryland during a political rally. At first, I made the mistake of likening assassins to serial killers. Even the assassins themselves denied that connection. But what I did find is that the assassin personality is similar to that of a celebrity stalker. Both tend to be paranoid, lacking trust in other individuals. Because of their highly suspicious nature, they can be difficult to interview. When I interviewed Bremer, I found myself trying not to make or hold eye contact because I could tell that it made him uncomfortable. Usually loners, they are not relaxed in the presence of others and not practiced or skilled in social interaction. Like many celebrity stalkers, though, in contrast to their inability or unwillingness to communicate through normal conversation, they keep a running dialogue with themselves, often painstakingly detailing their thoughts and fantasies in a diary. After the stalking and murder of a celebrity or politician, we tend to find that the offender has a thick diary (sometimes one he carries with him), with entry after entry about the attack— rationalizing it, planning it, fantasizing about it. It's like they're programming themselves to commit the crime, building courage to take action as they never have before.

Arthur Bremer kept such a diary, with entries that underscored his overwhelming feelings of insignificance and inadequacy, the primary motivators for most assassins and stalkers. In planning an assassination, the offender imagines that this one big event will prove once and for all that he has worth, that he can do and be something. It provides an identity and purpose as nothing in his life ever has. You can see this pathetic desperation in the fact that assassins are so focused on how people will receive them after they've acted on their fantasy that they don't always build in an escape plan. Many, like Ruth Steinhagen, want to be arrested and recognized at the scene of the crime. Bremer is another example of this. After spending time choosing a target and planning his attack, he never planned a way out. He simply needed to prove that this inadequate nobody was able to get in close enough range to get someone as important George Wallace. If he was unable to take that route to win himself significance in his life, in his diaries he wrote of another fantasy: after robbing a bank, police would catch up to him as he fled over a bridge. Before they could arrest him, he'd jump off the bridge and shoot himself in the head at the same time. It is key to his personality dysfunction that he couldn't just overdose and wait for someone to find his body or shoot himself out in the woods somewhere. He needed a spectacular end to draw attention to himself, much as the assassination attempt on Wallace would. It wasn't even a question of political ideology with Bremer. Before he stalked Wallace, he had stalked Richard Nixon and other national political figures, but concluded that getting close to them would be too formidable a challenge. It's ironic that some of Bremer's black fellow inmates held him in high regard for his assault on Wallace, who at the time was still espousing segregationist beliefs, when in fact he chose him as a target because he wasn't accomplished enough as an assassin to reach anyone of higher political stature.

Another trait shared by celebrity stalkers and assassins is their odd lack of loyalty to their cause. I know this sounds like a contradiction, given the years some will spend collecting intelligence and memorabilia on their chosen target, but the obsessive behavior and the planned final event are often far more important than their affiliation with a given person or political ideology, as we've just seen with Bremer. David Letterman's stalker, Margaret Ray, has apparently recently switched her attentions over to former astronaut Story Musgrave. After her arrest outside Musgrave's house, she reported that she was in love with Musgrave.

The issue of crazed fans stalking celebrities was brought back into public consciousness in 1980, when Mark David Chapman gunned down his idol, former Beatle John Lennon, on the street outside his apartment building in New York City. Like Steinhagen and Bremer, Chapman had no great ambition to escape after committing his crime because he, too, needed the identity he gained by murdering his victim. Unlike the other two, though, Chapman wasn't looking for public recognition of his accomplishment as much as he was acting out a final step in his deluded worship of Lennon. In Chapman's mind, the ultimate expression of his love for the man was to murder him, connecting his poor pathetic existence to the artist's forever. Chapman collected all of John Lennon's music and emulated him to the point that he reportedly formed relationships with women of Asian descent to mimic Lennon's marriage to Yoko Ono. A second motive, one even easier to understand, was simply the inadequate Chapman's profound jealousy of this man he admired so much. Basically, if he couldn't enjoy this life of fame, fortune, talent, and adulation, he would see to it that Lennon couldn't, either. Bringing about the superstar's death was for him the final, best way to ensure that his life would always be linked with that of the man he idolized.

Just three months after Lennon's murder, John Hinckley Jr. made his assassination attempt on Ronald Reagan as the president was leaving the Hilton Hotel in Washington, D.C., after a lunchtime speaking engagement. Hinckley's case is interesting because it shows both the unpredictability of the erotomaniac, love-obsession stalker and at the same time illustrates how nobody really knew how to deal with this type of criminal at the time.

Hinckley had been obsessed with movie star Jodie Foster. I met and got to know Foster while advising on the film of *The Silence of the Lambs*. She is a gifted, intelligent woman and I have extremely high regard for her both as an actress and a human being. I also have great compassion for her—that she became an innocent victim in one of the most appalling and potentially disastrous stalking incidents on record.

When Hinckley first began to contact her, she or her publicists responded simply by being nice to him as they would to anyone who wrote in, not realizing that the man who started out as just an enthusiastic fan was on a trajectory to violent behavior. When she became a college student at Yale, he obtained the telephone number of her dorm room. When he called her, she treated him cordially, as she would treat any fan who complimented her. Of course, she had no intention whatsoever of encouraging him into thinking that a relationship existed between them.

Unfortunately, things have reached such an alarming level today that many stalking and threat assessment experts, including Gavin de Becker, strongly discourage celebrities from contact with their fans, including sending out the signed photographs that are so popularly requested. This certainly penalizes the vast majority of genuine, respectful admirers because of the numerically small minority who might actually do the celebrity harm. But it's just too risky to take the chance any longer. In some cases, public figures have had to title property in other people's names to make their home locations more difficult to trace.

John Hinckley Jr. wrote to Jodie Foster, "You'll be proud of me, Jodie. Millions of Americans will love me—us." To put it plainly, he was coldly and callously willing to take the life of the president of the United States, as well anyone else who happened to be nearby, and conceivably alter history, to impress a girl who had no interest in him, in fact was only incidentally aware that he existed at all.

Although a failure as a political assassin, he achieved at least one part of his goal: his name is linked with Jodie Foster's. If he couldn't have her, this nobody could at least glory in the association.

Hinckley reportedly grew obsessed with Foster after seeing her performance in the movie *Taxi Driver*. Another actress had the misfortune to appear on-screen in a movie that would evoke similarly strong emotions in another disturbed individual. Although not yet a household name, twenty-seven-year-old Theresa Saldana had appeared in several films, including *Raging Bull* with Robert De Niro, by early 1982.

On the morning of March 15 of that year, a middle-aged man approached Saldana as she was unlocking her car outside her West Hollywood apartment. He said, "Excuse me," to get her attention, then asked if she was Theresa Saldana. When she answered yes, he took out a hunting knife he'd brought and began slashing and stabbing her repeatedly, using enough force that he actually bent the knife. A deliveryman who happened to be nearby, Jeff Fenn, heard her screams and immediately ran to her assistance, managing to get the knife away from her attacker. Paramedics rushed the young actress to Cedars-Sinai Medical Center, where she underwent heart-lung surgery and received twenty-six pints of blood. At one point, her heart stopped. Her assailant had almost accomplished what he would refer to as his "divine mission."

Police arrested and questioned Arthur Jackson, a drifter from Scotland in his midforties. They learned more about him and his crime from a diary he kept in his traveling knapsack. Like Arthur Bremer's, Jackson's diary provided a good look into the mind of a dedicated stalker whose obsession had become the be-all and end-all of his existence.

Investigation into his background—and from his own writings—revealed a history of disturbing behavior. The son of an alcoholic father and a reportedly schizophrenic mother, he was first hospitalized in his native Scotland with a nervous breakdown at age seventeen, which may have resulted when his romantic feelings went unreturned by the latest in a series of crushes he wrote about. After a year in the psychiatric hospital, he wandered through several countries and continents, holding down menial jobs in London, Toronto, and New York before joining the U.S. Army in the mid 1950s. There, he fell in love with another soldier and yet again the affection was one-sided. As he had back in his homeland, he suffered another nervous breakdown, and the Army sent him to Walter Reed Hospital in Washington, D.C., for treatment. He was released on a weekend pass for his twenty-first birthday, went to New York, and tried to kill himself with sleeping pills.

By 1961, Jackson had been discharged from the military and was transitioning from unrequited crushes on people he knew to throwing all his emotions into a fantasy life with famous individuals he had never met. Arrested that year by the U.S. Secret Service for threatening Pres. John F. Kennedy, Jackson was deported to Scotland, where he alternately lived with his mother and wandered around on the dole, spending much of his time and money on the movies. It was at this time that Theresa Saldana appeared in the films *I Wanna Hold Your Hand* and *Defiance,* the latter of which apparently inspired Jackson to focus his obsessive thoughts on her. According to Jackson's diaries, while watching a particularly violent part of the film, he had flashbacks to a similarly bloody real-life scene he saw while in the emergency room in 1956 following his suicide attempt. He transferred the excitement he got from the violence on Saldana and wrote that by "sending her into eternity" he hoped to win her love. This new focus held more emotional satisfaction than any of his previous "relationships," and it was here that he truly blossomed as a stalker.

For most stalkers, pursuing their prey becomes a full-time job, providing meaning in a life that previously had little or none. Arthur Jackson was no exception. The man who had been unable to keep menial jobs for long, who'd wandered around aimlessly through most of his life, suddenly had a mission and a goal for which he'd focus all his attention and travel thousands of miles—all in pursuit of a woman he'd never met. In 1982, he reentered the United States illegally and began trying to make contact with his target and potential victim. He started in New York. Posing as an agent with a great script—and as a producer, photographer, director's assistant, and publicist—he tried to get to the actress through her relatives and people she worked with, traveling to Los Angeles when his early attempts in New York failed. He would not be discouraged. After returning to New York, he learned that Saldana lived in Hollywood, so he hopped a bus out West to cross the country again.

When he got to the point where he realized he couldn't get any closer on his own, Jackson became more resourceful. In Hollywood, he hired a private investigator, who found Saldana's address for him. Fortunately, he was not as successful in weapons acquisition. Jackson originally wanted to shoot Saldana, thinking that would be a "more humane" way to end her life than by stab wounds. In his journeys across the country he tried several times to buy a gun, but without proper ID, such as a U.S. driver's license, he wasn't able to do so. As horrible as Saldana's injuries were, if Jackson had been able to fire a gun ten times at point-blank range, there would have been a very different end to this story.

Heroically, just two weeks after the vicious assault, Saldana showed up in court for a preliminary hearing, wheeled into the room with IV attached, bandaged and ready to testify against Jackson. He was convicted of attempted murder and of inflicting great bodily injury and was sentenced to twelve years—the maximum penalty available at the time. After serving his time in California, he was extradited to Britain, where he was wanted for murder in connection with a bank robbery in 1966. As of this writing, that trial is still pending.

At the time of her attack, Theresa Saldana's talent was being recognized and her career was gaining momentum, but she was certainly not the most popular or well-known actress in the movies or on television. She had never met Arthur Jackson before he showed up at her apartment. What made her the focus of his dangerous obsession seems to be that when he was ready to throw his energies and identity into the life of another, more successful human being, her image was there.

Because movie, television, music, and even sports stars make their living putting their image out before the public, they seem ready targets for the emotional attachment of lost souls.

In fact, many love-obsession stalkings involve ordinary citizens, including a case that resulted in one of California's largest mass killings, bringing the issue—as well as workplace harassment and violence—to the nation's attention.

In 1984, Laura Black was a twenty-two-year-old engineer and relatively new hire at ESL Inc. when she was introduced to Richard Wade Farley, a computer technician who worked in another department at the defense contractor. The petite, dark-haired Black was not only pretty but smart, pursuing an advanced degree while working at ESL. She was also athletic, a former award-winning gymnast who played on the company softball team. They had met when Farley visited a colleague in Black's department. The three went out to lunch, which meant little more to Black than expanding the number of faces she recognized at work, but apparently held much more significance to Farley. The lunch was certainly not a date—especially since they all paid for their own meal—and Laura Black couldn't have known that years later Farley would testify that "I fell instantly in love with her."

He began showing up at her desk regularly, inviting her on dates ranging from music concerts to comedy shows, even a tractor pull. She wasn't interested in him and, as she put it, "It made me uncomfortable. I don't like to deal with that type of situation at work." She politely tried to make the point that she was only interested in him as "a work friend." Still, Farley persisted, giving her gifts that were inappropriate for a casual acquaintance at the office, as well as just plain odd: a mirror shaped like a heart and a power shovel.

About a month after they'd been introduced, Farley demanded Black's home address and phone number, which she refused to give him. He became more and more persistent and she grew more concerned about his unwanted attention. The frustration level was increasing on both sides.

To point out just how difficult these cases can be, even experts who've studied stalking offenders offer different advice on how to deal with someone like Farley, which we'll get into more in the next chapter. Laura Black hoped that by being polite, honest, and firm in rejecting Farley's romantic pursuit, she would be able to defuse the uncomfortable situation. Unfortunately, Farley was not someone with whom she could negotiate rationally.

The people at the National Victim Center have outlined the patterns of behavior most stalkers like this follow, and it is almost eerie how well Farley's match their description. According to their model, many stalkers first try to win over the object of their affection with gifts, love letters, flowers, and the like. At this stage, the stalker desperately hopes he just has to show the person he's pursuing how much he loves her and that will be enough to win her. This is the motivation in cases where the offender has had a previous personal relationship with his victim, as well as in domestic violence situations, where his hope is to reestablish a relationship that existed previously. In either case, when they realize the gifts and invitations aren't working, they tend to resort to intimidation to pry their way into their victim's life. They may act possessive, jealous of the victim's other relationships, romantic or otherwise, however unjustified that reaction may be. Harassment turns to threats, either direct or indirect, that are communicated by the offender's words and/or actions. And when the threats don't work—after nothing else has worked—the stalker may grow violent. He may grow homicidal (and/or suicidal) either out of desperation, willing to try anything to prove his love and get his victim's attention, or out of anger and jealousy, determined that "if I can't have her, nobody will."

While it is predictable that a certain number of stalkers will follow this pattern to a violent end, nobody can say exactly what a given offender will do or when he will do it. Some may back off from threats and begin with flowers and love cards all over again. Others will jump through all the stages to violent or even deadly behavior within days. For some, it could take years before they grow violent. Still others may make threats, even confront their victim, then back off and stop their disturbing behavior for years, only to return when the victim least expects it. Experts may differ on their advice about how to treat stalkers, but the one thing upon which everyone agrees is that the unpredictability and the individuality of each case means that every one must be taken seriously.

Laura Black could not have known how serious the situation would grow. And to an outsider, before Farley grew threatening, his actions may have seemed sweet, if a bit odd. One of the most insidious aspects of the crime is that in the early stages, when only the victim realizes how inappropriate the stalker's behavior is, others (even some in law enforcement, I'm afraid) may react with confusion over the victim's alarm.

"You should be flattered by this attention," people say, thinking the man is merely smitten and will either give up when he realizes the woman is not interested or will eventually succeed and win her affection. That's the way it may have seemed to people around Laura Black, who saw that Richard Farley baked her blueberry bread, leaving it on her desk all buttered and ready to eat every Monday morning for seven weeks in a row. However, that bread was a sign to Black that something was not right with this man. This behavior was actually narcissistic: the antithesis of generous and caring. He was making it clear that he didn't care what she wanted, his will was going to prevail. For him, pursuit of Black was a power struggle that he could not afford to lose once he invested so much emotional energy.

At first, many people, possibly including his victim, may have thought he was just pathetic. In this, he fits the classic profile of other types of offenders, including both rapists and murderers who get their satisfaction from manipulating, dominating, and controlling another human being. It is also highly telling that Farley chose as his victim someone fourteen years younger than he was, a common practice with offenders who feel more comfortable and in control of the situation with a victim younger than themselves. Many serial killers select younger victims in early crimes, intimidated by people their own age.

After Black made it clear that Farley's feelings were not mutually shared, turning down dates, refusing to give him her phone number and address, even telling him in desperation that she wouldn't date him if he "were the last man on earth," he grew increasingly more harassing. As he would explain, "I had the right to ask her out. . . . When she did not refuse in a cordial way, I felt I had the right to bother her." And bother her he did, showing up in her office when she was there alone putting in overtime on weekends or at night. Like Arthur Jackson, he had a mission and was able to call up tremendous resourcefulness in its pursuit. He lied to a colleague in the personnel office at ESL just weeks after meeting Black and said he wanted to surprise her for her birthday. When the coworker called up Black's file on the computer, Farley memorized her address from the screen. He broke into Black's desk and traced her keys so he could make copies.

When he learned she was going to visit her parents for Christmas, he again gained access to her desk by telling corporate security he lost his desk key and giving them the number of her desk instead. Searching through her belongings, he found the address for her parents' place and sent one of the nearly two hundred letters she would receive from him—this one eight single-spaced pages long.

All these efforts served two purposes. First, like a rapist who breaks into women's homes when they're not there, stealing panties so he has a physical object to build his fantasies around before actually assaulting his victim, Farley was fueling his fantasy of possessing Laura Black. Sure, she wouldn't have anything to do with him by choice, but he was gathering intelligence, collecting details and snippets of her real personal life. As a star stalker painstakingly collects videos of every movie ever made by his love object, clipping magazine and newspaper articles and compiling a scrapbook, Farley was building an inventory of items and information that made him feel closer to Black. By copying down the license plate numbers of cars belonging to men who spent time with her and memorizing other details about her, he created in his mind the illusion of intimacy. This false sense later led him to the feeling, after he'd continued his stalking of Black for years, that they should go to a marriage counselor.

He stated, "We fight like an old married couple," revealing the degree to which his fantasy redefined their interaction, allowing him to fill in her side of the relationship he imagined them to have. Although not deluded like Hinckley, who was so adept at finding secret messages for him in Jodie Foster's every action that he wrote to her in 1980, "You didn't wear your plaid skirt today. . . . You have no right to disrupt our relationship in such a manner," Farley played the stalker's mind game fully, rationalizing his behavior with his belief that he could win Laura Black's attention. He didn't necessarily want her as his wife or girlfriend, but he wanted to know he could have her, that he wasn't the loser he and so many others took him to be.

With his intelligence-gathering and other stalking behavior, Farley also controlled how much privacy she had, taking that basic right away from her. And therein lies the second part of his motivation. Every piece of information he gathered, every intrusion he made into her life that she would have prevented, allowed him to reassert his control over the situation. She didn't want a relationship with him, but he was finding ways to make sure she thought of him day and night. There was no place she could go that he wouldn't be.

Farley revealed his need to control Black in 1985 when, frustrated that she had switched tactics from firmly refusing his advances to ignoring him altogether, he wrote, "I see you as much as six times a week, which doesn't give you much freedom, so I thought it would be nice to call when I wanted to see you, and the rest of the time is yours. But you don't seem to appreciate that. Now I'm thinking of changing the rules."

Much as other criminals find ways to rationalize and project the blame for their actions onto their victims, Farley was trying to justify his behavior, while at the same time intimating that he would step up his abuse. He would have her believe he'd tried to be accommodating, but that she had made things difficult—as though an adult in a normal, healthy relationship would have the inclination, let alone the right, to set up such "rules" for his or her partner.

It wasn't enough for him simply to observe her or learn personal details about her, he needed to make sure she was aware of his surveillance. He joined her gym, photographed her doing aerobics (and even including drawings of her in a leotard in one of his letters). He went to company softball games to watch her play and insinuated himself into after-game celebrations over pizza. He called her at home, often late in the evening, and would drive by when he was unable to get her on the phone.

Still, at times he would back off for a while, as though this might work where his campaign of intimidation had failed. Before too long, however, he would be following her again. In desperation, Black turned to the human resources department at ESL for assistance. Farley was told in no uncertain terms that if he wanted to keep his job, he had to leave her alone, as well as get psychiatric counseling.

We often find that when victims seek intervention from authorities one of two things happens: their situation either gets better or it gets worse. I know this statement sounds like hedging a bet, but the sad fact is that it's exactly true. As in all other aspects of their behavior, stalkers' reactions to their victims' seeking help from the authorities can be unpredictable. Both Linda Fairstein and David Beatty observe that sometimes a stalker can be persuaded to back off—although both add that this has to happen in the early stages of the stalker's career.

Fairstein notes, "I've seen when the guys have some tether to reality—family, job, something—and no criminal record and realize after the first law enforcement contact that they're likely to lose it all, some of them respond appropriately and it really stops the behavior." Of course, we always have to wonder with this type of obsessive personality if he hasn't simply moved on to a new victim. But it does appear that a percentage of stalking offenders will change their ways—again, depending on how much else they have going on in their lives, how well they recognize the consequences of getting in trouble with the law, and what was motivating their behavior to begin with. If they are mentally ill or simply stalk because they like it—much as a serial rapist enjoys overpowering and dominating his victims—they won't be deterred easily.

In some cases, actions on the part of the victim to get an offender punished (or simply to cut off his access to her, as when a victim seeks a restraining order against her stalker) can make things worse. Beatty notes that in many a stalker's mind, he's done nothing wrong.

"What's amazing," Beatty says, "is what you hear as they're being dragged off to jail, 'I never did anything to her. I only loved her.'" If an offender thinks he's done nothing wrong, he perceives the involvement of the authorities as an injustice perpetrated against him, and just one more way the victim—and society, through the criminal justice system—is harassing him.

In Black's case, seeking help from ESL management helped in that at least she'd finally gone on record with his harassment, but it did seem to escalate his behavior. It was shortly after Black reported him that Farley confronted her outside her apartment and first mentioned his gun collection. He told her how skillful he was at using his weapons. When she asked if he intended to kill her, he answered in person and in yet another letter that it wasn't his intention, although he warned that by threatening his job she had raised the stakes: "Time to remove the kid gloves."

He also wrote, "If I killed you, you won't be able to regret what you did. . . . In between the two extremes of doing nothing and having the police or someone kill me, there's a whole range of options, each getting worse and worse."

It was obvious that his therapy wasn't working. "Once I'm fired," Farley wrote Black, "you won't be able to control me ever again. . . . I'll crack under the pressure and run amok and destroy everything in my path. . . . Even if you don't crack up you will never again play with men with the same ease you do now, and I will win."

Even as he claimed his actions were motivated by unrequited love, he couldn't keep the all-important themes of domination and control from his manipulative letters to her. He was also unable to hide his obsession from ESL personnel, whom he advised that he owned guns that he could use to "take people with me."

Two years after a coworker innocently introduced them, the company fired Farley for harassment and poor job performance. At the same time, according to Black, she was told by the company she should get away for a while.

Loss of a job and loss of a wife or girlfriend are two of the precipitating stressors we look for in the life of a violent offender. When we're dealing with someone who already has personality problems, removal of the few anchors he has in his life can push him over the edge, as we've seen time and time again. Denied access to Black at work (even barred from the company parking lot), Farley's behavior grew more menacing as he sensed the threat of losing control over her. Although he and Black had never had a real relationship, in his mind he was facing loss of his job and his girl at the same time. He continued to follow her and, before he got another job, devoted his days to his full-time position as a stalker, showing up at her house and spending hours trying to figure out (through painstaking trial and error) the code to open her garage. He tried to get the manager of her apartment complex to rent him the place next door. When Black learned this, she moved, as she had done earlier in her ordeal. But, as before, somehow Farley was able to track her down again.

He continued to use letters to communicate his moods, from loving to menacing, and to manipulate his way into her thoughts, if not her life. In one, he set up a date and used her lack of response as an excuse to show up at her house, dressed to go out. When she wouldn't go, he took it as evidence of how she played games with him. She found herself in an impossible situation. If she called him to refuse the date, he'd found a way to get her to talk to him, which she knew he would interpret as encouraging. But if she didn't contact him, he'd be on her doorstep, ready and waiting.

And he set up another impossible scenario. Out of work, he told her he was running out of money and outlined his plan: "I get a job or I live with you, there is no alternative." Before that crisis arrived, however, he found another position in his field.

By the winter of 1987–88, three years after her ordeal began, Black was growing increasingly nervous and getting more signals from Farley. He'd lost a job, lost his home in foreclosure, and was being investigated by the IRS, to whom he owed some $40,000 in back taxes and penalties. "This is going to escalate and soon . . . ," Farley wrote to her. "The shit has hit the fan . . . all because you think I'm a joke and refuse to listen or understand that I'm gravely serious." He continued to project the blame onto his victim: it was her fault they were estranged. She was forcing him to do these things.

Ironically, while he was blaming her for his behavior, she was spending considerable time trying to figure out how not to escalate things. She was warned that her situation with Farley could cost her her government security clearance. It wasn't enough that she was living with the stress of Farley's direct threats against her and the way he'd managed to insinuate himself into her life, causing her to move, affecting her personal relationships, altering every aspect of her personal life. Now he was indirectly jeopardizing her job. Black considered going for a restraining order, but as she put it, "I was afraid that a restraining order would not protect me and that it might set him off." In early 1988, however, Farley left an envelope on her car windshield that contained a note and a copy he'd made of the key to her house.

Leaving her the key was just another way for him to assert his dominance, as if to say, "I didn't use this, but I could have and I still could." I've dealt with enough of these control types to know that he got off on imagining the fear it created when she realized he had access to her house and she hadn't even known it. He must have visualized the look on her face when she opened the envelope—if he wasn't off watching from a distance. Just as the sexual assault part of a rape is much less gratifying to a rapist than the planning, fantasizing, and physical and emotional control over his victim, actually breaking into Laura Black's home and killing her wouldn't have been nearly as satisfying to Farley as instilling the fear in her and fantasizing about it. Guys like this live for the hunt, for the power struggle.

But by playing that card, he moved Black to take legal action. On February 2, 1988, she sought help from the criminal justice system, asserting that she'd reached "the end of my rope" and pleading, "I need the court's assistance and the assistance of the appropriate police agencies to keep this man out of my life."

She was granted a temporary restraining order that prohibited Farley from threatening, following, surveilling, or calling her. He was also prohibited from getting closer than three hundred feet of her home, office, softball practices and games, and aerobics classes. A date of February 17 was set for the hearing on a permanent restraining order.

Laura Black had spent much of her adult life trying to rid herself of Richard Wade Farley, but this action was the last straw from his point of view. On February 9 he purchased a twelve-gauge semiautomatic shotgun for $600, along with plenty of ammunition for it and the other weapons he had at home. He had no trouble in the security check because he had FBI clearance from his former job and because the restraining order didn't even show up—in California at that time there would have been no record of the order until it had been violated.

The next day Farley dropped off an envelope for Black's attorney. In it, he asserted that he had proof of his and Black's relationship, including receipts from dinner dates, a garage door opener he said she gave him, and recordings of phone calls. As further proof, he claimed he knew where Black kept a secret stash of cocaine and described times they'd gone away together. None of it was convincing to Black's lawyer.

Obviously, all of that was completely false. But there's an important point here. Let's assume Farley's claims were only half BS and that at one time he and Black had dated. Let's further assume that he had proof of this relationship. As a former special agent of the Federal Bureau of Investigation, I know of no laws, statutes, or articles in the Constitution that allow someone to stalk and systematically terrorize another human being just because at one point they did have a relationship. We'll get into the dynamics of this type of stalking in the next chapter, but the reasoning behind Farley's claims is the same faulty logic other offenders use to justify acquaintance rape. Breaking the law, demoralizing and/or physically harming another individual in the process, isn't acceptable—ever. Although all rapes are not the same, and all stalkings are not the same, they are all criminal acts perpetrated against victims who in no way asked for or deserved the horrendous treatment they received.

As the day of the hearing approached, Farley got ready for a new mission: he either had to convince Laura Black to drop the court matter or he was going to commit suicide right in front of her. "I just felt she had to see the end result of what I felt she had done to me . . . not just read about it," Farley later said. He rented a motor home, which he stocked full of his guns and ammunition, along with photographic equipment—presumably to record the proceedings in case he was able to lure her to go with him.

That morning he started out following his daily routine, showering, shaving, and dressing, stopping at a local Jack in the Box for breakfast. After that, however, he prepared for combat. He returned home, where he left his last will and testament to be found if plans to talk Black out of the permanent restraining order were unsuccessful. That afternoon, suited up like a schleppy Rambo, he drove the motor home (now full of nearly one hundred pounds of weaponry and ammo) to ESL, where he planned to wait for Black to leave work. As 3:00 P.M. approached, now wearing an ammunition vest to go with the headband and fatigues, Farley tired of waiting. He filled the vest with clips, slipped a knife in his belt, and revolvers in holsters he wore. When he was ready to leave the motor home a few minutes later, he was wearing or carrying seven weapons, including his shotgun, the revolvers, two semiautomatic pistols, and a rifle. In final preparation for the hunt, he grabbed a pair of earplugs and leather gloves.

As he made his way across the parking lot and into the building, the first person he met up with was forty-six-year-old Larry Kane, a data-processing specialist Farley knew. Farley fired at him with his shotgun and killed him. He also fired at another employee, Randell Hemingway, but missed him, before shooting into an office and killing twenty-three-year-old, recently married Wayne "Buddy" Williams. Farley kept shooting as he moved closer to Black's office. He killed his third victim on the staircase to the second floor, where he shot five more people (three of whom died of their wounds) before he reached Black's office. Although he claimed it was his intention to make her witness his suicide, once he saw her, he started firing. He missed her with the first shot, but the second hit her shoulder, knocking her out. When she came to seconds later, she saw she was bleeding heavily and managed to kick her office door closed as she screamed. He didn't force his way back in, so Black tried calling 911. But she got a busy signal. When she heard his trail of gunfire move away down the hall, she slipped out of her office to escape.

By now, the entire floor was in chaos, covered in blood and smoky from gunfire. Along with his former coworkers, Farley had been firing at computers as he passed through the building. Black found her coworker and friend, twenty-seven-year-old Glenda Moritz, shot and dying on the floor. Software engineer Helen Lamparter, forty-nine, was also out there, lying facedown. As Black tried to stop her own bleeding from a wound the size of her fist, she hid with coworkers for the next half hour, in shock, blood making gurgling sounds in her lungs, as a police negotiator tried to talk Farley into giving himself up. He asked Farley to consider what his mother would be going through.

"It's gonna be real bad for her," Farley said of his mother, whom he claimed was the only person who ever loved him.

As Black fought for her life, hiding with colleagues who stuffed paper towels against her shoulder to slow the blood loss, Farley stressed to the police that he "never wanted to hurt her," claiming, "All she had to do was go out with me." He kept moving from one room to the next so the SWAT team couldn't zero in on his location, until at one point, Black could hear him on the phone in the next room and decided to make her escape. She managed to get down the hall, down the stairs, and into the street. A waiting ambulance took her to the hospital, where she was treated for a collapsed lung and broken arm, in addition to the massive injury to her shoulder.

More than five hours after the shooting began, hours in which Farley threatened suicide and then ordered a sandwich and Pepsi for dinner, Black's tormentor surrendered. By that time, seven people lay dead, another four wounded. As he gave himself up, he announced, "I'm the guy who is shooting people." But even then he tried to shift some of the responsibility for his actions, saying, "Tell Laura Black this is about her." The next day—the day of the scheduled hearing—a San Jose court commissioner granted the permanent restraining order against Farley.

The nightmare still wasn't over for Laura Black. After the assault, she was hospitalized for nineteen days, facing four operations to reconstruct and repair her shattered shoulder. Since then, she's been through at least three more surgeries, yet will probably never regain total mobility or muscle control of the shoulder and arm. If she could forget the entire four-year ordeal, the constant pain and the scars on her body (including some on her leg, hip, and stomach from skin grafts) would surely remind her.

And Farley continued to write to her from prison. In one letter, he told Black she'd finally won, although I doubt she greeted that with much enthusiasm given that she never agreed to the terms of his war.

When the case went to trial, both Black and Farley spent time on the witness stand. While Black never looked at her tormentor, merely glancing in his direction when asked to identify him, Farley spoke of their "relationship" in the present tense. Those in attendance described him as transfixed by her presence, taking notes as she testified. His attorneys argued that since the killings were not premeditated, Farley should not be found guilty of first-degree murder. And in his testimony, Farley tried to remove himself from the killings, saying, "I remember the gun going off once or twice. . . . I had to be firing it. There was no one else holding the gun." He also described the scene in Laura Black's office—where he shot her instead of carrying out his supposed plan to shoot himself. According to Farley, Black was smiling when she first looked to see who was entering her office, but "the smile is very fleeting . . . when she saw me, the smile disappeared."

As though to explain why he shot her, he again spoke in terms of the effect Black had on him, not the other way around. Her smile at that moment, Farley testified, "stuns me, basically, and the gun goes off." As in his letters to her, he was consciously missing the point again: the gun went off not because of her smile, but because he—who'd spent hundreds of dollars on ammunition and a new gun, rented a vehicle, dressed the part, and drove to her workplace, all in preparation for that very moment—consciously and willfully pulled the trigger.

Prosecutors wanted a verdict of guilt and a sentence of death. Police negotiator Lt. Ruben Grijalva was called to testify and recalled for the jury how Farley said he'd stopped shooting people because he didn't find it "fun anymore." The lieutenant reported that even when he was done firing at his former coworkers, Farley said he wasn't ready to surrender too quickly because he'd like to "gloat for a while." Between what they heard from Grijalva and from Farley's own testimony, the jurors got a good look at the chilling personality of the man. At one point Farley spelled out the terms of his near four-year reign of terror: "I win if I get to have Laura as a girlfriend, possibly a wife. . . . If she gets rid of me permanently, she's won."

The jury reached its verdict on October 21, 1991. Richard Farley was convicted of seven counts of first-degree murder. And although

Farley had previously promised in a letter, "I'll smile for the cameras on the way to the gas chamber," he was not smiling on November 1, when the jury recommended he be sentenced to die in said gas chamber. California's laws call for an automatic appeal in such cases, though, and as of now, Laura Black and all the survivors of Farley's rampage still await final justice.

I know there will be people who will say, "This poor man! Obviously he was terribly mentally disturbed. We should help him, not punish him." To them I say that this poor deranged mental case was somehow nonetheless able to hold down a full-time job at ESL and, after being fired, was able to get another job in his field. Then, while stalking Laura Black and working in the programming department of his new company, this poor man who so desperately needed help and compassion was also somehow able to take classes at San Jose State. He also met another woman—from whom he was able to keep his stalking of Black a secret—and got engaged. As he wrote in one of his letters to Black, "I'm really not insane, but I'm calculating. I just might scare us both with what I might do if I'm pushed into it." Some stalkers—many erotomaniacs among them—are mentally ill, and that's another story. But more, like Richard Farley, are master manipulators. They can use our compassion against us as we first fail to recognize dangerous behavior as more than simple pathetic, unrequited love, and then later as they try to evade punishment for their calculated and well-planned crimes.

The cases of Richard Wade Farley and Arthur Jackson offer prime examples of the importance of assessing dangerousness *before* a violent crime occurs. Clearly, Jackson suffered more severe personality defects (and possibly mental illness) than Farley. Farley was able to maintain (on the surface, at least) the image of a man who was self-sufficient and professionally successful, if not a social success, whereas Jackson was so dysfunctional and unstable that the only thing he ever succeeded in was the stalking of Theresa Saldana (and thankfully, he failed at his ultimate mission of killing her). But they were similar in terms of their single-minded obsessions with their chosen targets, and in the way they both gave off warning signals long before they committed their criminal acts.

Behavior reflects personality, and the two men revealed their potential for violence in different ways, consistent with their different personalities. Jackson's signs were more general, more related to his instability.

I believe, though, that when you're looking at someone whose identity is totally wrapped up in the lives of others (remember that Jackson had been obsessive over hopeless relationships from his early days as a schoolchild up to the day he tried to kill Theresa Saldana) and has nothing to lose, there's the potential for unpredictable behavior. Jackson had, after all, suffered several nervous breakdowns, tried committing suicide, and threatened the president of the United States. I think getting him out of the country was a good idea. It's just unfortunate that there was no system in place for the Secret Service to turn him over to authorities overseas in his own country who could appropriately monitor his behavior.

Although Richard Farley did not have a history as troubled as Jackson's, the signs were there in his letters and actions, as well as in the way he allowed his previously functional life to slip away. He was warned before he lost his job, but he persisted in his stalking behavior even as he knew his position, home, financial situation, and reputation all hung in the balance. If you start with a man whose behavior is already erratic and strip away all the remaining elements of normalcy in his life—giving him more anger to motivate him, and more time to fantasize—you're creating a recipe for disaster. Unfortunately, you don't need to have a rap sheet of previous violent crimes a mile long to be in a position to commit murder. Everyone who kills begins with a fantasy and a motivation, and if you read the signs, you can often see both.

California's antistalking legislation wasn't on the books when Farley was after Laura Black, but the case is a good example of why David Beatty says stalking-related behaviors need to be felony crimes. As he puts it, and as is so painfully evident from the Black case, stalking "is one of the rare opportunities where a potential murderer raises his hand and says, 'I'm gonna be killing somebody. Just wait. I'm on the path.'"

Beatty asks, "How difficult is it to prevent every other kind of murder? It's almost impossible." But stalking, he asserts, "leaves an opportunity to intervene in what seems to be in many cases an inevitable escalation towards violence and murder."

Laws weren't in place that were strong enough and specific enough to so identify Farley and stop him. We couldn't have predicted which seven individuals he would kill any more than we could have known that James Brady would pay for John Hinckley Jr.'s obsession with Jodie Foster for the rest of his life but we had indicators that *someone* was likely to pay dearly if no one intervened in either case. We can only hope now that enough people have died that we're ready to start picking these guys up and bringing them in when, as Beatty says, they first raise their hands.

Farley and Jackson can also give us some insight into how individual each stalking case is, depending on the offender. Jackson was so inadequate that he could not accomplish any intermediate stages in his stalking of Theresa Saldana: as soon as he found out where she was, he went for the kill. In some ways he was like David Carpenter, the socially inept, stuttering Trailside Killer, whom I profiled and pursued, and who murdered at least eight people in parks north of San Francisco before being apprehended. Carpenter betrayed his tremendously inadequate personality in his blitz style of attack, which gave his victims no time to react once the assault began, similar to Jackson's sudden, concentrated stabbing of Saldana.

Farley was in some ways more like Ronnie Shelton, with a similar combination of insecurity and arrogance. One former classmate described him as "one of those faceless people," and a "wimp," an image that would have been frustrating for a man who was also described by a former roommate as egotistical, "obsessed with always being right, with being macho." Where Shelton compensated for his insecurities by obsessively hitting on women, taking great pains with his appearance, and pursuing macho interests, getting into fights and collecting police paraphernalia, Farley joined the Navy. There, he was recognized for his marksmanship and good conduct and obviously got a lot out of the experience, since years later he alluded to how his training made him part of an "elite society," intimating that he'd been involved in secret surveillance operations that honed the skills he'd later use to keep track of and gather intelligence on Laura Black. Farley felt membership in this society made him special, allowing him to do things forbidden to others. Many of the serial offenders I've interviewed expressed a similar mix of feelings of invincibility and insecurity.

In the past (and to some extent even today) we have made it easy for stalkers to have those occasional feelings of invincibility. Unless they did something obviously dangerous to the victim, in many states no law had been broken for which they could be prosecuted. There were statutes against misdemeanors such as harassment, but even if someone was writing letters vowing to kill you, nothing could get the guy off the streets and remove the threat. It took one more tragic case for things to start to change.

As is often the case, when something happens to a famous person, the attendant publicity leads to heightened public awareness. The 1989 murder of Rebecca Schaeffer forced us all to look at stalking in a way we hadn't before. It forced the entertainment industry to recognize that anyone can be a victim, and it showed law enforcement just how dangerous these offenders can be.

Rebecca Schaeffer grew up in Portland, Oregon, the only child of a writer and a psychologist. A good student at Lincoln High School, she was also beautiful, with big brown eyes, a warm, friendly smile, dimples, and a ton of innocent charm. Schaeffer first tried her hand at modeling when she was in her early teens and landed roles in commercials as well as a part as an extra on a made-for-TV movie. She moved to New York City, where people in the modeling industry remember her as a "good kid" who, despite her youth, had a professional, serious approach to her work and was as clean-cut in her life as her image that appeared on the cover of *Seventeen* magazine.

Schaeffer's real career goal, though, was acting. She committed herself to acting lessons and the life of a struggling artist—even doing without phone service at one point because she couldn't afford it. With a regular part on a popular soap opera, she was soon offered a screen test for a role in the TV sitcom *My Sister Sam*. She landed the part and costarred with Pam Dawber, playing Dawber's younger sister on the show from 1986 to 1988. By the summer of 1989, she had also appeared in a feature film comedy, *Scenes from the Class Struggle in Beverly Hills,* and had just finished another film, directed by Dyan Cannon. That July she had a meeting scheduled with Francis Ford Coppola about a possible role in *The Godfather, Part III.* She was just twenty-one years old, with a life of unlimited potential ahead of her.

On the morning of July 18, 1989, the day after she'd thrown a party for her grandfather's seventy-first birthday, Schaeffer had reason to be in a good mood. In just under an hour she'd be meeting with the famous director about her possible next role. At about 10:15, someone rang the buzzer to her apartment. The intercom didn't work, so Schaeffer went to see who it was—still wearing her bathrobe. A young, white man with dark, bushy hair stood there waiting for her, a .357 magnum hidden in a bag. Probably before she had a chance to register what he was doing, the man drew his gun and shot her once in the chest at point-blank range. As she fell, screaming, he jogged down the block and disappeared. One of her neighbors ran to help her but could not find a pulse. She was taken to Cedars-Sinai Medical Center—the same hospital that had ministered to Theresa Saldana's wounds after her assault seven years earlier—where Schaeffer was pronounced dead just a half hour later. Her killer was still at large and her community—of neighbors, family, friends, fellow actors, and fans—was in shock.

Neighbors reported seeing a stranger hanging around in the hours before the murder, carrying a package. Some who'd walked by were approached by the young man in a yellow shirt, who showed them a publicity photo of Schaeffer and asked if they knew the actress and where she lived. At least one woman noticed him because she ran into him twice that morning and wondered what he was doing there. Another overheard him asking a cabdriver stopped in front of where Schaeffer lived if the structure was a house or apartment building. From all the descriptions of the UNSUB and his behavior—and from investigators' assessment that Schaeffer was not likely to have been killed by anyone she knew—the initial theory was that her killer was a disturbed fan.

These suspicions were confirmed the next day, when police in several jurisdictions worked together to identify and arrest a suspect: nineteen-year-old Robert John Bardo, an unemployed former fast-food-restaurant janitor from Tucson, Arizona. A friend of Bardo's who lived in Tennessee reported to police in L.A. that Bardo had talked about Schaeffer. The friend said Bardo had written a love letter to the young actress but that he'd also threatened her. The morning after the shooting, police in Tucson responded to reports of a man acting strangely in the middle of a major intersection. When they got there, they took Bardo into custody and faxed his picture to the LAPD, where several neighbors of Schaeffer's positively identified him as the young man they saw walking around outside her apartment. Bardo was charged with Schaeffer's murder.

Although police seemed to have the answer to the question of who killed Rebecca Schaeffer, the why was still a mystery. Bardo had a troubled history but no criminal, violent past, certainly nothing to indicate he would one day murder someone. Unless, that is, you knew what to look for. In retrospect, we can say that there were warning signs. But just as stalking was a little-reported and less understood crime than it is today, the telltale predictors that Robert John Bardo was potentially dangerous went unrecognized by those who might have helped protect Rebecca Schaeffer, both those who would have seen a disturbed pattern of behavior as Bardo grew up and those who would have shielded Schaeffer from any frightening contact with fans.

Robert John Bardo was the youngest child of seven in his family. His father, a noncommissioned Air Force officer, married a Korean woman living in Japan while at Yokota Air Force Base. As many military families do, the Bardos moved frequently before finally settling in Tucson when Robert was thirteen. Within months, Bardo started getting in trouble. That year, after stealing $140 from his mother, he hopped a bus to Maine in search of Samantha Smith, the young girl who had gained international attention with her letter to Mikhail Gorbachev. Bardo had written to Smith and she'd written back, which was apparently enough to send him on the journey across the country. Juvenile authorities found him before he was able to find Smith, however. Before he was returned home, he stabbed himself with a pen.

Although he earned straight A's in junior high school, his behavior was increasingly disturbing. A loner even then, he began writing letters to a teacher—at times more than one a day. Indicating he was already becoming more rooted in the world of fantasy than reality, he signed his letters in character as James Bond, Dirty Harry Callahan, and the like. He wrote of death—his own by suicide and the murder of his teacher and others. According to at least one published report, teachers tried to convince his parents he was in need of psychiatric intervention. But aside from one week of counseling at Palo Verde Hospital, the teachers' recommendations went unheeded.

Both Park Dietz and another psychiatrist, Dr. John Stalberg, indicated after studying Bardo's case that his family background was likely a contributing factor to his erratic, unsocial behavior. Although I wouldn't make the leap of logic to say that having a reportedly alcoholic father and/or paranoid mother leads to a child's becoming a stalker and a murderer, Bardo's disturbing background is consistent with those of so many criminals I've studied. According to one report, Bardo filled out a form sent by school officials to his parents and took the opportunity to ask for help: "This house is hell. . . . I can't handle it anymore. Please help. Fast." Bardo indicated to psychiatrists who interviewed him after the crime that an older brother abused him physically, allegedly forcing him to drink urine and shoplift. Whatever the source of Bardo's troubles, at the very least his parents seem to have been in denial about the extent of their son's problems.

By high school, his behavior was so disturbing that one former teacher characterized him as "a time bomb waiting to explode." Although still making A's, he wrote one teacher a ten-page letter in which he threatened to kill himself. After temporary placement in a foster home, he was returned to his parents. In 1985, he was hospitalized during the summer and was evaluated as "severely emotionally handicapped," and his family described as "pathological and dysfunctional." In general, though, he was regarded as a good patient, enthusiastic about treatment and therapy and in some ways a role model for other young patients, whom he discouraged from using illegal drugs. Although it seemed he was making progress, his parents took him home after a month. Just weeks later, he left high school for good.

At this point, his fantasy life grew increasingly important, and his career as a stalker (and ultimately a murderer) began to take form. He was a social outcast at school, but at least there he had his grades to help shore up his ego. Without that, all the insecurities and inadequacies overwhelmed him. This young man who was smart enough to get straight A's became a janitor at Jack in the Box, leaving his parents' house before five in the morning to start the two-mile walk to work. When he wasn't cleaning the fast-food restaurant, he was sleeping, playing guitar, or immersing himself in the alternative reality of TV and radio.

His introduction to Rebecca Schaeffer occurred in 1986. At this point, the asocial sixteen-year-old had never had a date, let alone a girlfriend, and never had sex. To someone like Bardo, Schaeffer represented an ideal: pretty, young, and innocent-looking, she was completely nonthreatening. Bardo watched her on *My Sister Sam* and would later say, "She just came into my life at the right time." He started writing letters to her. She answered one, in which he'd written his thoughts on friendship and spirituality, with a compliment on how nice and "real" his letter was and signed it "Love, Rebecca." This was for Bardo what lunch with Laura Black and another coworker was to Richard Farley. In Bardo's mind, the connection he'd felt watching her on TV had been solidified by this contact, the first time he'd had this with a woman.

Bardo remained obsessed with Schaeffer, but for a time in 1988 diverted some of his attention to other famous young celebrities, including the singers Tiffany and Debbie Gibson—both of whom offered the same blend of youthful innocence and budding femininity Schaeffer embodied. In 1989, though, he saw Schaeffer in a bedroom love scene in the film *Scenes from the Class Struggle in Beverly Hills*. Although he'd let his obsession wane, his attention—and fury—now turned back to Schaeffer. What had been for her just another role in her expanding career signified to Bardo that she was becoming, as he put it, "just another Hollywood whore."

Like Theresa Saldana and Laura Black, Rebecca Schaeffer was a low-risk victim. Although she was becoming famous, she lived a low-key lifestyle in an average, relatively safe neighborhood. According to her friends and coworkers, she was well liked, and her talent was greatly respected. Her *Sam* costar Pam Dawber adored her and was devastated by her death. She had no enemies. Or at least, no enemies that she knew of before Bardo killed her. Schaeffer had only seen early fan mail from Bardo. Her agent and people at the studio where she worked screened the mail and threw away frightening letters so as not to worry the young actress, who remained unaware of Bardo's growing obsession. Before he shot Schaeffer at her home, Bardo had tried to reach her at the Warner Brothers lot where they taped her show. The first time, he carried a large stuffed teddy bear and a letter for the actress, but was turned away by security guards. The second time, angry at what he perceived as Schaeffer's increasing arrogance, he carried a knife. This time, according to one account, the director of security drove Bardo back to his hotel and told him it was time to return to Arizona.

With his history of letters and visits, Bardo was sending a clear message to Schaeffer's people that he was desperate for contact with her. I'd like to believe that if the same thing happened today, someone with a solid background in threat assessment would be analyzing the situation. I know that Gavin de Becker, for one, would be, were she his client. Perhaps such an expert would have been able to predict that Schaeffer's name appeared frequently in Bardo's diary, where he wrote, "I feel that I want to become famous and impress her." I believe an expert would have known of Bardo's extensive collection of Schaeffer memorabilia, including videotapes and still more letters to the actress. And, perhaps, that expert would have read Bardo's letters and warned that the fan, although inadequate and unable to function well in society, was intelligent and resourceful enough to prove himself dangerous.

In fact, some of the same skills that served him well in school helped Bardo finally get to Schaeffer. He studied how Arthur Jackson gained access to his victim and hired his own private detective a month before the murder. It cost the PI just $4 to get Schaeffer's address at the California Department of Motor Vehicles, but the information was worth a lot more to Bardo, who paid $250. That, ultimately, was what Rebecca Schaeffer's precious life cost.

Like Jackson, Bardo was more resourceful and focused on the mission to kill Schaeffer than he had been with anything else in his life. In Arizona, you had to be twenty-one to purchase a firearm, so Bardo got an older brother to buy one for him. He wanted to make sure his attempt wasn't a failure, so he got hollow-point cartridges, designed to expand as they penetrate.

In 1991, Marcia Clark, now known for her role as chief prosecutor of the O. J. Simpson case, was the Los Angeles County deputy district attorney who handled the case against Bardo. Defense attorney Stephen Galindo was able to remove the possibility of a death sentence by waiving a jury trial. While not disputing the prosecution's assertion that Bardo pulled the trigger, the defense argued that Bardo was insane. To my knowledge, it was the only time Park Dietz testified for an insanity ruling in a murder case, and Park, whom I respect immensely, knew I disagreed with him on this one. Gavin de Becker worked with the prosecution, elucidating the planning, organization, and thought that went into the obsession and the crime.

As he pointed out in his fine book, *The Gift of Fear,* Gavin made clear that what might at first seem like insane, irrational, "sick" behavior is actually quite rational within the context of the personality of the stalker. "Assassins," he writes, "do not fear they are going to jail—*they fear they are going to fail,* and Bardo was no different. He had gotten all the components together: He had studied other assassins, he had researched his target, made his plan, gotten the gun, written the letters to be found after the attack. But like the daredevil, he was just a guy who worked at Jack in the Box until he made that jump, until the wheels left the ground, until he killed someone famous. Everything that goes with fame was waiting for him on the other side of the canyon, where, in his words, he'd finally be 'a peer' with celebrities."

Judge Dino Fulgoni found Robert John Bardo guilty of first-degree murder and sentenced him to life in prison without the possibility of parole. I hope that means what it says since he had, with great deliberation, sentenced Rebecca Shaeffer to death. His sentence is being served in California State Prison in Vacaville, which has also been home to Edmund Kemper.

Was Robert John Bardo a confused, disturbed, depressive personality? Yes. Was he damaged by a difficult upbringing? Possibly. Do I believe that these factors forced him to viciously take Rebecca Schaeffer's life, or in any way excuse his actions? Absolutely not. He chose to do this. He fantasized about it, he planned it, he premeditated it months ahead of time, and he carried it out. The day he killed her, he actually rang Schaeffer's buzzer twice. The first time the young woman came to the door they had a quick conversation, during which he gave her a note. She told him, "Take care," as she closed the door.

He had his audience with her then. He could have left, allowing that meeting to suffice. Instead, he went and got breakfast and then returned to kill her. Bardo himself later summed up his personality defects: "I'm not insane. . . . I'm just emotional." According to one report, he was able to look back objectively at his life from his jail cell and admit that dropping out of school was a mistake, that at that point he was completely isolated from real life, at home only in the world of movies and television. Truly delusional individuals do not recognize their retreat into fantasy as such. Marcia Clark thinks he's more a con man than someone who deserves sympathy. I have to agree with her, and with Gavin's assessment that he was primarily motivated by a need for fame, to draw attention to himself. In that way, he fits the assassin mold.

In the mid-1980s, Park Dietz researched and compiled a list of indicative behaviors commonly displayed by assassins. These include some sort of mental disorder, researching the target, keeping a diary, securing a weapon, communicating inappropriately with a public figure, narcissism and grandiosity, random travel, identifying with a previous assassin, getting around security and making repeated approaches to one or more public figures. As we see, this assassin behavior Park outlined applies equally to stalkers.

Gavin de Becker's research tells him that the most important single indicator of danger to the life of a celebrity or public figure from a stalker/assassin is what he calls "ability belief"—that is, the individual's belief that he can accomplish his mission. This seems to be the reason Bremer shifted his attentions from Richard Nixon to George Wallace. He didn't believe he could kill Nixon, but he did believe he could kill Wallace.

Before killing Schaeffer, Robert Bardo wrote to his sister, "I have an obsession with the unattainable . . . I have to eliminate what I cannot attain." As with Mark David Chapman's obsession with John Lennon, these statements, I believe, apply as much to the unattainability of the success and importance Ms. Schaeffer achieved in her life as they did to the unattainability of the actress as a girlfriend figure to Bardo. Again, we're dealing with an insignificant nobody—in this case, someone clearly living below his intellectual potential and frustrated by that— who can only achieve recognition by taking the life of someone famous.

Rebecca Schaeffer's murder had far-reaching effects for the Hollywood community and, on a larger scale, the criminal justice system in the United States. In this case, the senseless killing of one good person with a promising future before her caused outrage and concern that fueled positive changes. In 1990, California became the first state to pass specific antistalking legislation, which was a model for similar legislation throughout the country. Just months after Schaeffer's murder, the Conference of Personal Managers, a group composed of agents representing celebrities, met with experts in the security field and with officials from the Los Angeles Police Department. The goal was to highlight the concerns the agents had for their clients' safety and to discuss options open to them. It was the first step in the police department's development of a special unit to handle such cases of harassment. The LAPD's Threat Management Unit went into operation in July of 1990, the first unit of its kind in the United States.

There have been other consequences of Schaeffer's murder as well. The idea that Robert Bardo was able to "buy" Schaeffer's address (through a middleman) from the California DMV led that agency to increase restrictions on public access to its records. And the industry in general became even more sensitive to the advice of experts like Park Dietz and Gavin de Becker.

Even with antistalking legislation and a greater focus on the dangers, we still have a long way to go. De Becker estimates that internationally prominent stars such as Madonna may be recognized by more than a billion people, and with every detail of the star's personal life so well publicized, even those of us who are not obsessed can easily come to feel that we "know" her and others of her stature.

And the publicity machine surrounding the famous negotiates a delicate line between protecting the celebrity and keeping his or her image accessible to fans. Today, even after Saldana's attack, Schaeffer's death, and a great number of threats and deflected attempts, many in the entertainment industry seem unwilling to err on the side of caution.

With so large a group of celebrities in the New York area, Linda Fairstein naturally sees love-obsession stalking cases. "Part of the problem with a lot of the public figures," she says, "is they are discouraged from having the person arrested. It's going to be bad for their image. It's going to be in the tabloids. They're going to look like they're mean to someone who has a psych problem." But the laws won't protect anyone unless they're utilized.

Recent laws, too, offer no protection for Theresa Saldana. She was fortunate enough to survive her attack, but Arthur Jackson was also fortunate in terms of his timing. When he was convicted in connection with her assault, the maximum sentence was twelve years. Since then, California's sentencing guidelines have changed. The maximum sentence for the same crimes for which he was convicted today would be life imprisonment. But this revision is not retroactive.

Jackson was deemed dangerous enough to be denied parole during the twelve-year term, however. While imprisoned in Vacaville, at the same time that he reported he would "cross to the other side of the street" if he ever ran into Saldana again, he admitted that "by some extraordinary coincidence, I became enamored by a quasi-transsexual Puerto Rican inmate . . . who bore a vague resemblance to Ms. Saldana." Jackson also made it clear to prison officials and his fellow inmates that his obsession with Saldana was far from a relic of the past, expressing that someday he looked forward to "completing his mission."

Jackson even wrote to others on the subject, including a former producer for Geraldo Rivera's television show. In that 1988 letter, Jackson detailed his assassination plan, warning that "police or FBI protection for T.S. won't stop the hit squad." A year later he again voiced his intention to kill Saldana in a phone conversation with a Los Angeles–based reporter for the *Scottish Daily Record*.

It is sadly not surprising that Jackson's obsession with his victim did not let up even after he was convicted and imprisoned. Lt. John Lane, the founding head of the LAPD Threat Management Unit since its inception, has observed, "These are very long-term cases. . . . People can stay focused on an individual for one or more years." And this is true whether the victim is a celebrity or the woman next door.

David Beatty tells of one heartbreaking case where a victim was stalked for more than twenty years by the same man. He didn't just decide to leave her alone one day, and he wasn't arrested and put away. He simply died. The only way she was able to get relief was to outlive her stalker. But not every victim of stalking can count on that.

I am often frustrated when prison psychiatrists look at an offender's behavior in a controlled environment (where the inmate in question may be kept organized and safely medicated) and decide the guy's doing well and should be given another chance. In Jackson's case, I am pleased to report, officials who evaluated him recognized the true dangerousness of their patient. In 1988, the clinical and medical director at Atascadero State Hospital, Dr. Gordon W. Gritter, assessed Jackson as a "very dangerous man" after a psychiatric evaluation. Dr. V. Meenakshi, the chief psychiatrist at Vacaville, reported, "He's well-behaved, but he's crazy. . . . I'm uncomfortable about releasing him because he's still psychotic and still paranoid."

So in Jackson's case, with all this threatening behavior and expert opinions that he's still dangerous to Theresa Saldana and possibly others, he must still be locked up in California, right? Actually, although one would think the situation would be enough to trigger a judicial response beyond denying bail, Jackson's eventual freedom from the California prison system was essentially grandfathered when he was convicted for his crime. Once he served his twelve years, he was scheduled to be released. In fact, he had been given a parole date in March of 1990—the halfway point in his original sentence—because of "good behavior." As a frustrated and frightened Saldana noted in a 1989 interview, fearing Jackson's parole, "If he threw his food against the wall or used curse words to guards, that would count as bad behavior. But threatening Theresa Saldana or the Queen of England doesn't count." One might imagine the early parole was canceled because of his threats, but it was actually the result of other behavior, such as breaking windows and disobeying orders. These infractions resulted in the addition of 270 days to his sentence and eventual charges stemming from sixteen threatening letters he sent while still in prison.

As we'll see later, there are now laws that deal with this, thanks in large measure to the leadership and heroism of a family from Kansas whose daughter was brutally murdered by a paroled predator.

At this point, Jackson is being held not in connection with his threats, but because during his incarceration he wrote to police in London and confessed his involvement in a 1966 bank robbery in which one man was killed and two were wounded. After checking fingerprints and investigating the case, officials at Scotland Yard had enough information to issue a warrant for Jackson's arrest. In June of 1996, per British-U.S. extradition laws, he was released to officers from Scotland Yard. Then sixty-one years old, he was taken to Britain, where he faces charges.

Any of us can become the object of a stalker. And as we see from such offenders as Arthur Jackson, once launched on their quest, they do not easily give it up. If we are to prevent more of us from becoming victims of these maniacs, it is going to take real recognition of the extent of the problem and the concerted efforts and cooperation of law enforcement agencies, friends, family, neighbors, coworkers, and employers of the person being stalked, as well as the alertness of authorities in the institutions where some of these people may be being held.

If we all care, and we all work together, maybe we can get something valuable and lasting accomplished.

CHAPTER TEN

IF I CAN'T HAVE YOU, NOBODY WILL

California is not only the birthplace of current antistalking legislation in the United States, in 1991 it was home to the first ever felony arrest resulting from the still newly defined crime. The case didn't involve a famous celebrity but was related to domestic violence, which is actually more representative of most of these situations.

In May of 1991, police in the Sherman Oaks section of Los Angeles charged a man with the stalking of his ex-girlfriend. The two had dated for a couple of years, and when the woman tried to break up with the man, he wouldn't accept it. He began harassing her by telephone, vandalized her car, and even abducted her dog. The woman got a restraining order and filed a total of thirteen charges against her ex-boyfriend with the police before he finally called her at work with a direct threat: he was "ready to play hardball . . . [and] you'll be the next thing damaged."

After taking the man into custody, police discovered a .357 magnum under the bed in his apartment—the same caliber handgun Robert John Bardo used to shoot Rebecca Schaeffer in the heart. Under the new stalking law, the man was sentenced to a year in prison, plus six months in a rehabilitation facility. Is this sentence adequate for a man with a track record of threatening behavior and a clear intent to harm a woman? I'd say not. But it was the first arrest and conviction under the new law, and it was clearly a step in the right direction.

While the obviously mentally imbalanced love-obsession stalkers of celebrities may come to mind first, the National Victim Center believes that up to 80 percent of stalking cases involve a woman who is victimized by someone she knows well. This is known as "simple obsession" stalking, and in this type of crime the offender and victim had a relationship before the criminal behavior started. As frightening and unpredictable as an Arthur Jackson is, just as insidious are those who blend into the woodwork—say, a jealous ex-husband who is able to terrorize his estranged wife while keeping up appearances at work, church, and in social life. And as scary as it is to think that one of my daughters could run into a Richard Farley type, it's just as disturbing to imagine that one might go out on a few dates with the wrong guy and then find it virtually impossible to get him out of her life.

Simple obsession stalkers not only represent the majority of stalking cases, but are the most dangerous and, at times, deadly. While a percentage of love-obsession offenders hunt down the object of their obsession and attempt to physically harm them, many are too disorganized to launch such an effort or carry it out successfully. The majority are not career criminals. Simple obsession stalkers, on the other hand, can have a long history of abusive and/or violent behavior, although that may not be reflected in the form of a criminal record.

It's like Ronnie Shelton getting away with years of Peeping Tom activities. We've seen that for every serial rape case prosecuted, there may be a frightening number of lesser or even equal offenses committed that go unreported. Similarly, many simple obsession stalkers practice behaviors leading up to stalking that are abusive—emotionally and sometimes physically—for which they're never charged or punished. In some cases, this is because the offenses are minor and the victim is more concerned with getting out of the relationship than pursuing legal action. Other times, an abused wife may be too intimidated to report her husband's repeated violence to authorities until the one time her neighbors or children call 911.

Simple obsession stalking is so intimately related to domestic violence that they are virtually inseparable—different extensions of the same pattern of controlling, dominating behavior. Like love-obsession stalkers, though, the pace at which the offender's emotional dependence blossoms into a full-blown obsession can take anywhere from years down to weeks—or even just a few dates. And dangerousness can escalate remarkably quickly.

In cases where there has been a longer-term relationship between the victim and the stalker, the history of the offender's abusive behavior makes him all the more menacing as a stalker. He knows his victim as love-obsession stalkers cannot; he knows which buttons to push. He knows his victim's vulnerabilities. Even more frightening and dangerous, their past relationship has given him the intelligence data he needs. He already knows her patterns, her schedule, where she keeps her money, who her doctor is, whom she would count on and where she would go in an emergency.

There are warning signs before one of these guys begins stalking his victim, but, unfortunately, they are often not revealed until she is already somewhat involved with him, which is why intelligent, otherwise self-protective women can find themselves in this type of situation. These offenders are not obvious "bad guys" you can spot across a room. On the contrary, many can be quite charming at first, creating a favorable initial impression. Like certain other types of sexual predators, they are good at what they do.

In his relationship with the girlfriend who ended up testifying against him, Ronnie Shelton exhibited many of the domestic violence behaviors that mark the simple obsession stalker. Unlike his other rape victims, who saw only his frightening side, she had seen the charm he could exude when coming on to a new conquest. At first, he seemed polite, gentlemanly. In this regard, he was a classic domestic violence abuser. It wasn't until later in their relationship that his controlling, jealous, and insecure side began to show. Like many offenders of his type—including domestic abusers who go on to stalk their victims—he seemed not to believe normal social rules applied to him and therefore had no problem lying, cheating, or breaking the law to get what he wanted. Other typical characteristics of this type embodied by Shelton include a lack of conscience, empathy, or concern for others (both the partner he abused and the women he raped), as well as the manipulative behavior he used to keep his girlfriend in line and others fooled as to his true personality.

It is a common misperception that these types of stalkers—and domestic violence abusers in general—are generally under-educated, unemployed or holding menial jobs, and living close to the poverty level. But in fact, this is yet another crime where anybody can be an offender . . . or a victim—people from all races, socioeconomic backgrounds, even gender. According to one assessment, around a third of men undergoing counseling for physically abusing a wife or girlfriend held respectable, professional occupations and often enjoyed high status in the community as executives, doctors, even ministers.

And there are plenty of examples from the world of the rich and famous. In the case of O. J. Simpson, there is evidence of both his physical abuse of his ex-wife, Nicole, and of simple obsession stalking behavior: he interrupted her dates with other men and reportedly even watched her have sex from the shadows outside the home where she was murdered.

Another shocking case involved a highly regarded member of the criminal justice community—clearly not someone you'd expect to hear involved in such criminal behavior. Sol Wachtler, formerly chief judge of the New York State Court of Appeals, was ultimately jailed for his harassing behavior against a woman—his wife's cousin—with whom he'd had an extramarital affair.

Whether a successful businessman who stalks his estranged wife or—as we're seeing more and more often now—a high school teen who cannot let go of his first serious girlfriend, for the simple obsession stalker, criminal behavior grows out of a need to control and dominate his victim to boost his self-esteem. Like the love-obsession stalker who also suffers from extreme insecurity, this offender is often unable to develop and maintain personal and love relationships as others do. Some may have psychological problems, but for the majority, the problem is a personality disorder that manifests itself in inappropriate behavior and impaired social skills. They often feel powerless in everyday situations, and this, coupled with their inadequacies, makes them invest a lot of their emotions and sense of self-worth in their relationship with this other person. Stalking is just one manifestation of a jealous, paranoid husband's or lover's need to dominate his mate.

In a sense, both types of stalkers operate in the world of a fantasy relationship. Because although the simple obsession stalker actually had a relationship with his victim, what he is really obsessed with is the feeling of power he got out of the relationship, not the woman herself.

In profiling this type of stalker, compensation for insecurity and inadequacy is a primary characteristic worth noting. Some readers of *Mindhunter* and *Journey into Darkness* observed that it seemed as if virtually all the offenders we described shared variations on this theme. Sometimes their insecurity makes them seem cocky and act out, like Ronnie Shelton. Other times it overwhelms them to the point that the only way they feel they can vent is through a murderous, blitz-style attack, like Arthur Jackson. The universality of this characteristic on the part of so many different offenders makes it a critical observation. Obviously not all insecure men become serial killers, rapists, or stalkers, but it is an important element in the total picture and can often be the first warning sign we're given. And in a country where we know that about 12 percent of all couples will have some incident involving at least a "mild" form of violence, such as slapping or pushing, and where about 1,500 women are killed annually by a husband or lover, any clues we get are worth noting.

It is especially true in this particular crime category, because domestic abusers—including those who end up stalking their partners—often reveal their personality defects in subtle ways that don't set off warning buzzers. The future victim may be completely unaware of what she is getting into at first. The abuser can be so manipulative and cunning, the behavior so insidious, that she may not realize what is going on until she is enmeshed in a potentially dangerous relationship.

Before any physical and/or emotional abuse begins, the offender may first appear attentive, which soon reveals itself as truly more possessive and jealous than caring. He tries to control aspects of his mate or girlfriend's life—from picking out her clothing to trying to limit the time she spends away from him. An abusive husband or boyfriend may humiliate his victim, criticizing her appearance, downplaying her skills as a homemaker, mother, student, successful professional—whatever role she holds within and outside their relationship that gives her a sense of self-worth. He has the most strength if he can keep her off-balance, and playing mind games is one way he does this.

His most successful game involves switching moods: loving and tender one moment, angry and violent the next. His partner never knows whom she's dealing with, and while she fears and loathes the one side of his behavior, she cares for the other and thrives under his attention.

To increase his control over his partner, the abuser will try to put his victim in a situation where she is economically dependent on him. And if a child is involved, this makes it even easier for him to keep her under control as she may not feel able to support herself and her child on her own. She may also be afraid that if she leaves, he will get custody of—or outright kidnap—her children and she will never see them or be able to protect them from him again. There have even been cases where terrified mothers have escaped to a community "safe house," only to have the court force her to reveal her location when her husband sues for visitation rights. Thus, the same court system that a victim of domestic violence may turn to for protection has also been used by her abuser/stalker to exercise further control over her and maintain his presence in her life even after she's physically fled their home. Sadly, it is easy enough to see why some women, lacking the financial resources to fight what seems to them an endless legal war, either give up and return to face more abuse or disappear underground in desperation, giving up jobs, family, and friends.

As an abusive relationship continues, the offender grows increasingly critical of her friends and family, more and more jealous and controlling of the time she spends away from him. She may get to the point where she feels it's not worth the fight to see others, and if he has beaten her and the marks are visible, she may be too embarrassed to see them. There are cases where abusers force their victims to keep records of every minute of their day, check the mileage on the car, count the change in their purses—micromanaging every aspect of their lives and wearing them down completely.

In these cases, stalking and surveillance activities are already part of the domestic abuser's routine, his control and domination of his partner, much as Richard Farley's stalking of Laura Black was, to his way of thinking, a battle of wills that he was desperate to win. And just as Farley noted his frustration (as well as his "love") in his letters to Black, these abusers may well recognize their anger even if they can't admit to their inadequacy. Like Farley, they will not acknowledge the true reason for their dependence on this relationship—or that they are in a position of dependence at all—but will project any blame for their actions on their victim. They may see their need to control as either their duty as a "good" husband or their right. In the man's mind, violence occurs not because he is unable to cope with his emotions and lacks self-control, but because the victim did something wrong, something to set him off.

In one horrific example, as a Fort Worth man stabbed his wife to death in front of their two children, ages twelve and sixteen, he told her, "You did this to yourself." His rationale was that she and the children had started eating without him.

Before you shout, "This guy is nuts!" note that he held a responsible position as a computer specialist with the Federal Aviation Administration. This was probably not the first time he'd assaulted his wife, and I'm sure it was not the only time he found a way to justify his actions to himself.

As Gavin de Becker writes, "Why are we fascinated when a famous person is attacked by a stalker, which happens once every two or three years, yet uninterested when a woman is killed by a stalking husband or boyfriend, which happens once every two hours? Why does America have thousands of suicide prevention centers and not one homicide prevention center?"

When a woman escapes such a relationship, the abuser may rationalize his subsequent stalking behavior as either efforts to win her back—often trying first the charming, flowers-and-candy routine he used to win her the first time, like the gifts Richard Farley left for Laura Black—or as punishment she deserves for leaving him and treating him so unfairly. In his mind, she's his wife, and she'd better start acting like it.

The sexual sadist-killer of Ontario, Canada, Paul Bernardo, whose case we recounted in *Journey into Darkness,* treated his wife, Karla Homolka, in just such a fashion. She had to do all the work, accede to him sexually and in every other way, and submit to his beatings whenever he felt she deserved it. Even worse, he expected her to be a partner in rapes and murders, even the crime that led to the death of her sister, Tammy. Karla became his physical possession. When you think about it, if the abuser needs to make his victim even lower than himself, and he's a completely inadequate person, then his victim has to assume a subhuman role. She goes from being wife to property.

All of the abuser's personality defects and pathological rationalizations combine to make conditions extremely dangerous for a woman when she leaves a man like this. Overwhelmed with his own inadequacy and impotence, his emotions at that point also include rage that she would reject him and try to assert control, fear that he's been abandoned, and the drive for revenge. Threatened with losing the only aspect of his life that makes him feel powerful and in control, the abuser grows desperate. These are the cases where we hear variations on the practically stock phrase "If I can't have her, nobody will."

And statistics show that the most dangerous point in these situations is when the abused partner makes an effort to leave the relationship—whether they've been through this cycle together over a twenty-year marriage or a two-month dating courtship. The FBI's

1990 Uniform Crime Reports estimated that 30 percent of the female victims of homicide that year were killed by an intimate partner. Consider that along with the fact that victims of domestic violence who try to leave their abuser have a greater risk of being murdered by their spouse/partner, and you can see why it's critical that we recognize these potentially dangerous individuals early.

This brings us to the same good news/bad news scenario we have with the love-obsession stalker. The good news is that these guys tend to follow a basic pattern or cycle, and as with other types of offenders, if we know what we're looking for, we can predict the level of threat they represent to a potential victim. The bad news is that just as no one can predict when a love-obsession stalker will pass through specific stages in the cycle, or what behaviors he will exhibit in each, it is difficult to predict what a simple obsession stalker will do at any given moment. In many tragic cases, friends, family members, neighbors, coworkers tell investigators after a victim's been killed, "I knew he would kill her one of these days." Nicole Brown Simpson reportedly predicted she would die at the hands of her still-possessive ex-husband, O.J.

As public awareness of domestic violence and stalking grows—and as we get better legislation and more realistic sentencing guidelines to deal with these crimes—it's my hope that we'll more often take action *before* the victim is killed.

We can predict that the simple obsession stalker will run through the same basic pattern of behavior as the love-obsession stalker, beginning with the early stage where he tries to win his victim back using the flowers-and-charm routine. The next stage, intimidation, is reminiscent of the jealous, overly possessive and inappropriate behavior that led the victim to leave the relationship.

Like the love-obsession stalker, as the simple obsession stalker grows more frustrated by what he perceives as his victim's unwillingness to give him what he needs, he becomes increasingly harassing and threatening, in keeping with the abusive behavior he's accustomed to inflicting.

As David Beatty puts it, "The only thing that's changed is that the victim has inconveniently been removed from a venue where the offender can easily pursue and beat her in a physical fashion. He doesn't have the luxury of being able to just go across the room and commit violent acts and so is forced to create new tactics to do the same thing."

The offender's motivation and behavior is the same as it was before, only the specific strategies are different.

If the victim tries to permanently remove him from her life at this stage he may become violent in a last-ditch effort to reassert his control over their relationship. Laura Black's seeking a permanent restraining order against Richard Farley was just such a trigger. Think of all the cases you've read about where an unhappy, abuse-haunted marriage ends in a murder-suicide after the wife tries to move out or get a court order to keep her husband away from her and their children.

And simple obsession stalkings don't only happen to people who've been suffering in an emotionally and/or physically abusive relationship for years. It can be just as tragic when a victim spots the warning signs, acts on her growing awareness of danger early, and is still unable to save herself.

In 1982, twenty-two-year-old Dominique Dunne seemed to have it all. The daughter of writer and producer Dominick Dunne and Ellen Griffin Dunne, known as Lenny, and niece of writers Joan Didion and John Gregory Dunne, Dominique came from a background that was as loving and supportive as it was well connected. Youthful and pretty, smart and talented—at that stage where she could alternate between beautiful and girlish—Dunne had already appeared in many roles on television and that year costarred in the film *Poltergeist*. She had every reason to believe her career was taking off.

Her personal life, however, was conflicted. About a year before, she'd met John Thomas Sweeney, five years older and a chef at one of the "in" restaurants in L.A., Ma Maison. A full foot taller than Dunne, Sweeney was well built and handsome, and on the surface they seemed an excellent match. Both were talented and ambitious, and they shared many interests. Within a short time, they moved in together.

At first, Sweeney seemed quite the devoted boyfriend, going to Dominique's acting classes and appearing on the set where she was filming. They even went to the same therapist. But it became apparent that his actions were motivated by jealousy and a strong possessive streak. They would argue, and Dominique felt stifled. Sweeney grew ever more afraid that he would lose her. Threatened by her sophisticated friends and jealous of any man she might share a love scene with—although she gave him no cause to be—he reportedly accused her of having abortions, a claim that was completely unfounded.

There is no way to "talk sense" into an overly jealous lover ruled by his insecurities, although if she was like most normal, intelligent people, Dominique probably tried. The relationship became a battle as she tried to wrestle herself free and Sweeney vied for even greater control.

Her brother Alex related a scene in a restaurant during which a slightly tipsy fan who had seen her in *Poltergeist* approached her table while Sweeney was in the men's room. When he returned to the table and saw the man talking with her, he flew into a rage, physically lifted the fan off his feet, and began shaking him violently.

Her desperate understanding of the situation came through in an insightful letter she wrote, but apparently never sent him: "You do not love me. You are obsessed with me. The person you think you love is not me at all. It is someone you have made up in your head. . . . We only fight when images of me fade away and you are faced with the real me." She also wrote that she was afraid of him.

By August of 1982, he had grown violent, at one point reportedly grabbing her by the hair so hard he actually pulled out handfuls. She escaped to her mother's house in tears, and when he followed, Mrs. Dunne threatened to summon the police.

As is often the pattern in an abusive relationship, though, Sweeney was able to win Dominique back a few days later, no doubt after summoning up his most charming behavior. The bright and forgiving young woman simply did not have the experience yet to know that you can never go back to the "good old days" with a guy like this. Sooner or later, he will return to his jealousy, possessiveness, anger, and violence. And John Sweeney was no exception.

Within a few weeks they had another argument, during which he started choking her. Fortunately, a friend was staying with them at the time, heard what was happening, and interrupted the assault. Dominique escaped out a bathroom window, chased by Sweeney, who jumped onto her car to make her stop. But she got away and vowed that was the end. After days of hiding, she was able to get him to move out of her home and she changed the locks. She'd given him the "one more chance," and he'd blown it.

In a poignant and ironic coda, a few days after the funeral, her father, Dominick, was watching an episode of the television drama *Hill Street Blues* in which Dominique had guest-starred. The producers had dedicated the episode to her memory. In the show, she had played an abused teen. What viewers did not know, however, was that the marks on her neck were real, not makeup, having been put there by John Sweeney.

But Sweeney wasn't ready to give up. October 30, 1982, around eight-thirty at night, he had the operator interrupt a phone conversation between Dominique and a friend. Shortly after that, he showed up at her front door. At first, she left the chain on and spoke to him through the crack. But she was not alone that night—another young actor named David Packer was there to rehearse scenes with her—and that may have made her feel safe enough to open the door and go outside to talk with Sweeney.

From inside, Packer heard the sounds of a quarrel, screams, and a noise that frightened him enough to call the police, although he was told that he had called the wrong department; it was outside their jurisdiction. He then called a friend to say that if anything happened to him, the police should look for John Sweeney. As Packer fled the house, he ran into Sweeney, who told him to call the police.

When they arrived, Sweeney told them he had killed Dominique and had then tried to kill himself, claiming he took pills in an overdose attempt. There was, however, no indication that he'd taken anything.

Dominique Dunne was taken to the hospital, where doctors were able to restart her heart. But she was only being kept alive mechanically. Five days later, with the realization that she was registering no brain function, her anguished family allowed doctors to remove her from life support. They donated her heart and kidneys.

When police arrested Sweeney, they found him remorseful—but not about killing his girlfriend. I've observed that many offenders are remorseful when arrested simply because they're in custody. They mourn for themselves instead of their victim, and Sweeney went so far as to voice that concern to an arresting officer: "I fucked up. I can't believe I did something that will put me behind bars forever. . . . I didn't think I choked her that hard."

If there was little reason to believe Sweeney felt remorse over killing Dominique Dunne, there was even less to believe elements of the story he told interrogating officers and, later, the court. At the trial, Sweeney claimed he and Dunne had made up days before he went to her house and even talked about getting married. There is no evidence of this. And his version of what happened on the porch suffers from gaps of logic similar to those in Robert Chambers's story of how Jennifer Levin died. In his attempt to blame the victim, Sweeney claimed Dominique told him that night she'd been lying when she talked about getting married and having a family, and she admitted she was just leading him on.

Sweeney's reaction to her supposed lying, deceitful behavior: "I just exploded and lunged toward her." According to Sweeney, he could not remember what happened next. At some point he realized he was on Dunne, his hands grasping her neck. When he found she wasn't breathing, he said he tried to pick her up and get her to walk around, but she kept falling, so he tried doing CPR until they both threw up. He went inside, got two bottles' worth of pills to kill himself, pulled her tongue away from her throat (presumably to clear her airway), and lay down next to her.

Now, the first thing I have to say is that this is absolute and total bullshit. As Linda Fairstein noted in the Chambers-Levin case, it takes at least a few long moments to strangle someone to death. Strangulation victims stop resisting well before they actually die, so Sweeney had ample time to realize what he was doing and release her. Three experts called to evaluate the case said he had time to let up on his grasp so Dunne could have recovered. The coroner testified that it had taken between four and six minutes to strangle Dominique to death. Prosecutor Steve Barshop held up his watch for four solid minutes in court so that the jury could get a sense of how long that was and how much time Sweeney had to let go had he wanted to.

Sweeney's claim that he didn't remember anything about that part of the assault also doesn't match his comments to police and is an often-invoked defense ploy. Saying, "I didn't think I choked her that hard. I just kept on choking her," indicates he was at least partly aware of what he was doing.

In preparation for the trial, investigators found that he'd been through the same type of relationship with another woman between 1977 and 1980—although she was more fortunate than Dominique Dunne; she escaped with her life. John Sweeney was a classic abuser. Just as love-obsession stalkers keep to their obsessive behavior but may find other people to fixate on, domestic abusers and simple obsession stalkers often exhibit the same patterns in other relationships. Sweeney's first victim, a secretary, told the prosecution she'd been beaten by him no fewer than ten times and been hospitalized twice, including one occasion when she ended up with a collapsed lung and a perforated eardrum. Barshop tried to have the woman's testimony admitted as evidence, but Sweeney's court-appointed defense attorney, Michael Adelson, was able to get Judge Burton Katz to exclude it as more prejudicial than probative. The judge also ruled that Dominique's mother's testimony about the time Dominique came to her house after Sweeney beat her also could not be used for the same reason, and that anything Dominique had said in the last five weeks of her life to her friends and fellow actors about her fear of Sweeney was also not admissible because it was hearsay.

In other words, anything that pointed to the fact that Sweeney was a dangerous, habitual abuser who had given his victim reason to fear for her life would be prejudicial to the jury. And in the most stunning—and to me, inexplicable—ruling of all, Judge Katz agreed with a defense assertion that only charges of second-degree murder or manslaughter could be considered. In effect, this was saying that in those four to six minutes that he squeezed the life out of Dominique Dunne, John Sweeney had not legally formed the intent to kill her!

Writing in *Cosmopolitan* magazine after the trial, Dominick Dunne wrote, "It is always the murder victim who is placed on trial. John Sweeney, who claimed to have loved Dominique, and whose defense was that this was a crime of passion, slandered her in court as viciously and cruelly as he had strangled her. It was agonizing for us to listen to him—led on by Adelson—besmirch Dominique's name. His violent past remained sacrosanct and inviolate, but her name was allowed to be trampled upon and kicked, with unsubstantiated charges, by the man who killed her."

What the jury heard was a defense that the killing occurred in the "heat of passion" after Dominique confessed her lies. In other words, blame the victim for her murder. In his closing statement, Michael Adelson kept referring to his client as an "ordinarily reasonable person." What exactly did he mean by that—that Sweeney was a normal, okay guy except for those times when he was beating or strangling a woman in a violent rage?

The jury—which never learned of Sweeney's pattern of violence in his other relationship—was deadlocked for eight days before finally finding him guilty of voluntary manslaughter.

The verdict set off a firestorm of public outrage, during which time Judge Katz—whose rulings often favored the defense throughout the trial to the consternation of the prosecution—apparently thought it prudent to scramble to the opposite shore.

So at sentencing, while the defense tried pleading for leniency amounting to probation, Judge Katz, who had previously commended the jury by saying they'd "served justice well," wouldn't go for it. This time, he excoriated the jury and their verdict, saying, "I don't understand it for the life of me." I suspect Dominick and Lenny Dunne didn't understand it for the life of their daughter, either.

"This is a case of murder, pure and simple," Katz piously intoned before imposing the maximum allowable sentence of six and a half years. Compare that with a minimum of fifteen if he'd been found guilty of second-degree murder, or the potential life sentence for first. This is what the law says an innocent life is worth under these circumstances.

As it was, the sentence meant Sweeney need not serve more than two and a half years, given credit for time he had already served and with more time off for good behavior. He was sent to the California minimum-security correctional facility at Chico.

Steve Barshop commented, "He'll be out in time to cook someone a nice dinner and kill someone else."

The jurors, for their part, were dumbfounded. The foreman said Katz's criticisms were a cheap shot and that if they had heard all the evidence, they certainly would have found Sweeney guilty of murder. He stated that he felt justice had not been served.

As often it is not served in such cases, I'm afraid.

Once she'd seen his violent side and realized that he was not going to change, Dominique Dunne was sufficiently fearful of John Sweeney to end their relationship. She'd met him about a year after he'd split up with his former victim. In a more perfect world, he would have still been behind bars for what he did to her and wouldn't have had the opportunity to meet, much less murder, Dominique.

After serving the mandatory part of the sentence imposed by Judge Katz, John Sweeney was released from prison and began living under a new name—a new lease on life, so to speak. Dominique Dunne, it need hardly be added, is still dead.

When Sweeney went to her house that fatal night, though, she wasn't in fear for her life or she would never have gone outside to talk.

She did nothing wrong. When it came to protecting herself, she simply did not know that more was required than breaking up with him, getting him out of her house, and changing her locks.

Her sad naïveté was no match for his desperate cunning. Obviously, she wanted nothing more to do with him, but at one point she'd been in love with this man. He was skillful and manipulative enough to play on her compassion, her vulnerability, and her inexperience in dealing with people like him to get her to open the door. When she went out on the porch, she was probably attempting what many victims try: negotiation. Like others, Dunne probably hoped she could get him to leave her alone without causing further trouble. She didn't realize that you can't reason with someone like that—not at that stage.

We talked in the last chapter about the love-obsession stalkers who can be reasoned with: those who are rooted enough in reality that early threat of criminal charges and jail time or other punishment, plus potential loss of everything else in their life—job, home, relationships—may halt the stalking behavior. Unfortunately, these conditions are not present for most simple obsession stalkers. For one thing, they usually get away with abusive behavior for so long before they get in any trouble that the threat of police intervention isn't real to them. And when they are punished, it is typically not severe enough to make them change their ways. Domestic abuse crimes are still typically misdemeanors, so the offender knows that even if he can't get out of it, he won't be doing serious time. And if a victim does get law enforcement involved in what the offender perceives as her personal problem (it's definitely not his problem, in his mind), that just serves to make him angrier. She's not only disobeying and being disloyal, now she's hassling him with the law and causing him more trouble.

By the time a woman leaves an abuser, the two of them have often been through the cycle of courtship, intimidation, and violence more than once. It's almost as though they're both programmed in their roles. This is partly why it's so threatening to the abuser when the victim breaks the pattern. He doesn't like her to call any play changes—that's up to him—and he doesn't like the play she's called. It's a double threat. John Sweeney was angry that he couldn't control Dominique in their relationship, but it was even more threatening to his fragile ego that she could be the one to end the relationship. Nothing she could have said or done would have made the terms of their breakup acceptable to him.

Gavin de Becker has observed the futility of trying to reason with a delusional love-obsession celebrity stalker: "My basic philosophy is, you do not talk straight to crooked people. . . . A guy who has just left his wife, stolen a car, and driven three thousand miles because he got a message from Jesus that he should have a relationship with a famous singer doesn't have a whole helluva lot to lose. Do you think he'll end his trip [because] someone told him, 'You really have to leave her alone?'"

I think the same theory applies to guys who have a history of abusing the women in their lives. It's the pattern of behavior Stanton Samenow talks about, and it's the way underlying insecurities were expressed in the behavior and personality of every offender I interviewed in prison. Whether he's a sadistic serial killer who tortures and rapes children because he enjoys it, or a repeat domestic abuser who takes out his problems on the women in his life, he does what he does because it's who he is, and you won't be able to talk him out of it. On the contrary, if you are his victim, just by making yourself accessible to him you've given him a victory: he's regained a measure of control.

When Dominique Dunne walked outside that door, although she certainly didn't realize it, she weakened her position and strengthened Sweeney's. In giving even an inch, she inadvertently reinforced to him why he needed her in his life. Talking to him at all accomplished exactly the opposite of what she was trying to do.

To understand the complex dynamics of the situation, put yourself in her shoes. If someone came to your door and you went outside to tell him you didn't want to see him ever again, you wouldn't mean it as any sort of backhanded encouragement. You're only out there as a courtesy, trying not to be hurtful. It's like Laura Black first insisting she just wanted to be friends with Richard Farley.

But to understand the serial abuser/stalker, you have to walk in his shoes. And from his perspective, he sees that you don't want to be with him, yet you went outside anyway. He was able to make you do what he wanted. You had to acknowledge him. So your words don't turn him away. As Gavin and David Beatty have both pointed out, these are yellow lights he sees, not red. When he finally senses that you really mean "red," the only way he can handle it is by dealing an ultimatum of his own—in Dominique Dunne's case, that was death.

For this offender, remember, his "simple obsession" and sole purpose is to get this person back in his life. When he realizes he can't, he'll switch over to a fallback position, which may involve going out in a blaze of glory. Killing her becomes the ultimate act of control and oppression. Like assassins, many abusers keep diaries in which they write their plans as well as record their victim's movements.

Beatty describes a common entry: "I can't wait to see the expression on her face when she sees the gun. If she thinks she's won, I'll prove her wrong." As the situation they want slips farther and farther from their grasp, they embrace the fantasy of controlling the victim's very life and death.

If, in fact, the offender's identity is so tied up with his victim that he has no other means to possess her than to kill her, once he's done that, there's nowhere else for him to go emotionally, hence the frequency of murder-suicides. And I share the concern with others in the stalking victims' advocacy movement that this is just one reason why we have to make stalking crimes felonies with long-term sentencing options. If someone is willing to kill his victim and himself, threat of jail time isn't going to deter him. So we need to get these guys early and we have to be able to put them away for a long time. This means everyone involved—from the victim to law enforcement to prosecutors and judges—needs to really look at these offenders, recognize the danger, and act on their behavior as early as possible.

Ideally, the potential victim should cut off contact with the potential stalker as early as she realizes there may be a problem. And that means really cutting off contact. Gavin de Becker, who's got as much experience with this as anyone, recommends making it clear to the individual that you do not wish to have a relationship with him (or her) and are certain that this feeling will not change in the future; that you intend to pursue other avenues and trust that he will, too.

Then, stick to it. If someone calls you forty times and you relent and talk to him on the forty-first, if only to "clear the air" or "let him down gently," all you have told him is that forty-one phone calls are the price of one conversation with you, and the obsessed individual will gladly pay that price.

Walking in the shoes of any offender is difficult, but it's even harder if the one in question is your personal stalker. At least when I analyze a crime scene, as emotionally wrenching as it may be, I have a degree of objectivity. If, on the other hand, the crime were committed in my home—as part of an ongoing campaign of terror—it would be more stressful and more difficult not to react to the offender's action. And the average stalking victim does not have a background in behavioral analysis to help her in psyching out her opponent.

Stalking is a terribly difficult crime for a victim to deal with because it can be both long-term and unpredictable. Imagine waking up every day for twenty years—or even twenty days—and having as your first thought "Is this the day he gets me?" or "Is this the day he kills my kids?" Everywhere you go, you look around and expect to see him. Even if he isn't standing outside your window, watching you make your kids' lunch, you know he's always somewhere out there. Every time the phone rings you know who it could be. The mail could bring just bills and advertisements, or a photo of you taken one time you really thought he wasn't around. Maybe you got a restraining order and police threatened to arrest him so he's been quiet lately. That's no guarantee he isn't still watching and waiting for you to let your guard down. Statistically, overwhelmingly, he will be back.

Victims suffer all sorts of problems as a result of their experience, from depression, anxiety attacks, and physical ailments brought on by prolonged feelings of anger, stress, fear, and helplessness, to recurring nightmares and even post–traumatic stress disorder. Just as some rape victims suffer from rape trauma syndrome, stalking survivors subjected to repeated and unpredictable acts of personal terrorism against them may go through life in a permanently stressed state, traumatized by their experiences.

To make matters worse for already frightened and confused stalking victims, when they look for advice on how to deal with their stalkers, they face the added dilemma that the guidelines depend on which expert you talk to. The method promoted as the best approach by one may well be deemed a horrible mistake by another. Without knowing Sweeney's already violent past, some might even have advised Dominique Dunne to try a reasoning approach, negotiating terms so that he would leave her alone and she wouldn't get him in trouble with the police, which could cost him his job and make him angry.

And this doesn't just apply to stalkers who are unwilling to give up the objects of their so-called affections. A woman—or man—may be stalked by someone who has some other perceived grudge against her. It may be a shopkeeper the offender thinks cheated him. It could be a doctor or lawyer who the offender feels has not delivered the desired result. It could be practically anything. It is easy to become enmeshed from a position of total innocence.

One of the only points on which everyone agrees is that each stalking case is different, and strategies should be based on the particulars of the individual stalker involved. But even as the experts at the National Victim Center have done an excellent job outlining general steps stalking victims can take, they emphasize the importance of getting an expert involved immediately who can help tailor an approach to fit the specific situation.

The first step for any stalking victim, then, should be getting in touch with someone local, since stalking laws vary from state to state and what constitutes grounds for an arrest in one jurisdiction may be outside the arm of the law in another. In some cases—especially if the stalking behaviors cross jurisdictions, or threatening phone calls are made from one state to another—federal charges may apply under stalking and/or antiterrorism laws. Working alone, victims may be unaware of the procedures involved in filing a stalking or related complaint.

As at least one stalker put it, "This is my job." But most victims don't have the luxury—or the inclination—to make building a case against, reporting, and prosecuting a stalker their full-time job. But there are people out there who can help with these things, and there are additional resources, such as shelters and/or counseling groups.

In addition to its advocacy work, the National Victim Center provides referral services to victims of all categories of crime, including stalking. They welcome calls from anyone who needs to know where to turn. Even if you are just wondering if someone's disturbing behavior qualifies as stalking, they can answer your questions. The toll-free number for the National Victim Center is 1-800-FYI-CALL.

Something to keep in mind is a warning we hear from David Beatty, Gavin de Becker, and so many others: if you think you have a problem, you probably do.

This doesn't mean you should panic because some strange guy at work is flirting with you, but it does mean you need to be aware of what Beatty calls the "trigger point": the feeling Laura Black got when she saw Farley's home-baked bread. Beatty warns, "If you feel like you are getting unwelcome attention to the point where you feel so uncomfortable that you think your safety is at risk, that's the time in which to act."

You don't want to find yourself looking back later and realizing that you were right, something weird was happening. A future stalker was calling around, talking to coworkers and friends, asking inappropriate questions, gathering intelligence.

In many cases, early intervention is key. Beatty notes, "The potential positive outcome at the early stages of a stalking case are far better than at the last stages. If someone is overtly threatening you with violence, the options are pretty narrow." By then, he adds, probably the best that can be done is to press charges and get the offender locked up. But the chances are great that he'll be back out again and even angrier for having spent some time in prison or suffering some other punishment.

Tips that are widely offered by antistalking groups include using a post office box for your mail, being selective about giving out your telephone number and address, informing people (and organizations) that they are not to provide information about you to anyone, posting No Trespassing signs on your property, reporting threatening telephone calls to the phone company and having them traced, if possible, or using Caller ID, and reporting threatening mail to the FBI. These groups also suggest that you contact the Social Security Office to have your social security number changed if it can be proven that someone stalking you is using the number to find or harass you. If you have to move, they recommend ways you can avoid leaving a "paper trail" behind for a stalker to follow, including taking copies of your medical records with you (as well as your children's school and medical records), not leaving a forwarding address with the post office, and either personally picking up or giving up deposit money with your landlord.

If you are being stalked, experts also agree that you need to keep a record of everything. This means saving any letters from the stalker, any answering machine tapes with messages on them, items left for you, and the like. You should also keep a journal, with a record of the date, time, and place your stalker appeared, along with what he did, said, wore, what car he drove, its license plate number, and the names of anyone else who witnessed him being there. If you can get a photo of the stalker without placing yourself in danger, that could also be helpful, not just for showing where he was at a certain time, but to let your neighbors, coworkers, and others know to be on the lookout for this guy. Record-keeping can be critical because one of the by-products of long-term stress is impaired memory, as well as the fact that the case may have unfolded over considerable time. Like rape victims who don't remember everything that happened until details come back in bits and pieces, stalking victims may be misunderstood and even accused of lying if their story changes. A good log of everything that happens can help guard against this.

And unfortunately, stalking laws are still relatively new and, as literature you can obtain from the National Victim Center points out, victims may be in the position of first having to prove "probable cause" to police before they can get to the point of seeing the stalker prosecuted in court. Certainly, if you are being stalked, do not hold back from alerting authorities just because you don't have these pieces of evidence, but when they are available to you, don't throw them away.

The issue of when—and how—to enlist the help of law enforcement is one of the areas of greatest debate within the community of stalking experts, and the argument over the usefulness of restraining orders versus their risk to victims who take that route epitomizes the difficulties with trying to apply general rules. Experts and victims alike note wryly that a piece of paper can't act as a bulletproof shield in an emergency and point to Laura Black's case (as well as those where domestic violence victims have been found dead with a copy of their restraining order in their purse) as an example of their failure.

At the same time, David Beatty believes, "Protective orders are valuable for several purposes. They are not a protection. They don't stop offenders. In fact, in some cases, it can be the exacerbating trigger. But they do have other purposes. The one thing they do that's important is that they trigger the criminal justice process. It puts the process on notice that this is happening and that at least some judge somewhere has looked at the problem and said, 'Yes, there is a legitimate complaint here.'"

My Investigative Support Unit colleague Jim Wright, himself a leading expert on stalking, says, "The temporary restraining order essentially becomes not the solution but the means for employing the criminal justice system."

And, Beatty adds, "That may be the most important thing that a victim can get, because their hardest challenge often is simply getting the system to respond."

In an opposing view, especially with celebrity stalkers, Gavin de Becker advises a strategy of watching and waiting, rather than one that will "engage and enrage." De Becker warns that "confronting a stalker too early can aggravate the situation and possibly accelerate his violent tendencies."

Still others—including many in law enforcement—take the opposite view, believing that launching a campaign against the stalker can scare some off before the situation gets out of hand.

In my opinion, there's value in all these approaches, depending on the type of stalker. Just as I tailor proactive techniques to the specific UNSUB in a murder case, I believe the motivation of the stalker has to be considered, along with any signs of mental illness he or she may exhibit. And as with other types of cases, timing is crucial. An excellent response at one point might be a trigger to violence at another.

I also agree with David Beatty's assessment that "there's an important distinction to be made between a law enforcement/system response to stalking and an individualized victim response." As in profiling, we have to walk in the shoes of both the offender and the victim and consider the specific issues for both in planning to end the criminal behavior one way or another.

Sadly, there is still a lot of ground to be gained in terms of public education as well. We need to support victims of stalkers (both love-obsession and simple obsession), and in many cases that means first by recognizing criminal behavior. During the stages where the man is trying to regain control by courting the victim again, sending her flowers and gifts, unless an outsider recognizes this behavior as just one piece in a puzzle that can also involve deadly violence, it may seem that she is judging him too harshly. Just as Farley's gifts to Laura Black may have seemed generous, love notes and candy from an ex-boyfriend may appear as indicators that this poor guy is still head over heels in love with the woman. Only the victim recognizes them as creepy and controlling, because she understands the context and has lived through his other efforts to dominate her.

There is nothing any woman—or man—can do to deserve a beating at the hands of a spouse or lover. And neither does anyone deserve to be emotionally abused. It horrifies and completely confounds me when I hear of beating victims who seek help from family members or friends and instead get responses to the effect of "You must have made him awfully mad." I know the people who say these things are ignorant, but I don't accept that as an excuse and neither should any victim of violence. We cannot overstate that if you are being abused, you absolutely do not deserve that treatment and you do not have to live that way. If you can't find help locally listed in the front of your phone book (look under "Emergency Assistance" or "Community Services" for domestic violence shelters or rape crisis assistance), call the National Victim Center. In communities that have victim-witness units like the one we've looked at in Fairfax County, Virginia, call them. They'll be able to figure out what you should do or where you should go.

I also take issue with those who blame the abused victim for ever getting involved with that type of man. This is terribly unfair, especially since many times the same people were also initially fooled by the offender during his charming phase. Also, victims often receive the worst treatment at the hands of their abusers precisely because they are unwilling to put up with threatening and/or violent behavior.

What the victim needs in all these cases is the support of those around her. Questioning her judgment only strengthens the offender's position as it causes the victim to doubt herself. We don't blame burglary victims for not staying home to guard their possessions all day against a potential intruder. So why should we second-guess stalking victims, or rape victims?

Being stalked in any form is an incredibly stressful experience, and even if you feel that you can handle it, you should consider joining a support group. I find it a further testament to the courage of crime survivors that in many cases, when a victim did not find the support and understanding she needed from her community, law enforcement, and the criminal justice system, instead of giving up, she and others in similar situations founded their own support groups. Theresa Saldana founded Victims for Victims. Another survivor, Jane McAllister, founded Citizens Against Stalking. Try surfing the internet, looking for resources and information on stalking. You'll be amazed at what's available.

I know, though, that we still have a long way to go. The National Victim Center's "Helpful Guide for Stalking Victims," full of practical steps you can take to try to insulate yourself from the offender, is a depressing document, as are the similar lists you can get from other victims' groups. Reading these materials, you realize they all represent actions taken or planned by the victim—they're all reactive.

Because stalkers are adept at skirting the edges of lawful behavior, sometimes terrorizing a victim for years before doing anything they can be arrested for (even under the new laws), for the victim to improve her situation, she must change her behavior. He's the one doing something wrong, yet she's the one who's punished for it. She's the one who has to turn her home into a prison, with dead bolt locks, reinforced doors, extra outside lighting, minimal shrubbery, and maybe a guard dog for a pet. She's the one who needs to change her locks and unlisted phone number if she even suspects a breach in security. She loses her privacy, never traveling alone if at all possible, airing her "dirty laundry" by providing a photo or description of her stalker and his vehicle to people she works with, her neighbors, family, and close friends. She gives up outdoor interests like jogging and spends time and energy picking different routes to and from work, the food store, even church.

And she is the one who spends money she may not have in a desperate effort to stay safe, even as she knows she'll probably never really feel safe again. Even if her stalker dies, he has stolen time from her and irrevocably altered the way she sees the world. She can get to the point where she functions "normally" again, but like other crime survivors, there is no tremendous relief or peace when the crime itself passes. Sometimes, victims buy guns and learn how to use them.

Now, I think any one of the above developments is sickening. It enrages me to think that a decent, moral, contributing member of society has to pay such a high emotional, physical, and financial price—on a moment-by-moment basis—so some degenerate loser can have his fantasies and build up his own feeble, worthless ego. I think of Trudy Collins, the mother of bright, beautiful Suzanne Marie Collins, murdered at nineteen, who asks if we as a society realize what we're losing when we allow so many good people to be victimized.

David Beatty holds up his National Victim Center's "Helpful Guide" and states outright, "Everything in here is somehow a limitation on your liberty as a citizen. Every right that you have, basically, you give up, because the system cannot effectively respond in guaranteeing your protection."

To be fair, he notes, we can't even guarantee the safety of the president of the United States, on whose security we spend millions of dollars a year. But when a threat has been issued and a person has displayed a pattern of potentially dangerous behavior, we ought to be able to do more than we've been doing to make sure the stalker is the one locked up and deprived of his civil liberties, not the victim.

These cases have to be wake-up calls to all of us. If we are going to hold people in the social services and criminal justice system responsible for not focusing on the dangerousness of guys like Ronnie Shelton and Joseph Thompson in the past, then we also have to accept responsibility and start picking out the dangerous among us at the first warnings. And I'm hoping increased awareness and education will help. I can sympathize with the frustration of a cop on the street who's gone to the same house to investigate a domestic dispute a dozen times only to see the woman refuse to press charges, but I believe we have to look at why that happens instead of just getting angry at the victim. In many cases, when a victim of domestic violence/simple obsession stalking returns to her abuser, it's because she fears he'll be able to find her no matter where she is. We haven't been able to convince her we'll be able to keep her safe.

I keep coming back to David Beatty's penetrating observation that stalking is the only instance we know of where a future murderer identifies himself to police ahead of time.

That's not just an opportunity, it's a responsibility that cannot, and must not, be ignored.

CHAPTER ELEVEN

BUFFALO BILL
AND BEYOND

There can be little doubt that if one person were to be given credit (or responsibility, in certain circles) for placing behavioral science as it is practiced at Quantico squarely on the map and in the public imagination, that individual would have to be Thomas Harris, author of the best-selling novels *Black Sunday, Red Dragon,* and *The Silence of the Lambs,* all of which, of course, were also made into feature films. So completely have they become part of the collective psyche that I recently heard myself referred to on a television talk show as "that *Silence of the Lambs* guy." And even today, seldom does a week go by that I do not receive a letter from somewhere in the country asking how one goes about becoming a profiler and getting into the Investigative Support Unit, which I headed until I retired.

Harris definitely nailed the dark and constricting atmosphere of psychic tension under which we work—made all that much darker and more constricting by the fact that until recently, more than a year after I retired, the unit worked in a tight warren of offices sixty feet underground. He also captured a sense of the ultimately unexplainable evil that we try to identify and hunt down, largely through such memorable literary villains as Dr. Hannibal "the Cannibal" Lecter; Francis Dolarhyde, the "Tooth Fairy," and Jame Gumb, aka Buffalo Bill.

Fortunately for all of us, we have yet to come across in real life anyone quite as perversely brilliant and resourceful as the warped psychiatrist Dr. Lecter. As readers of our previous books undoubtedly know, I have come across a number of psychiatrists in my career whom I considered warped, but that had mainly to do with their professional unwillingness to look at the crime itself when evaluating the dangerousness and "rehabilitation" potential of the criminal. Thankfully, none of them in my experience ever went out and tried to duplicate the acts of the offenders in their charge. In fact, while we've certainly had doctors and dentists who've killed their wives or girlfriends (and were generally fairly easy to hunt down because they weren't as criminally sophisticated as they thought they were), I know of no serial-killer psychiatrists or other doctors. There is nothing to stop one from becoming another type of sexual predator, but our research has shown that serial killers, though often bright, tend to be inadequate underachievers. Most doctors wouldn't have to compensate in quite this way.

So while there seem to be no Hannibal Lecters in real life, there are, in a sense, some Buffalo Bills. Before writing *Red Dragon,* Thomas Harris came to see us in Quantico. He attended classes and spoke to a number of agents and listened carefully to what we had to tell him. The terrifying and repulsive character that emerged as Buffalo Bill—who lured women into his control by faking an injury with a cast on his arm, who kept them in a pit in his basement, and who then skinned them to create a female human "suit" for himself—is a composite of the traits, personalities, modi operandi, and signatures of three real sexual predator killers whom we had studied. We familiarized Harris with two of them while he was with us at Quantico. The third emerged years after *Red Dragon* had been published, while Harris was writing *Lambs.* Since each of the three represents a somewhat different type of predator, each displays varying levels of sophistication from the other two, and each brings up different aspects of the ongoing argument over whether people who kill for pleasure are "evil" or "sick," it is worthwhile for us to take a look at the three individuals who collectively contributed to Harris's character Buffalo Bill.

Edward Gein was born on August 8, 1906, in La Crosse, Wisconsin, and lived his entire life in the state. His father, George, was a frequently abusive alcoholic who worked intermittently as a carpenter, a tanner, and a farmer. When Ed was still a child, the family moved to a farm near the rural community of Plainfield to try to make a go of working their own land. Quite clearly, the dominant parent was Ed's mother, Augusta, who seemed to have pretty strong ideas about religion and morality and equally strong ideas about men in general and the kind of trouble they could get into. She fanatically impressed upon Ed and his brother, Henry, five years older than Ed, all of the sins they must avoid, and paramount on that list was any notion of sex outside of marriage, though Ed later recalled she seemed a little more lenient on the subject of masturbation. In any event, her message got across, and neither Ed nor Henry ever married, had sex, nor wandered far from home. As Ed later told a state psychiatrist, his mother had told him that "if a woman is good enough for intercourse, she is good enough for marriage."

Ed left school after the eighth grade, but remained an avid reader. He never had a regular job, but in addition to his work on the family farm, he would baby-sit in the Plainfield community and do odd jobs. Since he was quiet and fairly unworldly and unsophisticated, he was often taken advantage of and cheated out of his pay.

Within a span of five years, while in his thirties, Ed was left completely alone. In 1940, at age sixty-five, George died of heart disease. In 1944, Henry was burned to death in a marsh fire while trying to clear some land. And a year later, after her second stroke, Augusta passed away. Though she had been rigid and domineering, Ed was extremely attached to his mother and apparently felt lost without her. He boarded up his mother's bedroom and sitting room to be preserved, museum-style, as they had been while she was alive. As it turned out, this was not the only thing Ed Gein preserved.

No one thought much about this quiet, unassuming man who lived alone in the white clapboard house in the midst of a no-longer-working farm until late in the afternoon of November 16, 1957. It was a crisp, clear Saturday, the first day of deer-hunting season, and many, if not most, of the adult and teenaged males in the community of 642 were taking advantage of that event. Frank Worden, whose family owned the local hardware store on Main Street, was no exception. So his mother, fifty-eight-year-old widow Bernice Worden, took over for him in the store, as she often did when Frank had somewhere else he had to be.

Frank returned from hunting around 5 P.M. and found the store locked and dark. He was surprised, asked around, and someone at the filling station told him it had been that way most of the day. When he let himself in to investigate, he found the store empty, but there was a pool of blood on the floor and a bloody trail led to the back door. Outside, the store truck was missing. Frank immediately called Sheriff Art Schley, proclaiming his fear that his mother had been murdered.

Schley and his deputy Arnie Fritz rushed over to investigate, calling people from the state crime lab in Madison and other deputies and law officers to join them. When they arrived, they asked Frank if he suspected anyone.

"Ed Gein," he replied.

When they asked him why, he said that Ed Gein had been asking his mother to go roller-skating with him, and that he had been in the day before, asking about the price of antifreeze, and that while there, he had asked Frank if he was going hunting today. Frank responded that he was and that he'd be out all day. When the lawmen checked Bernice Worden's sales slips for the day, one was for antifreeze. This thin trail was the only evidence against Edward Gein, but it turned out to be all they needed to identify the UNSUB.

Gein wasn't home when the investigators came and knocked. But in a woodshed attached to the house, illuminated by their flashlights since there was no electricity, they came upon one of the grisliest and most notable scenes in the history of American law enforcement—one that was to rock this Middle American community of the 1950s to its core. There in the shed they found Mrs. Worden's headless body, hanging upside down with her ankles lashed to a wooden crosspiece, slit open from vagina to sternum, dressed like a newly bagged dear for skinning.

Sickened, the sheriff's men forced their way into the adjoining house where, if possible, their shock was even greater. The interior was a mess of clutter and trash. There were human skulls affixed to the posts of Ed's bed. Bernice Worden's heart was in a saucepan on the stove. Her head, eyes closed peacefully as if she were sleeping and already prepared with hooks through her ear sockets so it could be hung on display, was found in a corner in a burlap bag. Her other internal organs were in a box.

Capt. Lloyd Schoephoerster of the Green Lake County Sheriff's Department recalled it this way for the record:

> I had a feeling I never had before in my life because I had never seen anything like this. It was so horrible. We found skulls and masks; that is, the skin portion of the head that had been stripped from the skull and preserved and put in plastic bags. There were several of those skulls. We found a box that had women's organs in it and I noticed one small one was gilded a gold color with a ribbon tied on it; I believe a red ribbon. We found leg bones and discovered

the chair seats were made out of human skin. They were crudely made. The outside portion would be smooth and if you looked underneath you could see strips of fat. It wasn't a good job.

There was a knife handle made of bone and lamp shades from skin and there was one upper portion of a woman's torso from the shoulders, cut down both sides to the waist, with her breasts and everything completely tanned. It was stiff. You could set it up and it had everything attached.

This wasn't all. There were bowls made of the tops of human skulls, wastebaskets of stretched human skin, and a belt of female nipples.

They also found the "mask" of another woman, fully tanned and her face and hair preserved. Arnie Fritz noticed another bag, this one paper, behind the kitchen door. He opened it and shone his flashlight inside. Former sheriff Leon "Specks" Murty, who had come over to help his successor, gasped as he said, "By God, it's Mary Hogan."

Mary Hogan had disappeared nearly three years earlier—on December 8, 1954—from the tavern she managed in nearby Pine Grove. As with Bernice Worden's murder, there was a pool of blood on the tavern floor. And like Mrs. Worden, Mary Hogan was also in her fifties.

Sheriff Schley found Gein, arrested him, and subjected him to a brutal interrogation, at times grabbing the suspect and throwing him against the wall. Gein confessed to the two murders, having shot both women, but not to three other unsolved deaths the investigators thought could be related. He also admitted having robbed three cemeteries—Plainfield, Spiritland, and Hancock—taking all or parts of at least fifteen recently buried bodies, all women. He said he had known some of them in life. He might have killed others, however, since two preserved vaginas found on his premises did not match up with any cemetery records of recently buried bodies. He didn't recall much about the killings themselves, claiming he had been "in a daze." But he did allow as how both women reminded him of his mother.

That was the key to this bizarre predator. He was not a sexual sadist. He did not kill for the raw pleasure of it. He was not in search of power or manipulation, although he did admit that opening the graves gave him a thrill. What he was doing, it seems, was "re-creating" his mother out of random parts, many of which he could wear in an effort to "become" Augusta. Gein told another former sheriff, Dan Chase, that he used to put on the female torso with breasts attached that he had constructed and parade around his yard at night under the moonlight. He had begun killing when his grave-robbing wasn't sufficient to produce the "raw material" he needed.

As the psychiatrist who evaluated him upon his commitment, a Dr. Warmington, wrote, "The motivation is elusive and uncertain but several factors come to mind—hostility, sex, and a desire for a substitute for his mother in the form of a replica or body that could be kept indefinitely."

Dr. Warmington also noted that "since the death of his mother he has had feelings that things were unreal." Gein stated that he had heard his mother talking to him several times about a year after she died.

Other psychiatrists who examined the mild-mannered Gein for the state readily concluded that he was suffering from a severe psychosis, possibly schizophrenia. Within a week of Bernice Worden's murder, he had been committed to the Central State Hospital at Waupun and confined to a ward for the criminally insane, where he began living a quiet and uneventful life, always behaving cordially and amiably and giving the authorities no trouble.

But before long, his story had seized the popular imagination. He was proclaimed in the press the "Butcher of Plainfield." The car he had used in his grave-robbing expeditions was sold at auction and displayed at county fairs and carnivals throughout the Midwest. And novelist Robert Bloch wrote a thriller about a quiet, unassuming man who kept his late, domineering mother's remains intact and took on her persona, killing a woman who threatened to come between them. He called his book, simply, *Psycho*. The subsequent feature film, directed by Alfred Hitchcock and starring Anthony Perkins and Janet Leigh, quickly became a classic of its genre.

Ten years after Gein's commitment, psychiatrists at Central State Hospital declared him sufficiently lucid to stand trial for the murder of Bernice Worden. By mutual consent of the prosecution and the defense, a jury trial was waived in favor of a decision by Judge Robert H. Gollmar. After hearing all the evidence, Judge Gollmar concluded that while the murder was intentional (Gein claimed a shotgun he was looking at in the store and that he had loaded with his own ammunition had gone off accidentally), the defendant was legally insane.

This is not a decision I would disagree with. Though I don't believe that many repeat killers are actually insane in the legal sense, Gein certainly was. Like Richard Trenton Chase, the young man from Sacramento, California, who killed people in the late 1970s because he believed he needed their blood to keep his insides from turning to powder (he had previously experimented with injecting himself with rabbit blood but found it insufficient), Ed Gein was certifiably off his nut, a genuine psychotic who, I believe, committed the crimes as a direct result of his psychosis.

After the 1968 trial, Gein was returned to Central State Hospital. He died peacefully due to natural causes in the geriatric ward of the Mendota Mental Health Institute in 1984.

I first became interested in the Ed Gein case as a young special agent while working in the Milwaukee Field Office, my second assignment in the Bureau. Special Agent Jerry Southworth had dabbled in profiling, largely on his own, without resources or the research to back up his conclusions. This was the early 1970s and the shadow of J. Edgar Hoover was still long over operations. Hoover thought of profiling and other behavioral manifestations as voodoo and witchcraft.

But I saw what Jerry was doing and was fascinated by it. It dovetailed with my own early profiling efforts, which mainly involved debriefing bank robbers and other felons about why they committed the crimes they did, how they picked a particular target, what was going through their minds at the time, and the like. Gein seemed like a fascinating study of what seemed to be the strangest possible sexual predator. So in my spare time, I went to the state attorney general's office in Madison and petitioned to have the crime-scene photos and the rest of the records unsealed so that we in law enforcement could study them. I was successful, and we began teaching the Gein case when I was assigned to Quantico. I was never able to interview Gein in person as I wished, but I did speak at length with the psychiatrist who was supervising him at the time.

When we study a case like this, one of the things we do is try to figure out how we would have analyzed it if it had been brought to us as an UNSUB. In this instance, I think the two murder scenes—Hogan and Worden—would have told us a lot about the offender. In both cases, the body had been removed but no attempt had been made to clean up the blood or hide that a crime had been committed. Since it was obvious from the amount of blood that the victim had probably died on the spot, why would you remove the body? Normally, it's to prevent detection. But since that clearly wasn't the motivation in this setting, there had to be another reason. And when you start getting into removing bodies for purposes other than preventing detection of the crime, you're quickly moving into the realm of disorganized, perverse, and aberrational offenders.

I first taught the Gein case in 1976 as a special presentation to the FBI National Academy Class, made up of law enforcement officers from around the country. Though I have seen a lot worse crime scenes in terms of the sheer suffering of the victim, these shots of headless, naked bodies, human face masks, and other body parts are about as creepy as they come.

And this, I suspect, is what prompted Thomas Harris to build his own predator character around a recluse of ambiguous sexuality whose obsession was fashioning a female suit for himself out of pieces of real women.

While I will concede that Edward Gein was legally insane by any reasonable definition of the term, this is rare, and I would not make such a concession for the second model for Buffalo Bill, Theodore Robert Bundy. By the time Ted Bundy was executed in the electric chair of the Florida State Penitentiary at Starke on January 24, 1989, law enforcement authorities had tied him to more than thirty murders of young women across the length of the United States.

At first glance, Ted Bundy was almost a cliché, a poster boy for classic American middle-class success and happiness. He was good-looking and reasonably bright. He seemed to have an easy way with women, could turn on the charm, knew and appreciated the finer things in life, was active in politics, and enrolled in law school. Crime writer and former police officer Ann Rule worked next to him in a rape crisis center in Seattle.

But underlying that veneer was a much darker and more troubled existence. He was born on November 24, 1946, to twenty-one-year-old Louise Cowell in the Elizabeth Lund Home for Unwed Mothers in Burlington, Vermont. Louise had left her home in Philadelphia to avoid the scandal of the out-of-wedlock pregnancy. After considering putting the baby up for adoption, Louise and her parents, Sam and Eleanor Cowell, agreed that the parents would say the boy was adopted by them, making Louise his older sister. Though young Ted apparently knew the domestic situation wasn't exactly what it appeared to be, he adored his father/grandfather Sam, a landscape gardener by trade who many others remember for a bad temper, bigotry, cruelty, and intolerance for the weaknesses and shortcomings of others.

Though the family photos of Ted with tricycle and red wagon or sled and snowman, building sand castles at the beach, or trimming the Christmas tree seem typically idyllic and middle American, there were other warnings that things were not all okay with the youngster. When Louise's sister, Julia, was fifteen, she awoke on more than one occasion to find her three-year-old nephew placing kitchen knives in the bed next to her. Ted, she said, "just stood there and grinned."

The next year, again wanting to avoid scandal as Ted got older, Louise took him and moved from Philadelphia across the country to Tacoma, Washington. There she got a job as a secretary and met a cook named John Culpepper Bundy, whom she married in 1951, giving Ted his last name.

Ted grew into a handsome young man, joined the Boy Scouts, and did well in school, though several times Louise and John received notes from teachers about the boy's fierce temper. Louise might have thought he merely took after her father and apparently did nothing about it. She probably did not know that by the time Ted was in high school, he was clandestinely watching women through their windows as they undressed at night. He would also steal expensive clothing and other items, telling his mother they were given to him by the department store where he had a full-time job. From all evidence, Ted was acutely aware of his family's inability to afford a lifestyle he aspired to, and stealing was an easy and effective way to acquire it. This was a habit he maintained throughout his life.

Now clearly, not every young boy who has difficulty controlling his temper is going to grow up into a murderer—not even the ones who also get their kicks out of surreptitiously watching through windows as women take off their clothes or steal repeatedly to get the material things they want. None of these actions, on its own, is remarkably significant. But you'll note that we're starting to see a pattern here, and it's not one that offers a lot of confidence for the future.

We don't know exactly where antisocial behavior comes from, but such experts in child development as Stanton Samenow have observed that you can begin making it out at an early age. "I don't think that somebody wakes up one day and says, 'Gee, I'm going to become a criminal,'" he comments. "It's not a choice in the simple sense. But it is a choice in that the world presents to any child a number of options of what you should do, what you shouldn't do, what you can do, what you might do—all from a very early age. Children make choices in terms of what they internalize, what they heed, what they listen to."

Was his environment or upbringing a factor in the way Ted turned out? I've often said, as a result of all of my own research with serial killers, that they all come from inadequate or dysfunctional homes of one sort or another, many with physical and/or sexual abuse. In Bundy's case, while there is no evidence he was physically abused, he certainly had an abnormal and stressful childhood of dislocation and even name changing. What we also have is a family that was clearly ambivalent about the boy and his origins, and other family members, such as some contemporary cousins, who rubbed it in about his illegitimacy. Combine this with his aspiration for things he couldn't afford and his personality and inability to feel for or empathize with other people and, without intervention, you've got a recipe for a pretty dangerous character.

Which is exactly what he became. He graduated from high school in 1965, won a scholarship to the University of Puget Sound, then transferred to the University of Washington. He fell in love with a wealthy Stanford University coed, and when she broke off with him, he went into a depression, began neglecting his schoolwork, and soon dropped out of college. He couldn't stand the rejection and set about to re-create himself in the image he thought would be appealing to the likes of this rich and beautiful girl, just as obsessively as Ed Gein had tried to re-create himself as his own mother. This was one of the things that made Ted Bundy such an effective sexual predator: he could make himself over into whatever he needed to be.

He became active in state Republican politics. He made contacts. He once apprehended a purse-snatcher and another time saved a toddler from drowning in a lake. To all outward appearances, he was a model citizen. Ann Rule believes he actually helped people and saved lives working the hot line at the rape crisis center. After several missteps, he finally graduated from college in 1972 and then applied and got into the University of Utah Law School. But by the time he attended his first class there, he was already a murderer. On January 31, 1974, twenty-one-year-old Lynda Ann Healy, an attractive young woman with long, straight, blond hair, disappeared from her basement apartment near the University of Washington. The bedsheets were bloody and a bloodstained nightgown hung in the closet. A couple of weeks earlier and a couple of blocks away, eighteen-year-old Susan Clarke had been found assaulted, beaten, and sexually tortured, lying in her own blood. Though she would remain in a coma for months, Clarke did recover.

On March 12, 1974, a nineteen-year-old coed disappeared en route to a jazz concert in Olympia, Washington. On April 12, another young woman went missing, then another on May 6. On June 1, yet another disappeared after being seen leaving a tavern in Seattle with an unidentified man. And ten days later a college girl in Seattle left her boyfriend's apartment but never made it to the sorority house where she lived.

There were no bodies, but police were treating the disappearances as homicides. And there was a pattern. All of the apparent victims were college-age white females, all very attractive, with good figures and long, straight hair, parted in the middle.

Then, on July 14, two more young women—Janice Ott and Denise Naslund, both fitting the pretty, long-haired profile—disappeared from separate picnic gatherings on the shores of Lake Sammamish, a state park. But finally, police had a description to go on, from another pretty, long-haired young woman, Janice Graham. When questioned by police after the other women's disappearance, Graham reported encountering a good-looking young man in his early to mid twenties who introduced himself as Ted. He was polite and charming and was dressed in jeans and a white T-shirt. But the most memorable thing about him was the cast on his arm, suspended in a sling.

He said that he'd hurt his arm playing racquetball and needed help loading his sailboat onto his car. He was friendly and chatty, so Graham decided there'd be no harm in lending a hand. But when they walked to the parking lot and up to Ted's Volkswagen Beetle, there was no sailboat to be loaded. Ted explained that it was up the hill at his parents' house and asked her to get in and they would drive there to get it. At that point, she hesitated, and there is no question that this hesitation saved her life. She declared that she was running late and had to meet her husband and folks. Ted smiled and said it was okay. Several minutes later, she spotted Ted through the crowd, again heading toward the parking lot with another young woman by his side.

The cast was actually a successful and effective modus operandi for him. The combination of his glib patter and the cast on his arm would convince most attractive young women that he was "harmless," and he could get them to accompany him to the vicinity of his car, generally with the request for assistance in moving or carrying some heavy object that he could not manage himself in his temporarily handicapped condition. Most people want to help others, and Bundy took advantage of that instinct. When the woman was in reach and out of sight of others, the cast became a weapon. He would whack her with it, blitzing or disabling her. When she found herself in the passenger seat of his VW Bug, either willingly or unwillingly, she would also realize that the passenger-side door handle had been removed and she had no way out. Tom Harris employed this multipurpose cast as Buffalo Bill's MO for gaining control over his targeted female victims.

The police hunt intensified for a "Ted" fitting Graham's description. One of those who qualified was Ted Bundy. But this clean-cut Young Republican who had already been accepted in law school just didn't seem as if he could be the one, and he was fairly quickly discounted among a flood of other reported suspects.

In September, near the lake, hunters found the decomposed remains of three women buried in shallow graves. Dental records identified two of them as Janice Ott and Denise Naslund. The third could not be identified. The following month, the remains of two more victims were found. One was a missing woman from Vancouver, Washington. The other was unknown.

That same month, sixteen-year-old high school cheerleader Nancy Wilcox disappeared in Salt Lake City, Utah. Then several more, all in the general area. One woman—tall, beautiful Carol DaRonch—managed to jump out of Bundy's VW after he had abducted her from a shopping mall parking lot. He had posed as a police undercover officer and had handcuffed her. While he had her in the car, he had threatened to "blow [her] brains out" if she didn't stop screaming. That same evening, Debra Kent left a play at Salt Lake City's Viewmont High School and was never seen again.

The following January, the killing scene shifted to Colorado. Caryn Campbell disappeared in Snowmass Village. Her beaten and violated body was found the next month. In March, Julie Cunningham disappeared in Vail, another ski resort. Then Melanie Cooley a month later in

Nederland, and Shelly Robertson in July in Golden. Those bodies were both found, Nederland with her skull crushed and her jeans pulled down around her ankles, Robertson in an abandoned mine shaft.

The previous week, things had begun to come apart for Ted Bundy. He had been arrested in Salt Lake City on suspicion of burglary, one of his old standbys and a prime source of income and supplies for him. He'd been picked up for reckless driving, and a search of his car revealed handcuffs and a pair of panty hose cut into a stocking mask. Maps and gasoline receipts indicated he'd been in both Snowmass and Vail. Good police work tied him to the Carol DaRonch case. She was called in to see if she could identify him, which she did. He was convicted of attempted kidnapping, then extradited to Colorado for the murder of Caryn Campbell. Rather than seeming afraid or despondent, Bundy seemed to glory in the battle of wits with the law enforcement establishment. He was held for a while in the quaint old jail in the Pitkin County Courthouse in Aspen before being moved to the more modern Garfield County jail in nearby Glenwood Springs. While he was incarcerated, he was given access to the law library in the Pitkin Courthouse since he'd announced he wanted to prepare his own defense. On June 7, 1977, during a trial recess, Bundy wandered back to the library on the second floor, climbed out the window, and escaped.

He was picked up eight days later on the road and returned to jail under tighter security. But the following December, as his murder trial loomed, he escaped again, carving a small square out of the ceiling of his cell with a hacksaw, sneaking through a guard's apartment, stealing a car with the keys in the ignition, and headed away. When the car broke down, he got a bus to Denver and from there hopped a plane to Chicago. Then he went by train to Ann Arbor, Michigan, in time to watch the Rose Bowl on television in a local tavern. Tiring of the cold, he stole a car, which he drove to Atlanta, then abandoned it and got on a bus for Florida. There, his daring escape had not hit the papers.

One report had it that when Bundy was incarcerated in Colorado, he casually asked a jailer one day which states were most likely to execute a convicted murderer. The guard told him that the best chances would probably be in Texas or Florida. Now, some people have interpreted his decision to go to Florida as a death wish, an urge to be caught. I disagree with this assessment. I have seen very few obsessional predators who truly wanted to be caught. The few who actually seem to—such as William Heirens in Chicago, who scrawled, "cAtch Me BeFore I Kill More," on the wall of one scene with his victim's lipstick, or Ed Kemper in Santa Cruz, who called police from a phone booth in Colorado after he'd killed his mother and told them to come and get him—let you know in no uncertain terms.

What I do believe this exchange indicated was Bundy's tremendous arrogance, and his need not only to be able to manipulate, dominate, and control his victims, but the entire establishment as well. If he could go to a major capital-punishment state and continue his murderous ways, then he was every bit the superman above the law he thought himself to be. Of course, we have to couple that with the deep-set inadequacy about normal human relationships that motivated Bundy to want to kill in the first place.

As Dr. Samenow says, "What often happens in the mental health field is that they'll focus on what they call low self-esteem or sense of inadequacy. But that would be like saying, if you had a quarter, which is more important—heads or tails? They both make up the coin. What happens with the criminal is that he vacillates between an unrealistic view of himself as number one and an equally unrealistic view of himself as nothing."

Ted got a room near Florida State University in Tallahassee. Once again, he would have easy access to a ready supply of his victim of preference: beautiful, willowy girls with long, straight hair. This, in itself, is significant in terms of the criminal behavior of the serial offender. Even thousands of miles from his home base, he was still setting himself up to operate within his zone of comfort—a university campus—as he had several times before.

Late on Saturday night of January 14, 1978, dressed in black with a dark blue knit cap and carrying a wooden club, he stole into the Chi Omega sorority house, which had a reputation for some of the loveliest girls on campus. When he left fifteen minutes later, two of the girls were dead in their beds, ritualistically covered with blankets, and a third was severely injured in hers, all beaten, molested, and mutilated with his club and his teeth.

But that wasn't it for the night. A few blocks from the Chi Omega house, Bundy broke into an apartment and attacked another attractive young woman, leaving her lying diagonally across her bed in her own blood, her skull fractured in five places. Miraculously, she lived, but with deafness in one ear and permanent impairment to her balance, which prevented her from pursuing her dream of becoming a professional dancer.

Days later, while discussing the gruesome Chi Omega murders with some neighbors, Bundy casually asserted that he could get away with any crime he wanted to, even murder.

But by that point, Bundy was finally displaying the kind of postoffense behavior we have come to associate with many, if not most, serial killers. He was getting ragged, sloppy; others noticed his speech was slurred, and he was no longer dressing in the smart and fashionable style that had become his trademark. He had no job and had not yet paid any rent, but he was charging a lot of incidentals on credit cards he had stolen.

Even the style of his crimes had changed. While the earlier murders and attempted murders had shown a propensity for the thrill of the hunt, the thrill of control, and a desire to keep the victim alive and inflict punishment for as long as was practical, these Tallahassee murders were strictly blitz-style from beginning to end. By this point, the obsession had "degenerated" into a simple need to kill young women. Whether he realized it consciously or not, Ted was now playing an endgame strategy.

And his choice of his final victim shows a complete psychological degeneration. I would add "moral degeneration" to that if it were possible to descend further from the moral depths Bundy had already reached.

On February 6, driving a stolen Dodge van, Ted set out for Jacksonville. Along the way, he charged his needs on his stolen credit cards and left a new motel each morning without paying the bill. On February 9, beautiful little Kimberly Leach, a dark-haired twelve-year-old at Lake City Junior High, was seen in the school courtyard talking to a stranger, who motioned her toward a white van. Her body wasn't found until the first week of April, the neck sliced through, in an abandoned hog shed near Suwannee River State Park. Even after eight weeks of exposure, it was clear to the medical examiner that there had been massive trauma to the child's pelvic area. And the position of the body suggested that she had been slaughtered like a hog, meaning the killer's choice of locations was not accidental.

Bundy returned to Tallahassee the same day he took Kimberly's life. The next day, he was on the FBI's Ten Most-Wanted List for murder and interstate flight. He was picked up by the police for questioning after a date at an expensive restaurant, but when the officer stepped back to his squad car to run the license plates, Bundy bolted and escaped. He had no further problems with the law, probably thinking he was invincible, until February 12, when he decided to leave town. He stole an orange Volkswagen Beetle, the type of car he felt most comfortable in, and headed west out of the city.

In the alley of a closed restaurant, police finally caught up with him again. Pensacola police officer David Lee thought it odd that a car would be emerging from behind a place that was closed and turned on his flashers to pull the car over. But then the VW took off. Lee radioed in the plates, which came back as stolen. He chased the car and overtook it about a mile down the road. With his gun drawn, he ordered the driver out and facedown on the pavement.

Bundy tried to resist and a scuffle ensued. Lee fired a warning shot, but Bundy scrambled to his feet and ran. Finally, Lee got the cuffs on him, not realizing the significance of his collar. It was not until the next day that the FBI confirmed for the Pensacola Police that they had Theodore Bundy in custody.

That was when he began to negotiate. Without admitting guilt for anything, he attempted to continue his manipulation, domination, and control by implying that he could help clear up numerous open cases across the country in exchange for special treatment. The officers took this to mean not pursuing the death penalty and setting him up in some comfortable mental hospital. To prove his good intentions, one of the detectives suggested he tell them what he had done with Kimberly Leach's body, so that her family might have some closure.

After considering the matter for a moment, Bundy declined, commenting, "I'm the most cold-blooded son of a bitch you'll ever meet." He wasn't far off on that one.

There was some pretty compelling evidence, including bite marks on the buttocks of one of the Chi Omega victims that matched up perfectly with Bundy's dental impression. For the trial, Bundy, the failed law student, insisted on acting as his own attorney, as he'd been preparing to be in Colorado before his escape. He was "assisted" by Michael Minerva, a talented and well-thought-of public defender.

Back in form in the courtroom, Bundy was full of charm, and attracted an ever-increasing following of groupies for the widely covered trial. This is not an uncommon phenomenon, akin to the women who fall in love with convicted murderers in prison. But I never fail to be amazed by it, and I never fail to be disgusted by it.

At one point in the trial, the ever-manipulative Bundy indicated he was ready to confess to the Chi Omega and Kimberly Leach murders if he was spared the death penalty. But the ever-arrogant Bundy got into a disagreement with Minerva and moved to have him dismissed. The prosecution, now not wanting to take a chance on an appeal of a confession entered without counsel acceptable to the defendant, stopped bargaining.

With that, Bundy made the final choice that sealed his ultimate fate. On July 23, 1979, after six hours of deliberation, the jury found Theodore Robert Bundy guilty of murder in the first degree for the deaths of Margaret Bowman and Lisa Levy in the Chi Omega house. Judge Edward Court sentenced him to death by electrocution. The following year, Bundy was convicted of the murder of Kimberly Leach and again sentenced to death. During that trial, he even managed to marry his current girlfriend, Carole Ann Boone, who eventually bore him a daughter while he was in prison.

On death row of the Florida State Penitentiary at Starke, Bundy became something of a celebrity. Everyone wanted to "study" him, to see how such a handsome and intelligent young man could also be such a depraved killer. In this he resembled Tom Harris's Hannibal Lecter, the brilliant and evil killer psychiatrist whom the intellectuals wrote to and wanted to interview. Toward the end, as his appeals ran out over the years, Bundy began trying to barter information about unknown bodies and unsolved cases for more time.

Among those Bundy agreed to meet with was my Investigative Support Unit colleague Special Agent Bill Hagmaier. Bundy described for Bill his MO and what was going through his mind. As we'd suspected, the sex, even the murder, was incidental to the thrill of the hunt and the power of life or death over these innocent women. He even confirmed that when he had abducted Janice Ott and Denise Naslund from Lake Sammamish, back in Washington State, he had kept them alive as long as he felt he could and actually made one watch as he killed the other. This could be considered classic behavior for a depraved sexual sadist.

As is also typical for such types, Bundy's only sadness and remorse was for himself and for the fact that, despite all his manipulation and legal wrangling, he would apparently die for his sins. He begged for some intervention from both Bill Hagmaier and Bob Keppel, Ph.D., a well-respected criminal investigator from Washington with whom I had worked on the Green River murders. Desperate to buy time, Bundy had offered to work with Bob to help solve those crimes. Bill Hagmaier was with Bundy until the day before his execution.

Bundy had explained to Bill the simple though inexplicable fact that he killed beautiful young women because he wanted to; because he enjoyed it and it gave him satisfaction.

As someone who has spent a good part of his career trying to hunt down the Ted Bundys of the world, I can't say that I enjoyed the fact that he went to hell aided by two thousand volts from the Starke electric chair. But I would have to confess a certain satisfaction. Despite his incarceration for more than ten years, when, on the morning of January 24, 1989, I learned that Bundy had been executed, it was the first time I rested easy that he would never kill again.

Two things are particularly noteworthy about Gary Michael Heidnik's formative years, growing up in the Cleveland, Ohio, suburb of Eastlake in the late 1940s and early 1950s.

First, they were extremely dysfunctional. His father, Michael Heidnik, a tool and die maker, was cold and both physically and emotionally abusive, to Gary and his brother Terry, born less than two years later. When he wet his bed, Gary recalled as an adult, his father would hang the sheets out the window so the world would know of his crime. Gary claimed that when Michael felt Gary needed serious punishment, he would hang *him* out the window by his ankles, dangling him twenty feet above the pavement. Gary's mother, Ellen, a beautician by training and an alcoholic by avocation, divorced Michael in 1946, when Gary was just a little over two and Terry still a baby, for what she termed "gross neglect of duty." She would marry three more times before committing suicide in 1970. Her last two husbands were black, which, coupled with his hatred of his father, may partially explain why Gary felt more comfortable around blacks than whites as an adult. After the split, Gary and Terry went to live with their mother, but within a few years, her chronic alcoholism had sent them back to their hated father.

The other noteworthy aspect of Heidnik's youth was his twin preoccupations with the military and with business. He loved being a Boy

Scout and wearing a uniform, and he dreamed of going to West Point and a career as an Army officer. He also dreamed of being a millionaire businessman, and he avidly followed the financial section of the newspaper.

Gary was very bright. Ed Gein had an IQ of 99, just about normal. Ted Bundy, generally considered pretty slick and sophisticated by serial killer standards, was listed at 120. Gary Heidnik's IQ was 130, and on one test administered when he was an adult, he scored a remarkable 148! He did well at Staunton Military Academy in Virginia, but dropped out at the end of his junior year. He came back to Cleveland for a try at finishing school there, but lost interest after a month and joined the Army. This was 1961, and he wasn't sorry to be leaving.

He was trained as a medical corpsman at Fort Sam Houston in Texas, before being shipped out to West Germany. The abrupt transfer meant he couldn't collect on about $5,000 he'd loaned out to other soldiers at high interest rates, the beginning of his career in finance. He was never that careless with money again. When he got to Germany, Gary took the high school equivalency test and scored in the ninety-sixth percentile.

But he was also having both physical and emotional problems. He had headaches, dizzy spells, blurred vision, nausea. He also complained of hallucinations. Within months, he was back in a military hospital in Pennsylvania. In January 1963, he was diagnosed as having a schizoid personality disorder and was honorably discharged. His original 10 percent disability rating was ultimately raised to 100 percent, meaning he would receive a comfortable monthly pension for the rest of his life.

He enrolled in a practical nursing course in Philadelphia, graduating a year later and embarking on an internship at Philadelphia General Hospital. He'd put away enough money from his pension to buy a three-story house on Cedar Avenue near the University of Pennsylvania, and with typical thrift, he took one floor for himself and rented out the other two. But with all this, Heidnik's life was also taking a more disturbing turn.

For one thing, he was in and out of mental institutions. There was never any clear diagnosis of his problem, although the terms *schizoid* and *schizophrenic* kept cropping up. He was given various medications, including the antipsychotics Thorazine and Stelazine. He also socialized almost exclusively with retarded or mentally handicapped women, usually black or Hispanic, whom he would "pick up" at various institutions and homes, most notably the Elwyn Institute for the retarded. Under the guise of signing them out for a day's outing, Heidnik would generally bring them back to his house for sex.

In 1971, after driving cross-country to California on a momentary whim, Gary claimed to have been given a divine message, whereupon he returned to Philadelphia and established the United Church of the Ministries of God in his house, whose front yard also became a dumping ground for boats and cars in serious need of repair. He wrote up a charter, proclaimed himself "bishop," and secured proper IRS status. He drew his small but loyal congregation from retarded people from Elwyn and derelicts in his neighborhood. He stayed in that house until he got into a disagreement with his tenants in the fall of 1976, whereupon he barricaded himself in his basement with a rifle and handgun, and when one tenant tried to climb through the window to get to him, Gary shot at him, inflicting a superficial face wound. Aggravated assault charges were dismissed, but Gary had had enough. He sold the place, moved out, and bought another house in North Philadelphia. When the new owners of the Cedar Avenue house started looking around, they found not only mounds of trash and a sizable collection of bondage pornography, they also discovered a three-foot-deep hole dug through the concrete in the basement.

Gary opened an investment account in the church's name with Merrill Lynch. It was essentially a tax dodge, since the church was him. Over the years, he put about $35,000 into this account. By the time he was arrested for murder early in 1987, the account was valued at more than $577,000. With some of the proceeds of his shrewd investing, the "church" bought a couple of gaudy Cadillacs and a Rolls-Royce. He took in an illiterate retarded woman, Anjeanette Davidson, and together they had a baby girl in March of 1978, but the baby ended up in a foster home.

The following May, Gary and Anjeanette drove to the Selinsgrove Center near Harrisburg, to visit her much more severely retarded thirty-four-year-old sister, Alberta, who had lived there since she was fourteen. They were only to keep her out for the day, but they brought her back to the Marshall Street house where they kept her, denying vehemently that they had her, until authorities armed with a search warrant found her cowering in a storage room in the basement. Heidnik was arrested and charged with rape, kidnapping, endangerment, and unlawful restraint, among other charges.

The psychiatric report given Judge Charles P. Mirarchi Jr. (Heidnik waived a jury trial) was a pretty good summary of his mental status:

"He appears to be an extremely insecure and confused individual. Records indicate he is suffering from a major mental illness, which apparently has been of long standing. He is also psychosexually immature. He appears to be easily threatened by women whom he would consider to be equal to him either intellectually or emotionally. [He] cannot tolerate criticism. Gary needs constant acceptance and self-assurance that he is an intellectual, worthwhile human being."

The judge found Heidnik guilty and received some even more insightful and prescient evaluation in a presentencing report written by court-appointed investigator Joseph A. Tobin:

"Heidnik appears to be manipulative, and he is certainly lacking in judgment. He impresses me as one who sees himself as superior to others, although apparently he must involve himself with those distinctly inferior to himself to reinforce this. . . . It is my opinion . . . that he is not only a danger to himself, but perhaps a greater danger to others in the community, especially those who he perceives as being weak and dependent. Unfortunately, it seems to me that he will not significantly change his aberrant behavior pattern in the near future."

Judge Mirarchi took this report to heart and did the best he could—four to seven years in the state penitentiary. Heidnik served four years and four months, with three intervals of mental hospitalization for suicide attempts (drug overdose, carbon monoxide poisoning, chewing up and swallowing pieces of a light bulb) before being paroled in April 1983. The following year, he bought another house, this one at 3520 North Marshall Street.

The new house was rather impressive by the standards of the neighborhood, the only single-family stand-alone on a street of row houses. It would make a fine setting for his church. He had no particular girlfriend during this time, though he did have a brief relationship with a white woman in the neighborhood, who bore a son he used to refer to as Little Gary.

The next year, Gary decided to get married and was taken with the idea of having an Asian bride, since he had decided that Asian women knew their place with their husbands. So he essentially mail-ordered one from a service in the Philippines. He married pretty, twenty-two-year-old Betty Disto on October 3, 1985, in Elkton, Maryland, just days after she'd gotten off the plane from Manila.

After a week of wedded bliss, Betty came home one day to find Gary in bed naked with three black women. He tried to explain to the naive and morally straight Betty that this was how things were done in America. But Betty wasn't that naive. Though she stayed with him awhile, under threat of death if she left, she eventually got up the nerve to leave after making contact with other members of the Filipino community. Gary was charged with assault and spousal rape, but when Betty failed to show up at a preliminary hearing, the charges were dropped. The following September, Betty bore Gary's son, whom she named Jesse John. She sent Gary a postcard telling him.

By this point, Heidnik was no longer content merely being bishop of his own church. He also wanted to be master of his own harem. He thought ten wives and ten children would be a good start. On Thanksgiving Day, 1986, Gary began implementing his plan. When part-time prostitute Josephina Rivera, an attractive twenty-six-year-old woman who was half-black and half–Puerto Rican, agreed to come home with him for $20, he brought her to his bedroom, choked her unconscious, and confined her to his basement, naked and chained.

The key feature of this basement was a pit Gary had dug in the floor, similar to the one in the Cedar Street house, but wider and deeper—large enough, in fact, for several people to fit in. And there he kept her in the cold and filth. He raped her vaginally and anally daily, fed her poorly, and beat her with a wooden stick to maintain discipline.

Less than a week later, Heidnik secured his second captive, a mildly retarded, twenty-five-year-old black woman named Sandra Lindsay, whom he knew through Cyril Brown, a retarded black man Gary had befriended in the neighborhood and whom he used for odd jobs. And just before Christmas, he picked up a nineteen-year-old named Lisa Thomas, who agreed to go with him to McDonald's and then to Sears, where he said he would buy her new clothes. She joined the other two in the cellar.

On New Year's Day of 1987, Heidnik picked up twenty-three-year-old Deborah Johnson Dudley, another black woman. She turned out to be the most troublesome of all, constantly defying him and challenging his authority to imprison and rape her and the others. Consequently, as Gary dispassionately concluded, she needed even more punishment than the others. She was frequently beaten and either confined to the pit in the floor with a weighted cover on top, or suspended from a ceiling beam by her handcuffed wrist. When the others got out of line, they were given similar punishment. The rapes continued, and Gary checked regularly to see if any of the women showed any signs of pregnancy, indicating an initial success for his baby factory.

Occasionally, someone would come to the door looking for one of his captives. Of course, he would claim that he had not seen them, but just to make sure that their screams couldn't be heard, he took to leaving a radio blaring all the time. The captive women had to get used to the constant noise in addition to their rape, torture, and virtual starvation. Dog food had become a staple of their diet. Heidnik would also play them off against each other, demanding that one rat on the others so they could be punished. If the woman being asked had nothing negative to say, she herself would be punished.

An interesting sideline occurred during this period. Betty demanded support payments from Gary and took him to court. Like Bundy, Heidnik had enough confidence in his superiority and abilities to beat the system that he acted as his own lawyer, thoroughly ticking off family court judge Stephen E. Levin Jr. with his obfuscation of his financial resources, which were mostly hidden within the church.

On January 18, 1987, Heidnik picked up a young but streetwise prostitute, eighteen-year-old Jacqueline Askins. When he got her home, he followed his by now standard practice of dragging her down to the cellar and chaining her up. To impress on her what she could expect if she didn't cooperate, he whipped her across the buttocks with a plastic rod, then chained her ankles before going back upstairs.

Gary Heidnik became a murderer on February 7. Sandra Lindsay had been hung up by her handcuffed wrist from the overhead beam for several days as punishment for various perceived misbehaviors. She had been retching and feverish, but Gary thought it was all because she refused to eat. And since he was convinced she was pregnant with his child (she wasn't), she was simply being rebellious in not eating, meaning that the punishment had to continue. With the discipline of the others to think about, he could not afford to lose this battle of wills with her.

He uncuffed her and ordered her to stand. When she collapsed at his feet, he decided she was faking, so he kicked her into the pit. When he came back a few minutes later and dragged her back out again, she had no pulse. At that point, he acknowledged she was dead, so he hoisted her over his shoulder and carried her upstairs to figure out what to do with the body. He ended up cutting up as much as he could with a power saw, grinding it up to feed both to his dogs and his remaining captives, and placing the remaining parts in a freezer. When a rookie cop came to the door after neighbors began complaining of a horrible stench, Heidnik admitted he had burned his dinner and wasn't a very good cook. This was apparently sufficient explanation for the officer.

Heidnik didn't like the fact that the women could hear him walking around upstairs. If they always knew when he was in or out, it would be easier for them to plan an escape. The easiest way around that, he decided, would be if they couldn't hear him. So, after binding each one and securing her head with duct tape, he drove a screwdriver into their ears to damage their eardrums. By this time, he felt Josephina Rivera was a little more trustworthy than the others, and she was spared this particular torture.

But Deborah Dudley continued to be a problem. Gary was sure she was leading the others in planning rebellion against him. In an effort to scare her into submission, he dragged her upstairs and showed her Sandra Lindsay's head in a pot and her ribs in a roasting pan. That worked for a few days, but then she was back to her old ways and Gary realized there was no substitute for physical punishment.

Only this time he'd come up with a new method in addition to the frequent beatings. He found he could produce a painful electric shock with an ordinary electrical cord whose end he had stripped down to bare wire. All he had to do was plug it into a wall socket and touch the other end to one of the women's metal chains. On March 18, he came up with a refinement of the technique. Having decided that the women other than Rivera needed severe punishment, he forced them into the pit and had her fill it with water from a hose. He then placed the wire in the water and plugged it in. The women screamed in pain. The wire managed to touch Dudley's chain directly. She was electrocuted.

Heidnik didn't show any remorse, but he knew he had a problem. He wrote out a confession for himself and Rivera and forced her to sign it. This was his insurance policy. If she ever ratted on him, he figured, she would implicate herself at the same time. And he told her, "If I ever get caught, I'm going to act crazy. . . . I've learned so I can keep getting my government checks."

After leaving Dudley's body in the freezer for two days, he and Rivera dumped it in the woods in Wharton State Forest, near Camden, New Jersey. Realizing he could trust his first captive, he began giving her more freedom, even taking her out to eat in the local fast-food restaurants he favored. During one of these outings with her, he picked up another prostitute whom Rivera knew, named Agnes Adams. She became the newest member of the harem.

The next day, Rivera convinced Heidnik she needed to go see her family and tell them she was all right. He finally agreed, warning her he would kill the others if she tried to run away from him. Like Ted Bundy at his most grandiose, at the end of his career Heidnik had gotten sloppy and careless.

Rivera, in fact, went straight to her former boyfriend, Vincent Nelson, who couldn't believe how emaciated she looked. Nor could he fathom the incredible tale she related of rape, torture, and captivity. At first he was going to go over to North Marshall Street, and if her story turned out to be true, he'd take care of Heidnik himself. On the way over, though, he decided to call the police.

Within minutes, Officers David Savidge and John Cannon arrived at the house. They couldn't believe what their own eyes were telling them. As soon as they had freed the captives and secured the scene, they went after Heidnik, whom they found a couple of blocks away. Heidnik figured they were after him for child support, but when he saw their guns drawn on him, he realized the situation was somewhat more serious.

In prison, Heidnik tried to hang himself in a shower stall, but guards got to him in time. This may seem to be one more example of how "crazy" he was, but it is actually rational behavior within its context. I have often seen sexual predators, suddenly no longer in control and facing the prospect of fellow prisoners doing unto them what they have already done unto others, attempt to take their own lives.

Heidnik's attorney of choice, A. Charles Peruto Jr., was smart enough to know an innocent verdict wasn't in the cards—not with several eyewitness captives, rotting bodies, and other physical evidence. And the media was already going crazy with the sex slaves kept in the cellar dungeon by the evil genius and self-appointed minister of God. The only question was whether he could get a jury to go for an insanity or diminished-capacity plea, which would avoid the electric chair.

My unit was called in to consult with the prosecution team on strategies and how to get around a possible insanity plea. I went up to Philadelphia with Ron Walker. Ron, currently a squad supervisor in the Denver Field Office, was one of the two agents I'd taken with me to Seattle for the Green River case.

There was no question in my mind that Heidnik suffered from a mental illness—a rather severe one by my reckoning. But unlike the cases of Richard Trenton Chase or Edward Gein, I saw no evidence that he was delusional. His motives might not be fathomable to the rest of us, but clearly, he could appreciate the distinction between right and wrong and he was not *compelled* to abduct, rape, and torture women. In fact, both his planning of the abductions and the measures he took—loud radio music, blackout curtains, heavy cinder-block walls—show planning and organization rather than spontaneous, "crazy" behavior. He chose to do what he did because he wanted to.

Again, we can turn to Stanton Samenow for perspective: "You could say of a person who kills a bunch of people and cuts up the bodies and cannibalizes them, 'Well, that isn't normal.' That's true, but then you have to say, was there a mind that was purposeful? Was there a mind that was planning? Was there a mind that was in control? Was there a mind that knew the difference between right and wrong? And the answer to all would be yes.

"Sometimes people are so horrified by the crime that they say, 'He's got to be sick.' Well, it's *sickening,* but the act is not the product of a mind that is diseased. These people know right from wrong. In fact, they know the laws better than many regular people. But they have this uncanny capacity—almost like the way you could shut off an electric light switch—to shut off [the awareness] just long enough to do what they want to do, with the certainty they're going to get away with it this time, yet retain enough fear so that they're looking over their shoulders for the police. Crime is the oxygen of their lives. One man said to me, 'If you take away my crime, you take away my world.'"

During the entire time he was performing these depraved acts, Gary Heidnik was building his tidy nest egg with Merrill Lynch. When, during the trial, broker Robert Kirkpatrick took the stand, it became clear that Heidnik was a smart and shrewd investor. I know some psychiatrists will tell you that an individual can be rational and functioning in one area and out to lunch in another, but I think this rings pretty hollow. Gary Heidnik was okay with money—he just had this blind spot about kidnapping and torturing women? Sorry, I don't buy it.

I would go so far as to say that when you compare him with someone like Bundy, Heidnik's crimes were more sophisticated and more difficult to get away with, requiring greater skill and planning. Like John Wayne Gacy in Chicago, this guy was killing right in his own house. And unlike Gacy, he was keeping captives alive and still going about his "normal" business. This is not easy to accomplish, and I don't believe a strictly insane man could pull it off for long.

During the trial, Judge Lynne Abraham made clear to the jury that a mental illness, in and of itself, does not mean someone is legally insane. That is something the defense must prove.

And as far as the jury was concerned, it did not. They returned with a verdict of murder in the first degree. During the subsequent penalty phase, they decided unanimously that Gary Heidnik should pay for his crimes with his life.

In the early 1990s, my FBI colleague Jud Ray and I interviewed Heidnik in prison as part of a CBS *60 Minutes* program. I told the camera crew that, based on my experience, we were going to have to go through about five or six hours of bullshit before we could get down to the material that might mean something. Jud and I would first have to prove to Heidnik that he couldn't snow us.

He was very cordial, but there was a strange, strange look in his eyes. He was isolated from other prisoners because of what they might do to him. There had already been several attacks, which I'm sure only encouraged Heidnik's already well-developed paranoia. At first he denied everything, saying he'd even been testing electric wires in the toilet bowl of his cell to prove you couldn't kill anyone the way the prosecution said he'd killed Deborah Dudley.

Jud said to him, "You weren't mistreating these women?"

No, Heidnik insisted. They'd had birthday and Christmas parties down there, he'd brought them gifts and Chinese food and other delicacies. He'd even had a radio down there for them.

Jud reminded him it was to mask their screams. Gary denied it. He couldn't deny having these women in the basement, but he denied mistreating them. When we got him to admit some of the beatings, it was as if he had to punish these women for their own good, as you might slap a child who runs out into traffic. He described his plan for populating the world with little Garys. It was screwy as hell, but he was very articulate about it.

Jud and I glanced at each other. It was time to step up our attack. I leaned in close to Gary and said, "There's a problem in your background. Tell me about your relationship with your mother."

At that point Heidnik went nuts. The camera crew looked as if they were about to run out of the room in shock and surprise. Correspondent Leslie Stahl and the producer, watching on monitors from another room, couldn't believe it.

I kept pushing him. He stood up rigidly as if he wanted to leave, the microphone pulling on his shirt. I described the research we'd done that suggested that with most offenders like him, there'd been an abuse problem or other tragedy involving the mother.

He started crying, sobbing like a baby. My own theory is that as long as the mother is alive, there is always that sub- or semiconscious hope that the mother will accept and/or love the offender one day. That is why so many of them, such as Ed Kemper, strike out at other women as surrogates rather than the one who they feel is responsible for their pain. But when the woman dies, then the hope is over. In a peculiar way, when Kemper finally got up the courage to kill his own mother, he lost all hope; he had nothing left to live for. Perhaps that's why he turned himself in. By the same token, for all his weirdness, Heidnik didn't get into any irreversible trouble until after his mother committed suicide. In fact, it was the next year that he founded his church.

At this point in our research and knowledge, we really can't say with any degree of authority why an Edward Gein, Theodore Bundy, or Gary Heidnik does what he does, why he finds such satisfaction in the act that it takes over and subverts everything else in his life. And I'm not certain we ever will.

The one thing I do know is that, at this point, we have nothing effective to offer to get them to stop or to supplant the particular obsession with something less harmful and more productive. But until we do, we need to keep studying them and looking for answers—not because we *hope* we can help them, but because we *know* we've got to be able to stop them quicker and more effectively.

CHAPTER TWELVE

SPEAK OUT
FOR STEPHANIE

If there really were such a thing, the Schmidts of Leawood, Kansas, could have been considered the "all-American family." They certainly qualified for that designation until late in the afternoon of July 2, 1993, when their world turned upside down.

Gene Schmidt was from Hoisington, in the central part of the state, about ten miles north of where the Arkansas River takes its major turn at Great Bend—the center of the center of the country, the heart of the heart of America. Margaret Louise Dormois, universally known as Peggy, was from the southeastern Kansas city of Chanute, named for civil engineer and aviation pioneer Octave Chanute, who built the first bridge across the Missouri River at Kansas City and later influenced the Wright brothers in their understanding of flight. Gene and Peggy met in 1963 at Pittsburg State University, about an hour's drive from Chanute and due south of Kansas City. When they married in 1966, Gene became a student teacher in Missouri, right out of college, taking time out for a stint in the National Guard before resuming his teaching career in journalism and English in Kansas. He left teaching to go to work in Topeka for Jostens, the company noted for yearbooks and class rings, as a photographer and publishing consultant.

Their first child, whom they named Stephanie Rene, was born on the Fourth of July in 1973. "For the first three or four years of Stephanie's life, I let her believe all the fireworks were for her," Gene remembers. Their second daughter, Jennifer Anne, came along two years later, on October 9, 1975. Both girls were beautiful—angelic looking—Stephanie with thick, tight, blond curls and Jeni with straight, fine, blond hair.

Stephanie had colic for three months and kept her parents up virtually continuously. That turned out to be the most trouble she gave them for an extended period during her entire growing-up years.

Anticipating the first birth, Gene firmly expected a boy, and Peggy was hoping for one for his sake. But when Stephanie came along, Gene admits, "She stole my heart right away, so that when Jennifer was coming along, we were hoping for another girl."

As Peggy adds, "Boys are all right, but girls are very special."

Practically from the moment of Jeni's birth, she looked up to her big sister as her role model in life, and Stephanie tried her best to live up to the responsibility. As soon as they brought Jeni home from the hospital, Stephanie handed Peggy her diapers and said, "Give these to my little sister."

Peggy recalls, "She was a big help. She'd feed Jennifer. She was very maternal."

Jeni, for her part, didn't eat baby food very long because she wanted to be like Stephanie. She drew the line, though, at one of Steph's suggestions: "My mom would spray a big mountain of shaving cream on the kitchen table, and we'd play with it. And Stephanie would try and get me to eat it."

Jeni followed Stephanie everywhere; the two girls were inseparable. Jeni recalled the day Steph went off to kindergarten: "For three years I had her as my buddy all day long. And then one day this huge bus came to pick her up and take her away. I didn't understand. Kindergarten was only half a day and my mom said she'd be back soon, but it was so lonely without her. I waited on the front porch until she came back."

As they grew, Jeni both idolized and competed with her sister. She was often frustrated when she couldn't do things as well as Steph because of her age—whether it was swimming, gymnastics, piano lessons, or learning to ride a bike.

Eventually, the differences started to show. They were still close and completely devoted to each other, but Stephanie developed as a more outgoing, group-oriented person. She was always trying to lead and organize, wherever she went and whatever she was doing. Jeni was more sensitive and introspective and enjoyed doing things alone: reading, writing, cooking. But if Stephanie tried something and she was good at it, whether it was intellectual or athletic—and Steph was both a prize student and a good athlete—Jeni had to try it, too. Stephanie was a first-class swimmer and Jeni was somewhat afraid of the water, but when Stephanie won a trophy, Jeni had to try for a trophy, too. It wasn't resentment of her older sister's prowess; it was just that she admired Stephanie so much, she had to do "Stephanie things," too.

"Stephanie won the school spelling bee," says Gene. "Then, thank God, Jeni won the math flash-card contest. Otherwise, we were going to have to buy her a trophy!"

Even though Jeni was the serious one, Stephanie could be introspective, too. From the time she was young, she kept a journal and wrote down her deeply held feelings and beliefs. An entry from when she was ten records, "My Three Wishes: 1. I wish I was skinnier. 2. I wish I had long hair. 3. I wish I knew Ricky Schroder personally."

Though Stephanie ultimately turned into a thin and willowy beauty, wishes 2 and 3 went unfulfilled. Not only did teen heartthrob Schroder fail to come into her young life, her hair remained tight and curly. In fact, Janice Schuetz, her hairdresser in Topeka, remembered, "Stephanie was so cute, and she always wanted long hair. When she came to me for a haircut, she would climb up in the chair and say, in her dear little voice, 'Cut it long.'"

As parents, Gene and Peggy were completely devoted to their daughters. Gene, an accomplished professional photographer, captured virtually every aspect of family life on film. This included frequent visits to grandparents, family, and friends and trips to Disney World three years in a row.

After Gene left Jostens, he worked in a variety of fields, all taking advantage of his outgoing, larger-than-life personality and his natural salesmanship. For a while he sold real estate in Topeka. When his company split in two, he went with the half that aligned with RE/MAX and moved to the Kansas City area, buying a house in the upscale suburb of Leawood. Stephanie was in the eighth grade and Jeni in the fifth. The girls found adjustment to the move difficult, both in making new friends at school and in that they had moved into a more affluent, materialistic environment that neither was prepared for. It was harder on Steph, who was more peer-oriented. Jeni, who felt more comfortable being by herself, had a slightly easier time. Despite the affluent surroundings, both girls had part-time jobs at the local Hy-Vee grocery store. Steph graduated to working as a salesgirl at the Gap, which she enjoyed because she interacted with so many people. The clothing discounts were a large inducement, too.

Gene stayed with RE/MAX full-time for about three years, and all the while he and Peggy were designing promotional materials that he and other agents used in their selling. The demand for their services grew so great that Gene left real estate, and he and Peggy set up a thriving business as advertising and promotional consultants. Both beautiful blond girls served as occasional models for their parents' retail and real estate photographic spreads. They called the company Dormois Productions, utilizing Peggy's maiden name.

As the girls grew, the parents considered themselves neither strict nor lenient, and Jeni agrees. Their method of discipline had little to do with punishment or restriction. Instead, as Jeni recalls, her parents, and particularly her father, were continually challenging her and her sister's belief systems, making them articulate why they did what they did and felt the way they felt. If they could justify their thinking or behavior—whatever it was—in a way that sounded logical and reasonable when stated out loud, then it was okay. If not, the girls generally changed on their own. Even when the parents needed to impose discipline, both girls acknowledged their parents were always willing to listen, and every decision remained open to a well-reasoned appeal.

One night when Stephanie was fifteen, Gene and Peggy returned home with some friends to find her walking out of the garage with her boyfriend. Gene blew up. The rule was, you're not alone in the house with a boy when parents aren't home. In retrospect, Gene thinks he was probably as concerned with the impression on their friends as anything. But after he was finished with his tirade, Stephanie countered that he and Mom stressed trust. Had she done anything to violate that trust? Well, no, Gene admitted. Then why wasn't he trusting her now? Gene backed down.

Actually, the appeal that ended up working the best had nothing to do with discipline, but a lot to do with Gene's perception of family order and tranquillity. It involved the girls' quest for a dog. "I was not fond of dogs," Gene explains, "particularly selling real estate. I saw what they did to the values of homes."

"We always had an excuse," Peggy adds. "We kept buying stuffed animals, but after a while that didn't work anymore."

After several false starts, they finally ended up with a little white female bichon frise, in time for Jeni's seventh birthday. She was named Sandi and quickly became an integral member of the family.

Of the two girls, the more outgoing Stephanie was the prankster. Gene and Peggy used to play a game with the girls where they'd make one minor alteration to their clothing, such as putting a clothespin on the back of one of their coats, and see how long it took the girl to discover it. Then one day, Stephanie came home from school and said that Gene was supposed to call the principal. Gene asked what she had done.

"Well," she explained, "we had a substitute teacher today and I put a clothespin on the back of her skirt because I thought it would be funny."

"I called the principal and I was just irate that he was upset over something as stupid as a clothespin," says Gene. "And then he informed me that attached to the clothespin was a sign that said, 'I'm a dork.' So I looked at Stephanie and said, 'You left something out, didn't you?' "

It was a key part of Stephanie's personality that after she'd concocted a prank, she had to be there to laugh at it, meaning she was much more likely to get caught.

When Steph and Jeni got to the age where they were each attempting to monopolize, and therefore were fighting over, the phone, Gene and Peggy put in a second line and told the girls it was theirs, and to work out their own schedule. Like most other issues in the Schmidt household, initial arguments and bickering gave way to reason.

Gene and Peggy's basic philosophy with the kids was give-and-take, and that things would work out best if each party tried to understand and appreciate the position of the other. In music, for example, Gene was a traditional rock fan. Jeni was into the heavy-metal sound, and Steph liked softer, more romantic music and country western. Originally, there wasn't much crossover among the three distinct tastes. So Gene made it a point whenever he had one of the girls in the car with him to listen to her choice, and discuss what she liked about it, then to listen to one of his favorites and do the same. Gradually, all three of them began to appreciate the others' preferences.

All in all, Gene says, "Stephanie was a blast. She was just fun. I've never really seen that much unconditional love." And the ultimate success of the Schmidts' approach was reflected in another piece of Stephanie's writing:

"I hope someday I can be like my parents. I am excited to get married and want to have two to four children before I am thirty, but I want a couple of years to spend with my husband without any children. I want my family to be close-knit, caring and loving. I think it will be similar to how my family is now."

Jeni had always been more career-oriented, so Stephanie declared that she would have Jeni's kids for her. Despite her less maternal instincts, Jeni articulates her parents' influence just as directly: "Honesty and trust and a good sense of humor would probably be the three most important things my parents instilled in us. It just seemed very natural."

As they got into junior high and high school, Steph's and Jeni's tastes in boys also reflected their diverging personalities. "I liked boys with ponytails and who played guitars," says Jeni. "She liked guys with crew cuts and who threw footballs. But she always got along with the guys I'd bring home, and I always got along with her boyfriends."

Pretty much everything else, they shared. They borrowed each other's clothes, though Jeni's wardrobe was pretty pedestrian compared to the name labels Steph preferred, as Jeni saved her money while Stephanie quickly spent hers. Steph decided to teach Jeni "how to shop," which gave her a ready companion for one of her favorite activities in life.

Jeni's companionship was important to Stephanie. They shared friends, went swimming, saw movies, had lunch, and shopped. Recalls Jeni, "The day she graduated from high school, she took me out with her instead of just going out with her friends. That was pretty cool."

It seemed as if everyone loved Stephanie Schmidt. Heather Haas, her friend at Blue Valley North High School, says, "She was pretty much the one who was the core of the group. She was the one who was really outgoing and really a people person."

Stephanie didn't push herself academically in high school. She enjoyed the social side and the organizing too much. She declared that she wanted to go to the University of Kansas in Lawrence—KU in local parlance—but Gene was concerned that it was too big for her and that she chose it because so many of her friends would be going there. He said he would support any decision she made, but asked that she consider one or two smaller schools. He judiciously avoided suggesting his own alma mater for all the obvious reasons.

But since it was an obvious possibility and relatively close—about two hours' drive—Stephanie and her close friend Shannon Marsh decided to check out Pittsburg State. Instantly, they both fell in love with the school and decided it was what they wanted.

And they loved it when they got there. Stephanie reported that everyone seemed friendly and sincere. It was a fresh start and she loved the idea of being able to reinvent herself into anything she wanted. She also enjoyed the special treatment she got from the guys at the Sigma Chi chapter because her father was a prominent alumnus and former president of the fraternity chapter.

After her freshman year, Stephanie decided to stay for the summer and go to summer school. She and another girl moved out of the dorm and got their own apartment. As had been her practice, she continued talking to her parents or sister on the phone two or three times a day.

In December 1992, Stephanie got her first off-campus job, as a waitress at a new restaurant called Hamilton's. It was a small, family-oriented place where the waiters and waitresses wore starched white shirts and white aprons. It was downtown, at the other end of Broadway, the main drag, from the campus. It wasn't anywhere near her apartment, but by then she'd bought a shiny teal 1989 Honda with her parents' help and of which she was very proud.

Stephanie loved Hamilton's for the same reason she'd loved working at the Hy-Vee in high school: she got to interact with people. Stacey Payne, who worked with her at the restaurant, says, "She was hard to bring down. She was a happy person and made a joke out of everything."

When Peggy and Gene came to visit her the following March, they had lunch there, and Tom Hamilton, one of the three owners, told them how much he enjoyed having their daughter there.

When Gene asked her that night how she liked the other people at the restaurant, she told him that everybody was fine. Then she added, "There's one guy there we all feel kind of sorry for. He's older than the rest of us and he's been in jail."

"For what?" Gene asked.

"He was in a bar fight or something," Stephanie explained. "But he's very nice. He doesn't hit on any of the girls or anything." His name was Don Gideon. He was thirty-one, on parole, and he'd been living with his mother, but then when that didn't work out, Tom Hamilton gave him a place to live above the restaurant. He started out as a dishwasher, then graduated to busing tables and then helping out in the kitchen with such tasks as making salads. Hamilton considered him a good worker and dependable. Unlike most of the waitresses who were part-timing while going to college, Don was full-time and seemed to enjoy his job.

The summer of 1993, after her sophomore year, Stephanie decided to take a science course and keep her job in the restaurant. But before summer school started, she developed a sore throat so severe that it was almost swollen shut and a friend had to take her to the emergency room for a shot. By the time the infection cleared up, she'd missed the first four days of classes and it was too late to catch up. So when she came home for Father's Day, Gene and Peggy suggested that she could use a break, and since she couldn't take the course, she ought to stay home for the summer. But she really wanted to go back to the restaurant.

She still wasn't feeling well, but felt pressure to show up for her shifts. One day Tom Hamilton yelled at her for having spilled something, either gravy or sour cream. When she protested that she was trying her best even though she didn't feel well, Hamilton responded, "Well, why don't you just go home!"

Stephanie interpreted this to mean she was fired. A friend acted as an intermediary and persuaded Tom to tell her he hadn't fired her. But the encounter had left a bad taste, and when she learned that she couldn't have her birthday off in spite of having filled in every other weekend, she decided to leave and go home for the rest of the summer. Once Steph's mind was made up, that was it. But Tom didn't want to lose her and assured her that even though she was leaving, her job would be waiting for her whenever she was ready to come back. So she packed up her things and told her parents she'd drive home on Friday, July 2, after a date on Thursday with Matt Schicke, whom she'd been seeing for about two months; they'd had a lot of fun the previous weekend on a Sigma Chi canoe trip. Peggy planned a twentieth birthday celebration for Sunday, July 4.

Several of Steph's friends from the restaurant, including two who lived together with Stacey Payne—Sloane Kehl and Megan Ewing—wanted to take her out for an early birthday bash on Wednesday. They went out to dinner, after which Stephanie came back to her apartment. She called her parents at about ten-thirty and said she was getting ready to go out with some of her girlfriends to a local bar. Her throat was beginning to bother her again and she confided that she didn't really feel like going out, but she didn't want to disappoint the girls.

They picked her up about fifteen minutes later and took her to a place called Bootleggers Bar and Grill in Frontenac, where they joined other friends and coworkers. Frontenac adjoins Pittsburg on the north. Stacey, who was nineteen, came with another friend a year younger, and that night they weren't letting eighteen-year-olds into the bar, so the two of them left with Don Gideon and went to another bar, where they stayed until about midnight, then brought Don back to Bootleggers where his truck was parked. As it happened, Bootleggers was right across the street from the police station, something Stephanie would have noticed since she left at one point to buy some lozenges for her increasingly sore throat. Don went back into the bar, and when Stephanie declared that she wasn't feeling well and wanted to go home, Don offered to drive her.

Peggy and Gene and Jeni didn't hear from Stephanie on Thursday. Though she called regularly, they weren't overly alarmed. They knew she was busy getting ready to leave, they knew she had an appointment to see the doctor about her throat, and she'd undoubtedly be rushing to get ready for her date that night. It was okay, though. They knew she'd be home the next day because, earlier in the week, she and Jeni had arranged to go to the movies together Friday night. Jeni, who had a boyfriend who was an exchange student in Germany, had planned to go with his parents to meet him in Florida and so would miss Steph's birthday on Sunday.

Friday morning, excited by the prospect of her daughter's returning home that day, Peggy said to Gene, "Let's call Stephanie."

Gene replied, "No, let's let her sleep."

Later on in the day, they did call, and when they got no answer, they left numerous messages on her answering machine. There was a severe storm warning with high winds, and Peggy was worried about Stephanie's possibly having to drive through it.

When she hadn't arrived home and they hadn't heard from her by three o'clock, they began to be seriously concerned that she'd had an accident on the road. Jeni reached Matt at the grocery store in Pittsburg in which he worked and asked how late they'd been out the night before and if he knew when Steph had left to drive home.

Instantly, his voice sounded troubled. Stephanie hadn't shown up for their date the previous night. He'd tried calling and calling, then assumed she'd just forgotten about it and then had gone home the next day. In fact, he called Hamilton's and talked to Stacey. "Where's Steph?" he asked.

"She went home," Stacey replied, because that was what Stephanie had told her she was doing. But when Matt went over to check and found her car still parked at her apartment, he'd gotten very worried, too. He was about to call the Schmidts to ask them where Stephanie was.

Gene got on the phone. "Call the police right now," he told Matt. Then Peggy called Hamilton's. They were able to piece together that Stephanie and her friends had shown up at Bootleggers Wednesday night, and someone else recalled that she hadn't felt well, but that the girls she'd come with wanted to stay so she'd caught a ride with some guy—it might have been Don Gideon. He was there that night and was rumored to have a crush on one of the girls. Everyone was surprised to hear that Stephanie was missing. They hadn't expected to see her after that night for the rest of the summer, so no one thought anything of it.

That was when Stacey got worried.

Don Gideon had showed up at the restaurant Thursday morning looking tired and unshaved. They asked him if he knew what had happened to Stephanie since they thought he was the last one anyone had seen her with. He confirmed that it had been him leaving Bootleggers with her, but when they went outside to the parking lot, she'd gotten in a car with another friend of hers whom he didn't know. That was the last he'd seen of her.

The Schmidts' closest friend, and the best man at their wedding, Ron Seglie, was a doctor in Pittsburg. He always looked out for Stephanie, and he was the one she was to have seen on Thursday. Gene and Peggy called him at his medical office, and together with a police officer and a locksmith, he went over to Stephanie's apartment. They found no evidence of struggle, but they found no evidence of Stephanie, either. Her pocketbook was there. Only her keys and ID were missing—the two items she would have taken with her to the bar.

They called all the local hospital emergency rooms. None of them had seen her, either. The police had become convinced that Stephanie was not the type of person just to take off somewhere without telling anyone. "We're going to go full blast with this thing," a detective told Gene. They asked him to supply a good photograph. Searches were launched throughout much of the state. Kansas Wildlife and Parks officers handled the most remote and rural areas.

None of the Schmidts slept at all Friday night. Early Saturday morning, they had to make a collective decision about Jeni: Would she still go to Florida? Jeni wanted to stay with her parents and help them through the ordeal, but Peggy encouraged her to go. "I did it because I had no idea what was in store for us and how long this was going to be, and I thought maybe it would be better for Jeni—because I know Jennifer—to be away from all of this."

Jeni was torn. "Stephanie and I had a relationship of always looking out for each other. I didn't know if going away would be a good thing or if I was letting my parents down or not watching out for Steph. It was quite a decision to make."

When they'd confirmed that Jeni could fly back immediately if anything changed, she finally decided to go. The entire time she was in Florida, she had difficulty eating and sleeping. Her preoccupation was to find a nice birthday gift for Stephanie, and she looked for one every day, all the while knowing in the back of her mind that she might never see her sister again.

Eric Rittenhouse had met Stephanie at Pittsburg but knew of her dad even before she came since Eric was also a Sigma Chi and Gene had been one of the luminaries of the chapter. Eric and Stephanie had gone out together, but more than that, they were close friends. He was home for the summer in Overland Park, the community that adjoins Leawood, working in a Sherwin-Williams paint store, when his mother called him with the news that Stephanie was missing.

He immediately felt something was very wrong. He knew Stephanie too well to believe she would go off anywhere without telling her family. It would be totally out of character.

The rumors started almost immediately: that some of the tenants in Stephanie's apartment complex had a band, that they were involved with drugs, and that they wanted to take her away for the weekend with them, possibly to the Ozarks. Someone else had seen a young woman resembling Stephanie walking down a road near campus around midnight on Thursday. Gene checked her bank account. There was a routine $20 withdrawal, but no suspicious activity.

"I think in our minds, the worst-case scenario would be if Stephanie had to be in the hospital for a while," Gene said. "I don't think we ever thought of anything worse than that. It just wasn't possible." Using their promotional and photographic skills, he and Peggy sent a recent photo, which the Kansas Highway Patrol drove to Pittsburg for publication in newspapers.

A crisis response team was brought in to Blue Valley North High to help students and Stephanie's friends. Paul Chinn, the school psychologist who headed the effort, said, "They used to feel safe with one another. They grew up real fast. It's a loss of innocence."

"I'm running on hope," said Shannon Marsh.

Meanwhile, Don Gideon, the last person anyone had seen with Stephanie, had suddenly left town on Friday afternoon, having asked Tom Hamilton how he might go about renting a car. He was a material witness, and the police started looking for him. Monday was the legal Fourth of July holiday, so they would have to wait until Tuesday to see whether he contacted his probation officer as required or whether he broke parole.

The story hit the media on Sunday, July 4—Stephanie's twentieth birthday. Anyone with information was urged to contact the Pittsburg police or the Schmidts. It was a harrowing and agonizing day for Gene and Peggy. Flyers were distributed at Independence Day celebrations and fireworks displays. The search quickly became a huge media event, and the Schmidts' house became a nerve center, flooded with people. All of their friends and neighbors pitched in. Soon, thousands of cards and letters would begin pouring in. Stephanie's friends began calling and stopping by, which Gene and Peggy found immensely touching and comforting. Gene Fox, a media consultant and former television sportscaster and writer for the *Kansas City Star*, virtually took over. His daughter Kristi was a close friend of Stephanie's. Shannon Marsh organized the circulation of flyers around Pittsburg.

On Tuesday, Don Gideon failed to report in to his probation officer, and the Schmidts learned from Craig Hill, a local Leawood police detective who was acting as liaison, the specific nature of his criminal record. He hadn't been in a bar fight as he'd told the girls at the restaurant. He was a sex offender who had raped and sodomized a college coed in Parsons, Kansas, in 1983 while holding a straight razor against her throat and threatening to kill her if she resisted. He'd been granted early release from prison the previous November and got the job at Hamilton's when they opened a month later. Tom Hamilton reported that Gideon checked "no" on the employment application form that asked if he'd ever been convicted of a felony.

Gene urged the police to check Gideon's apartment, but they said they didn't have justification for a search warrant. Gene countered angrily, "If she's in there, I don't want my daughter dying because you don't have a warrant. There's got to be a way you can get in there." Tom Hamilton, the landlord, let police in. They found nothing. And since no one had actually seen Stephanie get into Don's truck outside of Bootleggers, they were pursuing the hope that maybe, as he'd said, she actually hadn't.

Gideon placed a collect call to his mother, Shirley, on Tuesday. She asked him point-blank, "Oh, Donny, what have you done? Did you kill this girl?"

"What girl?" he asked.

"The Stephanie Schmidt girl."

"I didn't kill anyone."

Shirley said he sounded surprised when she told him the police were looking for him. She called the police, who were eventually able to trace the call to a Safeway store in Crescent City, California, near the Oregon border. His abandoned pickup truck was found in Coos Bay, Oregon, about a hundred miles to the north. It was later learned that Gideon headed for the Canadian border, but was turned back by customs authorities at the Coutts, Alberta, crossing because of a prior felony conviction in the United States.

Another development, both frightening and disturbing in its implications, surfaced while Stephanie and Don were missing. A Crawford County, Kansas, woman in her early fifties came forward and told authorities that she had been raped by Gideon in April. He had been driving her home after a date. She hadn't reported the incident because she'd been afraid, but felt she had to once he was linked to another possible crime. She expressed great remorse that her hesitancy in reporting it might have allowed Gideon to assault again.

Gene and Peggy prepared a "missing" poster for wide circulation. It featured pictures of both Stephanie and the five-feet-ten, 160-pound Gideon. He was not officially a suspect, merely wanted for parole violation and questioning in Stephanie's disappearance. Stephanie's three companions the night she disappeared told a newspaper reporter they couldn't believe Don would be involved in her disappearance. They said he was like a big brother to them.

"He's been at our house and everything," said Sloane Kehl. "He never did anything. He never said anything that would lead us to believe he would be involved with something like this."

Gene Schmidt told reporters that even if Gideon had abducted his daughter, he took heart from the fact that Don released the other woman alive after the attack.

Shannon Gideon, Don's younger sister, told the Associated Press that even though there was some initial worry in the family that her brother was involved with Stephanie's disappearance, logic told her that he wouldn't be. "I admit, we wondered if something bad hadn't happened. But he knows that getting out of prison was his second chance and that he's lucky to get a second chance at all, so he can't blow it. He's working and being a good citizen." When asked about denying killing Stephanie to their mother, Shannon said, "I know he's got a past, but I believe him."

A number of friends and associates worked to get Stephanie's case featured on John Walsh's national television program, *America's Most Wanted,* most notably Larry Cukajti, a Sigma Chi friend of Gene's and an advertising account executive, who contacted the producer, Lance Heflin. The brief segment, including tape of Stephanie's summer boating excursion with their friends, the Foxes, ran on Friday, July 16, along with an interview with Gene and Peggy saying they were confident their daughter was still alive.

The next day, Donald Ray Gideon called Volusia County, Florida, sheriff's deputies from a hotel phone booth in Ormond Beach and turned himself in. Ironically, Jeni had been staying about five miles away. He didn't admit anything, merely told them, "I'm the guy you're looking for." He had told his older sister by phone that he had left Pittsburg when he did because he "just wanted to get away for a while and take a little vacation." Lead Pittsburg detective Ken Orender and Kansas Bureau of Investigation personnel drove to Florida. Gideon waived extradition and rode back with them to Kansas.

In Shawnee County Jail, he began to talk to detectives. State attorney general Bob Stephan was a friend of Gene's from Sigma Chi circles in Topeka, where Gene had started an alumni group. He called personally and tearfully said, "The son of a bitch confessed and it's not good. The police are on their way to talk to you now."

Local police, FBI, and KBI all came to the house. Police Chief Steve Cox asked everyone else to leave the living room and wait in the basement, then sat down with Gene and Peggy and Jeni. Craig Hill watched the basement door to make sure they weren't disturbed.

Chief Cox told them that Gideon had confessed to killing Stephanie, that he had drawn a map showing where he'd left the body, but that they couldn't find it so they were flying him down to show them. They would need Stephanie's dental records.

The confession was made to KBI agent Scott Teeselink and FBI agent Michael Napier. I know Mike Napier; he's a super guy, now working back in Quantico. Gideon admitted to the agents that he had offered Stephanie a ride home and that she'd willingly gotten in his truck with him. When he drove past the road leading to her house, he grabbed her hand so she couldn't jump out of the truck. He drove her to a field surrounded by woods, where he sexually assaulted her, then strangled her with his hands and tied her bra around her neck, all within an hour of leaving the bar. He said that he often went into rages, and according to Teeselink's and Napier's report, "When the rage hits, it is equivalent to and consists of 'pure power,' which he holds and exercises."

He claimed that after the rape, he led Stephanie by the hand out of the truck, gave her a screwdriver, and told her to kill him with it. She couldn't do it, he said, so he had to kill her. Let me say that this is not an uncommon type of embellishment to a predatory murder confession—an ex post facto attempt by the murderer to absolve himself of the blame—but it lacks all credence. Victimology in Stephanie Schmidt's case tells us that presented with this opportunity, she wouldn't have taken him up on his offer to kill him, but she would have run like hell.

In a telephone call from the jail, he also admitted the killing to his mother. He said he had killed Stephanie after assaulting her because he didn't want to go back to prison. He also admitted the rape of the Crawford County woman in April.

In spite of their worst fears, the pronouncement seemed unreal to all three Schmidts. Craig came over to them and mentioned Parents of Murdered Children. It was the first time Gene and Peggy had heard of the organization. "You'll get through this," Craig said.

After the announcement, the house began filling up with people again. Lynn Allen, the Johnson County victims' rights coordinator, who worked with the district attorney's office, came by to offer her help.

Stacey Payne could hardly believe the news. "I was sick. He had stayed the night in my dorm room not long before. Megan and I would be there; he'd sleep on our floor. I thought of him like a brother."

And when she thought about the events of June 30, her memories were even more chilling. "When my friend and I went to take Don back to Bootleggers, he was so persistent. He was just like, 'Take her home and let's go back out.' But she'd been upset about something, so I wouldn't do it. But I just thought back, you know? If I had taken her home and then gone back out with him, would I have found myself in the same situation as Stephanie? My mom still cries thinking about it, how close it was."

Eric Rittenhouse was devastated, not only by the confirmation of his friend's death, but by what he could have done to prevent it if he'd had more information. He would have looked out for Stephanie more intently. "I'd have felt a lot more protective. I would have said to her, 'Don't do anything with him. And if you need a ride, or anything, call me—any time of day or night, call anyone in the fraternity. We'll help you.' I just wish I could have known."

The media coverage ranged the entire spectrum of sensitivity. The Schmidts were infuriated by one story comparing their loss of a daughter with the Gideons' loss of a son. On the other hand, one local television reporter who'd recently lost her father came by simply to express her condolences. She and Gene and Peggy sat together in Stephanie's room and cried.

On July 27, acting on Gideon's instructions from the night before, investigators went to a field surrounded by woods in Cherokee County near the town of Weir, about ten miles southwest of Pittsburg. Fifty officers combed the area, and at about 4 P.M. they found Stephanie's body in a stand of tall weeds, decomposed from weeks of exposure to the elements. Within the hour, the Schmidts were told of the find. Because of the state of the body, Gene and Peggy and Jeni never had the opportunity to see Stephanie a final time after she died.

Donald Ray Gideon was charged with first-degree murder, aggravated kidnapping, and aggravated criminal sodomy and was transferred from Shawnee to the Crawford County Jail near Pittsburg.

Initially, authorities told the Schmidts they couldn't have Stephanie's body for burial because it constituted material evidence. They finally relented when the forensic report was done.

Stephanie Rene Schmidt, three days short of her twentieth birthday when she died, was laid to rest in Resurrection Cemetery on August 2, 1993. Gene and Peggy chose it because a close college Sigma Chi friend of Stephanie's who had committed suicide was buried there. His death was the first loss of a peer that group had experienced. Stephanie's, all too soon afterward, was the second. The preceding funeral service, held at Atonement Lutheran Church in Overland Park, was attended by an overflow gathering of more than eight hundred. Paul Clark, a professional musician and one of Stephanie's many, many friends, performed a song he had written for her entitled "Fallen Tree." The procession to the cemetery stretched over a mile.

As much as Gene's and Peggy's lives had already changed in the horrible weeks since Stephanie's disappearance, they were to change even more: agonizingly, magnificently, heroically. I suspect Gene and Peggy would just shrug and say they were doing what they knew had to be done, for Stephanie and others like her. But I defy anyone who has not been through this personally to minimize their mission or their accomplishment. Those who have will know all too well what I'm talking about.

Gene says, "We went from almost a complacent, quiet lifestyle to a highly public, financially challenged lifestyle. But it's not really for us. We've been guided a lot by Stephanie. Someone's got to do it. Not enough people are speaking out."

They went public the day after the funeral, going on radio to ask the critical question: Why was this violent man released from prison?

The fact of the matter was that Donald Gideon's release after serving ten years of his twenty-year sentence was mandatory, and it had nothing to do with his likelihood of hurting anyone else once he got out. It had only to do with "good time" in prison. The Schmidts couldn't understand how this could be allowed to happen. They approached the state Department of Corrections and were told they were not entitled to the information; in effect, if you want to know something, sue us.

"They were not at all sympathetic," Peggy remembers.

So when their friend, real estate agent Jim Blaufuss, approached them and said a group of legislators, attorneys, and business leaders were forming a task force focusing on violent sexual offenders and asked if they wanted to participate, they responded simultaneously, "Absolutely!" It would be called the Stephanie Schmidt Task Force, and its initial charge would be to see if they could change some laws to lessen the chances of this kind of tragedy happening to someone else's child. In addition to Blaufuss, the nucleus of the group included Johnson County district attorney Paul Morrison, state senator Bob Vancrum, and state representative Gary Haulmark.

But Gene and Peggy had already realized this new work they were doing would become a lifelong commitment, and they wanted something more permanent. "One of the things that shocked me initially," Gene explains, "was that since Stephanie was over eighteen, there was no organization like the Center for Missing and Exploited Children that would help her." So they set up their own foundation and called it Speak Out for Stephanie—S.O.S. They would concentrate their efforts on college campuses, trying to create awareness of sexual predators and increase personal safety.

On October 6, 1993, appearing before Cherokee County District Court judge David F. Brewster and over his attorney's formal objection, Don Gideon pled guilty to four felony counts. As he responded individually to the counts of premeditated first-degree murder, aggravated kidnapping, rape, and aggravated criminal sodomy, he sat expressionless. Gene and Peggy and about sixty of Stephanie's friends were also in the courtroom, most of them wearing Speak Out for Stephanie pins. They wept quietly as prosecutor John Bork recounted the events of June 30 and July 1. Bork said that the motive for the murder was to hide the rape. Judge Brewster then asked Gideon if he wanted to make any changes in the story. Gideon just shrugged and shook his head. Bork said he would ask for the maximum sentence to insure that the defendant never got out to prey on anyone else. He said that if Kansas had a death penalty, that was what he would have proposed.

As he left the courtroom, Gene told a reporter, "For the first time in my life, I felt I was in the presence of something evil. This guy has no remorse. He's a slug. He leaves a trail of pain wherever he goes."

The sentencing hearing was set for November 18. In spite of the guilty plea, Bork called witnesses and presented the graphic details of Stephanie's rape and murder in his effort to secure the longest prison term allowable.

Gene, Peggy, and Jeni all addressed Judge Brewster. Gene had wanted to play a poignant and moving video he had compiled of scenes from Stephanie's life, to demonstrate graphically what they had lost. But he was told it could be considered prejudicial and could be grounds for an appeal.

Since before Stephanie's death, Jeni had wanted to be a writer. It's an ironic tragedy that the first occasion in which her deep sensitivity and eloquence could be shared with the public had to be this one. But her message was powerful, and throughout her time before the court, she bravely riveted her eyes on Gideon, not letting him escape her condemnation, demanding, as it were, that all violent predators be forced to face the responsibility for what they have done. It was not Jeni who looked away; it was Gideon. Once again he proved himself to be the coward, one who could not dominate this eighteen-year-old young woman in an even test of wills.

"Your Honor," she began,

> Stephanie is not only my big sister, she is also my best friend. All my life Stephanie stood by my side. She has always been there for me: to protect me and do everything possible to help me out. I wish I could have been there that horrible night on July first. I wish I could have protected her somehow. So today I would like to take this opportunity in the courtroom to help my sister.
>
> I have sat down many times trying to think about what I want to say today. But I kept denying everything. I did not want to believe that I would never see my sister again. I did not want to believe she is dead. Nor did I want to believe that our justice system is also dead.
>
> It was and still is difficult to say what I want, because I am very confused. I am confused because I cannot understand why my sister was brutally murdered. I do not understand how any human being could hurt another in such a terrible way.
>
> Most of all I do not understand why it happened, knowing that our justice system could have prevented it from the start. This monster was already behind bars. Why was he released knowing he was a danger to society?
>
> Ever since that night I found out Stephanie was missing, I kept reaching out for one last string of hope. That she would be okay and home again. Time went by and Stephanie was still not home. I still kept reaching for a last string of hope, but I was let down, Stephanie was found—dead.
>
> I was let down continuously. I no longer have any dreams to reach out to. I always dreamt of the day I would be Steph's bridesmaid, or the aunt of her children. Stephanie will not see me graduate from high school, she won't be there to help me through college. I no

longer have my sister to call in the middle of the night for advice, or just a laugh to make me feel better.

This horrible creature took Stephanie's life, and mine! He destroyed our futures and our faith. Stephanie and I were both let down in faith of God, and most of all, our faith in the justice system!

My dad always told us that the government was there to protect the innocent. Yet this so-called justice system was more concerned for the well-being of some amoral creature like the one who murdered my sister!

Your Honor, I ask you to give me one last string of hope to hang on to. Please help restore my faith. Please make it so this coward never comes in contact with another Stephanie. Please do not let me down.

The courtroom was deathly silent as she spoke.

Judge Brewster got the message and he came through, sentencing Gideon to life in prison for murder with a "hard forty," meaning he would have to serve forty years before being eligible for parole. He added another 716 months—nearly sixty years—for the other charges, to run consecutively, which meant the thirty-one-year-old killer would have to serve eighty-eight years before he could be out on the street again.

"There's nothing more the judge could have done," John Bork commented approvingly. One year to the day after Stephanie's murder, a new death-penalty statute passed by the Kansas legislature took effect.

In March of 1995, Gideon's lawyers appealed the harshness of his sentence to the Kansas Supreme Court, claiming the judge may have been influenced by "inflammatory remarks by the victim's family." This was yet another example of the unfairness of a system that strives to totally depersonalize the innocent victim, while giving the guilty killer every opportunity to show what a generally decent guy he is. But in a ruling that affirmed the dictates of both justice and common sense, the high court in April unanimously rejected all of Gideon's thirteen issues of appeal. In approving the court ruling, an editorial in the *Topeka Capital-Journal* referred to Gideon as a "poster boy for Hard 40."

Peggy and Gene were no longer affluent Midwestern business people; they had become crusaders. "We had been doing advertising specialties across the United States," Gene says, "selling everything from ballpoint pens to postcards to magnets, you name it. Most of our clients were real estate agencies and schools and banks. We had done our semiannual business analysis. It had exceeded expectations and things were looking real good. That was June thirtieth. As soon as we were aware Stephanie was missing, we just put the business on stop. It wasn't even slow down. All our efforts were focused on finding her."

And they never went back. Living on their savings, doing just enough business to get by, they dedicated themselves to making people aware of the dangers they face from unknown predators and to changing laws to better protect the innocent.

Says Gene, "I think we were really impacted by those twenty-seven days when Stephanie was missing—at the number of her friends that reminded us so much of her. And friends of Jennifer's that reminded us so much of Jeni. And once we discovered there was nothing more we could do for Stephanie, we knew that we had to keep on going and get this kind of horror stopped. That was our whole objective."

The task force was in full operation. By December, they had written five proposed laws dealing with sexual offenders. In the process, they had realized that to accomplish what they felt needed to be done, both on a state and national level, they had to be politically active, something that would violate the Internal Revenue Service regulations regarding nonprofit—or 501(c)3—organizations, which is how S.O.S. was classified. So they set up a separate Stephanie Schmidt Foundation. S.O.S., no longer a 501(c)(3), would become the name of the campus chapters they intended to establish. Their motto: Changing Laws, Attitudes, and Lives.

Gene testified frequently to try to get the task force's bills passed. He and Peggy were determined to continue speaking out for Stephanie. During one appearance before a committee of the Kansas legislature, he recalls, "One of the representatives continually referred to the fact that we needed to take 'baby steps.' I was so infuriated that when we were contacted by the *Maury Povich* show, I said, 'Well, then, we'll show them what baby steps are like and let them know that we're serious.'"

Peggy and Gene and Jeni appeared on the nationally syndicated television program on February 15, 1994. With them were Jack and Trudy Collins, already respected national advocates of the victims' rights movement, and Stanton Samenow. Also on the program were Shirley Gideon and her daughter Shannon. It was a memorable encounter.

Before the broadcast, Povich had interviewed Don in prison. He accepted perfunctory responsibility for the murder, but there was no evidence of any genuine feeling. Like so many of these guys, the only genuine feeling he displayed was for himself and how he'd had "a problem" that no one was willing to fix.

"Do you feel any remorse at all?" Povich asked him.

"No comment," Gideon replied.

"What?" Povich pressed. "How could you say no comment?"

"Because I got ninety-nine and a half years. You know, I mean, does it matter whether I have any remorse? I mean, I got ninety-nine and a half years."

He recounted his troubled life, his repeated encounters with the law and incarceration, beginning in his teens. He seemed to place responsibility for his life of crime everywhere but in the choices he himself had made. Samenow listened to these excerpts of Povich's interview with Gideon, then commented that Stephanie's killer displayed the three traits he most associates with this kind of personality:

"One, a sense of ownership. You take whatever you want, regardless of the consequences. The second point is these are people who have no concept of injury to others. In fact, they regard themselves as the victim because they have been caught, and they will then blame the victim after the fact. And the third is, they all know what can happen to them. They know right from wrong.

"Crime is a matter of choice," Samenow explained to the studio and national audiences. "This man and others like him, after the fact, when they're held accountable, they will blame anything and everyone. This man blamed the system. But you know, everything but the federal deficit has been blamed for criminal behavior. The facts of what these people are like and what their motives are, are radically different from what they tell others after the fact."

Ironically, it was Shannon who expressed the feeling so many of us seem to have:

"You never think it can happen to you . . . but it can. . . . My brother won't get to be there for my graduation, my marriage—anything."

True. But as Gene pointed out, "Stephanie got the death penalty. There is a death penalty in every state, but it's in the hands of the criminals."

By April 1994, the Kansas State Legislature had passed four of the Schmidt Task Force's five proposed laws under the collective heading of the Stephanie Schmidt Sexual Predator Act. The only item that did not pass was a requirement for employer notification of an applicant's prior sexual offenses. Among the critical points in the legislation was a provision that after serving their prison term, offenders who have been psychologically determined to be sexual predators may be civilly committed to a mental institution while they are still deemed to be dangerous. Sex offenders released on parole must register. First-time offenders have to register for ten years, second-time offenders for life. This registration is public information, which the media may publish. Lying about previous sex offenses on a job application became a felony rather than a misdemeanor. And the standards of incarceration time were lengthened for most predatory sexual offenses.

At the same time that the Schmidts and their colleagues were working so hard to pass this legislation, the Schmidts also had to face an agency of the same state government over the specifics of their own case. It was hideous enough that Don Gideon could try to shift the blame onto Stephanie for her death. But when the Schmidts essentially found the Kansas Department of Corrections trying to pull the same stunt, they were outraged. In December of 1994, frustrated by the answers they were getting and the fact that they felt the same thing could happen to another young woman, they filed a civil suit against the Kansas Department of Corrections and Gideon's parole officer, Robert Schirk. Their friend and neighbor Jim Adler, an attorney with offices in Kansas City, agreed to represent them. Jim had known Stephanie for many years. She and Jeni used to baby-sit the Adler children.

The suit got to the heart of the matter: Are dangerous people routinely being let out of prison before serving their full sentences, and if so, who is then responsible for them and for keeping the public safe?

Court documents reflect Schirk's knowledge of his department's policy that if a parole officer determined a specific group of people, such as co-employees, to be at risk, he had to notify that group. Schirk indicated that the waitresses at Hamilton's were at risk but he failed to notify them. Why? Because he thought notification might cause Gideon to lose his job.

Even after Gideon had been working at Hamilton's for several months and had a good track record there, when Schirk admitted he no longer feared for his client's job, he still failed to notify the establishment.

In defending themselves against the suit, the Department of Corrections stated that American correctional policy over the past fifty years has turned away from the concept of vengeance and toward rehabilitation, and that knowledge of a criminal record is a serious handicap against the rehabilitation of an ex-offender. But is it not also a serious handicap against the safety of innocent people with whom he comes in contact?

Interestingly, Adler notes Kansas's position in this case seems to be different than the position it took in the highly publicized sexual registration case (which went to the Kansas Supreme Court) and the sexual predator case (which went to the United States Supreme Court). In those cases the state argued (and the courts agreed) that the public has a right to know and needs to know when convicted sex offenders are in the area and that sex offenders often are not reformed in prison.

In this suit the state seems to blame the Schmidts for Stephanie's death. The state's theory seems to be that since they knew that Gideon had been in jail for beating someone up, they should have taken precautions and perhaps not have allowed Stephanie to work at Hamilton's. But how does the Schmidts' limited knowledge compare with what the state knew? Aren't the correctional departments supposed to be the experts on criminal behavior?

It's worth noting here that a restaurant that employs attractive young college coeds could, and should, be considered a collecting point for Gideon's victims of preference. Whether or not Mr. Hamilton would have hired him had he been truthful on his employment application or if Robert Schirk had alerted Hamilton is a matter of speculation. But it is certainly fair to say that once Gideon was on the job and Hamilton's valued him as a regular, full-time employee, it would have at least increased the safety odds had Tom Hamilton been informed as to Gideon's status and could therefore both be on the lookout for disturbing behavior and/or inform workers one-on-one.

Of course, the old argument can be—and was—brought up that future violence is difficult to predict. But consider the following exchange during the deposition of April 27, 1995:

ADLER: In June of '93, would you have wanted your twenty-year-old daughter working with Mr. Gideon in a restaurant, not knowing he was a convicted rapist?

SCHIRK: No.

ADLER: You allowed Stephanie Schmidt to be in that situation, didn't you, sir?

SCHIRK: Yes.

ADLER: And why is it you wouldn't have wanted your twenty-year-old daughter to be working in a restaurant with him in June of '93?

LISA MENDOZA (Schirk's and Corrections Department's attorney): Object. Calls for the witness to speculate. Assumes facts not in evidence.

SCHIRK: Preferably I wouldn't want my twenty-year-old daughter close to anyone like that anywhere.

The parole officer did not notify Hamilton's as to Gideon's background. Court documents indicate that bells and whistles were going off that Gideon was a walking time bomb. They also show that Gideon's mother reported that his family was afraid of him and did not want him living with them any longer and that Gideon was having other problems—fighting at a bar, throwing a woman's purse down some stairs, slapping one woman, and insisting that another have oral sex with him.

Would Stephanie, as naive and good-hearted as she was, have continued working at Hamilton's had she known one of her coworkers was a convicted sexual predator? I don't know the answer to that, and I don't think her parents do, either.

But would she have gotten into the truck that night with him? Not a chance in hell.

The Schmidts' civil case is still pending. So far, the defendants have filed motions for summary judgment, which were overruled, except for the Schmidts' claim that the Department of Corrections' behavior was reckless to the point of shocking the conscience, thereby rising to the level of a substantive due-process violation. That portion of the case was dismissed. All sides appealed, and realizing that whatever they did would be appealed again, the Kansas Court of Appeals forwarded the case directly to the Kansas Supreme Court, where it currently awaits a ruling. Stanton Samenow has appeared as an expert witness for the Schmidts. Hamilton's has since closed.

These cases are tough to win because the courts have held that even if the parole officer's conduct is totally inept and irresponsible, the victim of a crime at the hands of a released offender has no claim unless the parole officer failed to follow his department's policy and unless there is a specific group, such as co-employees, that easily could have been notified. The Schmidts feel that both circumstances exist in this case.

To illustrate the reason there is a claim when a member of a specific group is injured as compared to someone in the population at large, consider the following analogy Adler used in one of his briefs. If a young boy has chicken pox, it would be impossible to notify everyone in the general public who may have come in contact with him at the grocery store, shopping mall, or elsewhere. However, the parents should notify his day care center or school of the risk to the children there as these are specific groups that are at risk and can be readily notified.

Through this case the Schmidts hope to once again make new law that will help prevent similar tragedies. They also hope to make state correctional departments responsible for following policies that they have implemented. In this case the Kansas correctional department had apparently determined that when the rights of the offender are balanced with the public safety, it is appropriate to notify employers when co-employees are at risk. Nonetheless, the parole officer did not notify because he thought it might cost Gideon his job. Despite the public outcry for notification and the courts stating that notification is appropriate, correctional departments seem to cling to the notion that employment is more important—as if sex crimes are only committed by the unemployed. We know this to be nonsense! If a rapist is employed, he can easily develop the trust of an array of unsuspecting prey with whom he works.

Why do parole officers seemingly place the offender's employment above public notification? Perhaps it is simply because they cling to the belief that their job is to "rehabilitate" the offender and not to protect the public. Whatever the reason, if this does not change, these tragedies will happen again and again.

There have been many ways that Stephanie's absence has been felt by the Schmidt family. Two of the most prominent were the laughter and the music. "We were just used to having a lot of laughter," Gene says. "And suddenly, it's gone."

Jeni adds, "I felt guilty. I didn't feel like I should be having any fun. I couldn't enjoy myself if I tried. I also found that music kind of left our lives. It had been a big part of our lives for a long time."

In spite of these recollections, Stephanie's friends remember how much Gene and Peggy comforted them during those long weeks of waiting. Heather Haas says, "They were just there for everybody."

Eric Rittenhouse adds, "Throughout the whole ordeal, they wanted us all around. We were welcome. And not only that, they made us feel so much at home. It always reminded me of Stephanie."

It was a year before the Schmidts found themselves laughing again or even able to listen to the music that they had shared with Stephanie. But finally, they decided, if they were to keep her alive in their hearts and souls, they had to be true to her. The quote under Stephanie's photo in her senior-class high school yearbook was "A day without laughter is a wasted day." For her sake, they resolved not to waste any more days.

But there was more to being true to Stephanie than continuing to delight in the things she delighted in.

Of all the provisions of the Stephanie Schmidt Sexual Predator Act, the most controversial was the one providing for civil commitment of some predators after the completion of their criminal sentences. This is a procedure that many states have looked into, and most were waiting to act until they saw how the Kansas law would hold up in the courts.

The Kansas law was first invoked to civilly commit Leroy Hendricks, an inmate soon scheduled to be released who had a long history of sexually molesting children. The law had established extremely strict guidelines for this commitment of "any person who has been convicted of or charged with a sexually violent offense and who suffers from a mental abnormality or personality disorder which makes that person likely to engage in the predatory acts of sexual violence." In addition, each case had to be decided on an individual basis by a judge, it had to be routinely reviewed each year, and the person under commitment could demand a special review at virtually any time. Despite these provisions, the Kansas Supreme Court struck down the act, declaring that it did not meet substantive due-process requirements. The Schmidts got behind a move to have the law reinstated.

Carla Stovall, a young and dynamic former Crawford County prosecutor and herself a graduate of Pittsburg State, is attorney general for the State of Kansas. One of her best friends had also been a homicide victim, which gave her an instant rapport with the Schmidts, whom she met through state representative Gary Haulmark. In fact, while she was running for office, she frequently stayed at the Schmidts' home and slept in Stephanie's room, which now functions as the guest room but which remains just as Steph left it, down to troll dolls and McDonald's Happy Meal toys she used to collect.

"My first thought," says Stovall, "was, 'Gee, I don't know if that's very healthy for them, to have left the room just the way it was.' But after staying there in that room, I understood that that's the only way to have left it, because Stephanie is still such a large part of their lives. She is very much a part of this family and a part, certainly, of our justice system now."

Stovall's office filed an appeal to the United States Supreme Court, which agreed to hear the case. Accompanied by Gene and Peggy, Jim Blaufuss, and others, Stovall went to Washington and argued the case before the nation's highest legal tribunal on December 10, 1996.

"For an attorney to have a chance to argue before the U.S. Supreme Court, you do your job as best you can. So I can't say that I prepared more for this because I cared, but I can certainly tell you the emotional commitment was greater than if it had been a tax case, say, that I was arguing, because Gene and Peggy and Jeni have become such good friends. And to understand them and what their mission was about— their belief, their courage, their commitment—it became something very special. And for them to have been back there with me the day of the argument is the only way that it was right. If they hadn't been back there, there would have been a huge chunk missing, because it was their work that we were arguing for. It was Stephanie's law that we were there asking for."

Then they all held their collective breath.

The high court handed down its ruling on June 23, 1997. By a five-to-four vote, the law was upheld, meaning it could be reinstated in Kansas and that other states would now consider statutes of their own to protect potential victims of sexual predators. Carla Stovall offered her office's help in drafting such legislation. In a concurring opinion finding that the Kansas law, with its attendant protections, was within the pattern and tradition of civil confinement, Justice Anthony Kennedy speculated that even the dissent "would validate the Kansas statute as to persons who committed the crime after its enactment, and it might even validate the statute as to Hendricks, assuming a reasonable level of treatment."

As Stovall pointed out, "During the ten years Hendricks was in a Kansas prison, he refused sex offender treatment. And he said that the only way to guarantee he wasn't going to molest again was to die. He had a forty-year history of molesting children—little kids, teenagers, boys, girls, family members, strangers. Sometimes the abuse was one time only; other times it lasted for years. Every child in this country was a potential victim of Leroy Hendricks."

Stanton Samenow says, "I think that it is humane what they're doing in Kansas. It does protect the community and it puts [predators] in a psychiatric facility. What is the alternative—to let these people out to molest and possibly kill again when we know we do not have the tools to effect lasting and permanent change? It's taken too long to come to this. Changing sexual orientation? I don't know that anybody knows how to do that. So I think that this was needed and I think if you know the minds of these people, you're not going to argue with this law and this practice."

The only thing I would add to this is to ask what message do we send children when we release their tormentors back into the community? By releasing someone like this, we only serve to reinforce his power and his victims' powerlessness.

When a reporter asked Jeni's reaction to the Supreme Court victory, she said simply, "Four years too late." But it was a stunning victory nonetheless.

And on a beautiful summer afternoon about two weeks after the verdict, around the time of Stephanie's birthday, the Schmidts held a "Supreme Celebration" for hundreds of guests. Their house and backyard were bedecked in red, white, and blue decoration for the occasion. It was the largest gathering there since Stephanie's funeral.

Carla Stovall spoke and helped Gene, Peggy, and Jeni cut a cake that had been elaborately decorated by one of Stephanie's friends and former coworkers at the Hy-Vee. The attorney general then presented them with a gift she said she had come across in a craft store in her hometown of Marion, Kansas. It was a homespun angel doll, to add to the sizable collection of angels the Schmidts already had. It was made of muslin, and dressed in muslin, as well, with cotton lace on the bottom, wooden wings, and curly blond hair like Stephanie's.

The angel is holding a heart, and on the heart is written, "Stephanie Smiled—June 23, 1997"—the date the Supreme Court decision was handed down.

Despite the differences in age, location, and family status, there are poignant analogies between the Stephanie Schmidt and Destiny Souza murders. Both Katie Souza and Stephanie Schmidt were betrayed by their own goodness and optimistic faith in people. Is there a way to preserve that goodness without sacrificing any more Destinys or Stephanies? What is the lesson here?

I think there is a lesson in the Stephanie Schmidt story for virtually everyone.

The lesson for young women, unfortunately, is that you can't be too trusting of human nature, that you have to do your best to understand the people around you and not place yourself in situations where your safety is compromised. This is a lot easier to accomplish if you're given the information you are entitled to have.

For parents, it is important to make your children—both girls and boys—aware and responsible.

For judges, the lesson is to become realistic, as Judge Brewster was, about what these offenders are really like and to use the sentence not only as a means to impose punishment, but as a means to protect the public as well.

For legislators, the lesson is to make sure that someone doesn't get out after serving only half his sentence merely because he has served "good time." There has to be a more effective and reliable gauge for determining when, if ever, a prisoner should be paroled.

For corrections officials, the lesson is simply to understand dangerousness and place the critical emphasis on not putting those under your control in a position in which they can hurt other people, once they've shown that propensity.

For friends of potential victims—and unfortunately this category includes virtually all women and children and even some men—the lesson is to be aware, look out, and always be willing to step in. As Eric Rittenhouse stated so clearly, knowledge is power, and lack of information is a severe handicap.

And for us, the public at large, we simply have to understand, understand so that we can demand that action be taken in this ongoing war. We have to stop excusing the inexcusable and insist that people be held accountable for their actions. Why is there such a tendency, I continue to wonder, to allow raw cruelty to masquerade as mental illness? It is an insult to the mentally ill to suggest that this is the main reason people commit violent crimes. Sexual predators do have an illness, but it is called a lack of conscience, not insanity.

And we have to examine closely our notions of rehabilitation. As Jeni said on the *Maury Povich* show, "Our government feels that people can be rehabilitated, and they continue to put the experiments out on the public. And I don't want to be an experiment anymore."

It would be nice to think that men like Donald Gideon could be "rehabilitated," that they would understand, as his sister Shannon suggested, that they'd been given a second chance and so couldn't blow it. But Shannon Gideon didn't get it. Neither, for that matter, did Gene Schmidt, when he took comfort from the fact that Don had not killed his first rape victim.

By my analysis, Donald Gideon *did* learn from the error of his ways, but not in the manner we would have hoped and the naive among us would have expected. He learned that if you abduct, rape, sodomize, and physically abuse a woman and then let her go, she's going to turn you in to the police and you're going to be punished. So if you want to avoid that you can either (a) not do it again or (b) eliminate the witness against you. Clearly, whatever made Don Gideon want to manipulate, dominate, and control through sexual attack, to feel, in his own words, "the pure power," had not been "rehabilitated" out of him by prison or therapy or personal resolve to be good.

In fact, when a friend and dorm mate of Gideon's first victim learned that Stephanie was missing and that Don was being sought, she told a reporter, "I knew that girl wasn't going to be found alive. This time," she explained, Gideon "wasn't going to leave [any] witnesses."

We know what Dr. Samenow thinks about rehabilitation. There is an equally interesting perspective from Fairfax County, Virginia, chief of police M. Douglas Scott, a man responsible not only for protecting the public's safety, but also for allocating the increasingly limited budgets which that public grants him.

"Over the course of my law enforcement career, I have seen very, very few examples where somebody could point out an offender to me and say, 'That person's clearly been rehabilitated; that even though they committed a serious felony, they're back out there leading a productive life today.'

"The public in general sees the good in all people and thinks that most people are capable of being good. The public even wants to believe that evil people can be rehabilitated or brought back into society with some level of assistance. But I think our society would go broke trying to rehabilitate the number of evil individuals that are out there on our streets today."

Let me put it another way. If you're one of those corrections or parole or good-hearted-in-general types who states that it is impossible to completely predict future violent behavior but wants to give these guys a second chance, to parole them into the community once they've served the requisite amount of "good time," I say this:

What is your acceptable failure rate?

Let's take a sample of one hundred offenders and let's let Don Gideon define that sample: men in their early thirties who have raped at knifepoint, threatening to kill their victim if she resisted, who then let her go, were identified, tried, convicted, and sent to prison. We'll forget about bad family backgrounds and other trouble with the law for the sake of this example.

Okay, now, if we parole each of these hundred men after having served half his sentence, what is your acceptable failure rate for this experiment in rehabilitation? In other words, how many of them can rape and murder innocent young women like Stephanie Schmidt before we call the experiment a failure?

Is two an acceptable failure rate? How about three? Five? More, maybe? Stated in these terms, I have yet to encounter anyone who will agree that the loss of even one life—one Stephanie Schmidt and all the joy and goodness that Don Gideon took out of the world when he killed her—is acceptable.

As David Beatty of the National Victim Center says, "We can all quote by heart since we were children that 'I'd rather see a hundred guilty men go free than one innocent man convicted.' And of course we all agree with that. But what about the at least hundred victims of these men? What about their innocence? Is anyone concerned about them? I was on a National Public Radio debate with someone who works with violent sexual offenders and he was talking about his fabulous success in treating them. He said sometimes the recidivism rates are as low as twenty percent! I said, 'Let me ask you a question. Do you have children?' He said, 'Yes, I do.'

"I said, 'Would you be willing to bet your child's life that you are right with any of the clients that you work with, and if you're wrong, your child is going to die or be sexually assaulted? Are you willing to take that risk?'

"He said, 'Well, that's not a fair question because I couldn't function objectively under those circumstances.' And I said, 'Every time you let someone out, you're betting somebody else's child. And that ought to be the standard we think about.'"

350

These predators aren't going to stop on their own. As Stanton Samenow, Park Dietz, and many others can tell you, they don't choose to, they don't care to, they have no normal conscience or feeling.

I just want to mention one item in our discussion of rehabilitation and its attendant question of remorse, and that is a letter Gideon wrote from prison to Jim Adler in response to his request that Gideon agree to a deposition in the civil suit. He refused, saying the Schmidt family was of no concern to him and suggested that they "let it go." Later, he said he felt in no way obligated to them.

The only thing that need be added about this letter is that it is punctuated with little hand-drawn smiley faces after a number of the exclamation points.

If we're going to let some of these guys back into society, as Don Gideon was let back after his first violent attack on a woman, don't we at least have a right to know about it?

Is it additional punishment to inform a community of a sexual offender now living in their midst? Is it an intrusion on his civil rights, his ability to make a fresh start after he's "paid his debt to society"? Well, first of all, anyone who willfully kills another human being can never fully pay his debt to society, and if he is ever let out on the street again, he is already way ahead of the game. But again we can turn to David Beatty for some perspective:

"We balance constitutional rights every day. The truth of the matter is, convicted offenders do not have the same rights as every other citizen. They can't vote; they have all kinds of limitations on their rights. And guess what? They chose. Unlike all the civil liberties that were taken away from their victims, the most heinous invasion of their privacy is to let other people know about them. And as for anyone who argues against things like public notification, what they're really arguing against is the principle of keeping criminal justice records. I've actually heard so-called civil liberties attorneys say, 'We ought to forgive and forget.'

"I nailed one of these guys in a debate. I said, 'Your position is that public records should be public and that access to government information is one of the most important protections against the evils of society.' Anyone can go down and get the criminal justice records. What this guy was complaining about was that by informing communities about sexual predators living there that we're doing too good a job of effectuating the principles that underlie the open-records laws."

351

In other words, this is information that the public already legally has a right to; just don't tell them about it.

"I tell people in the speeches I give all the time that Gene and Peggy Schmidt are heroes," says Carla Stovall. "They were absolutely a catalyst and the impetus for this law. A bill like this was introduced in the Kansas legislature prior to Stephanie's death. It didn't go anyplace, didn't even get out of committee. It was Gene's and Peggy's advocacy and the message of Stephanie—that is the reason this law was passed. They made a difference. Two people who were not rich or powerful or famous, who weren't elected officials, they were ordinary people who went to the legislature with a message. And the legislature responded. Our law was patterned after the State of Washington's. And I hope that the court's decision in upholding this will let other states take the courageous step of enacting this law now. It doesn't need courage now like it did for Kansas, but to enact this law now before any other tragedy happens—that demands a law and a response like this."

And it is only one of the many principles that have become the central focus of Gene and Peggy Schmidt's life. They should never have been placed into the situation of having to become heroes or fighters, but they have, without becoming bitter, without becoming strident, by still being simply the decent people they always were.

Stephanie is still very much part of a great many lives, and what they all say they miss is the unique sound of her laughter. Shannon Marsh, one of her best friends, says that Stephanie left a legacy of "years and years of great memories and a way to laugh at yourself and to laugh at some of your situations when things get too tough. I think of her every day."

Kelli Farha reminisces, "She would laugh so hard that her curly hair would stand up on its ends."

Darron Farha and the former Kelli Gariglietti are married to each other because of Stephanie, who knew Darron in high school, and like her, he decided to go to Pittsburg State. Kelli was from Pittsburg, and that was where Stephanie introduced them.

Their union is one of Stephanie's legacies, and they lit a candle for her at their wedding. "Even though she died, she's still working her goodness," Kelli comments.

Jeni is determined to make sure those people important to her know the kind of person Stephanie was. "If I ever have children," she says, "I think from the very beginning I would introduce them to who she is: pictures, sharing experiences, try and make her a part of their lives as if she were here. She's part of my life, and I think whether it's a child or a husband or whomever who comes in contact with me, they're going to know Stephanie through me; I'm not going to let that go. I want to live what she could not.

"It's kind of ironic that when she moved away to college, I felt that we became even closer, and now that she is far removed, I feel as if we are closer still. At the same time, I miss her physical presence and advice. And even though I grow older and she doesn't, she was my older sister and I will always feel an older-sisterly power about it. Even when she was alive, we knew each other in a spiritual sense, so I don't see why that would change. She'll definitely grow with me."

Gene and Peggy admit that while the love is still apparent, despite their best intentions there is less laughter. They still go through difficult times; some weeks are harder than others. It distresses them when other people just don't understand. They were saddened recently when a longtime friend couldn't empathize enough to comprehend why they couldn't handle going to his daughter's wedding. Ever since Stephanie died and a world of future possibilities was stolen from them, they have found weddings—particularly those of bright and beautiful and vivacious young women—exceedingly difficult.

They devote themselves nearly full-time to the foundation and Speak Out for Stephanie. "Why speak out?" they ask rhetorically. Because silence can kill.

The work of the Stephanie Schmidt Foundation goes on, and more and more campus chapters of Speak Out for Stephanie are being established. Peggy and Gene maintain an active speaking schedule on the critical issues of parole, notification, and the nature of sexual predators and have become prominent advocates in the national victims' rights movement. They publish a newsletter called *Speak Out,* and continue lobbying for a victims' rights amendment to the Constitution.

Employing Gene's experience with school photography and marketing, the Schmidt Foundation started out by developing a photo ID program for grades kindergarten through twelve. When it became clear that other organizations could serve this function, they shifted their focus to other programs. This is typical of the way they work. They look for voids and try to fill them.

If there is one word that summarizes all of the foundation's work, it would be *awareness*. Through programs they have developed for middle schools and the campus chapters of Speak Out for Stephanie, the Schmidts teach, preach, and, if necessary, screech the need for awareness. They teach college students to be able to extend their own reach, working with elementary and middle-school students. We'll concentrate on some of their suggestions in the next chapter.

On the college level, a particular focus lately has been awareness of Rohypnol, the so-called "date rape" drug. But overall, what they are working toward on college campuses is establishing both a sense of responsibility and a sense of community in which everyone looks out for everyone else. The first S.O.S. chapter was established at Pittsburg State, and Gene and Peggy are actively working to establish chapters throughout the United States.

As we were completing this chapter, the Schmidts' dog, Sandi, died at age fifteen. She was one of the last pure, innocent reminders of the wonderful way things used to be for them.

The fight continues. On the very day of the Schmidts' Supreme Celebration, an article appeared on the front page of the *Indianapolis Star* of a man who had a nine-year criminal record, including stabbing, escape history, and drug trafficking in prison. While he was awaiting trial on another charge, the judge released him from the county jail on his own recognizance. Nine days later, he molested and murdered a thirteen-year-old girl, stabbing her seventy-six times with the same knife he had used in an earlier assault. The judge stated he had no idea about this man's violent past. "This guy slipped through," he lamented.

How much more of this are we going to accept and tolerate? How many more Stephanie Schmidts have to die?

Tax-deductible contributions to the Stephanie Schmidt Foundation may be sent to P.O. Box 7829, Overland Park, Kansas 66207. To get more information, or to start a Speak Out for Stephanie chapter, the phone number for the Fax and Message Center is (913) 345-0362.

CHAPTER THIRTEEN

KNOWLEDGE IS POWER

Hans Hageman is one of those guys who seem to have everything going for them. Despite the sound of his name, he is dark with compelling good looks, a shaved head, and compact, muscular build, all this the legacy of his Midwestern white father and Puerto Rican mother, both of whom were missionaries. He is articulate, funny, impassioned. He went to tony Collegiate Prep, then Princeton University and Columbia Law School. Along the way he squeezed in an ROTC commission and married an equally intelligent, attractive, and charming wife. He joined a prestigious New York firm and specialized in corporate law, then went to Washington and worked on Capitol Hill for a while as counsel to a Senate subcommittee, where he made all the right connections. He came back to New York and became a narcotics prosecutor. With the combination of his intellect, experience, powerful charm, and social grace, he was courted by big Wall Street and Washington law firms, where he would become a major partner and power broker with a seven-figure annual salary.

But none of this is why we're writing about Hans Hageman. We're writing about him because of his particular obsession—an obsession to do good and make a difference. Because, you see, Hans walked away from the fancy firm, the fancy office, and the fancy income, and with his Harvard-educated brother, Ivan, established a private school on 103rd Street between First and Second Avenues, which he called the East Harlem School at Exodus House. Exodus House, the building in which the school was established, had been a residential drug treatment center founded by the Reverend Mr. and Mrs. Hageman. It was where Hans, Ivan, and their sister grew up. Hans is executive director and Ivan is principal. The assistant principal is Inge Hanson.

Ninety percent of the students come from families on public assistance, which means the Hagemans are always scrounging for funds. Hans had always been good with kids, and he first considered starting an elementary school. After all, logic dictates that the earlier you get the children, the more impact you're going to make. But he felt there were already programs and funding available for the early ages. The real challenge was the ones nobody wanted—middle-school and junior-high age: the kids who are the most difficult in the best of situations, and in this situation, kids to whom the damage has already been done and who already bear the scars of the neighborhood and environment. He knew that by undertaking this, he and Ivan would have to become not only educators but policemen, therapists, and warriors against the indigenous crack dealers who, at enormous physical risk, Hans confronted and turned away from the front of his school. Because of that, he became licensed to carry a firearm.

"The first two years were difficult," he admits, "but now I think even the bad guys in the neighborhood respect us."

East Harlem is a strict school with high standards. Hans believes that only in an atmosphere of discipline and structure and responsibility can personal freedom flourish. "We try to show the kids enough of what's out there and enough of the possibilities of life," he says.

The motto of the school is Competence With Character, and Hans says, "If these kids can physically and emotionally survive their adolescence, just in the Darwinian sense of survival of the fittest, they can be world-beaters." As I've said throughout this book, crime affects us all on so many different levels. "We can turn things around," Hans insists. "The only thing standing between some of these kids and success is a safe place. We want to provide the one caring, nurturing space in their lives."

He and Ivan know they're not going to succeed with all of them. One young man recently didn't graduate because he failed to complete his required ten-page paper. "It was his conscious decision not to finish, and he was given a lot of opportunity. Like a lot of other schools, we could have graduated him and said, 'Go on to high school, you're not our problem anymore.' But he did not graduate from this school. This is someone we have known since he was an infant, and it was a tough decision. We talked to him ad nauseam. There is a certain amount of triage which had to take place here. We don't give up on anyone as long as they don't give up on themselves. And even when they do, we're still available and they know that. But one of the hardest things for me is that we're going to lose some along the way. This kid is going to have to hit bottom, and the problem is that in a neighborhood like this one, when you hit bottom, you don't always return. He's smart enough to get himself into big trouble." As Hans made a choice against a lucrative career and a luxurious lifestyle, everybody makes a choice of some kind.

There is no question that the Hagemans have sacrificed for their obsession. Ivan is divorced and Hans is candid about the stress it has put on his own marriage. Often, he and his wife have had the additional strain of one or more young people living with them. But the most encouraging thing of all is that Hans believes "there are a lot of others out there like us; there certainly are."

One more example from the same neighborhood:

In 1992, our agent, Jay Acton, who is also a New York City attorney, minor league baseball team owner, and major baseball fan, founded Harlem RBI. It stands for Reviving Baseball in Inner Cities and was patterned after the first RBI program, begun in Los Angeles in 1989 by John Young, a professional baseball scout, in response to the problem of gang violence. Like Speak Out for Stephanie, RBI has grown, and there are now programs in more than fifty cities across America. Inge Hanson, aside from now being assistant principal of East Harlem School, is, like Jay, a lawyer and literary agent. She was the original Harlem RBI executive director. Jay and his associates located an abandoned lot on One Hundredth Street, off First Avenue in East Harlem, and with the help of the community turned it into a ball field.

The lure of the program is to provide organized, high-quality baseball experience for inner-city boys and girls between seven and eighteen years of age, divided into teams and leagues. But the real aim is to help young urban teens develop greater self-esteem while learning the values of teamwork and sportsmanship, and to motivate and help participating athletes study more effectively while offering them a strong incentive to stay in school. This last consideration is important. If you want to play, you have to maintain acceptable averages in your class work. To help achieve that, RBI has organized both a tutoring program and a mentoring program. They also publish a newsletter, written by the participants, with the advice and input of professional editors and reporters who have volunteered their time. And a speaker series exposes the young people to the outside world beyond their own neighborhoods—both good and bad—with topics that range from professional baseball and women in sports, to gun violence, drugs, AIDS, teen sexuality and responsibility, and great books. The entire operation is now under the auspices of the New York City Parks Council, and the current executive director of Harlem RBI is Richard Berlin, who holds a master's degree from the London School of Economics, but who developed the obsession to give something back when he started volunteering at RBI in 1993.

Having read this book, you know that two of the greatest weapons in the war on crime and predatory violence are increased individual feelings of self-esteem and an increased individual and collective sense of responsibility. With them, fewer young men will commit violent crime, and more young men will feel the obligation to step in and do something about the violence they see around them. Self-esteem will also make them less vulnerable targets for other predators. Programs such as Harlem RBI are going a long way in this direction. They're very much part of the effort to fight back.

We were going to call this final chapter "Fighting Back," except that we've already used that title in our last book, *Journey into Darkness*. So instead we are highlighting the basic theme of this book, which, in essence, means the same thing. As Hans Hageman has proved, knowledge is power, and there are many ways to fight back.

You can fight back the way Gene and Peggy Schmidt and Jack and Trudy Collins fight back. Or the way Linda Fairstein fights back. Or the way Carroll Ellis and Sandy Witt do. And then there are the more direct ways, the concepts and techniques that we each have to adopt to increase our chances of remaining safe.

Virtually all of the victims and survivors I encounter tell me how quickly they were forced to acquire their education in crime, the criminal justice system, and society's attitudes toward predators and their victims. What we need to do is arm ourselves with knowledge *before the fact,* and through that knowledge, try to even the odds. The following comments and suggestions are by no means intended to be complete or exhaustive. An entire book could easily be written on each topic. What I am trying to provide here are general attitudes, approaches, and concepts about sexual predators and obsessional violent crime.

With regard to attitudes toward rape, the first one we've got to get across is that it is *never* acceptable. This may seem pretty basic and elementary until we remember the survey of teenaged boys and girls who thought that forcing a woman to have sex was okay under certain circumstances—mainly having to do with the length of time the parties had known each other and how much money the boy had put out.

As Gene Schmidt says, "On all our visits to college campuses, we're finding that girls have to be taught that it's okay to say no, and that boys have to learn that no means just what it says. It doesn't need any interpretation."

Alarmingly, the 1995 National Survey of Family Growth, conducted by the U.S. Department of Health and Human Services, reported that 7 percent of the teenage girls surveyed who'd had sex indicated that their first sexual encounter was not one they participated in voluntarily, and almost another quarter said that their first sexual encounter was "voluntary but not wanted."

The other attitude we have to establish firmly is compassion for rape victims . . . even date rape victims . . . even prostitute victims. We've got to make sure they know that we understand that it was not their fault and that we provide an environment in which victims feel comfortable reporting and prosecuting the crime.

And *environment* is a key word in prevention, as well: awareness of your immediate environment can do more than any other single element in cutting down on sexual assaults. Remember Linda Fairstein's case of the rapist who was able to follow a woman into her own apartment building, even though his composite was posted in the lobby?

"Do you know the number of cases I have where the pizza deliveryman gets in, delivers to 25D, and then tries the other doors on the way out?" she asks. "I would like to think that I am not what I would call paranoid, but that I have a very healthy awareness of what goes on around me."

And, as Fairstein points out, "It isn't just a big-city phenomenon. There's not a week that goes by that I don't get calls from remote parts of the country about how to handle a case or situation that's going on there, or from victims disgruntled because it isn't being handled."

Before Stephanie Schmidt was killed, there hadn't been a murder of a young woman in Pittsburg, Kansas, in thirty years. Since then, there have been two more.

Wherever you live, it's important to keep windows and doors locked and entryways well lit. In and around the car, particularly in parking lots, always try to maintain a buffer zone around yourself and your car so that, if need be, you can drive quickly to a safe and well-lit area.

Now, you may not always be able to live your life so cautiously, and it may not even be possible for you to do so. But the one thing I do urge is that you evaluate and understand the circumstances in which you're operating. It comes down to a simple but universally applicable piece of advice:

If you're putting yourself at a potentially higher degree of risk, you need to put yourself on a higher level of awareness and precaution.

The Jennifer Levin and Stephanie Schmidt cases underscore the warning that you must never assume you know a person better than you do. Here were two bright and outgoing young women whose sole fault was trust—a quality we find admirable. Neither one of them did anything wrong, but because of their trust, both found themselves in situations that proved deadly.

Look after your friends and be aware of what they're doing. Stephanie Schmidt was the ideal victim from Don Gideon's perspective. Not only was she unaware of his predatory past, she was going home for the summer, so that none of her girlfriends would miss her in the next few days.

And don't assume that sexual predators are going to be obvious, any more than Robert Chambers or Alex Kelly or Don Gideon. A killer or rapist can look like anyone. Fairstein has had cases in which the defendants were doctors, lawyers, dentists, even ministers and rabbis, who assaulted their victims in "professional" surroundings. The best advice is what your mother told you ever since you can remember: Don't pick up hitchhikers, don't hitchhike yourself, and don't accept rides from people you don't know well. Don't accept drinks from people you don't know well. Obviously, this doesn't apply to professional waiters or bartenders, but the drug Rohypnol, for example, is easy to slip into a drink, takes effect quickly—sometimes within minutes—is hard to trace, and leaves victims unaware of their environment, with no memory later of what happened to them.

Det. Bob Murphy sums up all of this simply and well: "You try to take away the opportunity."

As we've noted, there are different kinds of rapists, and each one will react differently. So if you have enough presence of mind to be able to evaluate that individual during the crisis, by all means follow your instincts and react accordingly. The only score we keep is surviving. But since tailoring your reaction to a complex set of behavioral characteristics is difficult, there are a number of basic responses that have the odds in their favor.

If you are approached or attacked, do not get into a car with an offender. Scream, fight back, try to attract attention and/or get away. If he can remove you from a public place without any witnesses, your chances of getting out of this situation alive or unharmed are greatly diminished. Whenever you see the chance, take it.

In a stranger-rape situation, if he allows you to see his face, you get his name, or you can somehow otherwise identify your attacker and he knows it, it's all the more important to get away from him, even if he has a knife and you are risking injury. Because unless he's quite inexperienced, he's likely to kill you to leave no witnesses. As difficult as it may be to do, don't let your concentration falter. Channel your energies into survival.

If he knows you can identify him and you can't get away, then you've got to try to establish some kind of human connection. I always tell police officers, for instance, that if they find themselves in hostage situations, not to let the gunman get them facedown on the ground. In that posture, it's too easy for him to depersonalize you and then too easy to put a bullet through the back of your head—much easier than pulling the trigger when you're staring him in the eyes. By the same token, a rape is a hostage situation of sorts, and you could win survival points by not letting him depersonalize you, either. Even a predator as extreme as Gary Heidnik treated differently the one prisoner with whom he felt he had a human bond, and she was the one he allowed to get away and ultimately save herself and the remaining survivors.

I think our societal attitudes about stalking are beginning to change, but it's still important to understand that these men—and women— are not love-struck Casanovas. They are potential killers who, like all potential killers, are best dealt with sooner rather than later.

If you feel you are the object of an obsession, close the emotional door *as soon as* you begin to feel uncomfortable. Don't try to protect his or her feelings or "let him down easy." They're not worried about your feelings. And don't assume they'll "get over it."

Instead of trying to "negotiate," go into a protective mode immediately.

Cut off communication, screen phone calls, make sure your name isn't on the mailbox or assigned parking space at work, begin documenting any harassment or threats. Share information on potential stalkers with friends, neighbors, coworkers. Let them accompany you wherever and whenever possible so you don't have to confront the stalker alone. Let other people be your eyes, ears, and extended protection.

Know where the local police, fire, and rescue stations are so you can get to one quickly if someone is following you. Keep gasoline in the car and get a portable phone and keep it with you so you can call for help.

If you've secured a restraining order or any other relevant court orders or legal documents, keep a copy with you so you can show the police at any time. If the police will not help you, call the district attorney's office, the state attorney general, the victim-witness program in your area, or the National Victim Center—1-800-FYI-CALL—for help. This is a prosecutable crime.

On the related front of domestic violence, the best defense is always to recognize a man who is prone to violence or a need to control women *before* getting into a relationship. Never make excuses for his potentially violent or threatening behavior; he'll make plenty of excuses for himself. According to the Family Violence Prevention Fund, at least one out of every three murdered women is killed by her husband or boyfriend.

If he's overly jealous, insecure, possessive, and/or controlling, if he tries to isolate you from your family, friends, or co-workers, if he's hypersensitive and blames you or other people for all of his problems instead of taking responsibility, if he's cruel to children or pets, verbally abusive, hits or threatens to hit you (or kill you), uses force in settling arguments or in securing sex, if he can shift quickly and abruptly from loving to angry and violent and back again, or if he has a history of hitting or abusing any of his previous partners, the advice is simple: *GET OUT!* Whatever it takes. There are widely available support services like Fairfax County's Someplace Safe that can help you.

We should all be alert for the signs of domestic abuse in our friends and coworkers. Unexplained bruises, withdrawn or other unfamiliar behavior, or unusual absences from work are all things we should notice, and we should encourage an abused woman (or man) to seek help, while maintaining confidentiality.

The defense strategies are similar to the ones for stalking. Keep track of places you can go, such as police stations, churches, homes of friends whose location he doesn't know. Pack an emergency bag of things you and your children will need if you leave, such as ID, cash, credit cards, passports or birth certificates, medical records, and special toys. But if you think you may be in immediate danger, leave immediately, even if you don't have this kit prepared. Shelters, police and social service agencies, even rape crisis centers, are there to help you.

As Gavin de Becker urges, trust your instincts and gut reactions. You have them for a reason.

We've got to change our attitudes about crime in general, and in doing so, we've got to radically adjust some of our values. I was amazed, for example, that there seemed to be more public outrage (certainly more traffic on call-in shows) about the incident in which heavyweight boxer Mike Tyson bit opponent Evander Holyfield's ear in the ring than there was when he raped a young woman in a hotel room.

While I believe we are all responsible for the choices we make, sometimes those choices can be influenced by early intervention, as Samenow and others have pointed out. Had a Ronnie Shelton, a Joseph Thompson, an Alex Kelly, or a Robert Chambers, even a John Hinckley Jr. or a Jeffrey Dahmer—been recognized early enough, if the pattern of their early behavior had been detected, maybe something could have been done to change the way they thought. I certainly don't think this would have worked across the board, but in a certain percentage of cases, there would be a good chance. And if we can't change their thinking, we can certainly remove their opportunity to commit acts of violence.

So if you have or know of a child who is displaying early signs of aggressive or predatory behavior, seek help as early as possible, preferably before adolescence. There are some classic warning signs, such as what we call the homicidal triad: persistent late bed-wetting, starting fires, and cruelty to animals or other children. Maybe these symptoms are a passing phase in a particular case, but I've seen this presentation too frequently in the serial offenders I've interviewed and studied to ignore it. This triad is unquestionably a red flag and cause for alarm. Even if you don't see this in a child, there are many other indications, almost too numerous to list. But the important thing is that parents and teachers will recognize them instinctively in the context of an individual child's behavior and emotional development. The key is what Samenow refers to as "an expanding and intensifying pattern."

Aside from out-and-out behavior problems, we need to instill certain values and emulate sound role models. We've got to teach our kids that while sports and entertainment figures are glamorous and attractive, it's the Hans Hagemans and Linda Fairsteins and Carroll Ellises who are the real heroes and heroines, along with all the victims who find a way to help others in their grief—not using their misfortunes or tragedies as an excuse to hurt others. Katie Souza had a terrible background, much more than most people can imagine. But she didn't become a criminal or violent as a result. Rather, she dedicated her life to making things better for her children than they had been for her.

And there are certain things we have to learn to accept. We have to realistically recognize the limits of rehabilitation, and we have to create environments in which victims will feel safe.

Where I live, we have animal control ordinances that say, in essence, that your dog gets one "free" bite—after that, it's labeled dangerous, and you, as the owner, are held to the same standard of strict liability as with any other potentially dangerous situation. I've never encountered a dog yet as vicious as the sexual predators I've studied. How long are we going to continue giving them more than one free bite?

And we're not only talking about a permanent loss of a loved and vital person, though that alone can be unbearable. Keep in mind that when a person succumbs to disease or natural causes, or even an accident that does not kill her instantly, she is surrounded by family, loved ones, emotional and medical support. When a person dies as a result of violent crime, she dies alone, despairing, unloved by anyone nearby, terrified and in agonizing pain. And this is no act of God. Another human being chose to make this happen.

You may say that I'm overly emotional on this subject; you may call this hot-headed rhetoric. I plead guilty on both counts. But I've seen too much of this. I've spent too much time with wonderful people whose lives have been irretrievably shattered by one of these monsters, and each time I think about how it could be my own.

We've got to encourage victims' participation in the system and adjust that system so that it works for their benefit. Change the designation on serious crimes that are still classified as misdemeanors and make them felonies as they should be.

There is no conflict between civil liberties and victims' rights. There is no conflict between a fair trial and a balanced trial. By giving victims a stake in the criminal justice system, we need not take away any benefit currently accruing to a defendant. All we're calling for is balance. If a convicted defendant can tell the judge all the good things about himself in an attempt to avoid harsher punishment, why can't the family and friends of the victim tell all the good things about her and what has been taken out of the world? Defendants want fairness. So do I.

As David Beatty says, "Probably the most misunderstood concept about the victims movement is that it is a zero-sum game and that victims' rights can only be gained at the expense of offenders'. That is not the case. We are not challenging any of the basic core rights that are indelibly protected by the Constitution, things such as due process."

But one thing we should never do is let the perpetrators co-opt the status of victim. They made the choice that the crime be committed, not the victim.

That is one of the many reasons why I, like Gene and Peggy Schmidt, Jack and Trudy Collins, and an ever-growing groundswell across the nation support a Victims' Rights Amendment to the Constitution.

Again, David Beatty: "What I think is interesting is the way that people are beginning to see that the constitutional protections for offenders have always been sold to them as, 'These are your protections. If you're ever accused of a crime, you're going to want these protections.' Well, guess what? If you're ever the victim of a crime, you're going to want these basic protections, too. And that's what the amendment is all about. It's to protect all of society."

Stalking victims shouldn't have to change their names, abandon their lives, move out of town, or die.

Domestic violence victims shouldn't have to put up with ongoing punishment and abuse or have to resort to killing their abusers or being killed by them.

Victims shouldn't feel they cannot get information out of the criminal justice system because they have no "standing" in the process. As Kansas victims' rights coordinator Lynn Allen puts it, how would you feel going to a doctor who wouldn't give you any idea what was going on? You didn't ask to become sick, you didn't make a choice, but you are. And he says to you, "We'll do surgery and I'll see you in a couple of hours. That's all you have to know." Survey after survey tells us that even more than a favorable outcome of prosecution, victims want to be shown some compassion for their plight by the system. They don't want to be told, as Don Gideon told the Schmidts, to "get over it." They want to be shown that somebody understands and cares.

Sentences shouldn't be structured so that violent predators can go out and commit the same crime in relatively short order. If they are, as David Beatty states, then "the government comes close to being a coconspirator in the next crime that that person is going to commit. *Rights without remedies equal rhetoric.*"

We shouldn't be more interested in the privacy and reputation of convicted sexual offenders than we are in the safety of our children.

And our moral outrage at what some people do should not be eroded. Our obsession must be just as strong as the bad guys'. That's the only way we have a chance of winning this war.

INDEX

Abscam scandal, 132
Acton, Jay, 357
Adams, Agnes, 315
Adelson, Michael, 277
Adler, Jim, 341–43, 344, 351
Air Force, U.S., 168, 183, 186, 256
Allen, Lynn, 333, 365
Alley, Sedley, 166
American Law Institute Model Penal
    Code Test, 40
America's Most Wanted, 332
Anderson, Robin, 199
anger rapist, 93, 96–97, 104, 110
antipsychotic drugs, 309
anti-Semitism, 125, 140
antistalking laws, 223, 224, 227, 261–62,
    265
Army, U.S., 16, 36, 41, 42, 169, 209, 237,
    309
arson, 42
Askins, Jacqueline, 313
assassinations, political, 233
    attempts at, 233, 235–36
Atascadero State Hospital, 38, 263
Atlanta Child Murders, 44–47, 49
Attica State Prison, 42
Ault, Dick, 45
autopsies:
    photographs of, 16, 127, 176
    reports on, 16, 19, 127, 178

Baltazar, Patrick, 47
Barber, Aisha, 222
Bardo, Robert John, 254–61, 265

Barshop, Steve, 276–77, 278
Bates, Ruby, 139, 140
Bazan, Martha, 222
Beatty, David, 227, 230, 232, 243, 244,
    252–53, 263, 272, 280–81,
    283–86, 288–89, 350, 351–52,
    365, 366
Bell, Eldrin, 213
Berkowitz, David, 21, 26, 41–43
Berlin, Richard, 358
Bernardo, Paul, 271
Bhatia, Lucy, 200
Bhatia, Vinay, 200
Black, Laura, 239–53, 257, 270, 271, 273,
    280, 283, 285, 286
Black Sunday (Harris), 291
Blaufuss, Jim, 335–36, 346
Bloch, Robert, 296
bodies:
    condition of, 15, 19, 20, 23, 125–26,
        127, 173, 177, 334
    dumping of, 16, 44, 45, 48–49, 50,
        118, 170, 315, 333
    evidence of torture on, 23, 49
    mutilation and decapitation of, 38,
        39, 40, 101, 294–96, 314
    nude, 15, 19, 29, 49
body fluids, 126, 148, 154
    DNA analysis of, 56, 58, 60, 75
Boone, Carole Ann, 307
Bork, John, 336
Boston Strangler, 21
Bowman, Margaret, 307
Brady, James, 252

Branch Davidians, 36
Brannen, Melissa, 181
breaking and entering (B&E), 27, 52, 53, 55, 56, 62, 64, 67, 69–70, 71, 74, 80, 90, 94
Bremer, Arthur, 233–34, 237, 261
Brewster, David F., 336–38, 348
Brown, Cyril, 312
Brzonkala, Christy, 222
Bulow, Claus von, 132
Bundy, John Culpepper, 299
Bundy, Louise Cowell, 298–99
Bundy, Theodore Robert "Ted," 21, 81, 130, 298–308, 309, 315, 317, 318
Burgess, Allen, 93
Burgess, Ann Wolbert, 42, 93, 149–50, 151, 152
burglary, 17, 43–44, 59, 60, 76, 85, 101, 103, 105–6, 115, 124, 128, 130, 134, 160, 303
Butcher of Plainfield, 292–98
Butler, Marian, 67, 68

California Department of Motor Vehicles, 259, 261
California State Medical Facility at Vacaville, 38
California State Prison, 260
Campbell, Caryn, 302, 303
"Candlelight Vigil of Courage, Hope and Remembrance," 222
Cannon, Dyan, 254
Cannon, Joe, 66
Cannon, John, 315
cardiopulmonary resuscitation (CPR), 173, 276
Carpenter, David, 253
Carr, Sam, 43
Carter, Lester, 140
Cedars-Sinai Medical Center, 236, 255
Chambers, Robert, 118–30, 134, 136, 137, 146, 157, 160, 275–76, 360, 363
Chanute, Octave, 319
Chapman, Mark David, 234–35, 261
Charchenko, Andrew, 65
Chase, Dan, 295–96
Chase, Richard Trenton, 297, 316

child molesters, 44–47, 51–53, 54, 92, 101, 108, 109, 171, 193, 218–19, 346
Child Protective Services, 188
children, 101
    abuse and neglect of, 37, 41, 44, 55, 57, 60, 72, 77, 111–12, 161, 182–83, 184, 256–57
    custody of, 269–70
    problem, 35–36, 38–39, 59, 108, 111–12, 115, 363–64
    rape of, 51–54
    stalking of, 229–30, 256
    teaching of, 186, 364
    visitation rights and, 270
Children's Court (New Zealand), 111
Chinn, Paul, 330
Chi Omega murders, 304–5, 306–7
Citizens Against Stalking, 287
Clark, Marcia, 259, 260
Clark, Paul, 335
Clarke, Susan, 301
Cleveland Police Department, 63–83
    Scientific Investigations Unit of, 73, 75–76
    sex-crimes unit of, 70, 71, 74, 77
Cline, Dick, 217
Collins, Jack, 166–67, 199, 200, 208, 210–11, 215, 222, 339, 358, 365
Collins, Stephen, 166
Collins, Suzanne, 166, 199, 211, 215, 288
Collins, Trudy, 16–67, 199, 208, 211, 215, 288, 339, 358, 365
Conference of Personal Managers, 261
Congress, U.S., 150, 166, 210–11
conspiracy theories, 45
Constitution, U.S., 247, 365
Cooley, Melanie, 302–3
Coppola, Francis Ford, 254
Cowell, Eleanor and Sam, 298
Cowell, Julia, 299
Cox, Jeanette, 212
Cox, Steve, 332–33
Crime Classification Manual, 93
crimes:
    bragging about, 27–28
    claims of responsibility for, 17, 18, 20

compulsion and obsession in, 37,
39–40, 81, 86
congressional hearings on, 35–36
convictions and sentences for, 21, 30,
35, 36, 59–60
declaring war on, 34–35, 36
declines in types of, 35
environment and, 54–55
evidence of, 15–19
imposters claiming credit for, 46–47
opportunistic, 16, 33, 43, 95–97
planning of, 20, 23, 24, 27, 60
predictions of, 35, 47, 108, 109
prevention of, 34, 35, 282–89,
358–66
publicity on, 21–22, 29
repeat offenders of, 37, 38
visualization of, 23–24
crime scenes, 177, 297–98
collecting evidence from, 16, 56, 58,
80, 118
drawings of, 29, 30
maps of, 16
photographs of, 15–17, 19, 23, 24, 27,
30, 43, 176
"staging" of, 123, 126
taking souvenirs from, 43, 69, 95, 98,
105
Crimewatch, 89
Criminal Personality, The (Samenow and
Yochelson), 109–10
Criminal Personality Research Project,
18
crisis-intervention programs, 150, 162,
163, 330
Cukajti, Larry, 332
Cunningham, Julie, 302

Dahmer, Jeffrey, 363
DaRonch, Carol, 302, 303
Davidson, Alberta, 310
Davidson, Anjeanette, 310
Dawber, Pam, 254, 258
death threats, 60, 237, 244, 246, 312
de Becker, Gavin, 230, 232, 236, 258,
259, 260–62, 271, 280, 281, 283,
285–86, 363
De Niro, Robert, 236

Diana, Princess of Wales, 224
diaries, 42, 95, 233, 237, 258, 281
Didion, Joan, 273
Dietz, Park, 113, 224, 229, 256, 259, 260,
261, 351
DNA, 56, 58, 60, 75
domestic violence, 111, 169, 183,
220–21, 225, 266–89, 362
Dorrian's Red Hand, 118, 119, 121
Doyle, Jack, 119
Dreiser, Theodore, 140
Drug Enforcement Administration
(DEA), 168
drugs, 44, 69, 89, 93, 124–25, 128, 129,
130, 143, 145, 184, 329, 354
Dudley, Deborah Johnson, 312–13,
314–15, 317
Dunn, John, 78, 80
Dunne, Alex, 274
Dunne, Dominick, 273, 274, 277, 278
Dunne, Dominique, 273–81, 282
Dunne, Ellen Griffin "Lenny," 273,
278
Dunne, John Gregory, 273
Duvall, Lucie J., 70, 71, 73

East Harlem School at Exodus House,
355–58
education, 35, 36, 355–58
Einstein, Albert, 140
Elizabeth Lund Home for Unwed
Mothers, 298
Ellis, Carroll Ann, 165–71, 175–76,
178–82, 190–93, 197, 199–205,
205–7, 211–12, 214–18, 220–22,
222, 358
Ellis, Claude, 169, 179
Elwyn Institute for the retarded,
309–10
emergency services, 117, 173, 210, 225,
236, 248, 266, 287
ESL Inc., 239, 241, 244, 245, 248–49,
251
Evans, Alfred, 44
Ewing, Megan, 326, 334
exploitative rapist, 93, 95–96
extortion, 142, 143
extradition, 132, 264, 332

Fairfax County Circuit Court, 192–93
Fairfax County Police Department, 168, 217, 220
    Child Sex Crimes Unit of, 218
    Criminal Investigations Bureau of, 165, 205
Fairfax Victim-Witness Unit, 165–71, 175, 190–91, 193–94, 199–222, 287
Fairstein, Linda, 92, 99–101, 108, 115, 117–18, 122–29, 133, 136, 137, 143–46, 155–58, 160–63, 224–25, 243–44, 262, 358, 359, 364
"Fallen Tree" (Clark), 335
Farha, Darron, 352
Farha, Kelli Gariglietti, 352
Farley, Richard Wade, 239–53, 257, 266, 270, 271, 273, 280, 283, 286
Farrell, Frances, 19, 20, 25, 29, 31
Federal Bureau of Investigation (FBI), 88, 223, 284, 306, 332–33
    agents of, 16, 34, 48, 52, 78, 93, 226, 247, 333
    Behavioral Science Unit of, 16, 23, 33, 45
    Cleveland Field Office of, 78
    Denver Field Office of, 316
    Legal Unit of, 23
    Milwaukee Field Office of, 297
    multiagency and jurisdictional task forces of, 48
    1990 Uniform Crime Reports of, 271–72
    Ten Most-Wanted List of, 305
    Violent Criminal Apprehension Program (VICAP) of, 71
    see also Investigative Support Unit; National Academy of FBI
Fenn, Jeff, 236
fingerprints, 76, 78, 80, 87, 213, 264
Fitzpatrick, Johanna, 192–93
Florida State Penitentiary, 298, 307
forensic evidence, 122–23, 334
Foster, Jodie, 235–36, 242, 252
Fox, Gene, 330, 332
Fox, Kristi, 330, 332
Fritz, Arnie, 295
Fulgoni, Dino, 260

Gacy, John Wayne, 317
Gallagher, Lori, 19–20, 21, 28, 30, 31
Gein, Augusta, 292–93, 295–96
Gein, Edward, 292–98, 300, 309, 316, 318
Gein, George, 292
Gein, Henry, 293
gentleman rapist, 58, 94
Gibson, Debbie, 258
Gideon, Donald Ray "Don," 325–28, 330–38, 340–44, 349–55, 360, 366
Gideon, Shannon, 332, 339, 340, 349
Gideon, Shirley, 331, 333, 339, 343
Gift of Fear, The (de Becker), 259
Gill, Martin, 119–20
Godfather, Part III, The, 254
Gollmar, Robert H., 296
Gorbachev, Mikhail, 256
Gordon, Rosie, 181, 199
Graham, Janice, 301–2
grave robbing, 295–96
Gray, Ed, 70–72, 73, 78
Greenhaven Correctional Facility, 129
Green Lake County Sheriff's Department, 294–95
Green River Murders, 48–50, 308, 316
Grijalva, Ruben, 250
Gritter, Gordon W., 263
guns, 17, 19, 41–42, 72–73, 92, 99, 110, 225–26, 248–49

Haas, Heather, 324, 344
Hageman, Hans, 355–57, 358, 364
Hageman, Ivan, 355–57
Hagmaier, Bill, 307, 308
Hall, Rebecca "Becky," 172, 174, 182–83, 184–90
Hallett, Sally, 39
Hamilton, Tom, 325–26, 330–31, 342
Hanley, Kathleen "Katie," 171–97, 200–1, 203, 206, 208, 347, 364
Hanley, Steven, 171, 195–96
Hanson, Inge, 355, 357
Harlem RBI, 357–58
Harris, Dennis, 217–18
Harris, Thomas, 11, 291–92, 298, 302
hate groups, 45–46
Haulmark, Gary, 336, 345
Haynes, Rita, 81

Hazelwood, Robert "Roy," 16, 45–46, 93, 105, 151, 152, 154–55
Healy, Lynda Ann, 300–1
Heflin, Lance, 332
Heidnik, Betty Disto, 312, 313
Heidnik, Ellen, 308
Heidnik, Gary Michael, 308–18, 361
Heidnik, Jesse John, 312
Heidnik, Michael, 308
Heidnik, Terry, 308
Heirens, William, 17–18, 41, 304
"Helpful Guide for Stalking Victims," 287, 288
Hemingway, Randell, 248
Hendricks, Leroy, 345, 346
Henwood, Dave, 56, 57
Hill, Craig, 330, 333
Hillside Strangler, 21
Hill Street Blues, 274
Hinckley, John, Jr., 224, 235–36, 242, 252–53, 363
Hitchcock, Alfred, 296
HIV infection, 157
Hogan, Mary, 295, 297
Holderbaum, Robert, 181
Holyfield, Evander, 363
Holztrager, Karen, 69–70, 78
homicide-victim support program, 165–98, 199–224
Homolka, Karla, 271
homosexuality, 46, 49, 152
Hoover, J. Edgar, 45, 297
Horan, Robert, 190
Horton, James E., 140
Howell, Robert, 64
Hudock, Bruce, 133–34

I-40 Killer, 99
insanity defense, 41, 79, 80, 83
Inside the Criminal Mind (Samenow), 44
internet, 163, 287
Investigative Support Unit (FBI), 33, 44–45, 52, 68, 93, 117, 158, 230, 285, 307
    consultants in, 16, 45, 52, 56, 58, 113
    guiding principles of, 101
    see also psychological profiling program (FBI)

Ireland, Dana Marie, 199, 209–11, 212, 214
Ireland, John, 209, 210–11, 214
Ireland, Louise, 209, 210–11, 214
Ireland, Sandy, 209–10

Jackson, Arthur, 236–38, 251–53, 262–64, 266, 268
Jack the Ripper, 21, 232
Johnson, John Wesley, 212
Johnson, Laurene Dekle, 199, 212–13
Journey into Darkness (Douglas and Olshaker), 34, 38, 91, 97, 158, 166, 186, 214, 268, 271, 358
Justice Department, U.S., 211
Juvenile Crime Bill (1997), 35

Kane, Brett, 56
Kane, Larry, 248
Kansas Bureau of Investigation (KBI), 332–33
Kansas Court of Appeals, 343
Kansas Department of Corrections, 335, 341–44
Kansas State Legislature, 340–41
Kansas Supreme Court, 338, 342, 343, 345
Katz, Burton, 277–78
Kehl, Sloane, 326, 331–32
Kelly, Alex, 130–36, 137, 360, 363
Kelly, Chris, 135
Kelly, Joe, 135
Kemper, Clarnell, 38–39
Kemper, Edmund, Jr., 38
Kemper, Edmund Emil, III, 38–40, 43, 87, 304, 318
Kemper, Susan, 39
Kennedy, Anthony, 346
Kennedy, John F., 237
Kent, Debra, 302
Keppel, Bob, 308
kidnapping, 226, 269, 310, 334
    see also victims, abduction of
killers:
    alter egos of, 18, 41
    analysis of, 23–24, 25–29, 30, 33, 45–50
    code words of, 18, 21, 22

killers (*cont.*)
convictions and sentences of, 21,
40–41, 42, 47, 127–29, 212–13,
250–51, 259–60, 276–78
execution of, 298, 307–8
organized vs. disorganized, 24–25,
38–40
publicity craved by, 18, 20, 26, 27, 30,
324–35
responsibility claimed by, 17, 18,
20–22, 25
self-image of, 18, 21, 26, 29, 49
serial, *see* serial killers
urges of, 17, 21, 23
Kirkpatrick, Robert, 316
Knowlan, Michael, 81
Kole, Carla, 82
Koo, Aiko, 40
Kovacic, Vic, 75–76
Kravitz, Julius, 81
Ku Klux Klan, 45–46

Lafferty, John, 119
Lafon, John David, 170
Lamparter, Helen, 249
Lane, John, 262–63
Lanning, Ken, 93
Laven, Hans, 57
Leach, Kimberly, 305, 306, 307
Lee, David, 306
Leibowitz, Samuel, 140
Leigh, Janet, 296
Lennon, John, 100, 234–35, 261
Letterman, David, 223, 231, 234
Levin, Jennifer Dawn, 118–29, 136, 137,
160, 275–76, 360
Levin, Stephen E., Jr., 313
Levine, Michael, 81
Levy, Lisa, 307
Lindsay, Sandra, 312, 313–14
Litman, Jack, 128
Los Angeles Police Department
(LAPD), 255, 262–63, 265
Threat Management Unit of, 261, 263
Lyons, Thomas J., 175

McAllister, Jane, 287
McEntee, Mickey, 119

McGinty, Tim, 74, 77–80, 81–83,
86–87
McIlwain, Blaine, 48, 68, 69
McMonagle, Richard, 81–83, 86, 87
McVeigh, Timothy, 36–37
Madonna, 223–27, 261–62
Mann, Thomas, 140
Manning, John, 52, 58–59, 60
Mardigian, Steve, 52, 54, 58
Marine Corps, U.S., 166, 171
Marsh, Shannon, 324–25, 330
mass murder, 239–53
masturbation, 24, 25, 42, 43, 75, 81, 85,
94, 125, 293
Matuszny, Bob, 63, 64, 65–67, 68,
70–73, 77
Maury Povich show, 339–40, 348
Maxwell, Robert, 213
media:
crime coverage in, 29, 34, 47, 49, 55,
56, 60, 66, 69
killer's communication with, 17, 20,
27, 31, 46
medical examinations, 140, 144, 155–57
medical examiners (MEs), 16, 118, 122,
123, 176, 177
Meenakshi, V., 263
Mendota Mental Health Institute, 297
Mendoza, Lisa, 343
mental illness:
morality and, 37, 40–41, 43, 60,
296–97, 316–18
sexual predation and, 37, 38, 40–41,
43, 79, 80, 83
stalking and, 231, 233, 237, 251, 263,
265
mental institutions, 27, 30, 38, 182, 263,
296–97
mental retardation, 161–62, 310
Mergler, Mary Alice, 170–71, 200–3
Mergler, Meredith, 170, 199, 200
Merrill Lynch, 310, 316
Milano, Jerry, 77, 80, 81, 82, 83, 86
military service, 16, 26–27, 36, 41, 42
Miller, Robert A. "Rob," 172, 174–75,
179, 185–93, 196, 197
Mills, Stu, 57
Milton, John, 11

Mindhunter (Douglas and Olshaker), 34, 38, 48, 52, 112, 268
Minerva, Michael, 306, 307
Mirarchi, Charles P., Jr., 311
M'Naghten Rule of 1843, 40
MO (modus operandi), 18, 21, 28, 29, 30, 301–2, 307
   see also rape, MO in; sexual predators, MO of
Molitor, Amy, 132, 135
Moritz, Glenda, 249
Morrison, Paul, 336
mothers, 99, 249, 295–96
   anger against, 42, 87, 96, 146, 318
   dominance of, 26, 38–39, 69, 95, 292–93
Motivation X, 20, 22, 29
Moyer, Christopher, 204–5, 211
Moyer, Kimberly, 204–5, 208, 211
Murphy, Robert "Bob," 217, 360
Murty, Leon "Specks," 295
Musgrave, Story, 234
My Sister Sam, 254, 257, 258

Napier, Michael "Mike," 333
Naslund, Denise, 301, 302, 307
National Academy of FBI, 16, 37, 45, 68, 84, 151, 166, 298
National Center for the Analysis of Violent Crime (NCAVC), 93
National Center for Missing and Exploited Children, 336
National Crime Victims' Rights Week, 222
National Criminal Justice Association, 223
National Institute of Justice, 223, 224
National Survey of Family Growth, 359
National Victim Center, 223, 224, 227, 228, 240, 265, 283, 285, 287, 288, 350, 362
Navy, U.S., 185, 253
Neff, James, 62, 67, 73, 79, 80, 87, 102
Nelson, Vincent, 315
Neu, Tommy, 199
New York City District Attorney's Office Sex Crimes Unit, 92, 100

New York Police Department (NYPD), 117–19
New York State Court of Appeals, 268
New York Times, 117, 132
911 emergency, 117, 173, 225, 248, 266
Nixon, Richard, 234, 261

Ocilka, Betty, 62–63, 64, 65, 72–73
Oklahoma City bombing, 36
Ono, Yoko, 235
Operation Park, 52, 56–58
Orender, Ken, 332
Ortolano, Adrienne Bak, 136
Ott, Janice, 301, 302, 307

Packer, David, 275
paranoia, 43, 231, 233, 268
Parents of Murdered Children, 201, 333
parole, 90, 108, 129, 200, 263, 325, 349
Parrish, Phil, 63, 64, 65–67
Patterson, Haywood, 139
Payne, Stacey, 325, 326, 328, 333–34
Pennell, Steven, 99
Perkins, Anthony, 296
Peruto, A. Charles, Jr., 315–16
Peterson, Daniel "Danny," 15, 19, 20, 24, 25, 26, 29
Peterson, Kenneth, 15, 16, 24
Peterson, Melissa, 15, 17, 18, 20, 23–25
Peterson, Sarah, 15, 16, 17, 19, 24
photographs, 74, 75, 76, 77, 78, 122, 180–81, 243
   autopsy, 16, 127, 176
   crime-scene, 15–17, 19, 23, 24, 27, 30, 43, 176
   criminal use of, 19, 23, 27, 30, 84, 85, 243
Pittsburg State University, 319, 325–26, 329, 345, 352, 354
police:
   composite sketches by, 19, 29, 65, 72
   culture and jargon of, 23, 24, 26, 27, 28
   door-to-door interviews by, 56
   FBI collaboration with, 44
   impersonation of, 28
   interviewing of rape victims by, 63–65, 144–46, 150–51, 154–60

police (*cont.*)
  investigations and searches by, 16, 26, 27, 34, 46–47, 57–59, 63–83, 144–46, 150–51, 154–60, 173–75
  killers' communication with, 27, 29, 30, 39, 44, 46
  press conferences of, 21–22
  reporting crimes to, 54, 55, 61–63, 131, 141–46, 147, 148, 150–51, 152, 154–56
  special task forces of, 21, 66
  stakeouts and surveillance by, 47, 66, 105
  suspects among, 28–29
  undercover, 144
Poltergeist, 273, 274
pornography, 94, 99, 106
posttraumatic stress disorder (PTSD), 150
Povich, Maury, 339–40
power-reassurance rapist, 93–95, 96, 104, 105, 114–15
Practical Aspects of Rape Investigation: A Multidisciplinary Approach (Burgess and Hazelwood), 151
precipitating stressors, 57–58, 112, 114, 125, 126
pregnancy, 157, 158, 175, 179, 298, 313
Preppie Murder Case, 117–30
Price, Victoria, 139, 140
prisons, 30, 35, 36, 104, 129, 193
probation, 108, 330
prostitutes, 42, 48, 49, 99, 107, 112, 118, 145, 147, 149, 312, 313, 315
psychiatrists, 22, 43, 108–10, 115–16, 263, 293, 296, 316–17
Psycho, 296
psychological profiling program (FBI), 21–31, 34
  conferences and presentations of, 52, 91
  disclaimers in, 26
  evaluation of case linkages in, 33, 45, 47, 49, 52
  failures of, 30–31
  mental health methods vs., 22–23
  1979 establishment of, 16

proactive responses to, 27, 33, 49, 56, 58, 92
procedures of, 16, 22–29, 33–34, 42, 45–47, 48–50
  see also Investigative Support Unit (FBI)
psychologists, 22–23, 44, 79, 108, 330
Puccio, Thomas P., 132–33, 136
Pue, Terry, 47

racism, 45–46, 139–41, 234
Raging Bull, 236
rape, 27, 33, 40, 41, 45, 51–116, 130–37, 139–63, 171, 201, 220, 312–13, 333, 363
  avoidance of, 115, 116, 137
  brutality and violence of, 52–53, 54, 60–63, 73, 80, 91, 96, 97–99, 100, 104, 114, 144–45, 267
  categories of, 91–99, 101–5, 114–15, 130
  consensual foreplay and, 145, 147–48, 158
  counseling and treatment for, 150–51, 153, 155–57, 162, 163
  date and acquaintance, 91, 92, 115, 130, 137, 143–46, 147–49, 157–58, 228, 331
  devastating effects of, 91–92, 150–54
  expressive vs. guarded accounts of, 151
  false allegations of, 139–46, 147, 150, 151
  gang, 139–40
  gathering and linking evidence in cases of, 56, 57, 58, 60, 63, 65–66, 75, 78, 85, 126, 148, 156, 158–61
  mass, 146–47
  MO in, 52–54, 56–58, 61–66, 71, 73
  motivation in, 54, 56, 63, 68–69, 96–97
  personal relationships impacted by, 151–53, 163
  public attitudes toward, 92, 100–101, 146, 147–50, 161
  recovery from, 150–57, 162–63
  reporting and nonreporting of, 143, 147–49, 152, 154–56

research on, 93–99, 108–10
resistance to, 53, 61, 73, 152
serial, 52–90, 94, 101, 112, 115, 146,
    158–60
thwarting of, 53, 54, 73, 101–2
triggering events and, 57–58, 112,
    114
weapons involved in, 52, 62, 67, 69,
    70, 71, 74, 92, 94, 97, 98, 149
see also sexual predators
rape crisis centers, 162, 163
rape shield laws, 160–61
rape trauma syndrome (RTS), 150–51,
    153, 282
Ray, James Earl, 233
Ray, Jud, 317–18
Ray, Margaret, 234
Reagan, Ronald, 235
Redd, Terry Dale, 212–13
Red Dragon (Harris), 291, 292
Redmond, Lula, 201
rehabilitation, 348–49
    ineffectiveness of, 43–44, 109–10,
        115, 193, 342
Reilly, Pat, 117
RE/MAX, 321–22
remorse, 48–49, 60, 95, 114, 275, 340
Ressler, Robert, 16, 18, 93
Reviving Baseball in Inner Cities (RBI),
    357–58
Rissell, Monte, 112
Rittenhouse, Eric, 329, 334, 344, 348
Rivera, Geraldo, 262
Rivera, Josephina, 312, 314–15
robbery, 17, 44, 62, 63, 67, 74, 84, 90, 93,
    100, 105, 112, 238, 264
Roberts, Cynda, 172
Robertson, Shelly, 302–3
Rohypnol, 354, 360
Roper, Roberta, 201
Roper, Stephanie, 201
rough sex, 120, 122, 126, 160
Ruby, Jack, 81
Rudolph, Howard, 73
Rule, Ann, 298, 300

sadistic rapist, 93, 97–99, 108
sadomasochism, 99, 106

safe houses, 220, 269–70, 362
Saldana, Theresa, 236–38, 251, 252, 253,
    255, 262, 263, 287
Salp, Tom, 52, 54
Samenow, Stanton E., 44, 108–10, 193,
    223, 299–300, 304, 316, 339–40,
    343, 349, 351
Santamaria, Ross, 78
Savidge, David, 315
*Scenes from the Class Struggle in Beverly
    Hills,* 254, 258
Schaeffer, Rebecca, 254–62, 265
Schicke, Matt, 326, 327–28
Schirk, Robert, 341–43
schizophrenia, 43, 231, 237, 296, 309
Schley, Art, 293–94, 295
Schmidt, Gene, 319–36, 338–40,
    344–47, 349, 352–54, 358, 359,
    365, 366
Schmidt, Jennifer Anne "Jeni," 319–24,
    327–29, 332–34, 336–39, 344–47,
    348, 352–53
Schmidt, Margaret Louise Dormois
    "Peggy," 319–23, 325–36, 338–39,
    342–44, 346–47, 352–54, 358,
    365, 366
Schmidt, Stephanie Rene, 319–54, 359,
    360
Schoephoerster, Lloyd, 294–95
Schuetz, Janice, 321
Scotland Yard, 264
Scott, M. Douglas, 216, 349
Scottsboro Boys, 139–41
Search and Destroy murders, 15–31, 43,
    44, 46
Secret Service, U.S., 237
Seglie, Ron, 328
serial killers, 15–31, 37–50, 232, 241,
    292–318
    communications from, 17–18,
        20–22, 25, 27, 31, 46, 304
    interviews with, 18, 38, 42, 45, 112,
        307, 317–18
    MO of, 42, 301–2, 307
    pleas and defenses of, 41, 42
    studies of, 37, 38–40, 42–44
    see also killers; sexual predators; *spe-
        cific cases*

Sexual Homicide: Patterns and Motives (Douglas, Ressler and Burgess), 42

sexual predators, 15–31, 33–163
  apprehension of, 59–60, 76–77, 88–89, 101–2
  behavioral clues to, 54, 60–61, 103–8, 110–16, 154–55, 340
  choice, planning and control exhibited by, 38–40, 41, 43, 60
  consensual sexual relationships of, 79, 85–86, 94, 95–96, 107, 130
  criminal records of, 27, 59–60, 69, 78–79, 88, 90, 105–6, 110–13, 134, 158–59, 160, 325, 331, 332, 341–45, 351, 354
  distinguishing physical characteristics of, 61, 63, 64, 65–66, 70, 71, 78
  dysfunctional families of, 38–39, 60, 111–12
  enjoyment of crimes by, 40, 44, 96, 107, 113, 318
  informing communities about presence of, 341, 345–47, 351
  law-abiding siblings of, 38
  mental illness and, 37, 38, 40–41, 43, 79, 80, 83
  MO of, 52–54, 56–59, 61–66, 71, 73, 80–81, 83–85, 87–88, 94–95, 97–99, 147, 159
  motivation of, 39, 43–44, 46, 48–49, 54, 56, 63, 68–69, 92, 96–97, 99, 107, 130, 147
  obsessions of, 44, 46, 61, 85, 99, 107–8
  rehabilitation unlikely for, 43–44
  sadism of, 49, 85, 93, 97–99, 271
  sexual problems and arrested development of, 25, 26, 42, 49, 54, 57, 68–69, 79, 93–94, 95–96, 154, 158
  treatment of, 109–10
  trials and sentences of, 59–60, 78–87, 110, 130–36, 157–62, 166, 190–93, 336–39

Sexual Violence: Our War Against Rape (Fairstein), 100

Shank, Nadine, 212

Sharing and Caring, 194, 205

Shelton, Maria, 77, 82, 102

Shelton, Ronnie, 76–83, 85, 89–90, 96, 102, 110–11, 112, 136, 147, 253, 266, 267, 268, 289, 363

Sigma Chi, 325, 326, 329, 332, 335

Silence of the Lambs, The (film), 235, 291

Silence of the Lambs, The (Harris), 11, 291–92

"Silent No More" (Brzonkala and Barber), 222

Simpson, Nicole Brown, 268, 272

Simpson, O. J., 111, 259, 268, 272

Sirhan, Sirhan, 233

60 Minutes, 317–18

Smith, Edward, 44

Smith, Samantha, 256

Social Security Office, 284

sodomy, 155, 201, 334, 336

Someplace Safe, 220, 362

Son of Sam, *see* Berkowitz, David

South Auckland Rapist, 51–60, 88–89, 90, 95

Southworth, Jerry, 297

Souza, Destiny Ann "Dee," 171–81, 184–92, 191–93, 193–97, 199, 208, 347

Souza, Kathleen, *see* Hanley, Kathleen

Speak Out for Stephanie (S.O.S.), 336, 339, 353, 354

Spencer, Kathleen, 215

Spencer, Timothy, 97, 158

Stahl, Leslie, 318

Stalberg, John, 256

stalking, 33, 106–7, 221, 223
  attachment-seeking, 230, 239–61
  celebrity, 223–24, 225, 228–39, 254–62, 280
  defense strategies and, 282–89
  definitions of, 223, 227
  delusion-based, 230–31
  first felony arrest for, 265
  homicide and, 232–64
  identity-seeking, 230, 234–35, 258–59
  legal actions against, 225, 246–48
  legislation on, 223, 224, 227, 261–62, 265

love-obsession, 229–30, 231, 234, 236–62, 265–66, 268, 272, 279, 280
   mental illness and, 231, 233, 237, 251, 263, 265
   methods of, 223–24, 225–27, 240–46, 266–70
   profile elements and, 228–32
   rejection-based, 230
   shifting among target figures and, 234, 261
   simple obsession, 266–81
   statistics on, 224–25, 231, 265–66
Steinhagen, Ruth, 232–33, 234
St. Elizabeth's Hospital, 109
Stephan, Bob, 332
Stephanie Roper Foundation, 201
Stephanie Schmidt Foundation, 339, 354
Stephanie Schmidt Sexual Predator Law, 341, 345
Stephanie Schmidt Task Force, 335–36, 340–41
Stovall, Carla, 345–47, 352
strangulation, 118, 122–24, 276, 333
   compression asphyxiation, 127
   ligature, 15, 19, 20, 24, 25
Struyk, Virginia "Genny," 221
suicide, 62, 179, 207, 240, 308, 318, 335
   attempts at, 77, 79, 111, 182, 237, 275, 276, 311, 315
   threats of, 248, 249, 256
suicide prevention centers, 271
support groups, 150, 162, 163, 165–97, 199–222
Supreme Court, U.S., 140, 141, 162, 342, 346–47
survivors, 19, 20, 25, 29, 34
   counseling and support services for, 150–51, 153, 155–57, 162, 163, 165–97, 199–222
   desire for justice and closure by, 34, 153, 210–15
   rape, 143–63
   see also victims
suspects, 27, 59, 72
   criminal records of, 59–60, 76
   descriptions of, 57, 58–59

   interviewing of, 17, 27, 65–66, 77, 118–20
   lists of, 16, 17, 27, 59
   see also unknown subjects
SWAT teams, 249
Sweeney, John Thomas, 273–81, 282

Tanay, Emanuel, 81, 86–87
Taxi Driver, 236
Teeselink, Scott, 333
telephones, 19, 20, 25, 55, 227
   cutting lines to, 16, 19, 20, 28, 52
   portable, 362
   tracing calls from, 20, 105, 226
temporary restraining orders, 247, 265, 282, 285
terrorism, 36, 106
Teten, Howard, 45
Thomas, Lisa, 312
Thompson, Joseph Stephenson, 59–60, 87–89, 90, 94, 105, 111–12, 289, 363
Tiffany, 258
Tobin, Joseph A., 311
Trailside Killer, 253
"true detective" magazines, 28
TRW, 172
Tyson, Mike, 148–49, 363

Unfinished Murder (Neff), 62
unknown subjects (UNSUBs), 15, 255
   analysis of, 55–59, 93–116
   composite sketches of, 19, 29, 65, 72
   messages from, 17, 18, 20–22, 29, 44
   playing the game with, 33–34
   predicting actions of, 34, 47
   putting stress on, 28–29, 33–34
   suspicious activity of, 28, 29

Vancrum, Bob, 336
venereal disease (VD), 42, 80, 157
victim impact statements, 181, 191, 192, 211
victimology, 23–24, 45, 49, 103, 120–21, 124, 150, 203, 333
victims:
   abduction of, 46, 53, 91, 92, 98, 99, 161, 166, 210, 223, 225–27, 302

victims (*cont.*)
    analysis of, 16, 23–24, 45, 49, 57, 103,
      120–21, 124, 150, 203, 333
    binding of, 15, 19, 20, 24, 29, 53, 57,
      105
    blaming of, 62, 100–101, 136, 137,
      149, 151
    brutal treatment and torture of, 23,
      25, 49, 53–54, 166, 312–15,
      317–18
    burial and memorial services for, 29,
      173, 176, 180–81, 334–35
    communication with, 53, 63, 95,
      103–4
    compensation for, 205
    compliance of, 23, 92
    credibility of, 141–46, 147, 150, 151
    cries for help from, 53, 62, 91, 236
    defense strategies for, 358–66
    honoring the memory of, 211, 222,
      336–47
    humiliation of, 84, 95, 104, 107
    killers' identification with, 29
    legal trashing of, 128, 132–33, 137,
      160–61, 277
    lifestyles of, 16, 26, 49
    manipulation, domination and con-
      trol of, 18, 23, 25, 26, 30, 33, 43,
      47, 49, 56, 63, 77, 85, 147
    police interviews with, 57, 63–64, 68,
      70, 144–46, 150–51, 154–60
    potential, 34, 35, 92, 99, 348
    psychological stages experienced by,
      207–9
    resistance of, 19, 20, 34, 53, 61, 73,
      110, 123, 127, 361
    selection of, 20, 24, 27, 33, 49, 55, 56,
      57, 94, 96, 98, 114, 241
    "silent," 143, 147–49, 162, 163
    surveillance of, 24, 25, 70
    survival as goal of, 61, 361
    threatening of, 51, 53, 54, 61, 62, 65,
      67, 70, 71, 75, 131, 147
    verbal abuse of, 53
    vulnerability and terror of, 23–24, 26,
      34, 35, 49, 51, 53–54, 55, 60, 61
Victims for Victims, 287
victim's rights advocacy, 166, 287, 333,
    336–54, 358–59, 364–66
    legislation achieved by, 210–11, 223,
      224, 227, 261–62, 265, 340–41,
      345–47, 352
"Victim's Right to Speak, A," 210
Victim-Witness Assistance Program (V-
    WAP), 169
victim-witness units, *see* Fairfax Victim-
    Witness Unit
Viola, Frank, 72
Violent Criminal Apprehension Pro-
    gram (VICAP), 71
voyeurism, 25, 27, 69, 76, 89, 90, 94,
    105–6, 110, 111, 160

Wachtler, Sol, 268
Waco disaster, 36
Waitkus, Eddie, 232–33
Walker, Ron, 48, 316
Wallace, George, 233, 234, 261
Walsh, John, 332
war crimes, 146–47
Warmington, Dr., 296
watch groups, 55, 66, 74
Webb, Audrey, 212
Webb, Dick, 212, 213–14
Webster, William, 16
West Side Rapist, 61–90
    see also Shelton, Ronnie
Whildin, William "Bill," 174–75, 177,
    188–90
white supremacy, 45–46
Wiggins, George (Raheed Muhammed),
    200
Wilcox, Nancy, 302
Williams, Eugene, 140
Williams, Joyce, 169
Williams, Wayne Bertram, 47
Williams, Wayne "Buddy," 248
Witness and Victim Service (Cuyahoga
    County), 82
witnesses, 82
    expert testimony of, 80, 83–86
    statements of, 16, 19, 29, 115, 119
    youthful victims as, 217–19
Witt, Emily, 203
Witt, Paul, 203–4
Witt, Sandra S. "Sandy," 168, 169–71,

175, 181–82, 190–91, 201–5,
206–13, 215–17, 218–22, 358
women:
anger against, 42, 49, 53, 79, 85, 87,
96–97
demonstrations of power over, 43,
54, 56, 57, 58, 68–69, 79, 81, 85
troubled relationships with, 42, 49,
53, 58, 69, 79
women's movement, 92, 100
Worden, Bernice, 293–95, 296, 297
Worden, Frank, 293–94
Worden, William, 211

wounds, 17, 23, 122
compression, 127
defensive, 19, 20, 123, 127
Wright, Andrew, 139–40, 141
Wright, Jim, 285
Wright, Leroy, 140
Wright brothers, 319

Yochelson, Samuel, 108–9
Yorkshire Ripper, 56

Zbydniewski, Andrea "Zeb," 70–72, 77,
78